Library Technical Services

Library Technical Services

Adapting to a Changing Environment

Edited by Stacey Marien

Charleston Insights in
Library, Archival, and Information Sciences

Purdue University Press
West Lafayette, Indiana

Library of Congress Cataloging-in-Publication Data

Names: Marien, Stacey, 1962– editor.

Title: Library technical services : adapting to a changing environment / edited by Stacey Marien.

Identifiers: LCCN 2020018928 (print) | LCCN 2020018929 (ebook) | ISBN 9781557538420 (paperback) | ISBN 9781612495859 (epub) | ISBN 9781612495842 (pdf)

Subjects: LCSH: Technical services (Libraries)—United States.

Classification: LCC Z688.6.U6 T427 2020 (print) | LCC Z688.6.U6 (ebook) | DDC 025/.02—dc23

LC record available at https://lccn.loc.gov/2020018928

LC ebook record available at https://lccn.loc.gov/2020018929

Contents

Preface

In 2014 I co-presented with my colleague Alayne Mundt at the annual Charleston Conference for libraries. We described the first collaborative project between our two units, resource description and acquisitions. Alayne and I were relatively new as the heads of these units and we knew that we wanted to work more closely together. The presentation at the conference discussed how our units collaborated to develop a workflow that more quickly moved shelf-ready books out of technical services and into the library collection. At the same time, we submitted an article about the same project to the journal *Against the Grain*. Just before the conference, Katina Strauch, the editor of the journal, contacted us and requested to meet while in Charleston. At that meeting, she proposed that Alayne and I co-edit a column in the journal called Let's Get Technical that focused on technical services issues. Our column was first published in April 2015. Subsequent columns have focused on contemporary problems in technical services departments and how the units responded. Over the years, we have featured many stories from our own library at American University as well as contributions from other libraries. After being involved with *ATG* for a couple of years, Katina suggested a book as an extension of the column, with a variety of chapters from different contributors explaining their solutions to real-world problems. With her encouragement, I agreed and *Library Technical Services: Adapting to a Changing Environment* was born. As editor, I have recruited authors and solicited a variety of new chapters that I hope will be of interest to a wide range of librarians, library staff, and library and information science (LIS) educators and students. The chapters featured in this book have not appeared in the Let's Get Technical column for *ATG*. This book is intended primarily for practitioners working in library technical services, but when possible many of the contributing authors have provided scholarly citations to other relevant professional literature. Knowing most readers will likely not read the book from cover to cover, I have organized the chapters into meaningful categories of challenges faced by library technical services units. I hope this decision will make it easier for readers to find single chapters or subsections of most interest and relevance to their needs.

Library technical services operations, workflows, and tools are constantly evolving and changing. However, the challenges for technical services staff and managers are much greater than just constant evolution. Administrators, funders, and even library professional associations are questioning the relevance, utility, and viability of technical services in today's world of library services. It seems even those in our own libraries don't understand what we do or our contribution in curating, managing, and providing access to our collections. Technical services departments face serious existential threats in many libraries. Stories of technical services units and functions being relocated or even outsourced outside the library are common, with various justifications ranging from shrinking print collections to budgetary constraints and other reasons.

Thankfully, our community also is hearing more stories about technical services departments adapting and reinventing themselves in response to these challenges and threats. Strong advocates and innovators are embracing the opportunity to experiment, collaborate, and help our libraries adapt for the 21st century. This book contains many such stories. It begins with a conversation between a new librarian starting her career and her colleague, who is in the later stages of a long career. Following are a series of case studies of many different practical issues that technical service librarians are facing. There are chapters on diverse topics such as downsizing print collections, the relevance of government documents in a digital era, the challenges of supporting a distance education program, cataloging issues in a metadata world, staffing issues and challenges, effective collection development and management, and tips for setting boundaries when dealing with vendors. Other topics discussed in the book include how to manage the stresses of relocating technical services to off-site locations, reinventing technical services workflows, and creating new collaborations and partnerships. I hope that readers will find both inspiration and practical advice as well as examples for solving issues their technical services units may be facing.

Sadly, while this book was in its final editing phase, contributor Emily Hicks passed away on October 7, 2019, at the age of 50. She will be greatly missed by her friends and colleagues.

I wish to thank my colleague Alexandra Ogilvie for her thoughts and ideas on this project. Additionally, I must acknowledge several friends and colleagues for additional help with this book: Alayne Mundt, Michael Fernandez, Charles Thomas, and Lisa Kallman Hopkins, a contributor who put together the final bibliography. Special thanks go to my partner, Sean Casey, for all the support he gave me while I was working on this book.

Stacey Marien, Acquisitions Librarian
American University

The Challenges Facing Library Technical Services: A Dialogue

Rebecca Ciota and R. Cecilia Knight

In this introduction to *Library Technical Services: Adapting to a Changing Environment*, early career technical services librarian Rebecca Ciota and veteran technical services librarian R. Cecilia Knight discuss how we view library technical services. We provide our insights into what technical services are and the associated skill sets required. We also discuss our on-the-job as well as educational experiences that helped us arrive at our current positions at Grinnell College Libraries. And we ruminate on the past, present, and future changes in technical service work.

I am Rebecca Ciota, the discovery and integrated systems librarian at Grinnell College Libraries. I have served in that position since July of 2016. Previously I was at the University of Illinois at Urbana-Champaign (UIUC) as a graduate student and graduate assistant in the University Library's acquisitions unit. I graduated from UIUC's Graduate School of Library and Information Science (currently the iSchool) in May of 2016.

I am R. Cecilia Knight, the acquisitions and discovery librarian at Grinnell College Libraries and have worked at Grinnell since August of 1993. Previously I was principal catalog librarian at the University of Arizona Libraries and catalog librarian at Oklahoma State University Libraries. I earned my MLS at Rosary College (now Dominican University) in January of 1982.

We formulated the questions below through sitting down and discussing the changes we have seen in technical services work as well as attitudes toward such work.

Let's start out with the question of "What are technical services?"

REBECCA: Technical services can be difficult to define, since they are most often described in contrast to public services. Public services staff work directly with the patrons, whereas we in technical services seem to have a degree of separation between our work and the patron because we don't normally work face-to-face with our patrons. To define technical services without comparing them to public services, I would say technical services are library-related activities that ensure information is available and discoverable. Technical services staff select, identify, acquire, describe, organize, process, and provide continued access to the materials. We also maintain the technology that supports the organization and discovery of those materials.

CECILIA: I agree that this is the traditional perception of the division of work in libraries. A few years ago, our library decided to rename our technical services "library services" because these functions support and facilitate the overall work of the libraries. We provide library services to patrons via the many functions we perform, which include tasks requiring extensive technical skills such as acquisitions, cataloging, and systems; interpersonal skills such as supervising and negotiating; and research skills such as identifying content, doing overlap analysis, and tracking down resources.

You have established this dichotomy between technical and public services. Can you elaborate on the different skills needed for either one?

CECILIA: When I was pursuing my MLS in the early 1980s, it seemed technical services required focusing on details and following specific procedures. Technical services staff used computers and standard reference materials and wrote procedures. Public services required a person who could perform a reference interview and was comfortable with indefinite processes.

REBECCA: While pursuing my MLIS from fall of 2014 to spring of 2016, I did not notice such a distinct difference in skills between technical and public services. The people who seemed most committed to technical services studied data science, metadata, digital preservation, and audiovisual preservation. The people who seemed wholly interested in public services studied readers' advisory, services for diverse patrons, instruction, and children's librarianship. But most of my classmates took courses in both technical and public services functions.

The differences between Cecilia's and my graduate experiences is probably because the skills and aptitudes needed for all areas of librarianship have changed. As a heuristic, I like to think of functions like systems, cataloging, processing, acquisitions, preservation, and conservation as traditional technical services functions. But technical services have expanded beyond that. Now, we have new fields like e-resources management, digital preservation, data management, data science, digital publishing, and the definition-eluding digital humanities that could fall under the umbrella of technical services. Technical and public services librarians both need project management and social skills in much the same way, and public services librarians need a decent amount of technical skills to navigate the current information environment. It seems more positions in libraries are a hybridization of traditional technical services and public services roles.

How did you discover technical services work?

CECILIA: In library school, cataloging was seen as basic to librarianship. Therefore, we were required to take a class in cataloging in the first term; advanced classes were also offered. I wrote papers about thought leaders, like S. R. Ranganathan and Charles Ammi Cutter, and about library organizational topics. I am still influenced by these seminal ideas of focusing on the reader or user in my approach to library administration, management, and day-to-day work. I gained experience as a graduate assistant with various technologies, such as media production, computers with attached dot matrix printers, and OCLC terminals.

REBECCA: During graduate school, I held a preprofessional position in the University Library's acquisitions unit. The acquisitions unit purchased, cataloged, and processed most of the materials, both physical and electronic. In my role in the acquisitions unit, I gained experience selecting, ordering, and receiving items. I also worked on several e-resources management projects, and I even gained experience copy cataloging.

How did you acquire training for technical services work?

REBECCA: I received the bulk of my early training in technical services from my preprofessional position in a library acquisitions unit, a traditional technical services area. I also had coursework on technical services concepts. For example, I took courses in metadata creation and digital preservation. However, my impression was that my library school did not address the traditional technical services. I often knew more about technical services than my professors, who often had a somewhat outdated or ungrounded understanding of what technical services did. My professors often had never worked in a technical services role and therefore had never seen a complete picture of the work technical services librarians and staff do. And often, my professors had spent several years—if not decades—out of libraries, working on doctorates in a variety of fields and then teaching. Due to my preprofessional position, I had a much more up-to-date and grounded understanding of technical services.

CECILIA: As I went onto the job market my mentor counseled me to apply for jobs at large institutions to develop as a cataloger. My first professional position was at Oklahoma State University in 1982, where I received wonderful mentoring and training. The catalogers and library assistants were all in an open office area where we could easily consult. This was in the days of implementing the Anglo-American Cataloguing Rules (AACR2) and updating headings in the card catalog using sticky strips and typewriters. The knowledge, skills, and abilities that I brought were having up-to-date training on AACR2; being able to contribute to a request for proposal (RFP) for an online catalog due to my undergraduate computer science coursework; having experience with OCLC from interlibrary loan (ILL); and being familiar with media from doing classroom support as an undergraduate and graduate student.

REBECCA: Cecilia mentions being told by her mentors to go to a large library to develop herself as a cataloger. No one told me to do that. I went immediately to a small institution. I can see the benefits of starting somewhere large, where you can specialize in a field and have mentors who have moved up from your position to more senior ones. However, I wanted a wide variety of duties, and a smaller library like Grinnell College's offers a spectrum of opportunities.

How did the culture of the library where you had/have your first professional job affect your development?

REBECCA: In my current professional position, most of my training comes from the senior librarians at Grinnell College, who have taken it upon themselves to mentor me in technical services, server administration, and being a faculty member.

Cecilia also talks about the skills and aptitudes she had when entering the job market for the first time: up-to-date training on AACR2 and newer technologies. Like Cecilia, I had experience in technical services, though my experience was in acquisitions and e-resources management. I also had some experience with new technologies and platforms, having worked with self-checkout machines and video streaming in previous positions. The experience in acquisition and e-resources, I believe, was paramount to my success in interviews. My working style may have increased my appeal as a candidate. Former coworkers and references cited my willingness to experiment, document processes, and teach as one of my strengths. I was put in charge of more than 250 Chinese-language materials when the Chinese acquisitions specialist was on leave. Some people would have been overwhelmed by the characters; I simply developed a system to make sure all the books were accounted and paid for. In technical services, plenty of new and complex problems arise; it helps to be comfortable at least trying to resolve the problem in a calm and systematic manner.

CECILIA: In my first job, I sought out reasons to interact with the public services staff. My public services colleagues were very accommodating in providing cross-training opportunities at the various reference desks. This made it possible for my technical services work to be informed by how I observed and experienced the library being used. I have made sure to integrate public interaction, including research assistance, teaching, and providing backup for circulation service points, in each of my workplaces. These are locations where many patron needs and difficulties are identified.

How have technical services changed since you started your career?

CECILIA: In the first two libraries I worked in as a professional, the main card catalog held cards for the entire collection and then each service point had smaller card catalogs with cards related to the materials in that location. Library staff assistants filed cards in the card catalogs and the catalogers checked and dropped the cards. Alphabetization was an essential skill for technical services staff at all levels.

When we stopped filing cards and implemented an online catalog, we still maintained a card shelflist for several years. Staff jobs changed to spending almost all their time in front of screens. Work hours in these early years were structured by what system you were working in. You needed to schedule time at a different networked terminal for each system: one for OCLC, another for the integrated library system (ILS), and other for email. Technical services librarians and staff came in at odd hours to do systems backups and run updates and jobs. Later, Windows computers that allowed multiple client software installations allowed people to work at their own desks and move back and forth between systems as they worked. We integrated email and calendaring into our workflows as well and now use a variety of tools for database cleanup projects. Decisions are kept track of in email folders rather than on printouts, and reminders are added to online tools rather than paper calendars.

REBECCA: My career has been briefer and has not seen as much change. But I think the most interesting things that have changed in technical services during my career are not because of the changing information landscape or technology but because I made the switch from a large public research institution to a small liberal arts college.

At the large research institution, where I went to library school and worked as a graduate assistant in the University Library's acquisitions unit, there were so many resources—in terms of the sheer volume of print and e-resources we bought and provided access to, in terms of money spent, in terms of staff comparatively. At a smaller institution, resources are less extensive. Yet at both institutions I have seen increasing difficulties in accessing information. Having been in acquisitions, I know that one glaring difficulty is the increasing prices of e-resources and print serials, as library and institutional budgets either stagnate or shrink. Libraries of all types and sizes seem to innovate and collaborate on obtaining and accessing as much information as possible. Both institutions I have worked at are major players in various consortia that work to negotiate group pricing. Collection development, acquisitions, and e-resources librarians are pushing new buying models as well. Besides consortia and group purchasing, they have been experimenting with patron-driven, demand-driven, and evidence-based acquisitions to buy only what the patrons need, want, and use.

I have not been a systems librarian for very long, so it's difficult for me to discuss in detail how systems work has changed. But I do have somewhat of a historical perspective. Before ILSs became commercially available, there weren't systems librarians but instead head catalogers. With the implementation of ILS, the need for a librarian to manage the system emerged and the systems librarian was born. Cecilia mentions how first hardwired terminals were needed, and then the local area network (LAN) grew. More and more technology entered the library, and the mainstreaming of the Internet accelerated that further. The systems functions of technical services grew from no one (pre-ILS) to several people. Now, I have a staff that handles the ILS, the institutional repository (IR), virtual servers, and all variety of software and hardware.

As someone who grew up with the Internet, I had some sense that there was *so much* information available that patrons could be overwhelmed. Search engines can provide millions of results in mere milliseconds. In some ways, that's great. It means that technical services librarians can provide our patrons with more information than ever before: we are less constrained by geographic location and physical space. From my work in acquisitions, I saw plenty of the assessment and evaluation that goes into choosing and weeding resources.

Due to this incredible proliferation of information, I see how monumental the task is of making everything accessible and discoverable. Each system presents its own challenges. Technical services librarians work hard to ensure that all patrons can discover, access, and use information. Additionally, even in my short time as a technical services librarian, I have noted the increasing attention we are paying to accessibility in the resources we purchase as well as those we create.

CECILIA: I think that the biggest change in terms of performing and hiring for technical services jobs is how dynamic and far-reaching our jobs are now. I will contrast this with my first five to eight years in library technical services. Unlike the present, my work was highly structured: I knew what kind of work I would do, what technology I would use, when I would have access to each library system, and when I would take breaks and go home at night. As we moved into our first ILS that provided significant discovery opportunities to the public, we also started thinking about how to move from CD-ROMs and individual databases that we could log into remotely. Link resolvers were another necessary development to aid patrons in accessing the materials they were finding. This re-visioning of service to our users made our work life far less predictable. We are always making changes to how we do things as the various parts of the system shift and change.

We technical services librarians—and many staff members too—now need to be project managers capable of taking a solutions-based approach to responsibilities, identifying problems and the resources needed to resolve them, creating documentation, and supervising people. At the same time that the Internet can identify everything, we strive to find ways to put our solutions into users' workflows.

Initially the big changes for us were that more institutions had loaded their records into OCLC. This meant more records, more duplicates, more change requests, more merged records, more call numbers, more typo correcting, more series work, more authorities work, and so forth. As we moved from card catalogs to online catalogs, we had opportunities to provide additional access through entries for people, institutions, subjects, tables of contents, summaries, and the like. This ability has caused a philosophical shift from scarcity to abundance in technical services work.

Librarians mapped the card catalogs directly to the online catalogs that replaced them. As we wrote our first RFPs and dreamed of a new world of online discovery, we asked for the ability to search across multiple indexes, apply Boolean logic, and search by keywords. Keyword searching of records supplemented with abstracts and tables of contents provided greater depth in search and created some of the serendipity enjoyed when physically browsing the collections.

In acquisitions, we started sending orders electronically, rather than typing and mailing orders. Many libraries implemented approval plans and standing orders to cope with the explosion in publishing.

Another big shift came later as we got into the knowledge management and then digital scholarship business. Our technical skills are very much in demand for creating databases with the goal of identifying materials.

The shift to digital content caused significant change for technical services. We have spent years developing satisfactory workflows for materials we never touch, while continuing to ensure excellent service for patrons. We batch upload records and find ourselves trying to monitor intangible objects, all while we still have existing workflows for the physical collections. For print materials, any problems could be assumed to be unique to that individual record. With batch-loaded e-resources, we must go back and analyze the entire collection to make sure that this is not a systemic problem.

Over time, we added or repurposed staff positions to focus on the invisible but large task of managing e-resources. There is little sense of craft in relation to e-resources management. It is all about importing metadata, protecting data, and merging data to ensure and preserve access.

Acquisitions staff must ascertain, using a variety of databases and tools, that we don't already have each specific title that is requested. It is challenging for patrons to identify known items in our discovery systems. The staff handling the requests need to verify whether we truly don't have it against the catalog, as well as any electronic packages we have paid for.

The move to e-resources has also required the development of expertise in licenses and accessibility. Many libraries now have e-resource management specialists and electronic resource management systems (ERMS) to help keep track of this additional data and information. ILL and reserves are impacted by terms of use negotiated in licenses. These were not considerations with print books and serials.

REBECCA: I will follow up on some of Cecilia's comments because my remarks might provide some insight on how much technical services have changed. Cecilia started working when card catalogs were the system of discovery for library materials. I was born after the advent of the ILS, during the widespread implementation of online public access catalogs and in the twilight of card catalogs. I remember a card catalog at the local public library that no one used; and I remember encyclopedias on CD-ROMs. This was all before I turned 10 years old. I was in grade school and middle school when e-books became a viable option. By high school, I was reading popular fiction as e-books and my high school library staff constantly pushed e-resources.

Thinking about how much information dissemination and consumption has changed astonishes me. For example, I don't know what I would do when faced with making an encyclopedia on CD-ROM accessible for users. But it was my senior colleagues who wrangled that problem, and several other challenges. We will undoubtedly be challenged in the profession by new modes of information dissemination, and probably in the not too distant future.

How do you see technical services changing in the future?

REBECCA: Currently, technical services can be siloed, particularly at larger institutions. For example, when I was working in a large research library's acquisitions unit, I did not interact with the public. That, however, was starting to change as I left. I had been encouraged to work on the chat reference desk, and I know at least one of my former coworkers was encouraged to provide instruction sessions related to e-resources.

Now that I am at a small liberal arts institution, we do not have the personnel to silo people. I have my systems work, which includes managing people, the ILS, our IR, our virtual machines, and our hardware. But I am also required to liaise with academic departments and teach library instruction sessions. I see technical services librarians having roles that blend traditional public and technical services functions.

I predict that technical services functions will continue to integrate with public services functions. As e-resources become more and more the norm, either public services people will need to be trained on e-resources troubleshooting, or technical services people will be drawn out of their basement offices to provide on the spot support for digital materials. As digital institutional repositories grow in popularity, the work of scholarly communications and digital scholarship librarians will be crucial for improving and growing collections. We in technical services will need to work just as closely with collaborators to ensure that objects are discoverable and that the systems work appropriately.

I also foresee that nontraditional technical services functions will grow in prominence. Those nontraditional roles that are likely to grow are IR management and development, digitization, data science, bioinformatics, digital preservation, and e-resources librarianship. Much of our information is now digital, and our technologies for creating, storing, and accessing this information are changing at exponential rates. We risk losing our information if we no longer have the original technology to access it, so digitization and digital preservation will increase. Shared bibliographic records, like those from OCLC, will push records to become more generic, with a variety of origins and types of updates. That will make traditional cataloging rarer as institutions will only need catalogers for their original cataloging. This will further streamline various workflows in acquisitions, processing, and ILL. Libraries will likely always have those traditional technical services functions but not be staffed at current levels. My own position will grow more dependent on facility with coding languages and metadata schemas as systems grow to encompass both new and traditional technologies and resources.

CECILIA: As a technical services manager, I have always emphasized in all decision-making that the users are at the center and we need to take actions that will improve their experience. With the move to e-resources it has been difficult for staff to realign their work with new realities and perform new tasks.

Along with what Rebecca has mentioned, the major change that I see is the focus on the local. Pamphlet files and other small local collections were always the purview of public services staff and archivists. Special collections materials were held close and only the staff knew what wonders existed. Catalogers handled mostly mainstream published materials and focused on production and numbers. Now we focus on doing artisanal-level cataloging for our most unique items and we tell the whole world that we have them. Standard published materials arrive as e-publications or shelf-ready.

We have added IRs and digital asset management systems (DAMS) and created metadata for our local collections of pamphlets, posters, photographs, letters, and other primary documents, making them discoverable by the wider world. Large shops may have specialists for each of these systems, but at a small library we collaborate, and each bring our expertise to these systems.

We see this change reflected in our titles and job descriptions. A few years ago, when Grinnell College changed its logo and directed people to order new business cards, we decided to realign our titles with our librarian job duties. All the librarians changed their titles to communicate what their evolved positions now included. The systems librarian became the integrated systems and discovery librarian; the public services librarian became the humanities librarian and coordinator of research services.

Our firm orders enter our collections with minimum staff intervention as shelf-ready materials. Additionally, our e-book records come with the URLs for our institution created by the vendor. With the focus of OCLC WorldCat moving to be a global discovery tool for individuals, rather than primarily a tool for technical services staff, we are less attached to the records. It is now more important to have the most up-to-date version of each record to facilitate interlibrary lending, which is also far more patron driven now.

Our physical collections are no longer the largest part of our collection. Serials have moved almost exclusively online, and books are following, except for specific areas. Serials units are shrinking as we order, check in, and bind fewer print titles and use outside services to manage our aggregated subscriptions.

When I conduct interviews for technical services positions, I look for people who care about details, but I don't test their alphabetization skills. I am also looking for people who can interpret and apply guidelines rather than strictly follow rules. I need people who like to solve problems and puzzles, because that is where more of our time is focused. Instead of focusing on numbers of titles, we focus instead on how their work forwards the libraries' and the campus's strategic plans and goals.

CONCLUSION

Libraries have taken advantage of the opportunities afforded by the globalization of access to knowledge. Perhaps more than most local institutions, our day-to-day activities and services have been transformed by the Internet and the ability to deliver content in electronic formats.

Library technical services have found themselves bridging the physical and electronic collections. We are reaching a point now where we can deliver satisfactory service for both types of material. The skill set needed by technical services staff will continue to evolve as, for example, facility with coding languages and metadata schemas grows in importance.

The focus will continue to be on providing the best services to our communities, but with the added challenge of making our users aware that they are using their local libraries as they interact at a more global level.

CHALLENGE ONE

The Evolution of Library Cataloging and Metadata

CHAPTER 1

From Records to Data: The New Purposes of Cataloging

Kara D. Long

ABSTRACT

The MARC bibliographic standard debuted in the 1960s and quickly gained widespread adoption in libraries in the United States and Canada before being adapted for international use. Since then, MARC has remained the predominant bibliographic data standard and effectively made the library catalog computer searchable. The MARC standard did not, however, anticipate the emergence of the networked catalog or the possibilities posed by linked data. The development of new standards and formats for bibliographic records, such as Resource Description and Access (RDA) and BIBFRAME, seek to take advantage of these technologies. They also create new and emerging possibilities for library records beyond the administration and navigation of a local library collection. As library records become more like data—transportable outside of the catalog and more amenable to computational use and analysis—the purposes and goals of cataloging likewise are shifting

INTRODUCTION

Catalogers have moved from creating records for local use, to networked catalog environments, to contributing to massive, online, bibliographic datasets. Catalogers are witnessing not only the end of the MARC record but also the decline of the record, as a document, in favor of the record as data. Evidence for this can be seen in the ongoing development of BIBFRAME, the implementation of RDA, the changing core competencies for catalog librarians, and support for initiatives aimed at finding ways to use catalog records as datasets. These activities and others demonstrate a significant change in how we perceive of the library catalog, the role it plays, and the responsibilities of the cataloger. With this chapter, I hope to contextualize this shift in perception in the evolution of the library catalog and highlight that our current and ongoing transitions are laying the groundwork for a newly formed and forming expectations for our bibliographic data.

The impetus for many of these changes has been the adaptation of cataloging practices and systems for greater interoperability and use with web-based technologies. BIBFRAME, a model, vocabulary, and set of tools designed to replace the MARC standard, is one such adaptation.[1] The BIBFRAME project began in 2012, and as of this writing, participating institutions are about to begin to report the progress of the pilot for BIBFRAME 2.0. The BIBFRAME model has been presented in contrast to the MARC standard. For example, "instead of bundling everything neatly as a 'record' . . . the BIBFRAME Model relies heavily on relationships between resources."[2] This is a clear move away from the library catalog as a collection of records. This is an important distinction, carrying implications for the changing roles of catalogers. While there is significant overlap, there are material differences between records management, data management, and library cataloging, and the changing cataloging environments will require an expanding skill set that draws upon all three of these areas.

Emerging from the technological and operational changes to cataloging are new purposes and applications of the catalog that have yet to be defined or even fully explored. On May 16, 2017, the Library of Congress released over 25 million of its catalog records as a freely downloadable dataset on the data.gov site.[3] The press release quotes Dr. Carla Hayden, librarian of Congress: "Unlocking the rich data in the Library's online catalog is a great step forward. I'm excited to see how people will put this information to use." Her statement suggests that the library catalog as it stands, although freely accessible online, is locked and inaccessible or unsuitable for certain, undefined kinds of use.[4] The press release also quotes Beacher Wiggins, the Library of Congress director for acquisitions and bibliographic access, who reiterates this claim, stating, "The Library of Congress catalog is literally the gold standard for bibliographic data and we believe this treasure trove of information can be used for much more than its original purpose." He goes on to give an idea of what these uses might be: "From more efficient information-sharing and easier analysis to visualizations and other possibilities we cannot begin to predict, we hope this data will be put to work by social scientists, data analysts, developers, statisticians and everyone else doing innovative work with large datasets to enhance learning and the formation of new knowledge." The original purpose of the dataset is not defined in the press release, but it does position the use of the catalog *as* a dataset beyond or in addition to the catalog's intended or traditional purpose.

If the Library of Congress catalog records are a dataset, it is a messy one. The bibliographic data in the records was encoded by catalogers and machines across decades, during which cataloging standards and practices changed. And, while libraries often conduct retro conversion projects to bring old records up to new standards, they are imperfect. Without a familiarity with these changing practices, this data is unreliable at best and misleading at worst. We have privileged the opening of this data without necessarily having a wider conversation in library technical services about what it will require to make this data useable, interoperable, and comprehensible, and what it will take to do so in a sustainable way.

THE TRADITIONAL LIBRARY CATALOG

The purpose of the catalog has shifted as technologies have enhanced its capabilities and as the expectations of users and library personnel have changed. Looking back on the catalog's evolution can help us locate the traditional catalog, which is useful in that the catalog-as-dataset is defined in contrast to it. The catalog is a tool that mediates access between the collection and the user. It is also a tool for the administration and maintenance of the collection. It records the permutations of the collection over time. We cannot separate the purposes of the catalog from the broader goals of the library. As Karen Coyle and Diane Hillman remind us, it is difficult, if not impossible, to make a meaningful separation between the nature of the holdings of the library, the characteristics of the user population that the library is mandated to serve, and the library catalog. All these factors have been bound together to provide the service that embodies the main mission of the library: to put the desired resources into the hands of users.[5]

Ultimately, the utility of the library depends on access to its collections, done through the catalog, and made visible through the labor of its catalogers. It is as difficult to separate the library catalog from the aims of the library as it is to tease out the purposes of the catalog from the intentional and practical design decisions that have guided its evolution as a tool and as a concept.

The library catalog has a long history. The earliest known tools to administer collections were inventories and lists composed on clay tablets and scrolls. By the 16th century, the advent of the printing press necessitated more robust and comprehensive ways of keeping up with new and increasingly varied bibliographic materials.[6] Printed catalogs and indexes replaced handwritten inventories and lists. These printed and bound catalogs were eventually atomized into cards. Cards are portable, able to be arranged and rearranged into any configuration, including author, title, and subject.[7] By the mid-1800s, some libraries employed card-based systems for search and retrieval. Charles A. Cutter described the "objects and means" of the catalog in his *Rules for a Dictionary Catalog* (1876), a brief document in which he articulates what a library catalog should be able to do:

1. To enable a person to find a book of which either
    a. the author
    b. the title
    c. the subject
    . . . is known
2. To show what the library has
    d. by a given author
    e. on a given subject
    f. in each kind of literature.

3. To assist in the choice of a book
    g. as to its edition (bibliographically)
    h. as to its character (literary or topical).

Well over a century later, we still expect the library catalog to fulfill these same kinds of inquiries. And, for many years, these objectives generally guided the creation and maintenance of many library catalogs, even when practices were not universally standardized.

In the early 1960s, under the aegis of the International Federation of Library Associations (IFLA), representatives at the International Conference on Catalog Principles in Paris drafted their own criteria for the catalog.[8] According to the *Paris Principles* (1961), the catalog "should be an efficient instrument for ascertaining whether the library contains a particular book by *(a)* its author and title . . . and which works by a particular author and *(b)* which editions of a particular work are in the library."[9] These principles cover the same kinds of tasks that Cutter explicated. If we are to locate the so-called traditional catalog, it is necessary to ask whose tradition it represents. Broadly speaking, the library catalog has been based on Western ideas of knowledge organization and production. As such, the catalog and the organization of many libraries in the U.S. have been predicated on predominantly white, Western, male perspectives. This continued to be the case, even as a greater number of women entered the profession at the start of the 20th century; men continued to take on a greater number of leadership roles, including making high-level decisions around description, access, and cataloging.[10]

By the time the *Paris Principles* was released, the Library of Congress in the U.S. had already been experimenting with automating certain cataloging functions. Out of this effort, Henriette Avram, a computer programmer and systems analyst at the Library of Congress, developed the MARC (Machine Readable Cataloging) system, a "utility of the distribution of cataloging data in machine-readable form from LC to user libraries."[11] The MARC standard was designed to describe books and to facilitate the printing of cards for card catalogs. MARC was not designed to replace card-based systems or to describe materials other than books. In *MARC: Its History and Implications,* Avram acknowledges the magnitude and difficulty of developing a bibliographic model that includes multiple formats. Practical constraints and limits on time and funding inhibited the design and analysis of MARC for formats other than books. Changes and enhancements were made over time to incorporate nonbook formats, but these early design choices limited the extent to which nonbook and nonprint materials could be described.

The Library of Congress promoted centralized cataloging as an advantage of MARC; libraries across the country could order cards in the MARC format, describing materials held in their collections. This was endorsed as a time-saving measure for librarians in addition to the promise of more uniformity of catalog entries, which would ultimately result in easier sharing of records between libraries, better and more reliable union catalogs, less duplication of effort, and improved interlibrary loan service.[12] The near universal adoption of MARC was likewise an adoption of the descriptive practices that worked well in the MARC standard. The first edition of Anglo-American Cataloging Rules (AACR) was published in 1967, MARC was officially adopted by the Library of Congress in 1968, and generations of library catalogers in the U.S. and abroad acclimated to these tools and the catalog environment they created.

Although the development of MARC relied on computing, it predates the use of online public access catalogs (OPACs) as interfaces for user access to the catalog. This is an important distinction, as MARC data replicates the strictures of cards and card catalogs. In fact, MARC enshrined the practices purpose-built for card catalogs instead of expanding upon the card format or ditching it altogether. Essentially, the unit of measure in the MARC-based catalog is the card—not necessarily the bibliographic object. Early on, MARC facilitated the printing of cards, spine labels, and book pockets. One of the first computer-based MARC databases, MARC Retriever, was available for librarians and researchers at the Library of Congress, and it presaged the development of OPACs that brought the catalog online.[13]

In 1973 OCLC (then the Ohio College Library Center and now the Online Computer Library Center) distributed "beehive" computer terminals from which member libraries could catalog materials in a networked environment and allowed librarians to share, send, and retrieve records for online catalogs. OCLC's union catalog, WorldCat, has become the world's largest bibliographic database, and contributing to WorldCat has become a standard part of cataloging practice in many libraries.

For the past 50 years, the delivery of bibliographic data has been closely tied to MARC, and despite many OPACs delivering MARC records to library users daily, many online catalogs are based on relational database models, not MARC. This is an imperfect fit. In her review of FRBR (Functional Requirements for Bibliographic Records) and other bibliographic models, Karen Coyle sums up the situation: "The library profession models its data, but not the system solution that uses the data. This leads to an awkward situation where the goals of cataloging may not be the same as the functions of the catalog as implemented."[14] This depends entirely on what the catalog is for and what we would like it to do. But we lose our ability to set and pursue our own goals for our library catalogs when our models do not align with our systems.

Part of this misalignment is that MARC records are truly records. As Jason Thomale has pointed out, MARC records behave more like documents and less like structured data: "The fact: MARC is, at its heart, a data format built to contain catalog records; bibliographic items are described via the catalog records rather than directly via the structured MARC data."[15] Structured data is much more amenable to computation and use with web-based tools than are encoded text documents. And, without a way to play nicely with the web, the information encoded in MARC records is virtually invisible online, outside of a search through an online catalog or other dedicated library discovery tool. The current and ongoing evolution of the library catalog is a further atomization from text-based records to data.

THE CATALOG AS DATA

The promises of a linked data catalog have yet to be fully realized. The goal is that bibliographic data, liberated from the MARC record, will be more flexible, more visible on the web, and more amenable to interlinking. Currently, bibliographic data in records behave more like documents. The catalog relies on strings of text, formatted in specific ways to act as uniform identifiers for authors, geographic places, time periods, subject headings, and corporate bodies. This is not necessarily unique to documents, but it has deeply informed how the catalog works and how catalogers work in it. Every text string within every element of a MARC record is contextually situated in the record. The position or form of the contents of a single element can inform and is potentially informed by the position and form of other elements in the record. The full meaning of an element is lost if divorced from or read in isolation of the record in its entirety. Jason Thomale explains:

> Structured data formats are intended for machine consumption and tend to follow rules that are simple and consistent. . . . A document, however, is less straightforward, as the information it contains is meant more for human consumption; even if the document is marked up to aid machine-processing, the underlying structure is based on linguistics rather than a format that was designed to be machine-readable. The information in a marked-up document therefore behaves more like language than data. Meaning is not clear and encapsulated. The document contains semantic meaning beyond the sum of its marked-up data elements.[16]

Catalogers are accustomed to approaching records this way—as documents. While a linked data catalog offers a technical challenge to many catalogers, it also requires a different way of thinking about the records we produce and how we maintain them. This is much more than a technical change, or even a change of cataloging rules. This is a conceptual change.

A new code for descriptive cataloging is needed if we are to (1) relinquish the notion of the record as a document and (2) reorient our thinking about what cataloging is and what it can accomplish. RDA, a cataloging code to replace AACR2, was developed with this reorientation in mind and aims to be suitable for exchanging bibliographic information in the BIBFRAME format.[17] RDA is based on the bibliographic model put forward by IFLA and called Functional Requirements for Bibliographic Records (FRBR), which has again been revised as IFLA LRM (IFLA Library Reference Model).[18] RDA and BIBFRAME have both undergone major and minor revisions since 2012. The development of the FRBR model and these standards has been highly iterative, particularly to redress the ill fit between library data models and systems. Librarians, technologists, and other metadata practitioners have been vocal about the changes brought by RDA. Some believe these changes to be far less radical than what is truly needed: the language of RDA is too closely aligned with MARC and AACR2 to be a true departure and the inconsistencies between RDA and FRBR are confusing.[19] For catalogers on the ground, RDA has changed the content of some MARC elements and added others, but it has not brought about a change in how we think of records.

Many catalogers, myself included, still refer to elements of a record by their MARC code; a "245" is a title. This is hardly surprising to anyone who has spent time in technical services, but it shows how embedded MARC, and by extension the card, is in how we conceive of our work. So, when the Library of Congress released its catalog records in May, I read the press release with some trepidation. The Library of Congress and other media outlets described this as a "data release" or "dataset," but this is MARC data, record-like data; it needs to be converted into an easier to use format before any researcher could extract meaning. It is a good place to start, especially if sharing our records with researchers in new ways encourages us to approach the records as a dataset.

In her work on data scholarship and research in networked environments, Christine Borgman has written extensively about the uses of data and data-driven scholarship in various academic disciplines. She defines data as "representations of observations, objects, or other entities used as evidence of phenomena for the purposes of research of scholarship."[20] Yet, the act of cataloging has rarely, if ever, been perceived as a scholarly activity.[21] This does not preclude catalog records from being used for scholarly purposes; however, catalog records have not been created with this particular kind of use in mind. It remains to be seen if part of this paradigm shift to data brings with it new responsibilities for researchers that we had not previously envisioned.

Using library catalog records as a dataset requires some familiarity with cataloging codes, the rules by which observations are made about bibliographic materials and are then articulated in records. Cataloging codes, including RDA, have attempted to standardize the use and application of descriptive practice. These codes are numerous, have been applied inconsistently, and have undergone revisions, additions, and extensions over time. They are reflective of the goals of the catalogers and the limits of the catalogs that were in use when a record was created or edited. Ben Schmidt, a professor of history at Northeastern University, experimented with the Library of Congress records for his blog post "A Brief Visual History of MARC Cataloging at the Library of Congress."[22] He was interested in mapping out how the Library of Congress digitized catalog records over time. He used date information from the MARC 260 subfield c. This element usually contains the publication date for the work described. His visualization uncovered dates far into the future; contradictory dates within the same record; dates expressed in non-Roman calendars; a preponderance of materials dated to 1900. (It was standard cataloging practice to designate an item as published in 1900 when, in fact, the precise year could not be determined, but the item was published in the 20th century.) Projects designed to convert or migrate records from older systems can also affect the date in a record. Several catalogers responded to Schmidt's blog entry with explanations for some of these issues, and he was gracious in his responses. This was a relatively small-scale project, but it demonstrates how difficult it can be to analyze catalog data.

Even when cataloging codes are perfectly applied, the language used in catalog records requires some contextualization. In her seminal work *The Power to Name,* Hope Olson illustrates how racial and sexual biases are encoded into cataloging practice, particularly through the application of subject headings and classification determined in our cataloging codes.[23] Librarians continue to engage critically with these rules and subject vocabularies—especially now, as we can envision information infrastructures beyond MARC. Amber Billey, Emily Drabinksi, and K. R. Roberto have challenged the RDA and NACO rules that specify that the gender of a person should be recorded in name authority records.[24] Name authority records establish the standardized text string that must be replicated in each record associated with that person. In a linked data catalog, there could be other mechanisms for establishing authoritative description beyond the use of standardized text strings or authority records. Persistent, unique digital identifiers like online researcher IDs (ORCIDs) or uniform resource identifiers (URIs) can be associated with personal names, corporate entities, or geographic locations, or other named things. These identifiers can support automated links between an entity and the works associated with them, without using dates of birth or death or other personally identifying information. The Program for Cooperative Cataloging (PCC) has distributed information about using URIs in MARC records, but this practice is not currently widespread.[25]

The Library of Congress is not alone in this effort to frame catalog records as data. The Institute of Museum and Library Services (IMLS) has supported the collaborative project *Always Already Computation: Collections as Data.*[26] This group seeks to "foster a strategic approach to developing, describing, providing access to, and encouraging the reuse of collections that support computationally-driven research and teaching" through a series of talks and workshops that began in 2017. The group's work, spearheaded by Thomas Padilla, currently the interim head, knowledge production, at the University of Nevada, Las Vegas, has taken an iterative approach. The group has drafted guiding principles on establishing ethical commitments when developing data, a commitment to open documentation of data, interoperability, and data integrity. Here the integrity of data refers to its provenance, which "reflects how data were created, and modified, as well as the scope, and intended use of the data."[27] Catalog records have a complicated history, which I have only skimmed the surface of here. *Collections as Data* is not focused on MARC or even bibliographic data exclusively, but the questions arising from this work are important for library technical services to consider, especially if we expect our bibliographic data to be useful and meaningful *as data.*

A report from another IMLS-funded project, *Digging Deeper, Reaching Further: Libraries Empowering Users to Mine the HathiTrust Digital Library Resources* (DDRF), cites the Library of Congress Collections as Data forum and *Collections as Data* for recognizing the expanding role of librarians as stewards of data.[28] We perceive this shift as largely driven by researcher needs—namely a desire to engage in data-driven scholarship. Yet, as the report goes on to describe, many of these efforts at training and meeting these needs focus on support for digital scholarship services and positions. I would like to see more catalogers included in the development of these services and encouraged to share experiences in data transformation and assessment.

At my current institution, I have found building relationships with our digital scholarship librarians to be incredibly valuable.

These colleagues often work directly with students and faculty on data-driven projects. Our former digital scholarship librarian, Megan Martinsen, worked with a group of students to analyze collections data from the Tate Gallery. The students focused on how the size and scale of two-dimensional artworks changed over time. There was a notable outlier in their results, seeming to represent an artwork with extreme height. On closer inspection the group came to the realization that there was no such artwork in the dataset. The metadata for the dimensions had been entered incorrectly, and the painting was a standard height but had a panoramic length, which was less unusual. Martinsen and I were able to discuss how this specific example not only reinforced the importance of working with accurate and correct data, but also the importance of understanding context in which data gets recorded.[29] Institutions that encourage cross-departmental collaboration between technical services and other units of the library can benefit from the wide range of experiences that librarians in different units have with data.

Cultural heritage institutions have supported data-driven research in the humanities and other disciplines for years. The principles in development by *Collections as Data* seek to ground these activities in a set of shared values. If we hope libraries and library data to be truly unlocked from the catalog and the record, catalogers must engage with the discussions around the use and stewardship of this data beyond the life of the catalog. If the new purposes of cataloging include support for exploration of bibliographic data, then we must privilege formats and systems that make our data interoperable and accessible, our documentation openly available and comprehensible, and the provenance explicit.[30] This includes the work being done to interrogate our models and systems and it also must include the work being done to interrogate the biases embedded in our vocabularies and descriptive practices.

CONCLUSION

At the time of this writing, RDA is undergoing major revisions, and the second pilot of BIBFRAME has reported progress. Some of these changes will impact my day-to-day activities as a catalog and metadata librarian; many will not. It is still too early to assert whether these standards will align with the principles and commitments that guide *Collections as Data* or other groups seeking to establish best practices for data stewardship in academic libraries. What I am offering here is an idea: that we begin to think of our records as data and all that entails.

Creating a catalog from data that is fit for computational use and reflective of the values and goals of the library is an ambitious and ongoing goal. One of the first steps is to examine what it means for library records to be conceived as data. Based on the work of *Collections as Data* and even in looking at small experiments with bibliographic records, it is evident that our records must change if they are to be useful and reliable as a research dataset. Many changes have already been set in motion, but BIBFRAME and other changes to the catalog have not typically been presented as a move away from records toward data.

Practically speaking, many of the librarians and catalogers at my institution do not have the time or space in their workloads to take on a pilot project or to experiment with new cataloging models. That said, we frequently discuss project updates and conference reports on BIBFRAME and other efforts as a way of keeping up with potential changes. It has been helpful to begin talking about our records as data, and to be mindful of the terms we use when we do discuss bibliographic data. We still use MARC field tags as a shorthand, and if we catalog in MARC there is no sensible way to avoid talking in MARC. But this too can be a barrier when learning to catalog in a non-MARC environment or even imagining our data in a non-MARC environment.

Thinking of our records as records is also embedded in our assessment practices. Currently, each cataloger in our unit keeps a tally of their record count, and this number gets consolidated and added to our departmental record every month. This document can tell us only that—how many records are added and deleted each month. This document cannot and does not accurately reflect a large proportion of the work of our department. A great deal of work is spent cleaning, transforming, and generally wrestling with large record loads so that the data we ingest is meaningful and relevant to our users. This can mean long hours spent working with e-book loads, digital collections metadata, or special collections cataloging. We continue to record these numbers, but an hour spent on 60,000 e-book records and an hour spent on performing original cataloging of a single rare map are not easily reflected in the numbers alone. As we make this shift, we need to think about how we will assess ourselves and track our work with data—work that often cannot or should not be counted by the record.

My hope is that this new approach will provide many more opportunities to build context in ways that were constrained before. This is a much more expansive vision and introduces new goals and new responsibilities to technical services. We can no longer assume that the records we create in the context of our own libraries or institutions will be used in the ways we've imagined, or even used by human actors. What does cataloging fit for an API even look like? Increasing my contact with our digital scholarship librarians has given me an additional frame from which to view our bibliographic data. Keeping abreast of how students and faculty are using data in their research has encouraged me to look at our data from a different perspective. It is not enough to ask if a student can locate and identify a resource from the given data; we must also think about what other queries can be answered using bibliographic data and what that data looks like as a whole, not as a single record.

The catalog has undergone a slow dematerialization. Lists and inventories were broken down into cards. Card catalogs were broken down and transferred into computer terminals. Today, many of the resources available to our users are not described in the catalog at all. For example, our theses and dissertations are discoverable through our institutional repository and not the catalog. As library budgets have stretched, many libraries have increased their collections through licensed content and demand-driven acquisitions. Libraries providing licensed content to their users *may* ingest a MARC record for the licensed material, or metadata may simply be pushed to a discovery layer. There will be no MARC record, and none will appear in the library catalog. Perhaps one of the most provocative questions we ask when we receive a new resource is whether it should be described in MARC at all. This question is often met with some trepidation, but it is a question we are asking with more frequency. Some of the fear comes from change anxiety, some from anxiety about learning a new system or skill, but even with advanced training and mentoring and growing an expanding skillset, the move away from MARC is challenging. As catalogers, our professional identities have hewn so closely to the catalog and its traditions. I hope that by imagining our work and our data in a different way, we can also begin to imagine new trajectories and roles for the cataloger in the library and in the research process.

NOTES

1. BIBFRAME is perhaps the largest coordinated effort to develop a tool for linked data in libraries, but some libraries, archives, and museums have experimented with linked data in smaller, local applications. See the BIBFRAME site for more information: https://www.loc.gov /bibframe/.
2. "BIBFRAME Frequently Asked Questions," Library of Congress, accessed April 5, 2020, https://www.loc.gov/bibframe/faqs/.
3. Sheryl Cannady, "Library Offers Largest Release of Digital Catalog Records in History," *News From the Library of Congress,* accessed May 16, 2017, https://www.loc.gov/item/prn-17-068/.
4. Ibid.
5. Karen Coyle and Diane Hillman, "Resource Description and Access (RDA): Cataloging Rules for the 20th Century," *D-Lib Magazine,* 13, no. 1/2 (January/February 2007), http://dlib.org/dlib/january07 /coyle/01coyle.html.
6. Ann M. Blair, *Too Much to Know: Managing Scholarly Information Before the Modern Age* (New Haven: Yale University Press, 2010), 11–61.
7. Karen Coyle, "The Evolving Catalog: Cataloging Tech From Scrolls to Computers," *American Libraries Magazine,* January 4, 2016, https:// americanlibrariesmagazine.org/2016/01/04/cataloging-evolves/; Markus Krajewski, *Paper Machines: About Cards and Catalogs, 1548–1929* (Cambridge: The MIT Press, 2011); Amelia Abreu, "On Cards, Card-Based Systems, and the Material Cultures of Computing" (conference presentation, Systems We Love, San Francisco, CA, December 13, 2016).
8. Charles A. Cutter, *Rules for a Dictionary Catalog*, 4th ed. (Washington, DC: Government Printing Office, 1904); Ted Fons, "The

Tradition of Library Catalogs" *Library Technology Reports*, 52, no. 5 (July 2016), 15–19, https://doi.org/10.5860/ltr.52n5.

9. "Statement of Principles Adopted by The International Conference on Cataloging Principles Paris 1961," IFLA, accessed November 1, 2017, https://www.ifla.org/files/assets/cataloguing/IMEICC /IMEICC1/statement_principles_paris_1961.pdf.

10. Jessica Olin and Michelle Millet, "Gendered Expectations for Leadership in Libraries," *In the Library With the Lead Pipe* (November 4, 2015), http://www.inthelibrarywiththeleadpipe.org /2015/libleadgender/.

11. Henriette D. Avram, *MARC: Its History and Implications* (Washington, DC: Library of Congress, 1975), 4.

12. Ibid., 32.

13. Ibid., 26.

14. Karen Coyle, *FRBR, Before and After: A Look at Our Bibliographic Models* (Chicago: ALA Editions, 2016), 35.

15. Jason Thomale, "Interpreting MARC: Where's the Bibliographic Data?" *Code4Lib Journal*, no. 11 (2010), http://journal.code4lib.org /articles/3832.

16. Ibid.

17. "Resource Description and Access (RDA): Information and Resources in Preparation for RDA," Library of Congress, accessed October 24, 2017, https://www.loc.gov/aba/rda/.

18. Pat Riva, Patrick Le Bœuf, and Maja Žumer, IFLA Library Reference Model: A Conceptual Model for Bibliographic Information (The Hague, Netherlands: *IFLA*, 2017), accessed January 2020, https:// www.ifla.org/files/assets/cataloguing/frbr-lrm/ifla-lrm-august -2017.pdf.

19. Coyle and Hillman, "Resource Description and Access (RDA)."

20. Christine Borgman, *Big Data, Little Data, No Data: Scholarship in the Networked World* (Cambridge: The MIT Press, 2015), xviii.

21. Catalogers do participate in scholarly activity and produce scholarly work; however, in my experience catalog records produced by catalogers are not recognized as scholarly output by promotion and tenure committees in academia. I would love to be proven wrong about this.

22. Ben Schmidt, "A Brief Visual History of MARC Cataloging at the Library of Congress," *Sapping Attention* (blog), posted May 16,

2017, accessed May 20, 2017, http://sappingattention.blogspot.com /2017/05/a-brief-visual-history-of-marc.html.

23. Hope A. Olson, *Power to Name: Locating the Limits of Subject Representation in Libraries* (Dordrecht: Kluwer Academic, 2002).

24. Amber Billey, Emily Drabinski, and K. R. Roberto, "What's Gender Got to Do With It? A Critique of RDA 9.7," *Cataloging and Classification Quarterly*, 52, no. 4 (2014): 412–21, https://doi.org /10.1080/01639374.2014.882465.

25. Program for Cooperative Cataloging, *URI FAQs: PCC URI Task Group on URIs in MARC*, September 26, 2018, Library of Congress, http:// www.loc.gov/aba/pcc/bibframe/TaskGroups/URI%20FAQs.pdf.

26. *"Always Already Computational—Collections as Data,"* accessed November 1, 2017, https://collectionsasdata.github.io/.

27. Ibid.

28. Harriet Green and Eleanor Dickson, "Expanding the Librarian's Tech Toolbox: The 'Digging Deeper, Reaching Further: Librarians Empowering Users to Mine the HathiTrust Digital Library' Project," *D-Lib Magazine*, 23, no. 5/6 (May/June 2017), https://doi.org/10 .1045/may2017-green.

29. Megan Martinsen, personal communication, January 15, 2018.

30. In the IFLA Library Reference Model, an additional user task was added to the FRBR user tasks: explore. This task is considered open-ended, but it has the capacity to support a records-as-data turn.

CHAPTER 2

Measuring Metadata Quality: A User Research Approach

Erin Elzi and Kevin Clair

ABSTRACT

Usability testing is becoming more and more common in libraries, but the literature suggests that testing sessions conducted by, and used to improve the work of, cataloging and metadata departments are less ubiquitous. This chapter presents the testing methodology employed by the University of Denver Libraries for testing two of its discovery tools that are managed by the departments that conduct metadata work and how the results were used by those departments to improve the user experience for these tools via changes to its cataloging workflows.

INTRODUCTION

The idea of centering metadata creation around user needs dates to Ranganathan's law to "save the time of the user." However, in the library literature, this conversation has mostly focused on user-*generated* metadata, and for good reason. Tagging functions, wiki-a-thons, community events, and input from subject specialists are all methods for gathering metadata that have been implemented and written about extensively. These are great methods for several reasons, including application of natural language in search and retrieval, expert depth in describing materials, and application of authorized name and subject headings that reflect inclusive practices.

Efforts to move this conversation beyond user-generated metadata to the incorporation of user needs into methods for professional metadata creation have been largely confined to cataloging and metadata departments. Developing local practices that *seem* to best meet user needs, based on assumptions of what and how users search for, find, and select library resources, is certainly done with the best of intentions. Questioning the rules, standards, and practices that have been handed down over years is a great place to start, but more can be done to center the user in cataloging and metadata practice. If the users are not directly involved in the process, how do we know that their needs are being met?

This was the question that prompted the University of Denver Libraries to prioritize "invest[ment] in tools that simplify the user experience" in its strategic plan[1] and to assign this directive to its metadata and discovery steering committee (MAD). Led by representatives from all areas of technical services as well as from the access and research and instruction units, MAD is charged with improving the user experience of University Libraries' discovery tools through web design and metadata management practices. With the recent transition to a new library management system (LMS) and the implementation of a new public interface to the special collections and archives collections database, the authors saw this as the perfect opportunity to develop usability programs for the discovery tools they manage. This chapter is about our process for developing and refining user experience testing for library discovery applications, and how we have applied the findings of this testing toward the development of metadata management services at the University Libraries.

ABOUT THE UNIVERSITY OF DENVER LIBRARIES

With 16 faculty librarians and 50 staff members, University Libraries serves a community of 12,000 students, which comes close to a 50-50 split between undergraduate and graduate students. University Libraries also serves university staff, alumni, and 1,200 faculty members. In 2017 the Libraries created the position of design and discovery librarian. This position is housed in the scholarly communications and collections services division of the Libraries, along with more traditional technical services units such as cataloging, digitization, and library procurement and processing, and works closely with both public services and technical services to determine user needs and adjust systems and practices accordingly. The Cataloging unit, which works with MARC records and primarily uses RDA and Library of Congress standards, consists of the coordinator of cataloging and metadata services, 5 paraprofessionals, and 3 hourly employees. Its counterpart, Metadata and Digitization Services, is responsible for managing descriptive and inventory metadata for materials man-aged by special collections and archives, including the contents of the Special Collections @ DU repository of digitized and born-digital archival resources, and works primarily with non-MARC metadata schema such as Encoded Archival Description (EAD) and the Library of Congress Metadata Object Description Schema (MODS). It consists of the metadata and digitization librarian, 3 paraprofessionals, and anywhere from 3 to 5 graduate student hourly employees. University Libraries' collections consist of approximately 2,300,000 titles in three locations—the main library, the music library, and an off-site storage facility. The Cataloging and Metadata and Digitization units are responsible for the processing of material for all three locations.

LITERATURE REVIEW

This literature review is narrow in scope, focusing on studies directly involving technical services in the usability testing process. While there is no dearth of literature available about usability testing in libraries, there is a distinct lack of writings on tests that are managed by, or even call for any level of significant involvement by, cataloging and metadata departments.

As to be expected, most library usability testing focuses on the library website, related virtual tools that have a highly customizable architecture, or search strategies between librarians and students.[2] While testing of discovery tools has been done, often the resulting action was to ask the vendor to make changes, such as James Madison University asked of EBSCO,[3] rather than to change internal practice.

In *In Usability Testing: A Practical Guide for Librarians*, Rebecca Blakiston focuses on library websites. Blakiston recognizes that usabil-ity methodology can be applied beyond the website, in both virtual and physical library spaces. Her work includes "search for books on a topic"[4] as an example of usability testing tasks and mentions the possibility of workflow changes due to test results.[5] However, she does not mention metadata analysis via usability testing, or how testing results may affect daily workflows in metadata or technical services departments.

All the examples of library usability literature consulted were written by, discuss, or are aimed at librarians who do not manage metadata. Blakiston is self-described as a former reference and instruction librarian turned library website product manager.[6] Other authors included a library technologist, instructional design librarian, electronic resources librarian, research and assessment analyst, and collection management librarian. What was lacking from the list was cataloging and metadata specialists. Even in an article by Younghee Noh that focuses on metadata elements in reference resources systems using Dublin Core, those who participated in the testing and were most affected by the findings were reference librarians, not library users or technical services professionals.[7] Noh makes some great points about how metadata creation traditionally has been based on theories, and user testing did reveal disparity between existing metadata schema and the needs of a specific type of library tool. The article's focus on reference librarians as the users, metadata fields instead of their content, and lack of suggested action presented a literature gap that the authors of this chapter looked to fill.

Finally, a very recent article by Jessica Colbert shows that we at the University of Denver Libraries are not alone in our efforts in this area. Colbert suggests a multifaceted approach to applying patron-driven subject access. One of Colbert's methodologies consisted of user interviews that were recorded and then coded to pull out certain words;[8] it's a method that usability expert Nielsen Norman Group may classify as focus group and encourage as one technique to use in a larger usability study involving multiple sources of data.[9]

PILOT-TESTING PROGRAM

By coincidence, as University Libraries was investing in building a usability program, Metadata and Digitization Services and the Cataloging units each took on interns with an interest in usability issues. With some guidance from the librarians and the MAD committee, both interns were given almost free rein to design and implement usability tests in their areas of interest. One intern conducted testing for Compass, the Libraries' name for the LMS discovery layer, a customized instance of Ex Libris's Primo; another for the Special Collections @ DU digital repository for archival materials. They both opted for a think-aloud style of testing, based off the simple plans outlined in Steve Krug's *Rocket Surgery Made Easy: The Do-It-Yourself Guide to Finding and Fixing Usability Problems.* The think-aloud method calls for a space where participants can be observed (or it can be done entirely online), a set of tasks for the tester to complete, and a moderator who asks the tester to talk through the tasks as much as possible. While the moderator should not interfere with the participant by answering questions or guiding them to the correct answer, they can (and should) remind the participant to talk out loud if needed.[10]

Both interns worked independently to develop a script of tasks for each tester. On the day of the tests, each intern set up a testing station in a quiet study room on the main level of the library, using signage outside the room to attract participants with the offering of small incentives. Each intern set up shop for one day. Sessions lasted 10–15 minutes and attracted participants with a variety of research experience. While participant turnout was not something to brag about, it was enough to gather information to find patterns in the results; testing for each tool brought in five participants. Even though this sample size is sufficient according to Nielsen Norman Group,[11] one lesson learned was to expand our marketing reach for future sessions to increase diversity of the test participant pool.

Sessions were recorded on MacBook Pro laptop computers using the free version of the Silverback user testing application, which captures video recordings of both the screen and the user's reaction to it. Each intern reviewed the videos and submitted a full report to the MAD committee, including recommended changes based on their findings.

FROM PILOT TO PROCESS

The primary intent of these sessions was to explore the usability testing process itself; any actionable data gathered during the process was secondary. As a result, the pilot sessions were like those in the literature review above, focusing on architectural and navigational issues in each system, and the administrators followed their script of tasks to the letter. There was no intent to gather feedback on existing metadata.

Then there was the *aha!* moment. While we already had other functions that needed to be tested and were now able to fine-tune the testing process based on lessons learned from pilot testing, perhaps the second round of testing could provide insights into the metadata quality issues being discussed internally among MAD committee members and stakeholders. In the past, University Libraries had turned metadata fields on or off in the public user interface (PUI) based on a single person's request or continued the creation of local or enhanced fields simply because it had been done that way for years or because national standards call for it, or started new local practices because a cataloger thought it would be a good idea. But now that we were building a culture of usability testing, why couldn't we take our findings and use them to shape the answers to these everyday metadata issues? Even though the Cataloging and Metadata and Digitization units were already cognizant of user-centered metadata creation and were actively making decisions with the user in mind, we had not actually involved the user in shaping our practice.

The two units that create metadata for University Libraries use different systems to do so. The Cataloging unit works primarily in Ex Libris's Alma system, a vendor-hosted LMS with a customizable discovery layer holding MARC bibliographic records for published materials. Metadata and digitization services works primarily in the ArchivesSpace collection management system, which was built around the finding aid rather than the MARC record and with EAD as its underlying data model. Because these tools meet different needs for catalogers and end users alike, University Libraries planned separate usability testing sessions for each tool. The authors worked together on designing tests for each, gathering input from external stakeholders, writing a budget proposal, examining scripts for variables they held in common, test administration, and results analysis.

When both Compass and ArchivesSpace implemented new public user interfaces in the fall of 2017, it was decided that the time was right to plan a second round of testing, not only to reveal overall usability issues with these interfaces, but also to pose questions about the utility of their metadata to users. Since the second round of testing sessions was a joint endeavor by both the metadata and digitization librarian and the cataloging librarian, the format for the sessions and script was quite similar—with a few differences based on the content and types of material held in each. Due to the similarities, this case study focuses on the ArchivesSpace PUI session.

TESTING THE ARCHIVESSPACE PUBLIC USER INTERFACE

Because ArchivesSpace uses EAD rather than MARC as its underlying data model, it contains arrangement and description information for archival materials not available in Compass. For this reason, we conducted a separate round of user testing for it, with different tasks to complete for participants. In 2017, ArchivesSpace implemented a new public user interface, which is now the official special collections and archives discovery layer. This site is commonly used by archivists and researchers who work with University Libraries' archival materials, but it sees less use among students and the general public. User testing was designed to promote the site to a larger audience, identify and respond to questions users had about the site, and inform the development of guidelines for minimal viable description of materials in special collections and archives.

User testing was conducted in two six-hour sessions during November 2017, again using Silverback on a MacBook Pro for capturing screens and user reactions. For this round of testing we used version 2.1.1 of the ArchivesSpace application, the current production version at the time. Users had the option of walking in for short testing sessions, intended to highlight general observations about the quality of metadata and the discovery experience, or to sign up in advance for longer testing sessions involving searches geared toward specific topics. In order to attract participants, the user experience and outreach librarian sent emails to targeted departments on campus and posted via various social media outlets. We also placed invitations to participate in tests on the Libraries website and on digital signage displayed throughout Anderson Academic Commons. Interested participants could then sign up in advance via a Qualtrics survey. We used the same quiet study room as the initial pilot phase used and the same signage outside the door to attract walk-in participants. All participants were compensated with donuts from a well-known boutique donut shop, and those who had scheduled in advance for the longer tests received a gift card to a local restaurant—this information was included in all forms of marketing for the sessions. Over the two days of testing, 2 participants signed up for the longer tests, while 12 additional participants elected to walk in for testing.

While the clean and intuitive search interface was a positive according to test participants, it also results in little metadata appearing in records and search result summaries. Indeed, many participants requested that more metadata be present in search results when using the ArchivesSpace PUI. Table 2.1 represents observations made by test participants reflecting the use of various metadata elements in identifying materials useful for the research questions presented to them in their sessions.

Six users identified the description of an object as a key field in determining whether to use it in their research. Descriptions are very prominent in the ArchivesSpace PUI: they appear in result summaries when a search is first conducted and display in the basic information associated with a result when the user clicks through to its record page. ArchivesSpace looks first for a <scopecontent> note, then for an , when populating the description of a record; if neither is found, the description is blank. These notes are present in some collections but not in others, depending on the attention to detail they have received in the arrangement and description process; when they were present, respondents found them helpful in distinguishing among several otherwise identical search results and in selecting those that seemed to answer their research questions. It bears mention that there

Table 2.1 Number of Pilot-Test Participants Who Commented on Specific Metadata Fields in the ArchivesSpace Public User Interface

Field	Participant Mentions
Description	6
Subject headings	5
Form/genre headings	4
Titles	2
Notes	1

were limits to participants' use of the description field: one participant mentioned that they tended not to read past the first sentence of a description and therefore appreciated when a resource's description stated in the first sentence precisely what it contained.

Subject headings were identified by five participants as a useful field for both identifying relevant search results and finding related materials that did not necessarily appear in their initial search. Some participants noted that subject headings are difficult to find in the record view; elements not found in the basic information of a record, such as subjects, must be found via expanding the appropriate pane on the page, which was a problem for some participants. In addition to these interface concerns, the quantity and precision of subject headings were identified as key to identification of relevant search results. Many records had few or no subject headings attached, making it difficult for users to tell what the record they were viewing described (especially if text descriptions of it were also absent). In addition, one user had questions about the use of the term "consumption," both as a controlled subject heading and in resource descriptions, in the Jewish Consumptives' Relief Society Records. This user noted that without the use of the corresponding modern heading of "tuberculosis," these records might not be discovered by people who may find them useful. This is particularly so if metadata from the University Libraries' ArchivesSpace instance is indexed in external systems, such as search engines or Compass.

Form and genre headings were also cited by participants as helpful. The assistance provided by these headings took on many forms. Some users did not specifically request their presence among the subject headings but did tend to look for mentions of the form a resource took when identifying whether it was helpful for them (e.g., "photographs" or "audio recordings"). Others noted the absence of options to narrow a search by material type in the facets presented by ArchivesSpace in the right column of the search results view (ArchivesSpace gathers all subject headings, including form/genre headings, under the banner of "Subjects") and cited it as a key difficulty in narrowing results to just photographs or just audiovisual materials, as requested by some of the user tasks.

Titles were mentioned by two participants. Often, box titles include only the sequential box number in the context of its collection; occasionally a date range is also present. This presented problems for identifying relevant results in a search, particularly when boxes also lacked or <scopecontent> notes; one participant noted that more descriptive titles would assist in identifying relevant results, especially as titles appear in bold type on the page. Another participant, after viewing all available notes on a record, indicated that making these notes available in result summaries could also be of assistance. Test results also highlighted the need to focus on subject analysis and on the application of form/genre headings to more records within the database.

One motivation for ArchivesSpace PUI testing was that it is an underutilized library resource when compared to Compass or the Libraries website. Collections in ArchivesSpace have MARC records in Alma and are indexed in Compass, but as of this writing there is no method for indexing their components in Compass, so the ArchivesSpace PUI is the only place where metadata below the collection level—that is, for boxes, folders, and/or items—may be searched. Because of this, there was interest in determining how best to market it as a gateway to special collections and archives. Having made some general observations, we are now better positioned to target future user tests around specific functions of the site, such as faceted browsing, to determine whether our metadata application decisions are adequately meeting user needs and whether we need to make any feature requests to community developers to highlight the metadata we already have (or develop them in-house). As our testing moves from general observations about metadata to specific questions about how it is displayed and indexed by ArchivesSpace, we may also wish to develop a process for side-by-side testing of different metadata display options, a process known as "A/B testing." In this way we can gather comparative data that may be used to inform metadata quality improvement projects. During testing we also observed that some tasks were hard to understand for participants and required more explanation than expected. In future rounds of testing we will more clearly articulate these tasks to avoid such confusion.

No usability expertise? No problem!

Like University Libraries, other libraries likely have more than just metadata that would benefit from direct user feedback and analysis. As we found, it's possible, and quite easy, to fill a 10- to 30-minute session with questions that only address the quality of the metadata. However, if you can make improvements to the navigation, labels, usability in general, then it would be worth the time to include questions that address those. In fact, these may be the questions that get your project approved or encourage more stakeholder interest. In both tests, reference librarians provided input based on real-life queries they received at the reference desk that contributed to the development of the tasks used in the testing scripts. These tasks provided insights that may not have been revealed with the perspective of technical services alone.

To gather information pertinent to metadata, the test administrators remained flexible in their script. Krug refers to this as qualitative testing: "The purpose isn't to prove anything: it's to get insights to enable you to improve what you're building."[12] Still following the basic rules of think-aloud testing, the administrators went from a list of questions, tailoring which ones they asked based off how much feedback had been received for a specific element so far (i.e., if any patterns had emerged yet), and allowed some open-ended questions that addressed the metadata that was already visible in the PUIs.

The test results have been beneficial in decision-making about how to apply metadata in a user-centered manner. For example, they have been used to justify a change in practice that was already under consideration for our MARC records in the LMS, such as giving greater attention to summary and table of contents instead of relying on constrictive controlled vocabularies, or upon see also references (which were found to confuse users) to cover variances in terminologies. Testing on the ArchivesSpace PUI revealed that participants found portions of the site more useful than we expected. For example, many users found records for materials they wished to view in special collections by consulting Subject and Agent records, which provide links to any collection or item records where they are listed as subjects or creators. Currently these pages display very little contextual metadata to users; these findings indicate that more investment in such metadata may be beneficial for users.

In other cases, the results of testing reinforced metadata creation guidelines already in place. For ArchivesSpace, where the guidelines for minimal record metadata include and <scopecontent> notes at the collection level, as well as a certain degree of subject analysis per record, it was found that these guidelines reflected almost exactly the fields participants cited when making resource selection decisions. As users were sometimes disappointed when these fields were not present at lower levels of description, such as for boxes or items, testing provided evidence for future implementation of these guidelines at lower levels of collection hierarchy.

While the presented case study focused on ArchivesSpace, it should be noted that the testing did also result in rethinking which and how metadata fields are presented in University Libraries' instance of Primo. One unexpected result was how much users look for and rely upon the Summary field (MARC 520), and as a result the Cataloging unit has placed additional emphasis on ensuring new records have either a robust table of contents or summary note. Due to the breadth of material and volume of metadata found in Primo, Libraries runs testing sessions on this tool at least once a year, so analysis and improvements will continue indefinitely.

These test results do not live in a vacuum. For results that brought new issues to the table, we have consulted with other departments, presenting our findings and seeking approval before making any changes. This possibly has been the most important building block in creating an institutional culture that appreciates usability testing endeavors—the acquiring of institutional-wide buy-in and support— because metadata creation can only truly be user-centered when all types of users are consulted, including our colleagues on the front lines.

ACKNOWLEDGMENTS

The authors would like to thank and acknowledge Jessica Weatherby and Jennifer Eltringham, the two interns who did a fantastic job of designing and implementing the pilot tests. We would also like to thank Jenelys Cox for assisting with the ArchivesSpace usability testing, and Elia Trucks for help with marketing the test sessions.

NOTES

1. University of Denver University Libraries, *University Libraries Five Year Strategic Plan: 2017–2022*, 2017, https://library.du.edu/media /documents/university_libraries_strategic_plan_2017.pdf.

2. Nancy B. Turner, "Librarians Do It Differently: Comparative Usability Testing With Students and Library Staff," *Journal of Web Librarianship* 5, no. 4 (2011): 297, https://doi.org/10.1080/19322909.2011.624428.

3. Jody Condit Fagan et al., "Usability Test Results for a Discovery Tool in an Academic Library," *Information Technology and Libraries* 31, no. 1 (March 2012): 103, https://doi.org/10.6017/ital.v31i1.1855.

4. Rebecca Blakiston, *Usability Testing: A Practical Guide for Librarians* (Lanham, MD: Rowman & Littlefield, 2015), 24.

5. Ibid., 117.

6. Ibid., ix.

7. Younghee Noh, "A Study on Metadata Elements for Web-Based Reference Resources System Developed Through Usability Testing," *Library Hi Tech* 29, no. 2 (2011): 247, https://doi.org/10.1108/07378831111138161.

8. Jessica L. Colbert, "Patron-Driven Subject Access: How Librarians Can Mitigate That 'Power to Name,'" *In the Library With the Lead Pipe* (November 15, 2017). http://www.inthelibrarywiththeleadpipe.org/2017/patron-driven-subject-access-how-librarians-can-mitigate-that-power-to-name/.

9. Jakob Nielsen, "The Use and Misuse of Focus Group," Nielsen Norman Group, January 1, 1997, https://www.nngroup.com/articles/focus-groups/.

10. Steve Krug, *Rocket Surgery Made Easy: The Do-It-Yourself Guide to Finding and Fixing Usability Problems* (Berkeley, CA: New Riders, 2010), 63.

11. Jakob Nielsen, "Why You Only Need to Test With 5 Users," Nielsen Norman Group, March 19, 2000, https://www.nngroup.com/articles/why-you-only-need-to-test-with-5-users.

12. Krug, *Rocket Surgery Made Easy*, 14.

CHAPTER 3

Technical Services Advocacy: Partnerships in the Library and Beyond

Bridget Euliano, Peggy Griesinger, Kimberley A. Edwards, and Tricia Mackenzie

ABSTRACT

It can be challenging for technical services librarians to market their expertise internally, which can cause opportunities for collaboration to be missed. However, technical services leaders must connect their department's in-house metadata expertise with digital scholarship projects in which their subject librarian and special collection colleagues are engaged. In this chapter, the authors explore how building relationships and internally marketing your department's professional engagement can lead to technical services' metadata expertise being effectively leveraged to bring better access to key collections. Two projects will be explored that exemplify this effort. The chapter will further show that these examples did not happen in isolation but as part of a concerted and proactive technical services effort to market and promote its metadata expertise throughout George Mason University Libraries. This effort involved creating and disseminating a technical services newsletter, advocating for technical services representation on internal groups dealing with digital scholarship and discovery, and recasting existing librarian and staff positions toward a sole focus on metadata.

INTRODUCTION

To make key collections more accessible and widely used, technical services leaders must connect their department's in-house metadata expertise with their subject librarians' and special collections colleagues' digital scholarship endeavors. These connections are often missed because technical services librarians are not sure of the best way to market their expertise. In this chapter, the authors explore how building relationships and internally marketing your department's professional engagement can more effectively leverage technical services' metadata expertise and foster cross-departmental collaboration.

It can be challenging for technical services leaders to highlight what their departments can contribute when "technical services positions are most often behind the scenes" and "people do not understand the breadth of skills needed to perform the multiple tasks executed by a librarian serving in one of these positions."[1] However, this is an ideal time for technical services departments to demonstrate their value. Technical services work is experiencing a renaissance of sorts with the emphasis on the importance of metadata and linked data.[2] Metadata and cataloging librarians are taking the lead within the profession to transition libraries from reliance on the MARC standard and into the new world of possibilities that BIBFRAME offers.

In this chapter, the authors highlight two examples of collaborations between metadata librarians and subject specialists that led to innovative and robust ways of accessing two unique collections at George Mason University Libraries. One example involves a technical services department head designing a metadata profile to be used by a donor in creating metadata for an important donated collection. The *"Oh, Joy Unbounded . . .": A Celebration of Gilbert & Sullivan* online exhibit was created as a supplement to a physical exhibit of the same name. This collection included memorabilia from and related to Gilbert and Sullivan operas and the composers. In this instance, the donor was the subject specialist that worked directly with the head of resource description and metadata services.

A second example highlights a metadata librarian's involvement in a new digital scholarship project which transcribed and created metadata for select special collections materials. This project showcases a 17th- through 18th-century cookbook written primarily by early Virginia resident Elizabeth Fairfax offering numerous insights into domestic life in colonial Virginia. This involved close collaboration among the metadata librarian and four subject librarians, representing a coordination between two different organizational divisions within University Libraries.

The chapter will further show that these examples did not happen in isolation but as part of a concerted and proactive technical services effort to market and promote its metadata expertise throughout University Libraries. This effort involved creating and disseminating a technical services newsletter, advocating for technical services representation on internal groups dealing with digital scholarship and discovery, and recasting existing librarian and staff positions toward a sole focus on metadata.

TECHNICAL SERVICES AT GEORGE MASON

George Mason University (Mason) is a public university comprising a main campus located in Fairfax, Virginia, and distributed campuses in Arlington and Manassas. It has a total enrollment of nearly 36,000 students, about 30% of whom are graduate students.[3] University Libraries (Libraries) at Mason occupies four spaces across the three campuses and holds 3.4 million items in a wide variety of formats. Technical services in the Libraries is centralized, with all acquisitions and cataloging performed by the technical services group (TSG) from the main campus library.

TSG underwent a major reorganization in 2010. The primary goal was to improve workflows to more accurately reflect priorities within the Libraries, with additional goals of improving communication and creating a more flexible department structure. Planning and decisions regarding the restructuring were made by the TSG reorganization task force, which consisted of staff members from across the Libraries. They mapped systems, talked to focus groups, and conducted surveys. The new structure was implemented in 2012. It introduced a team-based approach, broader job descriptions to allow for increased flexibility in duties, and the creation of the position information analyst for technical services. The primary charges of the information analyst position were to work with TSG staff to improve data retrieval from the integrated library system (ILS) and to facilitate communication between TSG and the Libraries' digital programs and systems (DPS).[4]

Though, for example, there had long been a cataloging librarian who worked with staff in the Special Collections Research Center (SCRC),[5] the previously regimented job duties of other positions in resource description and metadata services (RDMS) had created a more siloed environment within the department and had limited the scope of the projects TSG could take on. The new team-based approach led to the formation of four distinct but interrelated departments within TSG: RDMS, resource acquisition (RA), payments, and gifts. The new approach laid the groundwork to allow for future collaborative work both inside and outside of TSG.

The revised structure of TSG after the reorganization, however, began to address the structural barriers between departments. For example, a new electronic resources–focused team was designed to include staff members from the collection development, RDMS, and systems departments, including e-resources specialists and the electronic resources librarian, thereby opening lines of regular communication among the departments. The increased fluidity among departments led to improved communication and workflows.

DONOR AS SUBJECT SPECIALIST

In the spring of 2017, Mason hosted a series of events, including performances, exhibits, and forums, to highlight the David and Annabelle Stone Gilbert and Sullivan Collection and celebrate the work of the legendary librettist W. S. Gilbert and composer Arthur Sullivan. Housed in the SCRC, the collection includes an extensive array of materials related to the operas of Gilbert and Sullivan and items once owned or created by the artists themselves.

In addition to the multipart physical exhibit, *"Oh, Joy Unbounded . . .": A Celebration of Gilbert and Sullivan*, a supplementary online exhibit was created, providing access to 241 items from the physical exhibition.[6] The online platform provided an opportunity not just for remote access to the collection but for a more complete description of the items than what is traditionally possible for items in a physical exhibit.

To make use of Mr. Stone's extensive knowledge of the collection, project staff decided that the donor would create the metadata for the online exhibit with the guidance of and in consultation with the head of RDMS. Though there was no formal training on metadata creation for the donor, the librarian had numerous discussions with him about the importance of following the best practice guidelines and provided instruction on how to enter the metadata into a spreadsheet. As further questions arose, the donor and librarian resolved them via email discussions. This sort of collaboration, between a donor and an RDMS librarian, was a first for the Libraries. As the former metadata librarian for the Libraries, however, the head of RDMS had a long working relationship with the SCRC, having created best practices documentation for digital collections, provided guidance in metadata creation, and performed quality control on metadata records. In both her former and current roles, the head of RDMS has worked to cultivate a collaborative relationship with the former head of the SCRC, has held regular meetings to discuss current and potential projects and workflows, and was tapped to serve on the search committee for the new director of the SCRC.[7]

While working on this project, collaboration was also needed with additional SCRC staff, particularly the digital collections archivist. The archivist was familiar with the donor and the Gilbert and Sullivan collection, as well as the digital platform slated for the online exhibit, Omeka.[8] It was helpful for the head of RDMS, who had no prior experience with Omeka, to gain a more robust understanding of the platform's capabilities and limitations before writing the metadata guidelines. The head of RDMS and the archivist met with the donor and other members of the Libraries to discuss the collection, the digital library platform, the level of description appropriate for an online exhibit, and the standard cataloging rules for description. Because Omeka is used for display and exhibition of cultural heritage objects, the head of RDMS decided that the descriptive metadata created for the online exhibit would focus on the artifacts owned by the donor and not on the digital objects/images. With the assistance of the cataloging and metadata services librarian responsible for special collections and music cataloging, metadata guidelines were created using an extended Dublin Core schema, appropriate content standards, and controlled vocabularies.[9] The guidelines and template were given to the donor so that he could create the collection metadata. There were a few follow-up exchanges between the head of RDMS and the donor, largely relating to conceptualizations of creators, contributors, and publishers and an appendix of controlled terms created for format headings. This was later followed by a review of the donor's metadata before the collection was uploaded into Omeka. The success of this collaboration has laid the groundwork for future collaborations between RDMS and donors or other individuals external to the Libraries.

WORKING WITH SUBJECT LIBRARIANS
AND THE DIGITAL SCHOLARSHIP CENTER

In March 2016, the dean of libraries and university librarian sent a memo to Libraries staff describing plans for the creation of the digital scholarship center (DiSC). This would include lab spaces and offices to facilitate cross-disciplinary digital research and scholarship throughout the university, focusing on consultation, workshops, and other events. DiSC was developed over the following year and officially opened in late August 2017.

Staff from across the library devote varying percentages of their work time to DiSC. This initially included arts and humanities subject librarians who apportioned some of their time to a specific digital humanities project that made use of the Libraries' digital collections. This project focused on a 17th- through 18th-century manuscript cookbook produced at least partially by an early Virginian named Elizabeth Fairfax and held by the SCRC. This manuscript, created at the end of the 17th century and added to throughout much of the 18th century, is a catalog of food and drink recipes as well as home remedies for a wide variety of illnesses and household maintenance issues.

The cookbook had already been digitized, so the goal of this project was to transcribe the handwritten recipes in the book and create metadata records for each recipe. This was complicated by several factors, including the fact that the cookbook authors used many words that are now obsolete and archaic, as well as British English words that have different definitions from the same words in American English. The handwriting was also not always able to be deciphered.

The current metadata librarian, who assumed this role after the previous metadata librarian left the position to become the head of

RDMS, was asked to assist in the project by creating a metadata profile[10] for the recipes. Previously, both the subject librarians and the metadata librarian had informally communicated about other projects to share expertise and problem-solve. Although these collaborations began as ad hoc efforts, they soon grew to be a natural part of the working relationship between the metadata librarian and the subject librarians. Furthermore, the metadata librarian had long worked side-by-side with the SCRC staff on their own digital projects, so she was familiar with their materials and the significant metadata properties that would likely be of interest in a special collections digital project. The establishment of these relationships over a period of years allowed for an organic extension of the collaborative teamwork between technical services and subject specialists.

Over the course of multiple meetings, the metadata librarian discussed the project with the subject librarians to gain an understanding of what information was necessary to record, what they would like to record if possible, and what information was unnecessary for these purposes. For example, although the digital object was a manuscript, and thus had important physical characteristics, it was not necessary to record physical information about the book for each recipe, as this information would be the same for the entire book. However, it was important to record very detailed subject heading information so that users could find recipes based on such topics as ingredients, preparation method, and purpose of recipe.

After initial discussions, the metadata librarian created a working best practices document for the subject librarians to review; this document recommended the use of the Dublin Core metadata standard and the American Folklore Society's Ethnographic Thesaurus (AFS ET) as a controlled vocabulary for subjects. The subject librarians brought up the issue of differing American and British versions of English words; the AFS ET used American versions of words, while the cookbook generally used the British version of words. The metadata librarian determined that the AFS ET was still the best applicable vocabulary to use and made provision to include the British version of words in a controlled set of tags in the metadata records. An explanatory note would be included on the digital exhibit page hosting the cookbook that explained the two vocabularies to users. This version of the best practices guidelines was deemed suitable for the project.

This project is currently ongoing, and the subject librarians are in regular contact with the metadata librarian to find solutions to issues encountered as the project naturally evolves beyond the scope of the initial best practices document. In the meantime, staff from technical services, DiSC, and the SCRC have extended the cookbook project to allow for further collaboration among their departments. The metadata librarian has begun to write best practices to encode the cookbook recipes using the Text Encoding Initiative (TEI), a standard that allows for myriad methods of marking up textual documents to further enhance their meaning. In this case, the focus will be on using TEI to encode, among other things, apparent errors and their normalizations, translations of foreign and/or obsolete words, and handwritten additions and deletions to the main text. Staff in both SCRC and TSG will be trained in scanning digital objects, performing optical character recognition (OCR) of handwritten text, and encoding text using TEI, allowing for a sharing of skills across the departments that will further strengthen cross-departmental relationships.

THE CONCERTED EFFORT AT TECHNICAL SERVICES ADVOCACY

As stated previously, these examples did not happen in isolation but as part of a concerted and proactive technical services effort to market and promote its metadata expertise throughout the Libraries, capitalizing on the opportunities created by the reorganization of TSG in 2010. This effort involved creating and disseminating a TSG newsletter, advocating for technical services representation on internal groups dealing with digital scholarship and resource discovery, and recasting existing positions toward a sole focus on metadata.

Metadata: A Monthly Newsletter for Technical Services Group

One of the first things that the current director of TSG did upon starting in her new role in January 2016 was to meet one-on-one with all full-time and part-time staff in TSG. This plan ended up comprising 23 individual meetings. It was a chance for the new director to get to know each person individually—an opportunity to learn about what they did and to find out if there were any pressing issues or concerns that should be attended to right away.

One impression that came out of those meetings was that some staff felt that they were not as connected to each other as they used to be and did not feel that they were as up-to-date regarding the work of other units within TSG. This was a good problem to have; it was related to the fact that TSG had moved into a new office space with enough room. TSG staff had previously been working in a cramped environment where one could not help but overhear and thus be aware of everything that was happening throughout TSG.

The director was also interested in making TSG less siloed amongst the various units it comprised, which, at that time, were RA, RDMS, gifts, and payments. The director came up with the idea of creating a monthly newsletter that would help explain and highlight the ongoing work and special achievements of TSG staff. For example, if RDMS was going through training on BIBFRAME, RA should be aware. Similarly, if RA was under tight deadlines due to the fiscal year close, then RDMS should know. In April 2016, the first issue of the newsletter, titled *Metadata*, was published and sent to all staff in TSG. The director also sent the newsletter to the associate university librarian for resources and collection management services and a few others in the Libraries that were interested reading it.[11]

Metadata has been well received within TSG. There is also a morale-boosting aspect to the newsletter, which seeks to highlight staff accomplishments and to thank staff for their work on projects. This is expressed via a regular feature called Director News. During various events, staff would often say, "We need a picture of this for our newsletter," demonstrating how comprehensively it has been accepted as a means of communicating within and outside of TSG. Staff have responded to *Metadata* so positively in part because of the great pride and care that is put into each issue. It has become a labor of love that requires thoughtful effort in order to produce a high-quality issue each month.

A wide range of articles has been published in *Metadata*—for example, an explanation of Name Authority Cooperative Program (NACO) work written by a cataloger, an update on BIBFRAME developments written by the head of RDMS, a linked data primer written by the metadata librarian, and an explanation on locating and ordering hard-to-find materials written by a staff member in RA. In addition, the newsletter has been a staff development opportunity in a variety of ways. The director and a staff member with a talent for graphic design and editing create and publish *Metadata* collaboratively each month, and the newsletter provides an opportunity for staff to write their own articles and reflections on the work they are doing or the groups with which they are involved.

After a few months, the newsletter started to get good word-of-mouth and was increasingly being forwarded to colleagues outside of TSG. It was shared with the dean of libraries and university librarian. The dean contacted the director and said that he felt the newsletter was so informative and well-produced that it should be shared monthly with all staff in University Libraries (about 130 people). Since November 2016, the TSG newsletter has been sent to all Libraries staff each month.

The wider distribution of the newsletter has led to some great collaborative opportunities. Colleagues outside of TSG have been asked to write articles on a variety of topics, from summaries of professional conferences they have attended to descriptions of collaboration on the acquiring and showcasing of artists' books. Perhaps most importantly, all Libraries staff see on a monthly basis the level of technical services' professional engagement. When the metadata librarian presented at the iPRES 2016 International Conference on Digital Preservation in Switzerland, it was not recorded solely as an entry on her CV; there was a picture of her standing at the podium presenting in Bern in the November 2016 issue of the TSG newsletter. In this impactful way, TSG effectively shows that we are not an insignificant behind-the-scenes unit but a vibrant, engaged, and valuable contributor to the forward-looking and forward-facing work of the Libraries.

Engaging With Internal Digital Scholarship and Resource Discovery Groups

Having a seat at the table and being aware of what is happening outside of technical services are both key to being able to see the possible opportunities to collaborate and contribute. TSG managers have encouraged and advocated for librarians to pursue collaborations with colleagues outside of what might be considered traditional technical services work. For example, TSG was an early and vocal supporter of DiSC when it was first proposed. TSG librarians offered their time to assist with digital projects, gave talks on linked data to the digital humanities working group, and learned new digital skills themselves through DiSC offerings. While TSG did not have a representative on the digital scholarship center committee, a vacancy came up on that group as it was transitioning to an implementation group, and the metadata librarian was chosen to serve. The metadata librarian had already distinguished herself by presenting at an international conference, publishing an article in a professional journal, being sponsored as one of the American Library Association's Emerging Leaders Class of 2016, and giving a presentation on linked data that was attended by all of the Libraries' associate university librarians (all accomplishments noted in various issues of the TSG newsletter).

The information analyst for technical services has also expanded her scope beyond traditional technical services roles by building a reputation as someone who understands data and is skilled at connecting what someone is looking to find with how to pull that data out of the system. The information analyst listens, asks questions, and tries to anticipate breakdowns between what is being sought and what is available. She is an expert at sussing out precisely the information that someone needs in the way they need it presented, even when the person may not be sure of those things themselves. Due to that expertise, the information analyst was chosen to serve as a member of the newly created library assessment group when it was formed in 2017.

The director of TSG has been appointed to chair several significant Libraries-wide committees, including the Alma implementation group, which leads all internal communication about the Libraries' migration from Voyager to Alma as part of the Washington Research Library Consortium. These types of assignments put TSG and its leaders front and center and give them a place at the table to contribute to shaping the future direction of University Libraries.

Recasting Positions With a Focus on Metadata

Vacancies often serve as an opportunity for an organization to reevaluate its current needs and to recast positions to better serve those needs. When the cataloging and metadata services librarian job opened in 2011, the head of the department restructured the position to focus on non-MARC metadata. Prior to 2011, except for transforming Dublin Core records for electronic theses and dissertations into MARC, the cataloging and metadata services librarian's work

focused exclusively on traditional MARC cataloging. When the adver-
tisement to replace this position was posted, there was an intentional
effort to attract candidates with non-MARC metadata skills. Those
skills were the priority requirements for the revised job. When it was
advertised again in 2014 after an internal promotion, the position was
modified to place an even greater emphasis on non-MARC metadata
and to require more advanced metadata skills such as XML transformation and editing. Eventually the position was renamed to the
more concise and appropriate "metadata librarian," demonstrating
the culmination of the Libraries' commitment to adapting to a post-
MARC environment.

Continuing in those same efforts, when a cataloging staff position
became vacant in 2017, the director of TSG and the head of RDMS
strongly advocated to recast the position as one that would solely work
on non-MARC metadata, such as Dublin Core–encoded records for
a collection of digitized images. This argument was successful and
allowed TSG to retain the position whereas, had it remained a cataloging position, it might have been repurposed in another Libraries
unit outside of TSG.

Reshaping this staff position filled out a cadre of positions within
TSG that have a metadata focus: a metadata specialist (staff position
working exclusively with non-MARC metadata), a metadata librarian
(focused mostly on metadata and doing a small amount of MARC cataloging), and a head of RDMS (who leads all the department's metadata
efforts and who has a background in non-MARC metadata herself).
These positions are illustrative of TSG's intentional direction set for
the RDMS department—that of a focus on metadata.

CONCLUSION

Collaborations between subject specialists and metadata librarians
are not always readily apparent; it takes effort and forethought to
identify and bring them to fruition. In this chapter we touched on the
aspects that led to these important collaborations at George Mason
University Libraries: recasting positions to fit changing organizational
needs over time; fostering awareness of what is happening outside of
technical services; ensuring technical services has a seat at the table

with representation on key organization-wide committees, working groups, and task forces; demonstrably showing the expertise of technical services librarians and staff; building internal relationships outside of technical services; and advocating for technical services librarians to have opportunities to develop new skills and be involved in innovative projects.

Technical services departments are at a precipice: they can either allow themselves to be outdated and prime for outsourcing, or they can be an integral part of what makes libraries most valuable and unique—our special collections and bringing them to the world. Because of the misperception that technical services work is purely behind the scenes and routine, technical services leaders must make a concerted effort to be valuable and innovative within their organizations.

APPENDIX

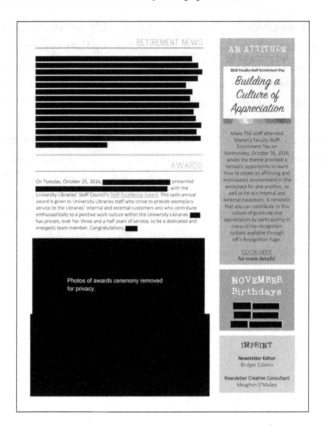

NOTES

1. Erin E. Boyd and Elyssa Gould, "Skills for the Future of Technical Services," in *Rethinking Library Technical Services: Redefining Our Profession for the Future*, ed. Mary Beth Weber (Lanham, MD: Rowman & Littlefield, 2015), 127.

2. For the purposes of this chapter, the term *metadata* is defined, as per Anne J. Gilliland, as "the value-added information that [cultural heritage information professionals] create to arrange, describe, track, and otherwise enhance access to information objects and the physical collections related to those objects." Anne J. Gilliland, "Setting the Stage" in *Introduction to Metadata*, ed. 2, ed. Murtha Baca (Los Angeles: Getty Publications, 2008), http://www.getty.edu/research/publications /electronic_publications/intrometadata/setting.html.

3. "Fall 2017 Official Census Student Enrollment Master Sheet," George Mason University Office of Institutional Research and Effectiveness, accessed December 4, 2017, https://irr2.gmu.edu/New/N_EnrollOff /EnrlSts.cfm.

4. Meg Manahan and Nathan B. Putnam, "Moving From Print-Centric to E-Centric Workflows: A Reorganization of the Technical Services Group at Mason Libraries" (presentation, Annual Meeting of the Potomac Technical Processing Librarians, Annapolis, MD, October 17, 2014), December 4, 2017, https://www.potomactechlibrarians.org /Resources/Documents/Annual%20Meeting%20Presentations /manahan_putnam.pdf.

5. Formerly known as Special Collections & Archives.

6. "Oh Joy Unbounded: A Celebration of Gilbert and Sullivan," George Mason University Libraries Special Collections Research Center, accessed December 14, 2017, http://gilbertandsullivan2017.gmu.edu/.

7. The title for this position was changed to director when the former head of the SCRC retired in 2016.

8. Omeka (https://omeka.org/) is a free, open source digital collection management platform created by the Roy Rosenzweig Center for History and New Media at George Mason University. It is used widely throughout the digital scholarship community to provide access to cultural heritage collections.

9. An Excel template based on the guidelines was also created for metadata input.

10. A metadata profile refers to a comprehensive set of guidelines that defines best practices for the creation of metadata records for a project, library, or set of objects. This includes guidance on the use of standards, controlled vocabularies, and data types.

11. The appendix to this chapter contains an example of a newsletter published in November 2016, with some redactions made for privacy.

CHAPTER 4

A Road Taken: A Cataloging Team Becomes a Metadata Team[1]

Scott M. Dutkiewicz and Jessica L. Serrao

ABSTRACT

This chapter describes the issues confronted along the "road taken" by a technical services team as it transitioned from traditional monographic cataloging to metadata for digital collections. To serve changing user needs, the team shifted focus to providing quality metadata. Along this road, the team confronted and welcomed several changes: a unit merger, off-site relocation, shedding the cataloging role, learning how to produce metadata, identifying areas for growth with a library-wide metadata summit, working with new stakeholders, and managing new staff and faculty. The chapter concludes with the lessons the team has learned and its prospects.

INTRODUCTION

This chapter presents a case study of the transformation of a traditional format-specific cataloging team into a metadata team at Clemson University Libraries. In response to changing technologies and user needs, the Libraries needed to rethink its organizational structure and team roles. It took Libraries' administration, faculty, and staff over two years to assess issues, plan, and implement changes, and it required four more years for the transformed teams to adjust to and learn new tasks.

To accomplish the transition from cataloging to digital collections metadata, multiple changes occurred. Two units merged to form the technical services and collection management (TSCM) unit, which was then physically relocated. Teams were reconfigured and cataloging and metadata responsibilities reassigned. Team members received new training, and new intra- and extra-unit collaborations formed. To further strengthen these collaborations and identify areas for improvement, two unit heads planned and held a metadata summit. What emerged was the metadata and monographic resources team (MMRT). The name reflected remnants of a role in cataloging while bringing new metadata responsibilities to the forefront. The resultant metadata team continues to assess and revise workflows and guidelines to ensure it is efficiently meeting user needs.

BACKGROUND

Clemson University is organized into seven colleges with a strong STEM-based curriculum; it recently received Research 1 status from the Carnegie Classification of Institutions of Higher Education. The Libraries' 30 faculty and 55 staff serve around 20,195 undergraduate students, 5,627 graduate students, and 1,659 faculty.[2] The central library has an average gate count of 9,000 visits a day. The Libraries operates five locations: its central library, the Robert Muldrow Cooper Library; the Education Media Center;[3] the Emery A. Gunnin Architecture Library; Special Collections and Archives (SC&A); and a remote storage facility. Prior to 2013, the Libraries was organized into eight units: acquisitions, administrative services, cataloging, interlibrary loan, office of library technology, reference, Gunnin Architecture Library, and Special Collections.

The two units pertinent to this case study were acquisitions and cataloging, from which the metadata team emerged. Being separate units, acquisitions and cataloging employees' offices were compartmentalized in six areas on Cooper Library's third floor. Each unit was broken down further into sections. The acquisitions unit had sections for monographs, electronic resources, and serials and bindery. The cataloging unit had a roughly parallel structure with sections for monographs and special formats, database maintenance and authority control, serials and government documents, and electronic resources and metadata. The special projects cataloger, section leader for electronic resources and metadata, had been cataloging archival collection-level records for inclusion in the library catalog. Naturally, he was the first to be assigned digital collections metadata for in-house special collections digital projects. This established a precedent for maintaining metadata for digital projects within the cataloging unit.

Though the Clemson Tigers have been on the athletic field since the 1890s, it can be said that the Libraries entered the "game" of digitization rather late. In 2007, the Libraries hired a digitization librarian who also served as the library technology unit head and it added a digital production librarian two years later.[4] The digitization librarian obtained an Institute of Museum and Library Services grant in 2010 for what would become the Open Parks Network (OPN), a digital repository containing materials from over 20 national and South Carolina parks.[5] However, both librarians resigned thereafter and the successor head of library technology and his staff carried the OPN grant forward. To handle the metadata load for this project, the unit head hired a staff-level metadata specialist who received assistance from student workers.

Between 2008 and 2011, the special projects cataloger led the production of metadata for six digital projects ranging from 85 to 1,664 images. He completed two of these projects, including the frequently viewed Carolina Textile Mills Collection of 366 images, with the help of two direct report assistants.[6] Nevertheless, the time-intensive management of electronic resources left little time for metadata work. Despite these accomplishments, after 2011 the special projects cataloger received no additional metadata assignments.

Users expect to find primary source materials online and increasingly rely on digital resources in their research. To meet these demands, special collections needed to digitize more collections to publish online. With more digital collections comes an increased need for improved descriptive metadata. Describing these unique collections would be time intensive. The structure of the Libraries' units, workflows, and cataloging load did not permit the cataloging unit to address this growing need.

STEPS TOWARD CHANGE

Planning Phase
In 2012, the Libraries commenced an eight-month library-wide planning process called the Future is Now. Formed by the dean of libraries, the task force was charged "to align Clemson University Libraries

(CUL) strategic priorities with changing technologies and user needs."[7] The task force comprised the associate dean as chair[8] with five staff and six faculty members who developed recommendations for collections, public/user services, technology/systems, technical services, communication/public relations/marketing, facilities/space, and library administrative activities. The task force report recommended that technical services "evaluate cataloging approaches with emphasis on metadata description [and] streamlined processing and embrace 'acceptable' copy cataloging."[9] They also noted that "the uniqueness of special collections resources and the increased need for discoverability require continuing efforts to catalog print, process archival work forms, and provide metadata for digitized collections."[10]

The task force recommended developing "team approaches where possible to draw upon expertise from both Acquisitions and Cataloging."[11] Consistent with this recommendation, a technical services consulting team evaluated the two technical services units in spring 2013. The consultants found areas of duplicate processes and multiple handling of materials, and their recommendation confirmed the dean's inclination to merge the acquisitions and cataloging units.

Unit Merger

TSCM formed in August 2013. Five teams, each headed by a librarian, were created within TSCM: standards and assessment, collection management, electronic resources, government documents and continuing resources, and metadata and monographic resources. TSCM had 6 faculty and 16 staff. The metadata and monographic resources team members came from the former monographs and special formats section, which followed a traditional format-specific cataloging workflow. The cataloging team that transferred to MMRT consisted of a librarian and two full-time technical assistants. The librarian cataloged special formats and original or complex copy for print monographs. One technical assistant copy-cataloged videodiscs and sound recordings, and the other assistant handled print monographs. No assistant had any metadata experience.

Although the new team had never engaged in any metadata work, the new name honored the importance placed on metadata in the Future is Now task force report. The naming also reflected the team's shrinking work with monographs since materials budgets remained flat, and a shelf-ready processing plan with the Libraries' primary book vendor was already in place. The organizational change created a new team, but physical arrangement did not reflect this change. As with the previous acquisition and cataloging units, the new TSCM unit remained dispersed across the third floor of Cooper Library.

Off-Campus Relocation

In August 2014, Libraries relocated TSCM (all teams but the government documents and continuing resources team) to a facility approximately nine miles from Cooper Library. Dubbed the Library Depot, the facility already housed the Libraries' digitization operations and high-density book and university records storage. The move was consistent with the Future is Now recommendation as it also freed up space for students, which is in high demand in many academic libraries. MMRT workspaces were purposefully situated in proximity to the digitization unit with the assumption that the two units would be working closely together.

TSCM members' initial reaction to the move was mixed (though ample parking at the Library Depot was a real plus). Over time, TSCM faculty and staff grew to appreciate the calm atmosphere conducive to concentration when separated from the bustling Cooper Library. On the other hand, Cooper Library faculty and staff were concerned about how the physical separation would affect communication. This is partially overcome with a once-daily courier service that transports mail and library materials. A shuttle also runs hourly between the Depot and campus. Efforts are also made to duplicate development activities at both the Library Depot and Cooper Library, and video-conferencing helps bridge the geographic divide. TSCM faculty and staff at the Library Depot must be intentional about their participation in library-related meetings and other service and training opportunities that occur on campus.

A NEW TEAM EMERGES

Initially, the team waited in anticipation of digitized archival metadata projects, but electronic theses and dissertations (ETDs) became the team's first assignment. Just after MMRT formed, Clemson Libraries launched the TigerPrints institutional repository and one of the first types of content ingested were records for theses and dissertations. This experience aptly bridged cataloging and digital collections metadata. The team lead collaborated with the principal cataloger on testing workflow and documentation for crosswalking current ETD metadata from TigerPrints into the library catalog using MarcEdit.[12] While still catalog-centric, this project helped the team lead apply new metadata competencies.

It was not yet defined how MMRT fit into previously established metadata workflows. Before relocating to the Library Depot, the team lead was assigned the first digital collections metadata project: a 282-image trial project for OPN. But it turned out that metadata projects for MMRT would proceed from SC&A rather than OPN. This development was connected to the arrival of a new head of special collections in 2014. In the fall of 2015, the special collections unit delegated the first metadata project to the team: Clemson University Historical Images (around 3,000 images described to date).[13] The team lead and the special formats copy cataloger worked on describing these digitized photographs. Involvement of the copy cataloger was part-time because she still had special formats materials in her workflow. In January 2016, this assistant retired, leaving the project in hiatus.

The team lead then enlisted the remaining assistant in the work, and at the same time a plan was set in motion about the vacant position—to simultaneously upgrade the classification and redefine it as primarily a metadata position, in contrast to the previous copy cataloger role. The remaining assistant's classification was upgraded to "library specialist" at about the same time to achieve parity on the team.[14] By June 2016, the newly hired library specialist was on board, the assistant's position was upgraded, and the team now had ETDs and three digital collections underway. In addition to the Clemson University Historical Images, work began on the Strom Thurmond Collection of speeches.[15] The A. Wolfe Davidson collection (1,070 images) was added soon afterward.[16]

Metadata was off and running and the team found they needed to balance the workload. The team lead had maintained ETDs for about three years until he delegated the task to the newly hired metadata specialist. When the digital projects team began a retrospective project to digitize older print theses and dissertations, the specialist also assumed responsibility for these records. In 2018, the senior specialist received ETD training, thereby splitting the retrospective project work. The current and retrospective ETD workflow enabled both specialists to learn MarcEdit and apply data manipulation techniques. Balancing the workload created variety in assignments and improved everyone's metadata skills. Having knowledge of each digital project also meant any team member could provide backup to maintain momentum and productivity.

GETTING ON THE SAME PAGE

When the first digital project began, the head of SC&A called a monthly meeting, which included the MMRT team lead, the head of digital scholarship, and the metadata manager (both from library technology's digital projects division). These meetings convened to track progress on various digitization projects and encompassed materials managed in the institutional repository as well as the digital objects described by MMRT. These meetings did not usually discuss the fine points of metadata for MMRT projects, but they were helpful from a broader standpoint. These meetings lasted until February 2017.

Early on, metadata generation and management for SC&A materials occurred within Excel spreadsheets. This technique caused issues when multiple users needed to edit the same record. The library technology unit had already adopted CollectiveAccess as the metadata management system for OPN collections. To allow for co-editing of record sets and conforming all digital projects to the same system, MMRT began using CollectiveAccess for SC&A collections as well. As an open source program, the library technology unit, with limited programming resources, was able to customize CollectiveAccess to fit SC&A metadata needs.

With the Clemson University Historical Images project reaching about 1,200 records completed and the two other projects starting to progress, SC&A expressed concern about the standards and best practices being followed. MMRT had proceeded with the understanding that standards were structured by CollectiveAccess and guided by cataloging and authority work experience. OPN metadata guidelines, written for a broad range of cultural institutions, were found to lack recommendations for situations MMRT encountered. For example, from the team lead's perspective, the practice of transcribing annotations uncritically from the back of photographs with little or no research was incompatible with robust metadata. This led the team lead to perceive that SC&A and MMRT lacked a shared understanding of the intended audience and depth of metadata for the projects. Were the projects extended finding aids, were they for local reference, or were they digital exhibits? MMRT and TSCM took a broad view, considering digital projects as intended for a broad audience needing robust description. SC&A supported less robust description to reduce the amount of time and research MMRT conducted in favor of quicker access.

Discussions between the team lead and SC&A led to an agreement that writing an application profile and best practices would be a step toward shared expectations. The team lead also felt that documentation would objectify metadata discussions so that conversations would rise above specific digital objects or the performance of a particular person. The application profile was drafted by the team lead, reviewed by the specialists, and transmitted to the head of special collections and the digital projects manager in March 2017. The team lead adapted the *SCDL (South Carolina Digital Library) Metadata Schema & Guidelines*, version 2016, used by OPN.[17] The application profile and best practices are available.[18]

One might argue that such a document should be developed before completing a single metadata record. In this case, practical experience with metadata problems informed the application profile and best practices. In addition to an analysis of 26 metadata elements with definitions and input standards, the MMRT document endeavored to guide the user in the decision-making process. It also provided examples of values to apply for both images and documents. After the completion of the application profile, digitization meetings were not held between March 2017 and May 2018. Not holding consistent meetings was detrimental to communication and collaboration between MMRT, SC&A, and library technology's digital projects division.

TRANSITIONING TEAM RESPONSIBILITIES

Cataloging

By early 2017, with three metadata projects underway, it became evident that work on monographs copy cataloging drew valuable time away from metadata work. This was particularly true for the one MMRT library specialist still conducting monographs copy cataloging, as well as working approximately one day a week assisting with government documents at Cooper Library. Acting on the encouragement of the TSCM unit head, the MMRT team lead explored shifting the print monograph copy cataloging to the collection management team, which retained some of the functions of the former acquisitions unit but also performed collection analysis, collection relocations, and management of gifts. This shift in workload proved effective because the collection management team enjoyed the advantage of recently hired specialists keen to learn new processes. While the collection management team already copy cataloged while using Library of Congress-Program for Cooperative Cataloging (LC-PCC) bibliographic copy, the two specialists needed a cycle of training to take up OCLC member-created copy for print materials. To support this transition, the MMRT team lead continued to review copy cataloging work and provide ongoing instruction on a case-by-case basis.

The next stage was to identify special formats materials that specialists could also copy catalog. Audiobooks on compact disc were targeted since they are expressions of the print resource. Videodiscs were also a candidate, but there were reservations about records without LC call numbers, which the Libraries requires for special formats. From a sample of 923 cataloged videodisc titles, the team lead found that 20% were documentary (nonfiction) titles that included an LC call number. The remaining 80% were dramatic films and television programs that might have contained LC call numbers in the original record. It was later decided to include these genres into the new videodisc cataloging workflow. Two specialists outside of MMRT trained to catalog these special formats.

At the end of this transition, MMRT specialists no longer cataloged print monographs and work with government documents discontinued. Reflecting this change in responsibilities, their performance goals no longer included cataloging, other than other duties as assigned. A shift in mentality occurred at this time as well. MMRT staff began to refer to themselves as metadata specialists rather than library specialists. The team lead's cataloging role with audiobooks and videodiscs was noticeably reduced. As part of the agreement with the collection management team, the team lead continues to train on and review print materials and supports cataloging high-priority items.

Metadata Training Gaps

Cataloging responsibilities may have shifted to another team, but the background and experience of MMRT members was still cataloging-centric. The team lead had 22 years of cataloging experience with 10 years' concentration in special formats, 7 years of Name Authority Cooperative experience, and 3 years with Resource Description and Access. The incumbent MMRT specialist had about 20 years of copy cataloging experience. The new specialist arrived with skills more aligned to metadata work. She held a bachelor's degree and a certificate in library and information science technology and had served an internship with an archive. The team lead's metadata training was about a decade old. He had attended two metadata workshops presented under the auspices of the California Digital Library, and after joining Clemson, completed a two-day course, Metadata Standards and Applications (in the Cataloging for the 21st Century series), in 2006. Upon taking over metadata responsibilities, MMRT members needed updated metadata training.

METADATA SUMMIT

Metadata at Clemson had been in existence for about a decade. During that time, problems were encountered, in part due to the number of units with shared metadata responsibilities. This formed the basis for holding a metadata summit. The summit, convened by the TSCM unit head and the library technology unit head, and conducted with an external facilitator, included 15 members drawn from the information and research services unit, the library technology unit, SC&A, and TSCM. From TSCM, the unit head and all members of MMRT attended, as well as librarians from two other teams (standards and assessment, and government documents and continuing resources). The purpose for the three-hour summit was "to bring together the different teams across the Libraries that contribute to or produce metadata and foster an open discussion about current practices, challenges, and communication channels" and "to discuss strategies for facing those challenges and creating new opportunities."[19]

The summit schedule included an overview of purpose and agenda, introductions, and ground rules. The first session was a summary of ongoing metadata projects and a metadata exercise. All participants received a brief metadata input form and an image, which they had not seen beforehand. The idea was to provide all participants with the experience of confronting an unfamiliar image with no previous coaching or standards. The intention of the exercise was to stimulate insight into the complexity of the activity from the metadata creator's standpoint.

The 15 participants were presorted into three groups of 5, and in the first of two breakout sessions each group considered a different metadata scenario. In the first session, each group concentrated on identifying the challenges involved with its assigned scenario. The second session focused on finding solutions to the challenges pinpointed in the first session. In both sessions, groups reported to all participants, so the insights of each group could be appreciated. A wrap-up discussion concluded the summit.

A post-summit summary noted several problems that surfaced during the discussions. Some of these problems reflected MMRT's previous concerns:

- Current staffing levels were not adequate for the increasing metadata needs
- Metadata operations needed a source of leadership
- Communication between metadata providers and practitioners had not been effective

The summary also suggested actions to address these problems:

- Improve communication within and across teams and units
- Provide access to better and more in-depth training
- Target metadata and technology professionals for future hires
- Bring in a consultant to identify areas of need and provide solutions
- Charter a metadata steering committee and working group

MMRT had great interest in the formation of the steering committee and the separate metadata practitioners working group. The steering committee was envisioned to "guide the development of standard procedures and to break down the communication and workflow silos between different metadata groups and providers. The committee would designate project-specific working groups to provide critical direction to new projects and to review practices of past and current projects. . . . The membership would include Libraries leadership, metadata practitioners, and metadata providers." The metadata practitioners working group would include those who created metadata, and it would "provide a forum for open communication about standards, workflows, procedures, and training opportunities."[20]

POST-SUMMIT OUTCOMES

The metadata summit led the MMRT team lead to expect changes in project management. All projects, proposed and active, should each have cross unit working groups that clearly define expectations for metadata, workflow, and time to completion. A common understanding of the metadata cultures in each unit and clear collection management priorities would enhance the Libraries' common purpose in digital projects. However, some of MMRT's expectations were not immediately fulfilled. One hope was to form the steering committee and the metadata practitioners working group. The steering committee proposal never moved past the library leadership team's approval stage. The practitioners working group, comprising MMRT and the OPN specialist, submitted a proposal for its charge to the leadership team, but this also was not acted on. This was likely due to turnover in the dean of libraries position.

Despite setbacks, TSCM fulfilled several summit recommendations. All three MMRT members received basic metadata training. They completed the Association for Library Collections and Technical Services web course, Fundamentals of Metadata. The recommendation "target metadata and technology professionals for future hires" became the springboard for a search for the Libraries' first metadata librarian. To fulfill this, TSCM's unit head applied for and received permission to reclassify a vacant staff position to a faculty position. In late 2017 and January 2018, the unit head and the team lead drafted a position posting. Interviews took place in May 2018. The all-day interview schedule included the customary general faculty and unit interviews based on a battery of prepared questions. However, MMRT, upon a suggestion from one of the specialists, decided to gauge how candidates thought about metadata problems. They devised a divergent approach inspired by the summit experience. Each candidate was presented with an image from the Clemson University Historical Images collection and asked to "think out loud" about what metadata elements would be required, and when the associated metadata was provided, to comment on the quality and possible improvements needed.

The new metadata librarian for digital collections was appointed effective August 2018. She is responsible for creating, enriching, and maintaining metadata for SC&A digital resources to support their discovery and accessibility. To accomplish this, she works collaboratively with MMRT, the library technology unit, and SC&A to develop and implement metadata standards, policies, and workflows. She quality controls and remediates current and legacy metadata and helps MMRT maintain awareness of current trends with metadata standards and digital library development.

On the initiative of the digital projects manager, meetings resumed between MMRT, SC&A, and the digital group in May 2018. Three groups now meet once a month. The digital projects collaboration group includes the unit head of SC&A, the digital projects manager, and the MMRT librarians. The Clemson University Historical Images working group includes the same members, plus the SC&A staff member responsible for processing the photographs, and the library specialists. The Thurmond Papers working group includes the unit head of SC&A, the digital projects manager, the archivist for political collections, and the MMRT team. Meetings alternate between the Library Depot and the Special Collections facility. The team lead did not initially expect the specialists to attend the campus meetings, but both specialists are motivated and attend whenever possible. Minutes taken at the meetings include action items, which are reviewed at the next meeting. Any revisions to documentation are noted, and a process has begun to integrate changes into the existing application profile and best practices.

IMPROVED WORKFLOWS

MMRT and SC&A needed to better define how complete to make metadata records. With MMRT's cataloging background and SC&A's

archival background, they had different presuppositions as to how detailed an object should be described. As a result, there was frequent and unreconciled discussion about the proper use of certain metadata elements. For example, what was the description field supposed to contain? Should it include original notes found on the back of photos, added archivist's notes, and notes made by metadata specialists? How would that mix of information be understood by the searcher? It also became evident that there were redundancies in descriptive work between SC&A and MMRT. Previously, MMRT created titles and descriptions. SC&A already created descriptions of the physical items prior to sending the materials to the digitization lab. SC&A and MMRT mutually agreed to test a new workflow in which SC&A provided select metadata fields and MMRT then concentrated on quality control and access points.

A new workflow assigned special collections staff, who were already processing the materials, to enter titles, dates, and descriptions into an Excel spreadsheet, which is ingested into CollectiveAccess. This change achieved many benefits: SC&A is curating what collections materials are digitized, which MMRT had difficulty doing; it reduced the number of fields MMRT needed to complete; it allowed SC&A to define the detail of description; and it allowed MMRT to concentrate on enriching the records with controlled access points, including local subject headings.

"BETTER TOGETHER"[21]

Changing technologies and user needs prompted Clemson University Libraries to rethink its strategies. The emergence of digital collections at the Libraries meant staff and faculty needed to transition their focus toward providing quality metadata for researchers to discover the University's unique and invaluable historical resources. Many steps were taken to solve this gap in service, and the newly formed metadata and monographic resources team continues to develop so it may provide the best service possible to the Clemson community.

As we look back on the "road taken" from cataloging team to metadata team, what did we learn? Approaching library transitions as opportunities for new collaborations is key to success. The TSCM unit merger and relocation were important because the two events contributed to the formulation of purpose and identity for MMRT. The transition of cataloging and metadata responsibilities to separate teams provided the resources necessary to build a sustainable metadata program. The formation of a digital projects collaboration working group and subgroups for each digital project allowed members of different units and teams to work closely together to achieve common goals. This also helped all collaborators bridge the cultural gap that existed between metadata from archival (such as more product, less process), cataloging, and technology viewpoints. In this regard, the addition of the metadata librarian was critical to forming a collaborative future in which the effective staging of new digital projects, the updating of documentation, and the evaluation of metadata can thrive.

The metadata team's purpose could only be achieved by shedding the cataloging role as much as possible, but team members found that letting go of customary activities was not as difficult as learning new skills. It was easier to transition cataloging responsibilities to another team than learn how to produce metadata in a collaborative environment. This was a steeper climb than expected. The cataloging-is-metadata mantra was a bit misleading in this case. Extensive cataloging skills did not transfer as easily to digital collections metadata work. While skills such as subject analysis and access point selection and creation are the core of both activities, the catalog-turned-metadata team required training to help in the transition. The team will need ongoing training as it continues to seek new learning opportunities to improve members' metadata proficiency and efficiency.

Documenting metadata standards and guidelines provided a successful avenue to define digital project goals and work toward consistent metadata practices. This was a step in the right direction for getting everyone on the same page, but MMRT found that defining standards (such as in the application profile) did not equate to shared understanding and implementation. What then is the essential factor for achieving shared goals? It would be trite to say "better communication," for as Barbara Rochen Renner and Lee Richardson suggest, communication is not the totality of collaboration.[22] Renner and Richardson also point out that we cannot assume one department understands the workflows of another department. Collaboration is more than documents, meetings, or working in a shared space. It is the process of discovering mutually developed solutions while traveling the same road together.

NOTES

1. The title references the famous poem by Robert Frost, *The Road Not Taken*. The poem is a reflection on choices made in an ambiguous environment. In this context, we intend to show how decisions, however arrived at, triggered a wave of later decisions and consequences. How we deal positively with those consequences is the important matter, hence, the "road taken."
2. Student (2019 data) and faculty (2019 data) totals from Clemson University Interactive Factbook, https://www.clemson.edu/institutional-effectiveness/oir/factbook/.
3. At that time, the Education Media Center was called the Tillman Media Center.
4. For an overview of the formation and collaborations of the digital initiatives unit (now part of library technology) see Emily Gore and Mandy Mastrovita, "Collaborative-Centered Digital Curation: A Case Study at Clemson University Libraries," in *Digitization in the Real World*, ed. Kwong Bor Ng and Jason Kucsma (New York: Metropolitan New York Library Council, 2010), 490–502.
5. See https://openparksnetwork.org/.
6. See https://digitalcollections.clemson.edu/explore/collections/textile-mills/.
7. Teri Alexander et al., *Transforming Clemson University Libraries for the 21st Century: Study and Recommendations by the Future Is Now Task Force*, August 9, 2012, p. 2, http://clemson.libguides.com/ld.php?content_id=9028659.
8. For the chair's view of the planning process see Eric C. Shoaf, "Transparency Means Greater Payoff in a Planning Process," *North Carolina Libraries* 71 (Spring–Summer 2013): 11–14, http://tigerprints.clemson.edu/cgi/viewcontent.cgi?article=1028&context=lib_pubs.
9. Alexander et al., *Transforming*, p. 13.

10. Ibid., p. 14.

11. Ibid., p. 13.

12. The metadata workflow used for ETDs is like that for patents described in Andrew Wesolek, Jan Comfort, and Lisa Bodenheimer, "Collaborate to Innovate: Expanding Access to Faculty Patents Through the Institutional Repository and the Library Catalog," *Collection Management* 40, no. 4 (2015), https://doi.org/10.1080/01462679 .2015.1093986.

13. See https://digitalcollections.clemson.edu/explore/collections /ua100/.

14. The Libraries uses a staff classification with ranks of library assistant and library specialist. Specialist positions are defined for more complex tasks with a broader range of decision-making in contrast to library assistant positions, in which only specifications are applied.

15. See https://tigerprints.clemson.edu/strom/.

16. See https://digitalcollections.clemson.edu/explore/collections/awd/.

17. See http://scmemory.org/wp-content/uploads/2018/05/SCDL MetadataSchema_2018.pdf.

18. See https://docs.google.com/document/d/1ibv58u6L_tnJyUNoIFJ KLCrwWY2L9xTLmzy6nskaXbo/edit?usp=sharing.

19. "Meeting Summary," email communication from Christopher Vinson, head of library technology, September 26, 2017.

20. Ibid.

21. The team lead credits Ivey Glendon for this felicitous phrase and her influential explanation of how project groups were formed at University of Virginia Library. See Ivey Glendon, "Better Together: Cataloging and Metadata Librarians, Archivists, and New Understandings for Description and Discovery" (presentation delivered at Association of Library Collections and Technical Services Cataloging Norms Interest Group, American Library Association Annual Conference, Chicago, IL, June 24, 2017).

22. Richardson, Lee M., and Barbara Rochen Renner, *Better Together: Technical Services & Public Services*, 2018, https://doi.org/10.17615 /h8tm-2s87.

CHALLENGE TWO

Improving Collection Evaluation and Management

CHAPTER 5

Assessing the Work of Technical Services Through an In-Depth Analysis of Physical Resource Usage

Laura Kirkland

ABSTRACT

This chapter describes an in-depth analysis of the circulating print collection at Stetson University.

This project was undertaken to determine how successful the library was in selecting resources for collection and how well those resources were being used. The analysis also grew out of the shifting of responsibility for the collection, from the public services unit to the technical services department. A variety of factors were used in analyzing the collection, including relative use compared to the size of subject areas and the number of new items added to subject areas and how often those new items were used. This analysis has enabled the technical services department to assess the impact of the work that is done and has provided insights into which areas of the collection would most benefit from purchases of new library materials.

INTRODUCTION

Stetson University, located in DeLand, Florida, is a small, liberal arts university with a population of 4,330 students, and 265 full-time faculty. The duPont-Ball Library holds just over 231,000 print volumes and subscribes to more than 100 databases. It utilizes the SirsiDynix integrated library system. We are a small academic library, with 8 full-time faculty librarians and 11 staff (some part-time). Due to our small size, there is overlap of responsibilities among various positions, and many of us have duties in more than one area. Our library's technical services department has four areas of responsibility:

- *Acquisitions*—deciding what books, periodicals, and videos the library needs and buying them[1]
- *Cataloging*—organizing materials in the library so that patrons can find them
- *Electronic services*—maintaining electronic access to the library's resources
- *Periodicals*—managing the electronic, paper, and microform journals

Personnel-wise, we have one staff member responsible for the purchasing of material, who also manages the print journal collection; one staff member who manages the e-book collections and maintains access to them; a new staff position (currently in the hiring process) to oversee e-journal collections, and access; one faculty member who oversees cataloging and processing of print and electronic resources; and the associate dean, who manages the technical services department. One other library faculty member works both in technical services to catalog music scores and recordings and in public services to provide reference service and library instruction.

In the past we have tracked technical services statistics based primarily on how many items we order, process, catalog, mend, and replace. But this is not a complete reflection of the work we do. Material requests come from many sources, such as faculty and other librarians, but the responsibility for budget allocation and spending of funds falls to the head of the department. She also approves all purchases. Since our department is responsible for the ordering of library material, the usage of that material is also a reflection of the results of the work we do.

As in many other libraries, there has been a marked decline in the use of print resources at our library during the past several years. Circulation has been decreasing 10%–15% each year since 2010,[2] and we recently weeded approximately 62,000 volumes from our circulating collection due to age, physical condition, and lack of use.[3] In FY 2008–2009 our library decided to shift our purchasing toward buying monographs in e-book format. We choose the print option only if the e-book is not available, if the electronic format is cost-prohibitive, or if the person making the request specifically requested the print book. This decision was prompted by several factors, including the need for reduced shelf space.[4] Cost was not a factor, as we found that most e-books cost the same (or sometimes more) than print books. However, we have found that utilizing patron-drive acquisition e-book collections has helped keep costs down, as we then only buy titles once our users have accessed them. The shift toward electronic purchasing also led to the replacement of a staff position (chiefly responsible for print copy cataloging) with an electronic collections specialist, whose primary responsibility is cataloging and managing e-book collections.

Despite a shift toward electronic resources, we have found that physical resources are still in demand in our library. Just over 17,000 items circulated during FY 2015–2016.[5] This represents a 1% *increase* in circulation from the previous fiscal year, for the first time in recent history. Similarly, although the number of books being added to our circulating collection has declined from 2,595 in 2010–2011 to 953 in 2013–2014,[6] over the past two years that number has been steadily increasing back up to 1,166.[7] This information led to the decision that an in-depth analysis of the usage of our print collection would be a worthwhile undertaking. It would show us how well our library is doing at selecting resources that our patrons use and to what extent they use them.

This idea grew out of the gradual shifting of some responsibilities for the circulating collection. Traditionally, responsibility for the management of the circulating collection has fallen to public services. In our library, as in most other libraries, public services circulates and shelves items, tracks down overdues, and so forth. But in recent years, our technical services department has assumed an increasing share of responsibility for the circulating collection. We put new items onto the New Books display and remove items from this display after six weeks. Since we catalog and process new materials, it seemed logical that we be the ones to then put them on display.

Technical services periodically takes inventory of the sections of the collection to identify missing items, reinstating many formerly lost items in the process. The circulation department does shelf read the collection and locates mis-shelved items. However, this process does not identify items on the shelves that are noted as missing or lost in the catalog. Very often, after buying a replacement item, the library would find the lost item back on the shelves, and we would then have duplicate copies. Since technical services is responsible for buying these replacement items, we began inventorying the collection, matching a printed list of items from the catalog against items on the shelves. As a result, we have identified many lost and missing items and have eliminated the need for unnecessary replacements.

Most recently we assumed responsibility for tracking missing items (i.e., items not found on the shelves in their designated space). Since we identify many missing items during our inventory, and we are responsible for withdrawing and replacing lost items, it seemed logical for us to track these missing items as well. This gradual assumption of these additional responsibilities was not the product of a single decision. Rather, it evolved out of the recognition that the library could benefit from additional attention to some areas of collection maintenance and oversight that were not currently being carried out. This shift in responsibilities involved no staffing changes; the library's move toward buying more electronic resources and fewer print items resulted in technical services personnel spending less time on acquisitions, cataloging, and processing. This enabled us to spend more time on maintaining and analyzing the collection.

Before the period of the present study, collecting data on the usage of our circulating collection was the purview of public services. However, data included in its annual reports has been limited to the total numbers of items borrowed, grouped by item formats (e.g., book, DVD, and compact disc). Data on how many times items have circulated can be obtained from reports in our integrated library system (ILS), but this information is usually only obtained by technical services personnel when deciding about whether to replace a lost or missing item, or whether to remove it from the collection due to low usage. Our process of tracking data only about purchases of materials, and numbers of items added to and removed from our collections, did not give us much insight into what sections of the circulating collection are most in demand. Also, it did not provide any guidance as to what new titles we should be acquiring.

After attending a workshop on using Excel to analyze library collections,[8] and learning about many more ways to use circulation data to analyze collection use, I decided to conduct an in-depth analysis of our circulating collection. I consulted the text co-written by the workshop presenter, Tony Greiner (along with Bob Cooper), *Analyzing Library Collection Use With Excel* (Chicago: American Library Association, 2007) in order to complete my analysis. Several libraries have conducted and published analyses of their collections, but most of those I identified were published over 20 years ago. I therefore chose to construct my analysis using methods solely based on the text by Greiner and Cooper.

Their collection analysis method examines not just overall circulation statistics but also the relative use of each section of the collection. *Relative use* is a ratio comparing the percentage of circulation of each subject area to the relative size of that area in terms of the overall collection. The idea is that if, for example, a section makes up 18% of the collection, it should account for 18% of overall collection use (a relative use of 100). If the relative use of a section is higher than 100, that section should be supported with more items. If the relative use is lower, the section might be examined for weeding of unused material, or fewer new items considered for purchase, or enhancement of different subjects within that section might be considered.[9]

My collection analysis also determined how many new items have been added to each subject area in the last two years, how often those newer items are used, and the relative use of these newest titles. I also calculated the correlation between the age of each item and its circulation usage. This helped me determine which areas of the collection are most used, which will benefit most from the addition of new titles, and how much the age of an item affects its usage.

It is my hope that this in-depth collection analysis will enable us to better assess the work we do in technical services, as well as give us insights into specific ways we can make better and more informed choices about the resources we provide to our users.

METHODOLOGY

To conduct my analysis, I ran usage reports in our ILS. This report gave me the following data on each item: author, title, publication information (including copyright date), call number, circulation data (total charges, date last charged, in-house charges,[10] and whether the item is currently on loan), home location, current location, and date the item was added to the online system. Items were separated into sections. Nonbook formats were separated by format into DVDs and compact discs. DVDs were further divided into feature films and non-fiction videos. These sections are classified differently and shelved separately.

Print items were then divided into subject groups by LC classification number. The H section was further divided into two sections, with business and economics (H-HJ) as one section and social sciences (HM-HX) as another since these subject areas are more distinct. Music scores (M classification) were separated from the music literature (ML-MT) since they are different formats (music scores and books about music) that are used in different ways. The juvenile books were separated into their own section, since they are shelved in their own area and are not generally used for research, as is most of the print collection. See Table 5.1 for a complete list of sections.

Noncirculating items were removed from the study consideration and not included in item totals. These include reference books and several special and archival collections. Items currently on reserve were excluded as well due to inflated checkout numbers. These items were chosen by instructors and made available for students' use in the library. Students were thus required to use these items, which were kept in the library, and each circulation accounted for only an hour or two of usage. I wished to study only those items chosen from the shelves by our users.

Each segment of the total collection is hereafter referred to as a section (e.g., all feature films, all items in E classification, all items in Q classification). Data was collected on November 9, 2017. "Recent" is defined as within the two-year period from November 9, 2015, to November 9, 2017.

RESULTS

Table 5.1 (relative use) shows that the section with the highest relative use is our feature films. This came as no surprise; this section is heavily used by students, staff, and faculty. Each DVD has been checked

Table 5.1 Relative Use of Circulating Collection

Section/LC Class	Items	% of Collection	Total Circulation	Average Lifetime Circulation	% of Lifetime Circulation	Relative Use
Feature Films	2,116	0.972	58,847	27.810	10.58	1087.826
Compact Discs	7,313	3.361	38,051	5.203	6.84	203.527
Videos	2,037	0.936	8,274	4.062	1.49	158.882
ML-MT (Books on Music)	8,749	4.021	28,874	3.300	5.19	129.092
R (Medicine)	4,216	1.938	13,342	3.165	2.40	123.786
Juvenile	5,027	2.310	15,627	3.109	2.81	121.596
HM-HX (Social Sciences)	9,674	4.446	29,423	3.041	5.29	118.968
B (Philosophy, Psychology, Religion)	22,570	10.372	58,774	2.604	10.57	101.860
G (Geography, Anthropology, Recreation)	4,564	2.097	11,871	2.601	2.13	101.740
F (American Local History)	4,098	1.883	10,398	2.537	1.87	99.250
N (Fine Arts)	9,560	4.393	23,093	2.416	4.15	94.487
J (Political Science)	5,087	2.338	11,735	2.307	2.11	90.234
E (American History)	8,377	3.850	19,113	2.282	3.44	89.247
D (General and Old World History)	15,938	7.325	34,363	2.156	6.18	84.335
T (Technology)	2,812	1.292	5,983	2.128	1.08	83.225
M (Music scores)	18,540	8.520	37,887	2.044	6.81	79.934
U (Military Science)	606	0.278	1,234	2.036	0.22	79.651
Z (Bibliography, Library Science)	533	0.245	1,040	1.951	0.19	76.323
C (Auxiliary Sciences of History)	909	0.418	1,689	1.858	0.30	72.680

(continued)

Table 5.1 (*continued*)

Section/LC Class	Items	% of Collection	Total Circulation	Average Lifetime Circulation	% of Lifetime Circulation	Relative Use
Q (Science)	9,904	4.552	18,349	1.853	3.30	72.469
P (Language and Literature)	52,286	24.029	93,825	1.794	16.87	70.191
H-HJ (Business)	11,333	5.208	18,006	1.589	3.24	62.147
V (Naval Science)	123	0.057	191	1.553	0.03	60.741
L (Education)	6,726	3.091	9,985	1.485	1.79	58.069
K (Law)	2,774	1.275	4,077	1.470	0.73	57.489
S (Agriculture)	1,420	0.653	1,934	1.362	0.35	53.274
A (General Works)	305	0.140	306	1.003	0.06	39.244
Total	217,597	100	556,291	2.557 (average)	100	n/a

Note: Items = total number of items in section; % of Collection = number of items in section account for what % of total collection; Total Circulation = total circulation of all items in section; Average Lifetime Circulation = total circulation of all items in section / number of items in section; % of Lifetime Circulation = total circulation of section / total circulation of collection; Relative Use = (% of total circulation / % total collection) × 100.

out an average of 27 times. Of our 2,116 feature films, only 37 have never circulated. The relative use of the feature films is extremely high because, although these items account for 10.58% of total use, this section accounts for only 0.972% of our circulating collection. The other nonbook format sections, compact discs (3.361% of the collection) and nonfiction videos (0.936% of the collection), account for the two next highest relative use categories (203.526 and 158.882 respectively).

I believe one reason the nonbook formats account for the most relative use is the nature of these items. Feature films can be watched in 90 minutes to 2 hours and then returned. Nonfiction videos are similarly used. Compact discs are 80 minutes long, and anecdotal evidence suggests these can be borrowed to listen to only a few tracks. So, these nonbook formats are intended for short-term use. This is reflected in their shorter checkout periods (one week for nonbook materials compared to four weeks for books.) This confirmation of the heavy use of these sections means we can confidently continue to purchase new items and replace damaged and lost materials from these areas in the future.

Comparison of the individual sections of the book collection will provide useful information about which of these sections are most heavily used. In terms of relative use, the book sections with the highest relative use are shown in Table 5.2. Each of these sections showed relative use above 100, meaning they accounted for a higher percentage of use despite accounting for a comparatively lower percentage of the overall collection.

The language and literature section (P), despite accounting for 16.87% of all lifetime circulation, has a relative use of only 70.191. This is due in part to the large size of the section. It contains 52,286 items,

Table 5.2 Sections With Highest Relative Use

Section	Relative Use
ML-MT (literature about music)	129.092
R (medical literature)	123.786
Juvenile	121.596
HM-HX (social sciences)	118.968
G (geography and recreation)	101.740
B (philosophy and religion)	101.860

more than twice as many items as any other section. I attribute the low relative use to the fact that many of the items in this section are classic works of literature and biographies and criticisms of well-known and frequently studied authors. Many of these titles are older and have not circulated as many times as newer titles. Nevertheless, we keep them as standard reference works we consider necessary for our collection and to support our English and Modern Language departments. The music scores (M) section is similarly situated. Our library owns 18,540 scores (the third largest section), which accounts for 6.81% of our total circulation. It has the fifth highest number of total circulations of any section. But because of the substantial size of the section, the relative use is only 79.934. As with the language and literature section, we own many scores that are considered "standard repertoire" and that we retain out of necessity to support our music program.

Science (Q) and business (H-HJ) both show lower relative use (72.469 and 62.147 respectively.) It has been our experience that patrons doing research in these areas tend to use journals and data-bases much more frequently than they use books. But it will be worth examining which existing titles in these areas currently get the most usage and determining whether we might add more titles in these specific subject areas. Books on women's and men's conversational styles (24 charges), social communication in advertising (20), and communication in the workplace (17) were among the highest-use items. So, communication in business would be worth looking into as a subject in which to invest more resources.

Some sections, such as law (K), naval and military science (V and U), agriculture (S), and general works (A), are just not as widely used in our library since they don't directly support a Stetson program. Although Stetson University does have an Army ROTC program, it does not have many students, and we are not aware of any writing or research assignments that would require these students to use resources in our military sections.

Some interesting observations can be found by comparing overall relative use (Table 5.2) to relative use of new items (Table 5.3). The books about music (ML-MT) accounted for the highest relative use of the book collection overall. But when only the newest items are examined (those added in the last two years), relative use drops from 129.092 to 25.421. Similarly, philosophy and religion (B) relative use

Table 5.3 Relative Use of New Items

Section/LC Class	No. of Recent Items Added	% of Items Added Last 2 Years	New Items Circulation	% of Recent Circulation by New Items	Relative Use of New Items	Items Out	% of Items Out	New Items Out	% of New Items Out
Feature Films	114	7.41	431	42.72	576.660	77	5.31	21	3.98
V (Naval Science)	1	0.06	3	0.30	457.582	1	0.07	1	0.19
U (Military Science)	2	0.13	2	0.20	152.527	2	0.14	0	0.00
E (American History)	25	1.62	23	2.28	140.325	46	3.17	5	0.95
Videos	38	2.47	34	3.37	136.472	9	0.62	2	0.38
R (Medicine)	14	0.91	12	1.19	130.738	7	0.48	0	0.00
H-HJ (Business)	20	1.30	13	1.29	99.143	40	2.76	6	1.14
K (Law)	7	0.45	4	0.40	87.158	3	0.21	1	0.19
Juvenile	349	22.68	184	18.24	80.416	134	9.24	184	34.85
Z (Bibliography, Library Science)	4	0.26	2	0.20	76.264	10	0.69	1	0.19
P (Language and Literature)	359	23.33	168	16.65	71.378	306	21.09	277	52.46
J (Political Science)	26	1.69	12	1.19	70.397	37	2.55	4	0.76
D (General and Old World History)	63	4.09	27	2.68	65.369	66	4.55	7	1.33
B (Philosophy, Psychology, Religion)	91	5.91	37	3.67	62.017	122	8.41	8	1.52
Q (Science)	48	3.12	16	1.59	50.842	31	2.14	3	0.57
T (Technology)	6	0.39	2	0.20	50.842	22	1.52	0	0.00
N (Fine Arts)	16	1.04	3	0.30	28.599	52	3.58	1	0.19

(continued)

Table 5.3 *(continued)*

Section/LC Class	No. of Recent Items Added	% of Items Added Last 2 Years	New Items Circulation	% of Recent Circulation by New Items	Relative Use of New Items	Items Out	% of Items Out	New Items Out	% of New Items Out
G (Geography, Anthropology, Recreation)	22	1.43	4	0.40	27.732	18	1.24	1	0.19
ML-MT (Books on Music)	60	3.90	10	0.99	25.421	139	9.58	2	0.38
M (Music Scores)	99	6.43	14	1.39	21.570	205	14.13	4	0.76
F (American Local History)	11	0.71	1	0.10	13.866	45	3.10	0	0.00
HM-HX (Social Sciences)	37	2.40	3	0.30	12.367	46	3.17	0	0.00
Compact Discs	112	7.28	4	0.40	5.447	0	0.00	0	0.00
A (General Works)	0	0.00	0	0.00	0.000	2	0.14	0	0.00
C (Auxiliary Sciences of History)	1	0.06	0	0.00	0.000	11	0.76	0	0.00
L (Education)	9	0.58	0	0.00	0.000	19	1.31	0	0.00
S (Agriculture)	5	0.32	0	0.00	0.000	1	0.07	0	0.00
Total	*1,539*	*100*	*1,009*	*100*	*n/a*	*1,451*	*100*	*528*	*100*

Note: No. of Recent Items Added = number of items added from Nov. 9, 2015, to Nov. 9, 2017; % of Recent Items Added Last 2 Years = number of items in section added in the last 2 years / total items added to collection in the last 2 years; New Items Circulation = how many times items added in last 2 years have circulated; % of Recent Circulation by New Items = circulation of new items in section / total circulation of collection in the last two years; Relative Use of New Items = (% of circulation by new items / % of total items added in the last 2 years) × 100; Items Out = total number of items currently checked out; % of Items Out = number of items currently checked out in section / total items out in collection; New Items Out = items added in last 2 years which are currently checked out; % of New Items Out = section new items out / total new items out.

drops from 101.860 overall to 62.017 for new books. I interpret these results to mean that the newness of an item may be less important when it comes to literature about music and philosophy/religion. Concentrating purchases on new items in these areas may not necessarily result in more use. In contrast, the medical literature section (R) has a 123.786 relative use overall, and 130.738 relative use for new items. Since the relative use numbers for the overall collection and the newer items are much closer, one could extrapolate that the relative newness of these books is a more important factor in predicting their use. This is supported by a comparison of the average copyright date of books in the music literature section (1977) and philosophy and religion (1972). The average copyright date of medical literature is 1989. This includes a range from 1889 to 2018, containing a few older classics, but overall these books are much more recent than those of either music or religion/philosophy. (See all average copyright dates in Table 5.5). Also, in the medical field, recent research often supersedes older research, resulting in older works being removed from the collection more regularly.

My analysis also helped identify sections that have zero relative use for items added in the last two years. Education (L) has a 58.069 relative use overall with 0 for recent items. This lack of usage is surprising, as the university offers both an undergraduate major and minor in education, as well as a master's degree in educational leadership. Our music librarian teaches an information literacy class to the music education majors and reports that she has been asked by the instructors to focus on teaching students to find journal articles, not books. So, this may be a factor in lower education book usage. Agricultural literature (S) shows a similar relative use of 53.274, also with 0 for recent items. But since the university does not offer either a major or a minor in agriculture, this lower usage is much less surprising. Also, the much smaller size of the agriculture section (1,420 items compared to 6,726 education items) indicates that the smaller relative use is much less noteworthy. One contributing factor to lower relative use for newer items might be the minimal addition of titles; in the last two years, only 9 items were added to the education section and 5 new items in the agriculture section. The library would be well-served to investigate why the education books are not used as heavily as other sections that support similarly sized academic programs.

In sections where newer items do not necessarily result in higher use, it might be worth considering adding more classic or standard works in these areas, even older titles. We regularly consult Resources for College Libraries and other similar sources that could provide suggestions for titles to consider adding.

Some sections with lower relative use overall had a much higher relative use of new books, as shown in Table 5.4. Since newer titles in these sections circulate considerably more than the older titles, adding new titles and heavier weeding of older titles might boost overall relative use in those areas.

I also used the analysis data to calculate the correlation between the age of items in each section and their usage. The results can be seen in Table 5.5.

Since the correlation is between the age of the item and the total number of checkouts, a negative correlation means newer items get more use and a positive one means older items get more use (higher age corresponds with higher use). Not surprisingly, most of the sections show a negative correlation between age and use, proving that newer items lead to higher circulation. However, all correlations were very small, ranging from −0.19366 to 0.181752. The greatest possible range would be from −1.00 to +1.00. So, it appears there is no real correlation between age and usage in the overall collection.

The nonbook sections show the highest correlation between age and use, which might seem unexpected. However, the average age of these three sections is much lower than that of the books. Therefore, most of even the oldest nonbook items are probably newer than many of the books.

The sections accounting for the highest percentage of recent circulation (in the last two years, 2015–2017) are shown in Table 5.6. These are among our highest relative use sections, so it is not at all surprising that they account for 59% of our circulation in the last two years.

Table 5.4 Relative Use of New Books

Section	Overall Relative Use	New Item Relative Use
Naval Science (V)	60.741	457.582
Military Science (U)	79.651	152.527
Business (H-HJ)	62.147	99.143

Table 5.5 Usage of New Items and Age Correlation

Section/LC Class	Recent Circulation	% of Recent Circulation	Average Copyright	Age/Use Correlation	No. of Recent Items Added	% of Items Added in Last 2 Years	Circulation of New Items
P (Language and Literature)	2,718	19.82	1971	−0.19366	359	23.33	168
N (Fine Arts)	378	2.76	1978	−0.19292	16	1.04	3
B (Philosophy, Psychology, Religion)	1,284	9.36	1972	−0.18823	91	5.91	37
D (General and Old World History)	1,013	7.39	1969	−0.16292	63	4.09	27
ML-MT (Books on Music)	1,186	8.65	1977	−0.16165	60	3.90	10
C (Auxiliary Sciences of History)	50	0.36	1975	−0.15731	1	0.06	0
E (American History)	57	0.42	1978	−0.1569	25	1.62	23
J (Political Science)	289	2.11	1987	−0.10969	26	1.69	12
L (Education)	180	1.31	1983	−0.10686	9	0.58	0
K (Law)	89	0.65	1987	−0.09674	7	0.45	4
G (Geography, Anthropology, Recreation)	292	2.13	1984	−0.09262	22	1.43	4
H-HJ (Business)	339	2.47	1985	−0.09023	20	1.30	13
R (Medicine)	207	1.51	1989	−0.08848	14	0.91	12
Q (Science)	430	3.14	1984	−0.0769	48	3.12	16
Juvenile	1,492	10.88	1985	−0.07405	349	22.68	184
F (American Local History)	275	2.00	1974	−0.07129	11	0.71	1
HM-HX (Social Sciences)	588	4.29	1987	−0.06815	37	2.40	3
T (Technology)	154	1.12	1989	−0.04341	6	0.39	2

(continued)

Table 5.5 (*continued*)

Section/LC Class	Recent Circulation	% of Recent Circulation	Average Copyright	Age/Use Correlation	No. of Recent Items Added	% of Items Added in Last 2 Years	Circulation of New Items
Z (Bibliography, Library Science)	25	0.18	1987	-0.02979	4	0.26	2
S (Agriculture)	58	0.42	1983	-0.02461	5	0.32	0
A (General Works)	12	0.09	1949	0	0	0.00	0
M (Music Scores)	815	5.94	1965	0.005588	99	6.43	14
V (Naval Science)	3	0.02	1986	0.06393	1	0.06	3
U (Military Science)	36	0.26	1988	0.086427	2	0.13	2
Feature Films	1,416	10.32	2008	0.149049	114	7.41	431
Videos	214	1.56	2006	0.164781	38	2.47	34
Compact Discs	116	0.85	1993	0.181752	112	7.28	4
Total	*13,716*	*100*	*1982*	*-0.056848 (average)*	*1,539*	*100*	*1,009*

Note: Recent Circulation = items checked out at least once in the last 2 years; % of Recent Circulation = recent circulation of section / total recent circulation of collection; Average Copyright = of items in section; Age/Use Correlation = relationship between age of item and number of circulations; No. of Recent Items added = items added in the last 2 years; Circulation of New Items = how many times items added in the last 2 years have circulated.

Table 5.6 Highest Percentage of Recent Circulation

Section	Recent Circulation	% of Recent Circulation
P (Language and Literature)	2,718	19.82
Juvenile	1,492	10.88
Feature Films	1,416	10.32
B (Philosophy, Psychology, Religion)	1,284	9.36
ML-MT (Books on Music)	1,186	8.65

CONCLUSION

Our library's public services personnel are currently conducting a usage study of our library space, determining which spaces are used most, noting both day of the week and time of day. Usage of our electronic collections is readily available from vendors. But before I conducted this study, we had only limited knowledge about the usage of the library's physical collection. This study has given us much more detailed and useful information.

It would have been interesting to compare usage statistics in the current study with those from the period before our weeding project. I was unable to do so due to the inability to distinguish those items removed during the recent large weeding project from every item ever withdrawn from the collection. Inclusion of the 62,000 little-used items most recently weeded would have given significantly different results. Comparing those numbers with those taken after the weeding would have illustrated the extent to which the weeding of little used items improved overall usage statistics.

Libraries routinely assume that patrons use newer books more. But is that always the case? If a section is regularly used but does not show a high correlation between newer books and more checkouts, then we can conclude that the older items are being used at the same rate as the newer purchases. Newer is not always better.

Additionally, seeing which titles are being used most will greatly enable us to make better qualified choices when it comes to ordering new titles. As an example, the analysis of the science literature showed that four of the most heavily used books dealt with the subject of sea turtles (27, 26, 23, and 22 checkouts). So, the library might consider purchasing more books on this subject.

As this study was being conducted, our library was in the process of migrating to a new cloud-based ILS. This new interface presents our users with new ways of searching for and exploring the library's resources. It will be instructive to repeat this usage analysis to analyze how this new interface may or may not have impacted usage of our collections.

I plan to repeat this collection analysis once each year. This will enable us to study circulation trends over time to see which sections are increasing or decreasing in use. It will also enable us to see the effects of any changes or adjustments we make to our choices for news materials purchasing. Since our current ILS does not track dates for all item circulations (only the latest one), yearly statistics will give us a better idea of how these circulation trends change from year to year. I will also consider dividing the language and literature (P) section into smaller sections. This would make the section sizes more consistent. Also, I believe some parts of this section are more heavily used than others. American and English literature likely gets much higher use than Greek or classical philology.

I am looking into ways to extend this collection analysis to new areas as well. To offset the extensive recent weeding of our print collection, the library has added over 150,000 digital resources. We can easily track usage of electronic resources purchased from vendors with vendor-provided statistics. But we have had no way to evaluate our library's other electronic resources. These fall into two categories. Many of the older titles that were weeded from our circulating collection are in the public domain and thus have free online access. We have been adding URLs for these titles to our catalog records, and in a future study we will track their usage to determine whether this practice is worth continuing. We will do the same thing with the websites we add to the catalog to determine whether this practice generates enough usage to continue adding these resources.

Tracking resource usage of these types of items (print and electronic resources that are not part of a packaged collection) is a new direction for our technical services department. In an era when data-driven analytics are permeating every aspect of library service, we see these new analyses as ways we can further document the work we do in technical services. They will also enable us to work toward making better informed choices that will provide more benefit to our users

NOTES

1. Although technical services is responsible for making the final determination regarding material purchases, faculty input in the development of the library's collection is highly encouraged. Faculty members may submit requests for book, journal, video, or other item purchases to the library at any time. We do not have library liaisons for department requests; our faculty make their requests directly, usually to the head of technical services, or occasionally to a librarian with whom they are personally acquainted. Faculty are also emailed reviews from Choice Reviews Online for possible library book purchases monthly. Library faculty and staff may also submit purchase requests. Toward the end of each fiscal year, the head of technical services submits purchase recommendations for areas of the collection from which we have received few (or no) requests.

2. Susan Ryan, *Public Services Annual Reports FY 2010–2011, 2011–2012, 2012–2013, 2013–2014, 2014–2015, 2015–2016,* https://www2.stetson.edu/library/about-us/library-publications/annual-reports/.

3. Withdrawn books were removed from the collection. Some were sent to Better World Books, some were given away, and others were recycled.

4. This was due to the addition of the University's Student Success Center and Writing Center into the existing library space.

5. Susan Ryan, *Public Services Annual Report FY 2016–2017.* https://www2.stetson.edu/library/about-us/library-publications/annual-reports/.

6. Debbi Dinkins, *Technical Services Department Annual Reports 2010–2011, 2011–2012, 2012–2013, 2013–2014,* https://www2.stetson.edu/library/about-us/library-publications/annual-reports/.

7. Debbi Dinkins, *Technical Services Department Annual Report 2016–2017,* https://www2.stetson.edu/library/about-us/library-publications/annual-reports/.

8. Tony Greiner, *Analyzing Library Collection Use With Excel* (presentation at the NEFLIN Workshop, Florida Coastal School of Law, Jacksonville, FL, July 8, 2016).

9. Tony Greiner and Bob Cooper, *Analyzing Library Collection Use With Excel* (Chicago: American Library Association, 2007), 117–18.

10. In-house usage has not been used consistently by the Library and thus this information was not analyzed.

CHAPTER 6

Building Better Collections Through Relationships: Sharing Expertise During Collection Downsizing

Mary C. Aagard, Nancy Rosenheim, Marlena Hooyboer, and Cheri A. Folkner

ABSTRACT

Boise State University's Albertsons Library undertook a substantial collection downsizing project in 2017. A survey tool was developed to investigate whether this project would strengthen working relationships between technical services staff and librarians. The survey would allow us to assess the process and its outcomes and gain insight into the emotions of those participating in the project. Survey results showed librarians and staff members had different experiences during the project. Librarians experienced more anxiety during the process than staff. More staff than librarians felt that there was a barrier to sharing their expertise due to their job role. Perceptions of technical services and librarians were not significantly changed throughout the process, although survey comments indicated an increased collegiality among staff and librarians as a result of the project. The comments of the survey respondents revealed that a high-level strategy for weeding and a shared understanding of objectives and best practices would have given the project more cohesion, supported buy-in, and increased participation. Using a survey such as this prior to undertaking a large-scale weeding process would help identify communication preferences, areas where training is needed, and best practices to use for the project. A similar survey after the project would evaluate the success of implantation from the perspective of library employees.

INTRODUCTION

In 2017, Boise State University's Albertsons Library undertook a substantial collection downsizing project to free up space for the expansion of the College of Innovation and Design. The magnitude of the project required the participation of most personnel within almost every library unit. While the Albertsons Library has conducted many collection management activities over the years, a project of this scope had not been undertaken before. To track the impact of the project on library staff, the authors developed a survey instrument to solicit feedback on the process and its outcomes and to assess how the feelings and working relationships of library personnel had been affected. This chapter will explore the results of that survey, with special focus on the impact of large-scale downsizing on relationships between technical services staff and librarians and the knowledge gained by survey respondents about collection management and the role technical services plays in that process.

BACKGROUND

Boise State University is a doctoral/research institution, with a student population of over 23,000 undergraduate and graduate students. Albertsons Library is centrally located on the 285-acre campus and is a hub for student and scholarly activity. The library's four floors contain collections, classrooms, open study space, and group study rooms. Visits average about 450,000 annually, and extensive online services are widely used.

In 2015 a new college, the College of Innovation and Design (CID), was established at Boise State University. As university administration had decided the CID was to be housed within the Albertsons Library building, in summer 2015 library collections were weeded and shifted to free up space. The library withdrew over 20,000 print journal volumes corresponding to JSTOR archival collections, as well as some curriculum materials. By the fall semester of 2016, the CID's enrollment and curriculum growth required additional space. The CID's expansion necessitated that the library free up 10,000 additional square feet, requiring the rehousing or withdrawal of 110,000 volumes/items. A newly available retrieval facility could hold approximately 30,000 volumes, but the library would need to withdraw approximately 78,000 additional volumes. The initial time frame for completion of the project was ambiguous but tight. The goal was to have the volumes withdrawn before the start of the 2017 fall semester.

Planning for the downsizing project started in February 2017. Almost all library units were involved in the project in some manner, although most of the effort was handled by three units: acquisitions and collections, instruction and research support, and access services. The traditional functions of technical services are handled by the acquisitions and collections unit and the cataloging unit. The acquisitions and collections unit is organized by the functional areas of serials; receiving and collections; and ordering, interlibrary loan, and gifts. The cataloging unit handles complex copy and original cataloging. As of the writing of this chapter, the acquisitions and collections unit comprises 16 professional and classified staff while the cataloging unit comprises 1 librarian and 2 classified staff. Overall collection decisions are made by the library's collections council. The council is chaired by the head of acquisitions and collections with membership of the dean, the associate dean, and the heads of access services, instruction and research, and cataloging. All Albertsons librarians have collection responsibilities in their assigned liaison areas. Although several library classified staff members have MLS degrees, throughout this chapter "librarian" refers to tenured and tenure-track library faculty.

Collection responsibilities of Albertsons librarians varied widely, as did their collection management experience. Some had extensive experience with collection management and had been weeding their collections on an ongoing basis throughout the years. Some, particularly those who had been hired within the past eight years, had little experience with collection management and weeding at Albertsons Library. Over that eight-year time span, the increase in demand-driven acquisitions (DDA) and the decrease in print monograph budgets have reduced opportunities for the traditional collection roles of budget management and selection of items for the collection. Technical services staff continued to receive and process purchasing suggestions and requests from librarians but also established procedures for purchasing items requested directly from patrons for DDA titles. Librarians were consulted about database and e-journal packages and worked with faculty who requested materials, but they were not involved extensively in developing and curating the collections in their subject areas.

THE DOWNSIZING PROJECT

The collections council concluded that there were obvious candidates for weeding in the print collection, including back files of print journals for which the library had perpetual online access. Librarians were responsible for reviewing the print collection in their assigned subject areas, with an eye toward weeding unused titles and those not relevant to the teaching and research mission of the University. As a starting point, acquisitions and collections generated print collection lists in Excel that corresponded to the subject areas assigned to each librarian. Each collection spreadsheet included bibliographic information and usage statistics for print titles within specific call number ranges. Librarians developed their own methods to evaluate their lists and determined selection criteria for withdrawal. Once decisions were made, most librarians recorded their retention decisions on the collection lists and returned the lists to acquisitions and collections so that items marked for withdrawal could be pulled from the shelves by acquisitions and collections staff or access services staff. Some librarians pulled the materials they wished to be withdrawn themselves and brought the items to acquisitions and collections. Once the decisions or the items were brought to acquisitions and collections, the receiving and collections section manager coordinated the process of preparing the materials for withdrawal. Depending on the list and subject area, some items were immediately pulled, some were sent to other subject librarians for review because of the interdisciplinary nature of the subject, and some were sent to the collections council for review. Once the decisions were finalized, acquisitions and collections staff prepared the materials for withdrawal and access services staff shifted the remaining materials. The collections council acted as a guide and the ultimate decision-maker about retention decisions.

As of the writing of this chapter, 78,000 print volumes and many sets in microform have been withdrawn from the collection. The required space will be vacated by the library and the College of

Innovation will be able to begin renovations in spring 2018. The goal of the downsizing project was met, but not without some speed bumps and concerns.

SURVEY METHODOLOGY

To fully understand the impact of the downsizing project on staff and interdepartmental relations, a survey instrument was developed and administered to current librarians and staff members and former librarians and staff who had been employed during the project. Reviewing library literature revealed a few examples of surveys being used to query library staff about working relationships. Claire Hill, a librarian in Perth, Australia, conducted a study of over 200 library workers, examining the relationships between librarians and library technicians/paraprofessionals. Hill asked questions about tensions and difficulties in working relationships between the two groups. Respondents were also asked if they felt working relationships could be improved.[1] A group of librarians in Canada conducted a study in 2015 using a survey that asked about changing roles and perceptions of librarians and paraprofessionals. Using a Likert scale, they asked respondents to agree or disagree with various statements about different job roles.[2] After reviewing these articles, a decision was made to build a new survey instrument to use the prism of the downsizing project to examine staff members' attitudes and perceptions of each other.

The survey questions were grouped into seven sections: experience and involvement, confidence, methodology, feelings, relationships, process improvement, and outcomes. The experience and involvement section asked questions about years of service and whether the respondent had taken a collection management course and, if so, whether that course included information about weeding and deselection. The confidence section asked about the respondent's confidence in making weeding decisions. The section on methodology asked questions about how weeding decisions were made, including whether the respondent had worked with faculty from their liaison areas to make deselection decisions. In the feelings section, we asked how the respondents felt about the process and whether there were emotional reactions to their assigned tasks and responsibilities. The relationships section focused on how librarians and technical services staff worked together, to determine whether each group's perceptions of each other changed because of the work that was done on this project. Questions about the process sought feedback about how the weeding and collection management processes could be improved. Lastly, we sought to identify project outcomes that could inform future weeding efforts.

Qualtrics software was used to create the survey instrument. The survey and survey process were submitted to and approved by the authors' institutional review board. On October 9, 2017, the survey was distributed to Albertsons Library current and former librarians and staff who had been employed during the project. Survey recipients were given until October 17, 2017, to respond, with a reminder sent on October 12 to those who had not yet completed the survey.

RESULTS AND DISCUSSION

Of the 51 staff members who received the survey, 38 (75%) completed it. Twenty-four respondents indicated they were staff, and 14 were librarians. Fourteen respondents classified themselves as working in technical services, and 24 said they were not members of a technical services unit.

Questions on the experience and involvement of staff and librarians revealed that overall staff members involved in the project had longer tenures at Albertsons Library than the librarians. As table 6.1 shows, over half of the staff members (13 = 54%) have more than 10 years of service at Albertsons Library, while less than a quarter of the librarians (3 = 21%) have been employed here that long. Total years of library experience did not reflect that disparity.

When asked about involvement in the weeding process, all librarian respondents felt involved at some level, with half indicating that they were highly involved. In terms of raw numbers, the group somewhat or highly involved in the project was composed almost equally of staff (11) and librarians (12).

Equal numbers of staff and librarians remembered taking collection management coursework. Of those who remembered whether their coursework covered weeding or deselection, only 25% had coursework that thoroughly covered weeding. More staff than librarians

Table 6.1 Experience and Involvement of Staff and Librarians

	n	Staff	Librarians
Length of service at Albertsons Library			
0 to 5 years	13	8	5
6 to 10 years	9	3	6
11 to 15 years	1	1	0
More than 15 years	15	12	3
Years of library experience			
0 to 5 years	4	3	1
6 to 10 years	8	4	4
11 to 15 years	4	3	1
More than 15 years	22	14	8
Taken courses in collection management			
Yes	16	8	8
No	19	16	3
Don't remember	3	0	3
Course characterization (16 respondents selected all that applied)			
Collection management a primary focus	13	6	7
Collection management only a small part	1	0	1
Weeding only touched upon	6	2	4
Weeding was thoroughly covered	4	3	1
Don't remember much	1	1	0
Applied principles from coursework to this process			
Yes	11	5	6
No	2	2	0
Unsure	3	1	2
Level of involvement in the weeding process			
Not involved at all	3	3	0
Involved at a peripheral level	11	9	2
Somewhat involved	14	9	5
Highly involved	9	2	7

indicated that weeding had been thoroughly covered in their coursework. Almost equal numbers of staff and librarians applied what they had learned to the weeding process.

As table 6.2 shows, 9 of the 14 librarians had participated in a collection review in the past, with most withdrawing between 6% and 15% of the reviewed collection. Just over half of the librarians felt they had above average subject expertise for their collection areas, and a similar

Table 6.2 Weeding Experience, Confidence, and Future Program Likelihood of Librarians

	n	%
Previous collection review experience that included weeding		
Yes	9	64
No	5	36
Size of collection reviewed in previous experience		
1 to 10,000 volumes	0	0
10,001 to 20,000 volumes	4	44
20,001 to 50,000 volumes	3	33
More than 50,000 volumes	2	22
Quantity withdrawn in previous experience		
0% to 5%	0	0
6% to 10%	3	33
11% to 15%	3	33
More than 15%	3	33
Subject expertise in assigned collection area where you have the most knowledge		
1—No expertise	0	0
2	0	0
3	6	43
4	4	27
5—Lots of expertise	4	27
Confidence level regarding weeding before this project		
1—Not confident	1	7
2	1	7
3	5	36
4	4	29
5—Very confident	3	21
Confidence level regarding weeding at project's current stage		
1—Not confident	0	0
2	1	7
3	2	14
4	7	50
5—Very confident	4	29
Frequency of second-guessing your decisions		
Never	0	0
Sometimes	10	71
Frequently	4	29

(continued)

	n	%
Confidence level in ability to conduct a future systematic weeding program in assigned collection area		
1—Not confident	0	0
2	1	7
3	2	14
4	5	36
5—Very confident	6	43
Likelihood to regularly weed collection		
Not at all likely	1	8
Somewhat likely	8	62
Highly likely	4	31

Note: Some percentages do not total 100 due to rounding.

percentage felt above average confidence in weeding before starting this project. At the time of the survey, after most of the librarians had completed their review, over 75% had above average confidence in their weeding evaluation process. All librarians indicated that they "sometimes" (71% of the respondents) or "frequently" (29%) second-guessed themselves as they made decisions. When asked about their confidence level for future systematic review, over 75% of the librarians felt above average confidence to do future systematic reviews.

Table 6.3 shows librarians' responses regarding their decision methodology. As librarians developed their criteria for withdrawal, over half consulted faculty in their collection areas, either by email or in person. All of those who consulted faculty received a response, with half feeling the response was helpful and half feeling the response was limited. Almost all of the librarians used resources other than collection statistics when making withdrawal decisions, with over half consulting other library staff or fellow librarians. Half of the librarians considered the holdings of other libraries. A little under half of the group did a literature search, and a few librarians consulted colleagues outside the library and/or subject bibliographies. Some librarians asked their librarian colleagues and technical services staff about how they made decisions and whether they had suggestions for evaluation. A few based their decisions solely on usage and other collection data. Over 75% of the librarians physically assessed the collection. Most

Table 6.3 Weeding Methodology of Librarians

	n	%
Consulted faculty in assigned collection areas		
Yes, for all assigned collection areas	5	39
Yes, but for only some assigned collection areas	2	15
No	6	46
For those who consulted faculty, characterization of feedback received (7 respondents selected all that applied)		
Helpful	5	71
Limited	5	71
Angry	0	0
Received no feedback from faculty	0	0
Other	2	29
Resources consulted besides faculty in assigned collection areas (14 respondents selected all that applied)		
Usage and other collection statistics	14	100
Library staff	9	64
Fellow library faculty	8	57
Literature search	6	43
Colleagues outside the university	2	14
Subject bibliographies	2	14
Other	7	50
None	1	7
Physically assessed collection when making weeding decisions		
Yes	11	79
No	3	21
Considered other holdings in call number areas		
Yes, considered both print and online holdings	12	86
Yes, considered print holdings only	0	0
Yes, considered online holdings only	0	0
No	2	14
Considered holdings of other libraries		
Yes	7	50.0
No	7	50.0
Worked with technical services staff beyond receiving usage collection lists		
Yes	10	77
No	3	23

Note: Some percentages do not total 100 due to rounding or multiple responses.

considered other holdings, regardless of whether print or electronic, when making weeding decisions. Over 75% of the librarians indicated that they consulted with technical services staff beyond receiving the initial subject lists.

The survey asked staff about their associations with the material that was to be weeded and how they felt during the process. Fifteen percent of respondents said their weeding decisions were made harder when they had personally purchased, processed, or taught from the item. Just over 60% of the respondents expressed no frustration with the process, though a greater percentage of librarians (45%) were frustrated than staff (35%).

Comments indicated that frustration commonly grew from a perceived lack of a higher-level strategy and the absence of a shared understanding of objectives and best practices. Each part of the process was largely seen by only one group. Some staff seemed to be frustrated by not being privy to the evaluation criteria that the different librarians used for their selection decisions. Because these criteria varied widely, there was some frustration with not understanding why some items were pulled and some left on the shelf. Some librarians may have been given in-depth guidance about the withdrawal process from the subject area faculty, and technical services staff would not have known that. Staff also physically touched each withdrawn item. They were able to evaluate condition and physical use in a way the librarians were not. It is said to never to judge a book by its cover, but doing so is unavoidable when a person is tasked with removing selected books from the shelves. Some books were in extremely poor condition, and others had a deep accumulation of dust on top. Many technical services staff felt they had a direct connection to the full life cycle of the book, from purchase through withdrawal. Most librarians didn't see the physical condition of the books. Librarians also didn't see the extensive backend database work it takes to remove an item from the collection.

Over 70% of librarians felt anxiety during the process, while just over 20% of staff felt anxiety. This may be because the librarians have direct relationships with subject area faculty; if a faculty member misses an item that has been removed from the shelves, the subject librarian is typically the first person to hear about it. Just over 30% of staff felt there was a barrier to sharing expertise due to their job role; only 14% of librarians felt that way. While most of technical services staff felt their skills were valued, over 25% did not.

When asked about the cohesiveness of the process, almost 75% of staff felt like the process was cohesive; only 50% of librarians did. Just over a third of both staff and librarians felt that the lack of an updated collection management policy inhibited the process.

Responses to questions on interactions between librarians and technical services indicated that 36% of the librarians were consulted by technical services staff, but only one technical services respondent indicated they were consulted by librarians. This result is mitigated by the fact that the two technical services staff members who had the most contact with librarians are authors of this article. As authors these two were unable to participate in the survey, and their extensive communication with librarians was not captured. These two staff members provided mentorship and guidance to librarians and staff alike. To some extent their experiences and perceptions have been incorporated into the conclusions and interpretation of the findings.

Because this project involved staff who do not often work together, the survey asked about changes in the perceptions of librarians and technical services staff of their coworkers. Less than 15% overall had a changed perception of technical services, both between librarians and staff. More than 25% of staff overall had a changed perception of librarians. When asked about working relationships between librarians and staff, over 90% of librarians and 68% of staff felt working relationships could be improved.

The comments about benefits that were gained from participation in the project revealed a common set of themes. The most frequently heard was that librarians and staff gained a greater understanding of the collection and resources. Looking at thousands of titles with associated usage data and evaluating the physical collection helped expose staff and librarians to resources they may have forgotten or not known about. Many respondents indicated that a benefit of the process was the removal of dated or biased content. The second most common theme was increased collegiality among staff and librarians as an outcome of the project.

Although 75% of librarians reported that they physically assessed the collection before making their decisions, most decisions seemed to be made on paper using usage statistics and dates of last use. For some librarians, the task for reviewing titles was immense; the largest section included over 47,000 titles. Technical services staff were tasked with pulling the items from the shelf and were able to see the collection in context as they were pulling titles for withdrawal.

Only certain aspects of the process of making room for the CID's expansion were under library control. The bottom line was that significant collection space was to be reassigned to the College, and the collection had to be moved. The access services unit and acquisitions and collections unit determined when to shift the collection into different areas of the building and when to weed the collection. Project timing was affected by not having firm dates for the renovation timeline. There was a sense of urgency to move quickly because of funding that needed to be spent before the end of the fiscal year, but no dates were set by the University on when projects needed to be accomplished. All librarians, except for the dean and associate dean, have liaison responsibilities. Though most librarians work in the instruction and research support unit, a few work in different units.

There were many factors in our library's culture and environment that affected our ability to accomplish our goals. Most importantly, library administration supported our strategy to weed the collection as we prepared to shift the stacks. Funds were made available to provide for student shifters and for shredding and recycling the withdrawn print materials. The library also has strong middle management that kept the project moving. Most librarians saw the need for a systematic evaluation of the print collection. Their work with scholars and learners across campus helped them see how print collections were and were not used.

As we approached the project, we encountered several challenges. We had financial support from library administration but no specified objectives other than to relocate the volumes from the area designated for CID expansion. We did not know ahead of time the level of skills that would be needed for this project. Participants turned out to have differing levels of expertise with Excel and in using the catalog. Another challenge was the lack of a defined timeline. We had no choice but to work as quickly as possible in case the renovations were able to start before anticipated.

Librarians approached the weeding process in vastly different ways. Some weeded based solely on usage data, while others did extensive physical reviews, looking at condition, multiple editions, and so forth. Each librarian decided what publication dates and usage statistics to use as guidelines for withdrawal, depending upon their subject areas and/or personal values. This process exposed the need for revised/revisited collection development policies and more guidance in collection management principles for liaison librarians. Future projects will need to include a mechanism for accountability. Acquisitions and collections staff became the driving force in right-sizing the collection because of their expertise in the collection maintenance process.

CONCLUSION

The survey coupled with our own project experience led us to some interesting conclusions about the collection and its use, staffing patterns and needs, and interunit relations and dependencies. Usage data and physical reviews of the print materials brought home just how necessary a thorough review of the collection had been, given the widespread and substantial changes that have taken place in the use of all print resources. The comments of the survey respondents revealed that a high-level strategy for weeding and a shared understanding of objectives and best practices would have given the project more cohesion, supported buy-in, and increased participation. The project and the survey brought to light limitations and opportunities in job duties and roles and highlighted potential limits to collaboration because of staff classification. Comments suggested that more frequent in-person meetings about the project to share experiences and challenges and to offer guidance might have made the process smoother. Communication about the project needed to be more frequent and delivered via email, in one-on-one meetings, in all staff meetings, and in other formats as appropriate. For many respondents the short project timeline proved to be a hindrance to participation, either because they did not have enough time in their own schedules or they didn't know how to prioritize the withdrawal work without knowing the renovation timeline. Balancing project responsibilities with day-to-day job duties was a concern for many.

We also concluded that the project would have gone more smoothly if the librarians and staff members possessed (1) a shared understanding of best practices for approaching weeding; (2) knowledge of past weeding or collection management efforts at the Albertsons Library; (3) background and contextualizing information about the collection and its different phases of development; and (4) the technical skills needed to perform the tasks assigned to them. The project leadership assumed that all librarians had a robust understanding of collection management and were already using strategies for evaluating their subject areas. We found this wasn't always the case. It was also assumed, sometimes incorrectly, that everyone had the necessary level of expertise with using Excel. Bringing everyone to the same starting point may have alleviated some of the pain points in the deselection process. Finally, we learned how much everyone supports cross-unit collaborations, or at least cross-unit understanding of work. All library staff want to see the whole picture and want to work together to achieve library-wide initiatives. A positive outcome listed by multiple respondents was gaining a better understanding of each other's job duties. Staff got to know each other better and achieved a sense of greater collegiality.

While the urgency of this project did not allow for establishment of best practices and communication of a higher-level strategy, the collections council is developing these for future collection reviews. In support of ongoing collection management efforts, the acquisitions and collection unit is developing a methodology to provide liaison librarians regular print and electronic collection reports. The authors will be presenting the results from this survey to our library colleagues; we anticipate receiving feedback that will be used in our path forward.

Despite the frustrations of library staff, challenges with communication, and the inevitable loss of library space, Albertsons Library was successful in accomplishing its objectives. Librarians and technical services staff were able to band together to manage a huge deselection project. We hope this is just a stepping stone to continuing cross-unit collaboration.

As other academic libraries contemplate embarking on large scale, all-library or multi-unit weeding projects, they might consider using this survey as a template for conducting a preassessment of library staff. Library leadership can ask specific questions about communication preferences, the weeding process, and technical skills needed to do the work. The results of the pre-survey would be a tool to craft best practices for approaching weeding and reveal areas of technical skill that would need additional training. Taking into consideration that a common theme of many large-scale weeding projects is a compressed timeline, a preassessment may help libraries save time in the long run by identifying areas of concern, allaying assumptions, and laying a foundation for success.

NOTES

1. Claire Hill, "The Professional Divide: Examining Workplace Relationships Between Librarians and Library Technicians," *The Australian Library Journal* 63, no. 1 (2013): 23–34, https://doi.org/10.1080/00049670.2014.890020.
2. Norene James, Lisa Shamchuk, and Kathrine Koch, "Changing Roles of Librarians and Library Technicians," *Canadian Journal of Library and Information Practice and Research* 10, no. 2 (2015), https://doi.org/10.21083/partnership.v10i2.3333.

CHAPTER 7

Bound for the Stacks: Strategic Rightsizing and Classification of Print Journals Collections

Emily A. Hicks and Fred W. Jenkins

ABSTRACT

Many libraries are struggling to adapt to changing user needs and expectations, along with the space and resource constraints that have become the new normal. Library users want more space for group and private study, transdisciplinary collaboration, and social interaction. This chapter will discuss the major rethinking of a bound journal collection at the University of Dayton Libraries. Plans for a major renovation were taking shape and the bound journal collection needed to move to an on-campus storage facility. Print journals were being transitioned to online access and our subject librarians made two complete sweeps of the bound journals looking for titles that were fragmentary runs or no longer in scope. This multistage review of our bound journal collections encompassed the visual inspection of each journal, the identification of the appropriate Library of Congress (LC) classification, the barcoding of volumes, the creation of item records, and the labeling of volumes. A long-overdue comprehensive review of the print periodicals required the ability to solve problems and adapt to change throughout the project. As we continue the process of rightsizing our collection, we are both expanding our electronic holdings and making our physical collections more user-friendly by making them accessible via the library stacks.

INTRODUCTION

Many libraries are struggling to adapt to changing user needs and expectations, along with the space and resource constraints that have become the new normal. Our library is no exception. Library users want more space for group and private study, more spaces for transdisciplinary collaboration, more spaces for social interaction. The shelves in our stacks are packed with little room for growth of print collections. The traditional approach of maintaining large local physical collections, including many items that are used seldom or never, no longer works. Although new acquisitions have become largely electronic over time, a new strategic plan that emphasizes rethinking collections for twenty-first century teaching and scholarship,[1] new university priorities, and impending renovations has accelerated our need to reassess collections holistically and to reduce space devoted to legacy print collections. As a member of a large library consortium (OhioLINK) we have also come to view our local collections in the context of the statewide collection that is readily available to our users.[2] As a result, we are in a multistage review of collections that began with our journals collections and will continue with a full review of our circulating monographic collections using OCLC's GreenGlass software.[3]

WHO WE ARE

The University of Dayton (UD), a top-tier Catholic university, was founded in 1850 by the Society of Mary (the Marianists) in Dayton, Ohio. UD is a highly residential campus with an undergraduate enrollment topping 8,000 full-time student and a graduate (including law) enrollment of over 2,300. The University Libraries, comprising Roesch Library, Marian Library, the International Marian Research Institute, and University Archives and Special Collections,[4] includes 19 faculty (16 tenure-leading and 3 lecturers) and 32 staff.

WHERE WE STARTED

Until the mid-1990s, our journal collection was entirely print, comprising approximately 3,000 current subscriptions and 6,600 titles in all. It consumed almost an entire floor, including processing space, a current periodicals/reserve area, and stacks for bound journals. We acquired our first electronic journals, a package from Academic Press, through OhioLINK in 1996. More consortial packages arrived in subsequent years.[5] We cautiously dropped local print subscriptions but kept print backfiles. Later OhioLINK acquired several publisher backfile packages and we locally acquired several JSTOR modules.[6] As space pressures mounted, we began to discard print backfiles for which we now had secure long-term access to the online versions, except for a few titles with high-quality images and those in a few narrowly focused areas in which we have exceptionally deep collections.[7] Our approach remained largely opportunistic and ad hoc.

About three years ago, the University Libraries began taking a more systematic approach to acquiring online backfiles, since plans for major renovations, which required moving the bound journal collection to an on-campus storage facility, began to take shape. We acquired all remaining JSTOR journal modules available at the time, in part because these include many smaller publishers across all disciplines. We examined subject packages from major publishers whose backfiles are not included in the OhioLINK Electronic Journal Center. In previous purchases, core titles and usage were key factors. As space became the most pressing issue, the amount of real estate recovered became equally important. At first we measured this by number of volumes, but we soon found that was not a reliable indicator due to the wide variation in size of volumes. We then moved to number of shelves/linear feet. While quality and relevance remained essential, cost per linear foot recovered became the deciding factor in whether to purchase a package. All in all, we acquired 16 subject collections and custom packages from seven different publishers, in addition to four JSTOR modules not yet in our collection.

At the same time, our subject librarians made two complete sweeps of the bound journals looking for titles that were no longer in scope or fragmentary runs. The fact that our bound journals were physically arranged alphabetically by title on the shelves made scanning by subject more difficult. As retention decisions were made on these titles, we verified that there was adequate access to them through OhioLINK and the Center for Research Libraries (CRL). In some cases, additional titles were identified for replacement with electronic backfiles. The librarians also identified many titles for transfer to special collections.

BOUND JOURNAL PROJECT

As renovation planning progressed, it was soon clear that we would need to repurpose second floor stack space to meet new user expectations including more and larger group study spaces, a scholars commons, and more natural light. Once the decision was made to permanently move the bound periodicals off the second floor of the library, a series of other decisions followed. The decision about where to move the collection during renovation was beyond the scope of this project. No matter where the periodicals were stored, we needed an efficient system to access the journals. Removing the collection from public view had implications for how we tracked and labeled the periodicals. Our journal holdings were displayed in the public catalog as a range of dates and volumes as appropriate. Information acquisition and organization (IAO) staff checked in current subscriptions and shelved them unbound either in a small current periodicals space with soft furniture conducive to browsing or alphabetically in the stacks in boxes alongside the bound volumes. Bound volumes were labeled with a simple local call number indicating the type of material (i.e., PERIOD). The idea to classify and reorder the journals according to Library of Congress (LC) classification had been discussed and tabled several times over the years due to resource constraints. The renovation planning necessitated revisiting this issue.

PROS AND CONS OF CLASSIFICATION

One advantage of a classified journal collection is providing continuity by shelving a title in one place no matter how many title changes have occurred. Classification aids subject access by collocating all the journals on a topic. Classification also gives us the option to interfile print journals and print books, which is integral to opening space on the second floor of the library for new functions. This step is contingent upon the review of our circulating monographic collections resulting in the removal of a significant number of print books from the upper floors of the library. LC classification arrangement facilitates serendipitous browsing of the general print book together with the journal collections.[8]

Unfortunately, classified bound journal collections require more shifting, particularly when they are interfiled with the print book collection.[9] Glaser points out that over the course of a long publication history, the focus of a journal could change, rendering the subject access misleading or obsolete.[10] A major disadvantage to retrospectively classifying a bound journal collection is the amount of work involved. The scope of this project required touching each title, volume, and catalog record, sometimes multiple times. The project also required a significant investment of labor and resources in addition to the already substantial workload of evaluating bound journal collections for digital replacement and deselection. Timing of a retrospective conversion project is critical. At what point do the advantages outweigh the disadvantages? For us, the timeline was dictated by the upcoming renovation project, not the size of the bound journal collection.

PROS AND CONS OF ALPHABETICAL ARRANGEMENT

Some people say that shelving in alphabetical order requires less shifting of collections. Others believe that shelving print journals in alphabetical order makes access easier because if you know the title, you can bypass the catalog and go straight to the stacks to find the journal.[11] However, you must know the exact title, and changes in titling may necessitate multiple locations for what is, essentially, the same journal. Local practice and binding conventions may cause variations in titles that may be hard for users to predict.

The main advantage of keeping the collection in alphabetical order was the fact that it was already arranged that way. This choice would have saved labor and supply costs in the short term but limited our options in the future by virtually ensuring that the print journals would remain off site indefinitely and that access to the collection would be staff only. Without classification, the bound journals could not be interfiled with the print books on the upper floors of the library. Title changes would have continued to be a source of confusion since the continuation of a title may or may not be shelved near the previous title. The space previously occupied by bound journals will be repurposed during and after the renovations. Ultimately, the needs of our users would be best served by classifying the bound journals and interfiling them with the print monographs on the fourth, fifth, and sixth floors of the library.

SCOPE OF THE PROJECT

The scope of the bound journal classification project was determined after much discussion among library staff, faculty, and administrators. The project was related to, but separate from, the systematic approach to acquiring online backfiles. The project encompassed the visual inspection of each journal, the identification of the appropriate LC classification, the barcoding of volumes, the creation of item records, and the labeling of volumes. Item record creation, barcoding, and labeling facilitated the circulation of individual bound journal volumes while the collection was off-site during renovations as well as after the collection returned post-renovations. We made a conscious decision to start the project during the acquisition of online backfile collections and weeding. Any lost work due to that project would be weighed against needing to meet the renovation deadlines. Both weeding and online backfile acquisition are ongoing initiatives. Although the increased acquisition of electronic journal files and the subsequent removal of duplicate print titles had decreased the size of the collection, the bound journal project was still monumental.

PROJECT STAFFING

The Libraries' collaborative culture made the project possible. The project's success required coordinated teamwork between collections, IAO, education and information delivery (EID), and information systems and digital access (ISDA).

Technical Services

The IAO division includes seven full-time staff, one part-time staff, two full-time faculty, and one full-time faculty division director. We employ between 6 and 12 student assistants each semester as well as 2 to 6 student assistants during the summer. IAO division functions include acquisitions, electronic resources management, cataloging, book processing, book repair, catalog management, authority control, and metadata for Roesch Library, University Archives and Special Collections, and Marian Library.

Starting the project in the fall of 2015 was not coincidental. We had sabbatical funds to pay for a catalog and electronic resources assistant, a part-time temporary position, at 20 hours a week to help launch the project. Special projects funding from our student budget initially supported one graduate student position. When the catalog and electronic resources assistant moved to a full-time position elsewhere in the library in the spring of 2016, the catalog management assistant, an existing part-time employee in IAO, assumed the day-to-day project management and three additional graduate student assistants were hired. In addition to the catalog management assistant, the project involved significant time investment of the coordinator of cataloging, the information resources specialist, the technical services assistant, the material processing and book repair specialist, several undergraduate students, and the director of IAO.

Collections

IAO staff and faculty work closely with the associate dean for collections and operations, who manages the collections budgets, licensing for electronic resources, and assessment of collections. For the project, the associate dean's systematic approach to assessing our print journal holdings and acquiring online backfiles was integral. Some years ago, the university library committee agreed to a policy that the libraries did not need to keep print if there was secure online access to journal backfiles, which removed the need to consult faculty on the removal of most individual print titles. The subject librarians' efforts to review journals for scope and completeness contributed a much-needed high-level evaluation. The subject librarians work in all areas of the libraries, including collections, EID, ISDA, IAO, and Marian Library.

Access Services

Access services, a part of EID, manages circulation, OhioLINK borrowing, interlibrary loan, and stacks maintenance. The stacks maintenance and administrative specialist and the stacks maintenance student assistants coordinated and performed the location transfers, including the discarding of journal holdings as needed. Once the project was completed, the stacks maintenance and administrative specialist and the stacks maintenance student assistants reorganized the bound journal collection by LC classification to facilitate moving the collection off site.

Systems

The library systems support specialist, a member of ISDA, performed the necessary changes to the catalog coding, circulation policies, and public interfaces to facilitate the location and use of the bound journal collection during the renovation.

PROJECT OVERVIEW

The project was completed in phases: journals were evaluated one-by-one for condition and OhioLINK availability, LC classification was determined, item records created, barcodes attached, and labels printed and applied. Many discrepancies in journal records were fixed and old catalog records were updated. Evaluation for transfer, discard, binding, or repair occurred throughout the process. Some titles were identified for transfer to special collections. Sometimes the decision to acquire the online version or discard a journal would not happen until after the classification and item record creation was completed. This was to be expected since the projects were running concurrently. Problems found during the project often prompted us to send the title to the associate dean and information resources specialist for evaluation. The journal was either returned to the work-flow for this project, prepared for binding, or marked for discard. Many of the same staff and faculty were involved in both projects so communication and documentation were vital. We used email to communicate questions and decisions because it was an effective way to communicate the same information to several people at once. It was important to communicate the ongoing changes in a timely way to avoid unnecessary work and keep a written trail to follow if clarification was needed.

PROJECT WORKFLOW

The catalog and electronic resources assistant and graduate student, and later the catalog management assistant and four graduate students, were tasked with visually confirming that the titles and holdings of bound journals located in the stacks on the second floor matched the list of print journals generated from the online catalog. Each person started with a different letter of the alphabet to avoid confusion. Once a title was located and holdings confirmed, the OCLC bibliographic record was checked for LC classification. If no LC class number was found, the catalog and electronic resources assistant established one according to library standards. The LC classification was added to the existing or updated catalog records as needed. Item records with the LC class number were created and barcodes attached to all bound volumes. The volumes were relabeled with the new LC class number. The material processing and book repair specialist coordinated the labeling completed by several undergraduate students. Near the end of the project, we circled back to the journals evaluated during the early part of the project to fix problems that had been set aside. The coordinator of cataloging used the master spreadsheet and a visual inspection of journals to confirm that all titles had been completed. We celebrated the end of the two-year project with a pizza party for everyone involved. We began the project with a list of just over 4,500 print journal titles. After acquiring backfiles, eliminating duplication, and deselection, we now have just over 1,560 print titles with just over 28,400 volumes. Over the course of the two-year project, we classified over 200 additional titles and created item records including barcodes for the related bound volumes that were subsequently deselected. In most, but not all, cases, this happened before the bound volumes were labeled with the LC classification.

CHALLENGES

We knew that surprises and challenges were likely to surface along the way. We were not disappointed. The size of the collection combined with the ambitious goals of the project was daunting. The print periodicals had not been comprehensively reviewed in many years, if ever. Some journals predated automation. Others were incomplete or inconsistent due to changing processes and priorities throughout the years. Parts of the collection had been weeded over the years using differing criteria. In some cases, catalog records had been removed, but the corresponding volumes had not been removed from the shelves. In other cases, volumes had been removed without the systematic removal of catalog records and OCLC holdings. Binding anomalies further complicated the project.

These hidden variations from the past necessitated a reevaluation of our processes and often required a change to our methods. The ability to solve problems and adapt to change was vital to the project. It was important for the staff and faculty to have the freedom to try different processes and procedures as we encountered issues and problems. The final processes and procedures were the result of a collaboration of everyone who worked on the project. This process was an excellent learning opportunity. However, it was time-consuming and sometimes frustrating for the staff, faculty, and students working on the project to adjust the processes to accommodate the unanticipated discrepancies.

LESSONS LEARNED

Libraries planning to tackle a project of this size and complexity should approach the endeavor with flexibility, patience, and a sense of humor. We planned as best we could for the unexpected and when it happened, we reevaluated our plans and workflows to adapt. The master spreadsheet reflected the decisions and accommodations we made throughout the process. We used quality control measures throughout the project that were extremely important, since we employed many student assistants who worked varied schedules. Regular QC checks enabled us to catch errors before they became systematic and large-scale. QC checks involved reviewing selected titles for accuracy and consistency across the corresponding catalog records and physical volumes. Recurring mistakes with specific student assistants were addressed in a timely fashion. A visual inspection of each journal near the end of the project identified any lingering issues. Although

QC is time-consuming, it was an important step in our process. We now have an accurate picture of the size and scope of our bound journal collection for future planning. Effective communication was vital throughout the project. We used group emails and occasional face-to-face meetings to inform, ask questions, and discuss workflow changes.

NEXT STEPS

Even as the journal project was winding down, we were already engaged in licensing OCLC's GreenGlass software to assess our print monographic collections. Our general monographic collections occupy three full floors; many shelves are so packed that it is difficult to remove or reshelve books. Shifting has become very difficult. At the same time, our print circulation has been on a long slow decline in keeping with national trends.[12] Many books have never been used and are readily available in many copies across OhioLINK. We have now started reviewing print monographs and identifying titles that are candidates for discard. GreenGlass enables us to easily identify duplicates across our collections. It also provides a wealth of data on usage; availability in OhioLINK, Ohio, and the U.S.; and several custom peer groups. We are currently in the process of preparing title lists for faculty consultation and then discard. Our goal is to create enough space to integrate bound journals and monographs post-renovation, as well as provide 5 to 10 years' growth space for print collections.

CONCLUSION

Remaking collections for the 21st century is on the agenda at many libraries, but massive legacy print collections make this a daunting task. When an impending renovation made addressing our legacy print (and practices) imperative, we found a well-designed workflow and close collaboration across all library units to be essential. In addition to freeing space for new uses, we have cleaned up many long-standing discrepancies in the catalog and moved many scarce and fragile items to special collections. As we continue the process of rightsizing our collection, we are both expanding our electronic holdings and making our physical collections more user-friendly. During the renovation, bound print journals may be requested via the library catalog. Post-renovation print journals will be publicly accessible via the library stacks. Going forward, print journals will be classified, barcoded, labeled, and shelved upon return from the commercial bindery.

NOTES

1. University of Dayton Libraries, *Strategic Plan 2017–2020*, 2017, https://www.udayton.edu/libraries/_resources/docs/strategic-plan-2017-20.pdf.

2. OhioLINK (https://www.ohiolink.edu/) is a consortium of 120 Ohio academic libraries. In addition to shared physical collections of more than 46 million items, OhioLINK provides access to over 24 million electronic journal articles and 100,000 e-books.

3. See https://www.oclc.org/en/sustainable-collections.html.

4. The Marian Library (https://udayton.edu/marianlibrary/), separate division within the University of Dayton Libraries, is the world's largest collection devoted to Mary, the Mother of Jesus; the International Marian Research Institute (https://udayton.edu/imri/index.php) is devoted to academic research on Mary and is closely associated with the Marian Library.

5. Thomas J. Sanville, "A Method out of the Madness: OhioLINK's Collaborative Response to the Serials Crisis," *Serials* 14 no. 2 (July 2001): 167–68, https://doi.org/10.1629/14163.

6. JSTOR (https://www.jstor.org/) is an online archive of academic journals, books, and primary sources.

7. Roger C. Schonfeld and Ross Houseright, *What to Withdraw? Print Collection Management in the Wake of Digitization* (New York: Ithaka S+R, 2009). Provides a good overview of the rationale and possible criteria for replacing print journal backfiles with electronic versions.

8. Robbin Glaser, "To Classify or Alphabetize: The Arrangement of Print Periodicals in Academic Libraries," *Serials Review* 33, no. 2 (2007): 91–96, https://doi.org/10.1016/j.serrev.2007.03.002; and Amy K. Weiss, John P. Abbott, and Joseph C. Harmon, "Print Journals: Off

Site? Out of Site? Out of Mind?" *Serials Librarian* 44, no. 3/4 (2003): 271–78, https://doi.org/10.1300/J123v44n03_19.

9. Weiss, Abbott, and Harmon, "Print Journals: Off Site?" 277.

10. Glaser, "To Classify or Alphabetize," 92.

11. Weiss, Abbott, and Harmon, "Print Journals: Off Site?" 276.

12. Rick Anderson, *Can't Buy Us Love: The Declining Importance of Library Books and the Rising Importance of Special Collections* (New York: Ithaka S+R, 2013), 1–3, https://doi.org/10.18665/sr .24613; and Suzanne M. Ward, *Rightsizing the Academic Library Collection* (Chicago: ALA Editions, 2015), 25–33.

CHAPTER 8

Space Reclamation: The Cataloging Department's Role in Weeding Projects

Muriel D. Nero and Jia He

ABSTRACT

Since its founding in 1968, the Marx Library was committed to the practice of acquiring books through purchases and gift donations, filling shelves to maximum capacity. Decades later as space and resource concerns evolved, the library embarked on several weeding projects to drastically change its physical landscape. The motives behind each project, their outline and execution, and the role of the cataloging department throughout all processes is recounted here.

INTRODUCTION

The Marx Library at the University of South Alabama embarked on several weeding initiatives to provide space for the relocation of the university's archives, to develop a more relevant collection of resources for student and faculty research, and to create a learning commons to provide more seating as well as support student collaboration. With these weeding endeavors, the cataloging department played an essential part in the planning, implementation, and workflow of these projects. This chapter discusses why the weeding began, the parties involved, and the workflow of the serials, main and reference collections, VHS, and CD discard projects, as well as the lessons learned from these undertakings and the status of weeding in the Marx Library.

BACKGROUND

Founded in 1963, the University of South Alabama is a 1,200-acre campus with an enrollment of more than 15,500 students and offers over 100 academic programs.[1] There are three libraries on campus that are under the umbrella of university libraries: the Marx Library, the Biomedical Library, and the Mitchell College of Business Learning Resource Center. The Doy Leale McCall Rare Book and Manuscript Library is also part of the university libraries organization. The seventeen librarians at the University of South Alabama have faculty status and follow the same promotion and tenure requirements as teaching faculty.

The first president of the University of South Alabama, Dr. Frederick Whiddon, wanted a firstclass academic library and viewed the library as one of the most important facilities on campus. Prior to the opening of the four-story university library on September 15, 1968, $610,000 was budgeted for the purchase of more than 100,000 books to build a collection to support the various undergraduate and graduate programs offered by the university.[2] In the following years, with a much smaller budget, collection development was mostly done by acquiring print materials through purchases and gifts. No thought was given to the problem of multiple copies. The philosophy was if one copy was good, two copies were better. If a third copy happened to show up, it was also cataloged and added to the collection for good measure. It was considered impolite to turn down book donations from retiring professors or anybody affiliated with the university; after all, these people could be potential donors to the library. Over the years, the library has received some monetary donations. One benefactor had a study room named for him. The other benefactor, a former reference librarian, had the reference department named for her.

From 1968 to 2014, books were consistently being added to the shelves, but there was never a concerted effort to weed the general stacks. This was something most of the librarians knew needed to happen but finding the extra time to perform the daunting task of weeding was not a high priority. Some very traditional librarians were reluctant to remove or throw away a single book from the shelves.

Because the cataloging librarians and staff are responsible for adding these purchases, gifts, and multiple copies to the collection, they were not surprised by the condition of the book stacks or by the multiple copies of so many titles.

Fast-forward to the 1990s and several key factors prompted the library to reevaluate the print collections. First, the Internet and World Wide Web completely revolutionized how libraries access resources. Print-only resources like indices were made available electronically, which later evolved to the current full-text academic databases.[3] Along with acquiring more databases, the library began purchasing large packages of ebooks that covered a myriad of disciplines in the early 2000s. With the popularity of iPads, tablets, and e-readers like the Amazon Kindle and the Nook by Barnes & Noble, reading a book on a device was a very easy transition for most students and faculty. With this shift to eresources, the students no longer relied solely on the physical books to complete research assignments.

THE CATALOGING DEPARTMENT

Behind the scenes, the cataloging department worked to catalog and manage the bibliographic footprint for these print and eresources. This is a four-member unit with two cataloging librarians and two full-time staff: the head of cataloging, the cataloging electronic resources librarian, an LTA (library technical assistant) II, and an LTA I. The department also has the invaluable assistance of two student assistants each scheduled to work 20 hours a week.

Because this is a small department, each member has specific and shared cataloging responsibilities. The head of cataloging and the cataloging electronic resources librarian perform most of the original cataloging as well as copy cataloging for monographs, serials, government documents, maps, archival resources, and any other formats. The cataloging electronic resources librarian is primarily responsible for cataloging e-resources and item types with the media location, such as DVDs. The LTA II and LTA I both perform copy cataloging of monographs and serials; however, they do not have copy cataloging responsibilities for the e-resources or media titles.

THE ARCHIVES

In 2011, the University of South Alabama archives, located on the Springhill campus in downtown Mobile, Alabama, acquired a collection of historical documents from the family of Doy Leale McCall Sr., who was the owner of a lumber mill with his father and brother in Selma, Alabama. In his spare time, he collected bottles and historical materials. Along with materials passed down through his wife's family, Mr. McCall amassed a priceless collection of artifacts. Appraised at $3.1 million, this collection comprised historical documents and papers relating to Alabama from the 17th through the 20th centuries, and it included such items as presidential land grants, slavery and Reconstruction papers, plantation records, and Civil War diaries.[4] Because of this immense collection, the archives were renamed the Doy Leale McCall Rare Book and Manuscript Library. There was also one significant requirement of this agreement between the university and the McCall family: the archives had to move to the main campus. After two years of trying to find a new home for the archives on campus, the university administration decided the best place for the archives was the third floor on the south side of the library, which housed the serials collection and valuable student study space. This was not well received by the librarians or the archivist because both parties would be losing valuable space. For the librarians, this meant the loss of student study space and the downsizing of a print collection. Although the archivist was told by representatives from university administration that the new location within Marx Library was large enough for years of growth, this was not a realistic portrayal of the space. What did this mean for the library? It was time to weed, and time was a definite factor. As noted by Christine L. Ferguson, "often libraries wait to embark upon weeding projects until space is at a premium. . . ."[5] This was the case for the Marx Library; librarians needed to weed extensively, and quickly as well.

In 2013, during this same time frame of the decision to move the archives into the library, the library received a $3 million pledge from the Julien E. Marx Foundation Trust. In recognition of this generous gift as well as to honor the Marx family of Mobile, Alabama, the library's name changed to Marx Library. With this gift, $1 million was designated to the renovation of the third floor south library space to relocate the Doy Leale McCall Rare Book and Manuscript Library.[6]

THE BOUND SERIALS

The archives had a new destination, and now it had the money to renovate. The only task left was to weed and relocate the bound serials collection. The dean of university libraries emailed the other deans on campus to notify them of the changes about to take place in the Marx Library. Before any title was removed from the shelves, the head of government documents and serials, the leader of this massive undertaking, created a spreadsheet of available serial titles and identified titles within the collection available through our databases. In consultation with reference or subject liaison librarians, decisions were made about whether to keep or discard for each title as well as some titles to cancel. Along with the availability of titles via databases, there were other factors in the evaluation process. Following are some of the questions asked to help determine what to weed: Are they seminal works for the field? What years are available electronically? What is the preference of faculty for print versus electronic in different fields of study? What is the best value for the current budget?

After this process, the head of government documents and serials supervised the student assistants with the flagging of titles and volumes to keep or withdraw. Then, she created a final list of titles being withdrawn. This list was attached to a memo sent to the faculty library representatives by the subject liaison librarians. If a department wanted something on the list, the titles would be boxed for pickup by that department. Only very few departments accepted this offer.

The government documents department, with help from librarians and staff from other departments, did the physical labor involved with this project. The serial titles the library would retain would be moved to the second floor south across from the reference department. Because this project was so well organized, the cataloging department's role was to simply delete the weeded serial titles from the catalog and remove the library's holdings symbol from the corresponding OCLC records. The head of government documents and serials provided printouts of the titles to be deleted from the OPAC (online public access catalog) and the corresponding title found in the cataloging module of Voyager, so the physical titles were never brought to the cataloging department. The Voyager printouts contained bibliographic and holding numbers so cataloging personnel could correctly identify the titles and holdings to be deleted. The head of government documents and serials also provided excellent notation on the printouts to prevent confusion about what was to be withdrawn.

The student assistants from the government documents department took the deleted titles to the dumpster. The deadline for this project was the end of June 2015 so that the renovation of the third floor south could begin. The Marx Library originally held 3,229 serial titles. After weeding and relocation to the second floor south, the serial collection was reduced to 1,128 titles; approximately 1,961 titles were withdrawn from the collection. When the dust cleared from weeding and relocating the serials and the renovation of the third floor south was completed, the Doy Leale McCall Rare Book and Manuscript Library moved into the Marx Library in April 2016.

THE BOOK STACKS

During the weeding and relocating taking place on the second and third floors, the head of access services, who is also a subject liaison for education, noticed the aged collection of titles in her subject area. In December 2014, she proposed a weeding inventory project that would require all the subject liaisons to begin weeding their subject areas in the book stacks. She was in communication with all department heads and subject liaisons on the planning and workflow for this project. The main collection had never been weeded and the shelves were overrun with books with outdated information, titles that had very few checkouts or had never been checked out, and in some instances physically damaged books. The phrase she would often use to describe this monumental undertaking was to "start with the low-hanging fruit." This meant starting with multiple copies, books in terrible condition, some of the smaller subject areas, and computer science, where it was obvious the information was outdated. The weeding began with the liaison librarians browsing the shelves of their subject areas and physically removing books.

The head of access services and the head of cataloging worked together to develop a workflow for the transportation of these weeded books to the cataloging department for removal from the catalog. After the subject liaisons pulled the weeded books from the shelves and placed them on book trucks, these trucks went to a holding station on the first floor north for review. After the review period, the subject liaisons consulted with the head of cataloging to determine the best time to bring the book trucks to the department for removal from the catalog. Generally, the end of the week was preferred by all parties involved. So as not to get the weeded books mixed in with incoming new acquisitions, all weeded book trucks were placed in the cataloging librarians' office area. At times the office was overrun with book trucks. However, this state of disarray did not last long because the cataloging librarians and staff knew what to expect by the end of the week and made changes to their schedule to quickly dispense of these dust-covered forgotten titles. After these books were removed from the catalog, the cataloging department's student assistants were on recycle bin duty.

The head of cataloging also created a three-column spreadsheet with the following headings: LC classification range(s), books withdrawn from the main collection, and month/year. This spreadsheet served the purpose of tracking the quantity of books withdrawn and from what subject areas in the book stacks. The spreadsheet count did not include a breakdown by title, volume, or number of copies. This information was recorded on each cataloger's own personal monthly statistics sheet for submission for the cataloging department's monthly totals.

This workflow allowed the cataloging librarians and staff to incorporate the deletion of books into their daily routine and weekly schedules. This was also necessary because the cataloging of new materials and faculty requests are the cataloging priority when the subject liaisons are purchasing new materials to spend the allotted funds for their subject areas for the fiscal year. (The fiscal year for the University of South Alabama is October 1 to September 30.) As soon as funding is available, the subject liaisons begin ordering for their respective areas and are expected to spend half the allotted funds for their departments by the end of January, with the rest being spent by July 1. The subject liaisons seem to do the most weeding after they have exhausted the book funding for the fiscal year. From December 2014 through November 2017, 13,489 books were weeded from the main collection. Weeding has moved up on the priority list. Although this massive weeding project ended, the subject liaisons are still weeding LC classification ranges and specific collections such as the Alabama Gulf Coast section.

THE REFERENCE COLLECTION

Inspired by the progress of the weeding inventory project, the head of reference began critically analyzing what was on the shelves in the reference department. Since most of the traditional reference resources are available online or through databases, it was time for these print resources to be weeded. As with the weeding inventory project, the same workflow was used with the cataloging department. However, the head of cataloging did make one modification that greatly streamlined the process for both departments. Instead of removing large multivolume sets to multiple book trucks to take to the cataloging department, the persistent link record from the OPAC for these large multivolume sets would be emailed to the head of cataloging. After the head of cataloging checked the bibliographic, holdings, and items records in the cataloging module of Voyager to make sure there were no issues with deleting the title, she would notify the sender of the email that the title could be disposed of. This greatly improved the disposal part of the workflow. Instead of the books taking a trip to the first floor, where they would sit and wait to be deleted and recycled, they were removed from the reference shelves and taken directly to the recycle bins by reference staff and student assistants. Because the head of reference, who also has a background in cataloging, reviewed each title pulled for withdrawal and checked the catalog, the head of cataloging was confident the links to records emailed were correct.

Another facet of the reference weeding project was that some titles were designated to be relocated to the main collection instead of recycled. These titles were placed on separate book trucks because they would need more attention from the catalogers. None of the titles removed for withdrawal or relocation were part of standing orders or approval plans so there were no cancellations to deal with. If the bibliographic records for transfers are in poor condition, the records are updated to comply with the current cataloging rules and practices of RDA (Resource Description and Access). The cataloging student assistants create new spine labels to denote their new location in the book stacks.

THE MEDIA COLLECTION

With weeding taking place on the second through fourth floors, the collections on the first floor remained untouched until university administration directed the Marx Library to find a space and plan the layout for a learning commons. For many years, one of the most popular comments from students was the need to have quieter and group study spaces with comfortable seating. Although there was limited space and financial resources, the librarians did their best to carve out some quiet study areas and make small enhancements to group collaboration spaces, such as adding whiteboards. However, this was not enough to meet the high demands from students. The directive from university administration came with funding as well, so with this financial backing, the library would use the learning commons to provide the space the students needed.

The only space available for a learning common in the library was in the Instructional Media Center (IMC) on the first floor north, which housed the media collections (DVDs, CDs, VHS tapes), the children/young adult collection, and music books. The music books would be relocated to the main collection in the book stacks. Since the reference department had some free shelf space due to weeding, the DVDs and children/young adult books would be relocated to this area. However, the VHS tapes and CDs had reached their expiration date years ago and were merely taking up valuable space. These collections would be completely removed from the collection. The liaisons who weeded the VHS tapes made lists of titles for replacement and gave them to the head of reference to purchase. Because money is not limitless, these lists were prioritized in order of necessity to the collection. The only departments with significant numbers of DVD replacements were English and Foreign Languages. The other subject liaisons did not feel the need to replace much of the VHS content. If a DVD could not be purchased, the VHS tapes would still be taken out of the collection but located in the subject liaison's office. The rationale behind this move was to make sure the tapes were in safe location until the library investigated ways to transfer the tapes to another viable format.

Following the same workflow as the previous weeding projects, we completed the withdrawal of the CD collection in two months. It was a very small collection of 1,151 titles. The removal of the VHS tapes collection had some hang-ups. First, there was a master Excel spreadsheet of every tape that had been cataloged with an assigned number. The only people who had access to this spreadsheet located on the library's shared drive were the circulation supervisor, the head of cataloging, and the cataloging electronic resources librarian. Also, only one person at a time could view this spreadsheet. Many years ago this spreadsheet was set up with limited access to prevent other users of the shared drive from making changes to it. This spreadsheet was the only list of media titles owned by the library. Second, the cases were in such bad shape from years of exposure to sunlight that the plastic was disintegrating. There were trails of plastic pieces on book trucks, carpets, and any space the cases were on. The disposal of these tapes was also an issue. We could not put these tapes in the recycle bin because they were not recyclable.

Since the circulation staff would be removing these tapes from the shelf in IMC, it was decided that the best way to handle the spreadsheet was for a circulation staff member to be the only person working on the spreadsheet to mark titles withdrawn. As for the disintegrating cases, gloves were used to protect hands and the vacuum cleaner was kept nearby to clean the carpets. Disposal of these tapes was solved by using large trash bags before placing them in the recycle bins. If we used the trash bags, the custodians knew to place them in trash and not recycle. After all these processes were followed, over 4,000 VHS tapes were withdrawn. The IMC was completely empty of materials and shelving before the beginning of the 2017 fall semester. The renovation of this space to a learning commons began in January 2018 and was open to students in August 2018.

LESSONS LEARNED

Communication among all departments is the key to success when undertaking a weeding project. There must be a well-defined plan, actions for implementation, and progress reports along the way. No matter which department leads the weeding, the cataloging department must be involved to carry out the final steps of removing the weeded materials from the catalog and holding symbol from OCLC records, and in some instances the disposal of the materials. If the plan is to retain but relocate titles, the cataloging department needs these books to be clearly marked and separated. Because some of our weeding projects were time-sensitive, the removal of weeded materials became a higher priority for the librarians pulling the materials and the catalogers deleting the materials. In cataloging, it's much easier to delete a bibliographic record than it is to add or create a new one. Because of this, our cataloging librarians and staff were able to find a balance between cataloging new resources and deleting old resources. Some preferred daily or weekly schedules for when they would do what task. With these weeding projects, reports from all parties involved were given in biweekly or monthly department head meetings, so there was always communication about what stage the project was in.

Cross-training staff outside of cataloging is also an option to consider if help is needed to delete materials from the catalog. However, proceed with caution. This was a viable option for our head of cataloging because the acquisitions staff had access to OCLC Connexion client and used the cataloging module of Voyager to perform some actions associated with acquisitions. Another deciding factor for cross-training was that one staff member had prior cataloging experience, and they also shared an office space with cataloging staff, which was helpful when they had questions. A staff member from acquisitions did assist with the deletion of weeded books, but the student assistants were responsible only for the disposal of weeded materials. There is too much to risk to the catalog to allow haphazard deletion of bibliographic, holdings, and item records.

Finally, learn how and when the weeded materials will be disposed of. Our serials project was so massive, library administration had a dumpster brought to the library. After this project ended and the dumpster was removed, the library got nine recycle bins for the other weeding projects. There were some pickup issues with the bins. They would be overflowing for days before library administration intervened to get a regularly scheduled pickup.

ADDITIONAL CONSIDERATIONS

To contain all the books being removed from the shelves or relocated to other areas, extra book trucks were necessary. At the height of the serial and weeding inventory projects, book trucks became a hot commodity, and librarians and staff were looking for empty trucks in every department. More book trucks were ordered to facilitate these rapidly moving projects, but when weeding is on hiatus, each department needs to have someplace to store the empty trucks.

Another thing to consider: If you have people with allergies or skin issues in the department, invest in gloves and masks. Books are dust magnets. Our cataloging librarians and staff used a duster and the small attachment on the vacuum cleaner to clean dusty books before handling them.

Finally, get to know the custodial staff in your library. Whenever we needed more trash bags or the vacuum cleaner, or the floor was covered with plastic pieces from VHS cases, the library custodial staff were more than willing to assist us. Most librarians do not want their spaces covered in weeding debris for any length of time.

CONCLUSION

University library real estate is limited, and the demand is high. No longer are our libraries viewed as quiet, musty storage spaces to house books. Library spaces are being repurposed for student collaboration and engagement and other user services that are beneficial to university communities. "Libraries simply can no longer afford, both literally and figuratively, to devote so much of their physical space to storing monographs, reference works, and bound journals when the demands on space and for other user-oriented services is so high."[7]

With the loss of tangible materials and efforts to repurpose spaces, the Marx Library is purchasing more e-resources such as ebook packages and single titles as well as video streaming subscriptions. Print monographs will still be preferred by some disciplines, but the acquisition of these titles must be managed and the titles periodically evaluated for relevance. Although weeding is completed for the archives move and for a learning commons, the weeding of the general stacks and reference collection is ongoing. The librarians have incorporated weeding their subject areas into their goals and periodically will evaluate these collections. Whatever direction the Marx Library's collection will take in the future, the cataloging department will always play an integral part in the addition, deletion, and the bibliographic maintenance of print and eresources.

NOTES

1. "About USA," University of South Alabama, accessed January 25, 2018, http://www.southalabama.edu/aboutusa/.

2. *History of the University Libraries, University of South Alabama*, University of South Alabama, last updated June 5, 2015, http://www.southalabama.edu/departments/library/resources/libraries-history.pdf.

3. Cristina Caminita and Andrea Hebert, "The Weeding Planner: How a Research Library Weeded Approximately 2.76 Miles of Print Materials From Shelves to Repurpose Library Space or Much Ado About the New Normal," *Against the Grain* 28, no. 4 (2016): 34, https://doi.org/10.7771/2380-176X.7457.

4. *History of the University Libraries.*

5. Christine L. Ferguson, "In Favor of Weeding," *Serials Review* 41, no. 4 (2015): 223, https://doi.org/10.1080/00987913.2015.1103573.

6. *History of the University Libraries.*

7. Ferguson, "In Favor of Weeding," 223.

CHAPTER 9

Relocating, Downsizing, and Merging: Inventory Projects to Manage Change in a Digital Environment

Gail Perkins Barton and Rachel Elizabeth Scott

ABSTRACT

With a new library location and newly created librarian position, the Health Sciences Library (HSL) of the University Libraries at the University of Memphis needed a comprehensive inventory. Having previously completed a small-scale inventory, technical services librarians led the project to assess the HSL collection before the newly hired librarian arrived. Beyond ensuring that all materials were in the collection and reflected properly in the integrated library system (ILS), an up-to-date inventory asserts the value of the physical collections to a variety of campus stakeholders. This chapter offers ideas for working collaboratively with personnel across library departments to conduct and complete a major technical services project.

INTRODUCTION

The role of technical services in the modern academic library is con-textual. The functions, services, workflows, and priorities must be defined by the vision and mission of the library and larger institution. Nonetheless, one of the constants across diverse academic librar-ies and their component departments is change. Technical services departments must respond agilely to an unpredictable future and its often unknowable needs. When technical services librarians can help prepare for the future, and not merely respond to change, they can add immense value.

A colleague recently identified the perception that technical services librarians serve as gatekeepers of opaque processes. This may create the impression that they are change-averse and move slowly. One of the misconceptions that the authors recently heard regarding technical services at our own institution is that it does not directly support the mission of the university. Perhaps this misconception is because technical services employees often work behind the scenes and infrequently teach or serve students face-to-face. By proposing, and quickly completing, an inventory project that had clear implications for public services, the authors and their technical services colleagues at the University of Memphis proved themselves partners in fulfilling the mission and vision of the university. The inventory project was part of an effort to prepare the University of Memphis's health sciences collection for a newly created health sciences librarian position. This collection had been created approximately two years prior, from the merger of a now-defunct branch library and a subset of materials from the main library and is housed in the newly constructed Health Sciences Library (HSL). By embracing this opportunity to help, not only a new colleague, but also the university, the technical services librarians demonstrated their willingness and ability to act quickly and to support the university's broader mission. Completing this project in two months, before the arrival of the new health sciences librarian, influenced public services staff's, as well as our own, perceptions of technical services within University of Memphis libraries.

LITERATURE REVIEW

The evolution and future of technical services has been a common theme throughout the literature. Considering the dynamic nature of technical processes in the digital age, it makes good sense that those of us engaged in the work ponder its future. Several librarians have written about the positive and negative impact of automation software on library technical services.[1] Beyond the initial automation of shared cataloging applications feeding into online public access catalogs (OPAC), opportunities to partially or fully automate technical services have only increased. The future is unpredictable, but despite the vast changes in the past several decades, the need for information professionals to mediate the information deluge has been established. According to Bradford Lee Eden, "technical services staff, with their unique skills, talents, abilities, and knowledge in relation to the organization and description of information, are desperately needed in the new information environment."[2] Automation has also brought considerable change to inventory processing in the past decades. Several libraries began to conduct inventories with handheld devices in the 1990s.[3] Both Martha Loesch and Jim Womack documented the use of integrated library system (ILS)–generated lists to conduct large-scale inventories at their respective institutions.[4] Ernick documented the use of Innovative Interfaces' Millennium inventory control processes to conduct inventory in a small academic library setting.[5] Greenwood discussed the automation and modification of University of Mississippi's inventory processes, including the adoption of Sung, Whisler, and Sung's[6] 2009 electronic inventory and shelf-reading program, Library Stacks Management System.[7] Many authors have written about the inventory implications for radio frequency identification (RFID) in libraries.[8] For libraries whose collections are not yet RFID tagged or who are reluctant to fully automate inventory processing, locally defined inventory processes with varying degrees of automation should be pursued. This chapter documents the challenges and opportunities of inventorying dynamic collections to manage change.

STATEMENT OF PROBLEM

The University of Memphis is an urban research university with a fall 2019 enrollment of 21,685 and a Carnegie Classification of Doctoral Universities: Higher Research Activity. The university does not have a medical school, but the expansion and strength of existing health science programs helped to ensure the funding of a new Community Health Building, which officially opened August 2015. By approving for hire a new health sciences librarian position, the administration seemed to prioritize library support for the newly constructed Community Health Building and the academic programs housed therein.

The University Libraries at the University of Memphis comprises three branch libraries and Ned R. McWherter Library (McWherter), the main library. There were previously several branch libraries whose collections were extensively weeded before being subsumed into the main collection. Unfortunately, not all of the weeding and transfer processing was accurately reflected in the ILS. Within McWherter, the primary public services departmental divisions include circulation, special collections, administration, and research and instructional services (which comprises learning commons and government publications). There is no official technical services unit or designated head; cataloging, library information systems, and collection management (which includes interlibrary loan, acquisitions, electronic resources, and collection development) perform traditional technical services work. All these unit department heads report directly to the associate dean. The inventory project was spearheaded by Gail Perkins Barton, then interim head of collection management and Rachel Scott, ILS librarian.

The authors knew that the new incoming health sciences librarian would benefit from a recently inventoried collection. After all, conducting inventory is how one determines what is available, and by omission, what is no longer available. One of the primary responsibilities of the subject librarian is to be familiar with resources relevant to their discipline and know which resources are available within the local collection.[9] The accuracy of the health sciences collection as represented in the ILS would facilitate the incoming health sciences librarian's familiarity with available resources and provide concrete data concerning prior use and acquisition of these materials. Preparing the collection for an incoming colleague would empower him or her to understand the scope of the collection and facilitate the future public services work.

Another concern was ensuring that all items in this collection were cataloged, even if they were historically browsing collections. In addition to expanding and supporting the health sciences, the University of Memphis has an initiative, UofM Global, to expand and support distance education offerings. This means that some health sciences students and faculty may never browse the physical library shelves, which heightens the need for all titles and resources to be adequately described in online catalogs. In the next section, the authors will explain how personnel worked collaboratively across technical services units to process the relocated, downsized, and merged collection.

CHANGE IN THE ILS

The ILS librarian must continually learn how best to leverage the library system as the powerful tool it can be and investigate when processes might be automated. Innovative Interface Inc.'s Sierra database reporting and inventory functions were essential to the success of this project. Additionally, MARC record editing tools facilitated the bulk creation of bibliographic and item records for the previously unprocessed dissertations based on minimal data. Before the newly hired health sciences librarian arrived at the University of Memphis, the authors coordinated efforts to ensure that the collection was accurately represented in the ILS. Prior inventories had been conducted from print shelf lists or using an ILS-specific inventory product called Circa. No comprehensive inventory had been completed in the institutional memory of the University Libraries. This project is the first complete inventory project to be conducted not using the endorsed ILS product, but by uploading files of barcodes directly to the ILS to update the fixed-length field "inventory date" in the item record.

Circa, the ILS inventory function, requires a steady wireless signal and was found to be too cumbersome. The person conducting inventory with Circa must understand the various fixed- and variable-length fields in the item record. When, for example, an item that has been marked as lost, withdrawn, or in-transit is scanned in Circa, an error message is prompted. The person scanning must know enough about the collection and the relative importance of this message to respond appropriately. The authors were concerned that if this product were used to conduct inventory, too many items would be pulled for further investigation. To simplify inventory processing on the front-end, the ILS librarian used Sierra Admin's off-line circulation "compare inventory to shelf list" process to add an inventory date to the item record of each record with a barcode scanned. This feature allows a text file (.txt) of barcodes to be uploaded to the circbatch directory on the application server. Therefore, participants with little or no technical system training in reading the various fields could still contribute in a robust manner to this project by scanning the barcode of each book into a text file to share with the ILS librarian.

Several problems were encountered and addressed along the way. When preparing to consolidate materials from the defunct speech and hearing branch and main library into the newly built HSL two years ago, attempts to weed and withdraw some of the content had left materials that were still on the shelf suppressed from online public access catalogs and discovery layers. Conversely, several titles marked as available in the ILS were not inventoried and not found in any library collection. Interdepartmental communication and collaboration were essential as problem items, including previously uncatalogued theses and obsolete formats, were discovered and systematically processed. Collection management staff were trained to use the newly created workflows for the project to be completed in a timely manner. They continued their daily duties as they worked part-time on the project, which was located approximately two miles away from the main library. In the end, over 6,400 items were inventoried, 150 titles were added, and several hundred incorrect item statuses were updated in the ILS.

One of the main factors that propelled this project forward quickly was the urgency and support displayed by senior library faculty and administration. With all health sciences librarian candidate interviews complete, and an offer imminent, there was tremendous acceptance by library faculty who saw wisdom in having a collection that was orderly and properly reflected in the ILS. Having already completed a very small but successful scanning project a few months earlier in the main library, the two technical services librarians and many staff involved in this project were pleased to see the urgency expressed in tackling the inventory at the HSL. With the encouragement and support of the library faculty and expertise from a previous small project, planning began immediately. The collection management department already had a student employee in place for a few weeks of summer work and immediately redirected responsibilities to the scanning at the HSL. One of the experienced staff members was asked to oversee the schedule and encourage others to sign up for a regular shift to work at the HSL. This broadened the investment of many whose schedule allowed for participation in the extra project.

The authors adjusted, acknowledging challenges encountered, for example: designating a devoted laptop, barcode scanner, an extra-long power cord, and a portable station, as well as addressing uncata-logued dissertations with no records or spine labels. However, some challenges were unavoidable. Since the HSL is located on the south campus, away from the main part of the university and the University Libraries, it was difficult to orchestrate the continual scanning since employees had to travel to the location, set up the computer, resume scanning a section, close and send the files, and then return to the main campus and daily duties. It would have been ideal for one person to oversee the project on south campus, but that was not possible. Even though the student employee scanned some each day, oversight of the project was difficult from afar. The health sciences staff in that library are not part of technical services and needed to continue with regular duties, assisting students and other library users, because summer school was in session at the time this project began, although they did provide some background knowledge and history that was quite useful.

CHANGE IN PHYSICAL COLLECTIONS

One surprise on the first inventory planning trip to the HSL was the discovery of a browsing section of uncatalogued dissertations that had been provided by students or professors throughout the years. Some of those in the browsing section also had a duplicate already cataloged and on the shelf; others did not. One result of this project was the cata-loging of those dissertations and completion of the necessary physical processing. They were then moved to the oversize section for books that exceed 27 centimeters in height, which follows the same model as the main library. In addition to preparing and later moving the brows-ing section, other dissertations that were interfiled in the regular size collection were identified by the ILS librarian, pulled, and prepared for the oversize location with additional labels created by cataloging.

The HSL collection was already configured with shelf height estab-lished like that used in the main campus library, which includes a separate oversize area. With that collection increasing by over 150 items, it was important to have enough room available. However, that section was unable to shift forward due to the periodical section being directly adjacent to it. In collaboration with the HSL staff, a decision was made to shift the oversize items backward by one section because there were several empty in that area. This small change helped to accommodate oversize section growth; considering changes to local collection development policies to acquire more textbooks, this move was prudent.

Inventory participants across technical service units brought helpful expertise to the project. Staff in cataloging had knowledge of some HSL items that were awaiting corrections in their backlog and not reflected properly in the library catalog. They worked to resolve the issues and returned the books to the HSL after inventory. Also, there were personnel in collection management that had knowledge of the transfer process and even participated in preparing many nursing-related items from the main library to the HSL two years ago. Having the experience of working to transfer the items from the main campus library to the HSL was a benefit to the project; several books were found that never made it to the HSL and remained in McWherter. These were discovered when staff searched McWherter for items listed as "not on the shelf" or "missing" after scanning was complete. In brief, there were items in the HSL with a McWherter location listed in the catalog and vice versa. Many were identified, the location corrected, and the book physically placed in the correct location. Having a deeply ingrained desire to link patrons with needed material, the collection management personnel worked regularly to correct the physical issues discovered and ensure that the book was properly labeled and readied for discovery and use.

Occasionally, however, specific processes slowed the inventory project. For example, the authors initially considered moving the 150 uncatalogued dissertations to McWherter so that they could be more fully cataloged. Instead, the ILS librarian went to the HSL, applied temporary handwritten spine labels, and added barcodes to item records after bulk creating brief bibliographic and item records, which greatly expedited the record creation process. Cataloging created new and permanent spine labels and collection management personnel applied the labels before shelving the dissertations in their new location in the oversize area. Another label project was discussed, but ultimately postponed. During inventory scanning, several participants remarked on severely faded spine labels that were difficult to read. Though a worthwhile project, replacing the faded labels would have been a competing focus. No technical services personnel have individual spine label printers and all label printing goes through cataloging. After the first attempt at compiling a text file for cataloging, it was evident that the task would be quite large and take focus off the main effort at hand. It was decided that the spine labels could easily be identified later simply by walking through the stacks.

CONCLUSION

The timing was right for this project. It was inspiring to collaborate with colleagues to ensure a warm welcome and smooth transition for a new colleague. It was also just before the beginning of the summer term, when fewer users were in the library. When working on a project that involves barcode scanner beeping, physical processing of materials in the main reading room, and occasional discussions among workers, it is best to do so during a time when fewer library users are attempting to work or study in that location. A way to silence the barcode scanner was found in the barcode operation manual, but it also was determined that the person scanning depends on the sound as an auditory cue to move on to the next barcode. A regular glance to the screen is needed to verify whether the whole barcode is registered into the text file, so a re-scan can be done before moving too far along. Without the sound from the barcode reader, the person scanning is too occupied by watching the screen to see when the barcode displays and causes a slight delay. Another important consideration is the amount of activity within the collection while a project of this type is ongoing. For returning items to be included in the inventory, HSL staff emptied the book drop and assembled returned items on a designated cart to be scanned on a regular basis.

Open communication and support from leaders are essential to successful project management, especially in transitions. In this case, the two technical services librarians were in constant communication and offered praise and recognition of team members for the accomplishment of tasks along the way, reminding them of the importance of this project to the incoming HSL librarian as well as to all University Libraries users. The lead librarians remained positive and flexible and provided support as needed.

Though it was not a part of their regular workflow, many collection management staff went to the HSL and completed the physical processing of dissertations, which had been added to the catalog. This required adding tattle tape and the property stamp, applying newly created spine labels, and relocating the dissertations to the oversize area in the library. Working from a list created by the ILS librarian, collection management staff pulled the dissertations, which were processed but still located in the regular shelves, and moved them to the oversize area as well. In addition, employees from collection management checked the main library as well as the HSL for items that were missing or not found in the expected location, involving the staff there when their schedules allowed. Being a small team, communication about the progress was not complex. Each week, and often daily, the department received an update either in person or by email from the librarians. The team was diligent and willing to assist with various tasks as needed, which expanded the expertise of the collection management personnel, including several who were somewhat new to the department.

Working closely together, cataloging, collection management, and ILS librarians and staff gained a deeper respect for each other and the work accomplished in technical services. More importantly, the impact of this work on library users was made quite clear. When items are incorrectly labeled, missing, or otherwise unable to be found as reflected in the ILS, the resource may as well never have been purchased. The two librarians leading this project were careful to be supportive, provide feedback, and keep the purpose of the project ever before the team members. As the project ended, those who participated expressed a sense of accomplishment for their part in the project and said that it was rewarding to have collaborated to realize such an impactful change. This initial inventory project has changed attitudes about technical services and has already created considerable buy-in for an ongoing inventory. Employees in both technical and public services now collaborate on inventory projects, large and small.

Overall, the importance of knowing what is on the shelf and how it is reflected in the ILS is essential to quality library service. Librarians and staff of technical services units are vital in keeping the collection organized and ready for discovery and use. The functions of the public services areas depend on the work of technical services.

However, this work is largely invisible; few outside technical services are even aware of the decisions, processes, and maintenance that go into achieving seamless access to materials. When resource problems arise, technical services come to the forefront quickly to investigate and solve the problem. They then again calmly retreat behind the scenes to continue the quality control that creates smooth access for libraries and users alike. Adapting to change and having a plan to address upheavals such as closing and/or merging collections, deep deselection, or the other collection crises is crucial in guiding one's library through uncertainty and keeping the collection healthy today and for many tomorrows.

The relevance of this case study might not be immediately applicable to readers. Indeed, the local circumstances and institution-specific details may render the outlined approach to conducting inventory less useful to other institutions. Nonetheless, the authors conclude with five recommendations that are more broadly useful for a variety of technical services projects.

1. *Timing is everything:* consider staffing and user schedules and tap into projects with momentum.
2. *Communication is key:* before personnel can provide support or buy into a project, they must be informed about it.
3. *Many hands make light work:* the more people supporting and engaged in the project, the quicker and more accurate the work.
4. *Variety is the spice of life:* technical services work can lack variety and short-term projects can provide a welcome break.
5. *R-E-S-P-E-C-T:* taking the time to coordinate interdepartmental projects instills a deeper understanding and respect for our technical services colleagues.

NOTES

1. Gregor A. Preston, "How Will Automation Affect Cataloging Staff?" *Technical Services Quarterly* 1, no. 1–2 (Fall/Winter 1983): 129–36, https://doi.org/10.1300/J124v01n01_21; Hong Xu, "The Impact of Automation on Job Requirements and Qualifications for Catalogers

and Reference Librarians in Academic Libraries," *Library Resources & Technical Services* 40, no. 1 (2011): 9–31, https://doi.org/10.5860/lrts.40n1.9.

2. Bradford Lee Eden, "The New User Environment: The End of Technical Services?" *Information Technology and Libraries* 29, no. 2 (2010): 99, https://doi.org/10.6017/ital.v29i2.3148.

3. Charles David Emery, "The Use of Portable Barcode Scanners in Collections Inventory," *Collection Management* 13, no. 4 (January 5, 1990): 1–17, https://doi.org/10.1300/J105v13n04_01; Li Chen and Yongli Ma, "Library Inventory Using Palm Pilot," *Technical Services Quarterly* 22, no. 2 (2004): 15–23, https://doi.org/10.1300/J124v22n02_02.

4. Martha Fallahay Loesch, "Inventory Redux: A Twenty-First Century Adaptation," *Technical Services Quarterly* 28, no. 3 (2011): 301–11, https://doi.org/10.1080/07317131.2011.571636; Jim Womack, "Inventory or Stockcheck?" *Christian Librarian* 53, no. 3 (2010): 111–13, https://digitalcommons.georgefox.edu/tcl/vol53/iss3/4.

5. Linda Ernick, "Floating Bibs and Orphan Barcodes: Benefits of an Inventory at a Small College," *Library Resources & Technical Services* 49, no. 3 (2005): 210–16.

6. Jan S. Sung, John A. Whisler, and Nackil Sung, "A Cost-Benefit Analysis of a Collections Inventory Project: A Statistical Analysis of Inventory Data From a Medium-Sized Academic Library," *Journal of Academic Librarianship* 35, no. 4 (2009): 314–23, https://doi.org/10.1016/j.acalib.2009.04.002.

7. Judy T. Greenwood, "Taking It to the Stacks: An Inventory Project at the University of Mississippi Libraries," *Journal of Access Services* 10, no. 2 (2013): 77–89, https://doi.org/10.1080/15367967.2013.762266.

8. Sadanand Y. Bansode and Sanjay K. Desale, "Implementation of RFID Technology in University of Pune Library," *Program-Electronic Library and Information Systems* 43, no. 2 (2009): 202–14, https://doi.org/10.1108/00330330910954406; Yogesh K. Dwivedi et al., "RFID Systems in Libraries: An Empirical Examination of Factors Affecting System Use and User Satisfaction," *International Journal of Information Management* 33, no. 2 (2013): 367–77, https://doi.org/10.1016/j.ijinfomgt.2012.10.008.

9. Stephen Pinfield, "The Changing Role of Subject Librarians in Academic Libraries," *Journal of Librarianship and Information Science* 33, no. 1 (2001): 32–38, https://doi.org/10.1177/096100060103300104; Tom Glynn and Connie Wu, "New Roles and Opportunities for Academic Library Liaisons: A Survey and Recommendations," *Reference Services Review* 31, no. 2 (2003): 122–28, https://doi.org/10.1108/00907320310476594.

CHALLENGE THREE
Rethinking Library Space Usage

CHAPTER 10

For Efficiency's Sake: Consolidating Workflows, Managing Change, and Positioning Ourselves for the Future

Mary S. Laskowski and Jennifer A. Maddox Abbott

ABSTRACT

Managing institutional change is challenging and can often result in unintended consequences. This chapter illustrates best practices and lessons learned through a series of changes in a technical services unit at a large research university to help to inform others facing similar challenges and opportunities at their own institution. The overall goal is to create models for ongoing change that are flexible and nimble enough to adjust rapidly as strategic priorities, resources, and support structures evolve over time.

INTRODUCTION

The collection management services (CMS) unit within technical services at the University of Illinois at Urbana-Champaign recently combined formerly dispersed staffing operations and relocated to remodeled space at our high-density storage facility, the Oak Street Library. Much of the impetus and planning regarding this move was predicated on finding efficiencies in staffing and operations that could help ensure provision of excellent production and patron services while maximizing available resources and preparing ourselves to meet upcoming technical services challenges, both known and projected. A key component in the long-term planning for this consolidation was streamlining several workflows formerly dispersed throughout the library and across various staffing levels under one umbrella operation, with staff trained to handle projects as part of their normal daily operations. Rather than solely focusing on current needs, we are now poised to effectively manage change in an always evolving technical services environment.

In this chapter we discuss the overall goals we hoped to achieve, the planning and preparation required, and the implementation and success of the consolidation to date, with the goal of providing information that may be helpful to other institutions who may not be physically relocating but have project work or workflows that could benefit from shared expertise. Specifically, this chapter relates how we aligned the transition with existing and future project workflows, including ongoing support for mass digitization and increased participation in consortial collection management, such as hosting a consortial shared print repository. We discuss the challenges and opportunities in tiered staffing models and the necessity for increased communication. Our overall goal is to create a model that works well to support current and future large-scale projects while being flexible enough to adapt rapidly to changing institutional needs. By capitalizing on the trend toward consortial collection management and the changing nature of high-density storage facilities, we proactively demonstrate the key role that technical services can play in leading academic libraries' participation in new, exciting initiatives.

BACKGROUND INFORMATION

Initially, the University Library's focus on technical services project work grew from the understanding that some work, such as peak acquisitions, cataloging, and reserve processing periods, are cyclical in nature. That understanding, combined with other needs throughout the library for short-term assistance, led to the creation of what was called the cyclical and makeshift logistics squad (CAMELS) in 2004. CAMELS's purpose was twofold: to assist libraries with occasional heavy workload duties during peak service periods and to assist with short-term work, such as opening libraries each morning, that requires immediate action and coverage for understaffed libraries. All assistance was provided on a temporary basis and took place in public service units throughout the library system during the regular workweek. As the work of the team progressed, the original assumption was eventually almost completely reversed. While it was true that reserves work, for example, was cyclical in nature, training staff on the team to assist on a temporary basis proved problematic, as each departmental library had slightly different expectations and standards for reserves services. In a smaller environment, with fewer discrete, separate units with differing policies and procedures, this model may still be worth pursuing. However, due to the unique nature of many services within our library, eventually the team was disbanded. The process generated a greater understanding that many of the technical services staff involved with cyclical work had extensive skill sets that could be applied to growing priorities in collection shifts, transfers, consolidations, cataloging of backlogs, and so on. In other words, the groups that were originally slated to receive help, such as the reserve processing team, became the group that now focuses on providing project assistance to others throughout the library.[1]

In 2008, the group of staff from the undergraduate library that had worked predominantly on e-reserve processing for the University Library became a stand-alone technical services unit, at that time called information processing and management. This group continued with their responsibilities for e-reserve processing but in nonpeak periods assisted with other cyclical tasks. In contrast to the conclusions drawn by Lihong Zhu, who indicated that "while permanent teams could be used to replace traditional hierarchical structures, project teams were not meant to replace existing structures since they were often used to deal with important short-term objectives and initiatives,"[2] the University Library in effect created a permanent project team built on the understanding that though work scoped as a project will, by definition, end, there is always the next project in the queue, and having a permanent, dedicated project team with appropriate skill sets maximizes efficiencies. Although creating a dedicated project team or unit may seem cost-prohibitive, the local finding was that it was much more cost-effective in the long term due to minimizing the costs of hiring, training, and supervising project work on a one-off basis.

In addition to reserve processing (print and electronic), the unit became responsible for gift and last copy processing, major collection transfers throughout the library, and working with consortial initiatives such as mass digitization and shared collections. Support for the library's New Service Model initiatives[3] became a staple of the unit's workload, providing skilled project management and a workforce accustomed to complicated cataloging backlogs as well as large-scale shifts and transfers. As Feeney and Sult indicate, "Managing projects is not a new topic for libraries; however, because of the changing nature of library work, along with resource constraints and expectations for accountability, the need for effective project management has increased."[4]

As of July 1, 2012, the unit took on management of the library's high-density storage facility and changed its name to collection management services (CMS) to better reflect the growing role of the unit in the large-scale collection management of the University Library collections. The high-density storage facility (Oak Street Library) houses roughly a third of the library's physical holdings at over four million volumes, and most of the major collection management projects involve at least some aspect of selecting and transferring items into or out of high-density storage for long-term preservation and access. For the next five years, however, the unit was split across two physical locations, with a few staff housed at Oak Street to handle storage retrievals, refiles, and general vault work and most of the staff housed in the main library building, concentrating on reserve processing, transfers, gift processing, and most of the consortial project work.

CMS is one of four centralized technical services units in the University Library, the others being content access management (cataloging and metadata), acquisitions, and preservation services. Almost all technical services work has been consolidated in the four technical services units, with some few processes related to special collections remaining with individual units. The technical services units are production oriented and currently comprise 27 faculty and academic professionals, 57 civil service staff, and various graduate assistants, graduate hourly employees, and student workers.

RATIONALE FOR COMBINING COLLECTION MANAGEMENT SERVICES AND OAK STREET OPERATIONS

There were many benefits to consolidating CMS from two locations to one. One of the most obvious advantages was the increase in the number of staff available for a variety of tasks. Consolidating staff allowed for additional people to be trained to operate the industrial lifts used for retrieving materials from the high-density shelving, and increasing the number of lift operators scheduled daily contributed to increased productivity within the Oak Street vaults. Because of the cold conditions (50 degrees Fahrenheit), the amount of time staff are allowed to work retrieving or refiling library materials in the vaults must be limited; the consolidation increased the number of certified lift operators at Oak Street from 7 to 12, allowing more staff to spend part of the day in the vaults and part of the day in the workroom preparing materials to be shelved or in the staff workspace working on cataloging-related projects. While not all staff were willing or able to become certified to use the industrial lifts, there was enough interest from volunteers and new positions hired to allow for this increase. The Oak Street Library not only is a high-density storage unit but also operates as a full public service unit. So, much in the same way the unit benefited from having more lift operators, it also benefited from having more staff to cover shifts at the circulation desk or serve as backup to cover for illness, breaks, lunches, or vacation time. Also, staff who previously were unfamiliar with cataloging had an opportunity to branch out and expand their skill sets, learning various aspects of library materials processing. Cross-training not only provided staff with more variety in their day and management with more flexibility in assigning tasks but also enhanced each staff member's overall understanding of workflows they were previously unfamiliar with, therefore giving them greater familiarity into why particular details or steps in the process matter. While individual staff had varying responses to this increased diversity of tasks, the consensus after the fact is that more flexibility and knowledge increased job satisfaction.

CMS management has for many years worked to push work down to student and hourly employees when possible, freeing up permanent staff time for more complicated and rigorous tasks. An hourly or student workforce allows for flexibility when more staff are needed, following the ebb and flow of projects. Cross-training permanent employees as much as possible also helps create an environment that not only addresses current priorities but is as flexible as possible to accommodate rapid changes necessary to meet future needs. Jeehyun Yun Davis, who conducted a study in 2013–2014 investigating the transforming nature of technical services, found that "budget constraints and rapid technological innovations are the major driving forces that have been bringing change to technical services, and these trends are likely to continue into the near future. Efforts to reduce costs result in resolutions to improve existing workflows, which lead to increased efficiency and greater collaboration within the library, on campus, and among universities."[5]

Large-scale collection management projects, as well as the overall growth of the collections held in the facility, have significantly changed the workflows at the Oak Street Library. The number of items retrieved continues to increase each year, both due to increased collection size in storage and improved discoverability, which also increases the number of items that need to be refiled in the vaults. In addition to increasing circulation numbers, nearly 30,000 items were de-accessioned from the facility in 2015 as part of a shared print repository project and were sent for deposit at the consortial level, as the University Library high-density storage only housed locally owned content. This was followed by a deduplication project, withdrawing more than 63,000 serial volumes from the Oak Street collection that were duplicates of the shared collection and for which patrons have electronic access through the library. Withdrawing these materials and then reclaiming the space in the Oak Street vaults was a large undertaking that required a lot of coordination, and having all members of management and staff in one location allowed for significant streamlining of the workflows. As storage facilities at other institutions reach maximum capacity, these types of space reclamation and shared storage options will continue to increase.

CMS has also been the unit most heavily involved in the library's participation in a consortial large-scale digitization project for several years. Library materials have been retrieved and scanned from several library locations, but most of the remaining materials to be scanned are located at Oak Street and so are being retrieved by our Oak Street staff. Now that all staff are in the same building, we no longer need to retrieve the materials and have them delivered to the main library for processing. The entire workflow happens in one building, requiring carts of materials to be taken upstairs instead of across campus. This saves time and reduces the physical impact on staff and the library materials.

PLANNING AND PREPARATION TO ALIGN WITH
EXISTING AND FUTURE PROJECT WORKFLOWS

Planning for physically relocating the CMS staff from the main library to the Oak Street Library began during the summer of 2016. To ease the transition, the unit maintained a footprint in the main library for storing book trucks and gift donations. It also continued to run a large-scale digitization project from that space for an additional nine months after the permanent faculty, academic professionals, and staff moved locations in order to meet scheduled deadlines and to maintain proximity to the collection that was being digitized at the time. As is often the case with campus facilities projects, there were a lot of variables that could impact the timeline for this move, so staff had to be prepared to move as soon as early September, knowing that the move might not take place until much later in the fall. In the meantime, unit management's planning for the move was already underway.

The management team, which consisted of the unit head and two additional professionals—one at each location of the unit—actively explored options for desk and workspaces, cross-training on various tasks that were currently being completed on one end of the unit or the other and streamlining projects and workflows to discover new efficiencies. Management began meeting more regularly to better understand each other's work and to identify places where staff could be cross-trained. Information regarding project progress and priorities at the different ends of the unit were shared more consistently so that staff would begin to develop a better understanding of all the tasks, projects, and functions that took place across the unit. A major goal was to make the transition as smooth as possible for the staff. It was understood that change and not knowing could be stressful, so management shared as many details as possible as they became available, even if it was just to update the staff that progress had stalled, or lights had been installed. Staff were repeatedly encouraged to approach any of the managers with questions or concerns.

Scoping the consolidation as a project within a unit that was already accustomed to project work allowed for a great deal of buy-in from both the administration and the staff involved, as there was more context to understand the rationale and decisions from top to bottom. As more and more work of the unit is scoped as projects, it allows for both the sense of completion in accomplishing a specific task (whether it be a task that takes a few days, a few months, or a year) and an enhanced understanding of the need for communication and ongoing training to pick up new responsibilities on short notice. A common thread in technical services discussions across institutions is the need for increased flexibility within existing workforces, and scoping more work as projects is a great way to challenge employees to engage and encourage greater job satisfaction.

IMPLEMENTATION—THE ACTUAL MOVE

An obstacle that was known in advance was the distance the unit would be from other units that CMS visits frequently, particularly the main stacks and the library's cataloging unit. Although most of the unit's projects involve material housed at Oak Street, projects require staff to visit the main stacks, even if it is just to compare copies, as well as to pass materials to the cataloging unit, particularly materials CMS does not have the ability to catalog (e.g., foreign language materials). This new distance required some changes to workflows when working with other units.

An obstacle to success that was initially underestimated, though, was the impact that the specific physical location of the newly remodeled space would have on staff morale. No longer working in a building that is in the heart of campus and no longer being surrounded by so many colleagues and friends in the main library was a harder adjustment than was anticipated. The Oak Street Library is approximately one mile away and houses only one other (small) library unit. While this was a known factor in the planning stages, overall the staff themselves were surprised at the effect this had on them after the move. The relative proximity and ongoing collaboration with other library units, as well as enthusiasm for relocating to newly remodeled, nicer workspaces, initially overshadowed the impact that being removed from the main library building would have.

As Jeanie Daniel Duck noted, "Empowerment does not mean abandonment. Giving people permission to do something differently is not helpful if they are unable to do it. That permission just set them up to fail. Setting the context for change means preparing the players, understanding what they do and don't know, working with them, watching their performance, giving them feedback, creating an ongoing dialogue with them."[6] One of the things the management team would change if we had the move to do over is to try to accomplish more cross-training of the staff ahead of time so that not as many tasks and workflows are completely new at once. There were a lot of logistical problems in that regard because the staff were in separate buildings, but reassigning a few staff in each direction a few months ahead of the major consolidation may have reduced the amount of training needed immediately following the move, and therefore some of the associated stress as well.

Although the move caused some stress, there were many positive outcomes as well. Management had worked hard to create a seating chart that made sense for grouping tasks but also mixed staff from both halves of the unit. Staff were encouraged to share any seating preferences before the plan was finalized, and all requests received were able to be accommodated. There was a concerted effort to ensure that there would not be an us-versus-them atmosphere, and it was great to see new work friendships develop and people eating lunch together who before the move had only known each other's names and met briefly at periodic staff meetings.

Since the consolidation, management has more flexibility in planning out projects. There are now more staff available to pitch in on a project, such as preparing shipments for off-site digitization, and more options available when trying to coordinate who will work on what while juggling multiple simultaneous project workflows. For example, if it is determined that an all-hands-on-deck approach is what is needed to quickly work through and complete a project, whether quickly means a few hours or several weeks, there is the opportunity to do just that. This was not as easy before the consolidation took place. Before the move, if a project was in the queue behind a similar project, it would need to wait until the appropriate staff person was free to work on it. There are now more cross-trained staff and therefore more flexibility in scheduling projects based on other factors. Current major projects include hosting the next phase of the Big Ten Academic Alliance (BTAA) Shared Print Repository, ongoing participation in the BTAA Google Book Search project, and internal major transfers from other departmental libraries.

Another benefit relates to working with the library materials that typically are coming out of the Oak Street vaults or are being transferred into them. Most of the project work completed by CMS involves materials at Oak Street, and those materials come from all departmental libraries that constitute the University Library. Having catalogers in a location other than where these materials were housed required multiple trips per week of materials coming or going. CMS has a box truck to help alleviate the impact of project work on library facilities, but management knew that the resources—staff time and supplies—required to move materials back and forth could be better utilized if the unit were consolidated in one location. To transport large quantities of books, staff must load the materials onto book trucks, which are then wrapped in shipping plastic to ensure items don't fall off during transport. Wrapping, loading, driving, unloading, and unwrapping have now been cut out of the workflow for most of the unit's project work.

CONCLUSIONS

Moving all staff and operations to one location, the Oak Street Library, was a successful project, and improvements in workflows have already been achieved. As Sheila S. Intner notes regarding risk, "The fact that deciding on goals and objectives involves risk is something no librarian likes to think about, perhaps, especially not technical services managers. Moreover, managing risk is not only part of establishing goals and objectives, but it also figures importantly in evaluating the performance of a department."[7] While it was a risk to move further away from other technical services units of the library, it was one that was worth taking.

In place of a strategic plan, the University Library currently has adopted the *Framework for Strategic Action, 2015–2021*, which helps inform strategic directions, budget allocations, and so forth. The work of CMS falls under points (2A) "Optimize discovery of, access to, and accessibility of all library resources, collections, and services"; (4A) "Lead regional and national efforts to shape cooperative collections and related services"; and (4B) "Expand access to unique collections and resources."[8] Early indications suggest that all goals of the consolidation were achieved at least to some degree and that the unit is poised to fulfill the longer-term goals in relation to the strategic framework, which will allow CMS to continue to optimize accessibility, expand access to our unique holdings, and lead in cooperative collection efforts. Though not all problems can be anticipated, making sure that there is significant time for planning and ongoing conversations with all individuals affected by the consolidation will help ensure project success. It is perhaps helpful to note that sometimes it is the smallest changes that cause the greatest discontent, and sometimes small changes can help address major issues. Allowing the greatest possible staff empowerment in the decision-making process goes a long way toward building a collaborative team that is poised to address new challenges.

NOTES

1. Jennifer A. Maddox Abbott and Mary S. Laskowski, "So Many Projects, So Few Resources: Using Effective Project Management in Technical Services," *Collection Management* 39, no. 2/3 (July 2014): 161–76, https://doi.org/10.1080/01462679.2014.891492.
2. Lihong Zhu, "Use of Teams in Technical Services in Academic Libraries," *Library Collections, Acquisitions, & Technical Services* 35, no. 2–3 (June 2011): 80, https://doi.org/10.1016/j.lcats.2011.03.013.
3. See https://www.library.illinois.edu/staff/administration/new-service-model/.
4. Mary Feeney and Leslie Sult, "Project Management in Practice: Implementing a Process to Ensure Accountability and Success," *Journal of Library Administration* 51, no. 7–8 (October 2011): 745, https://doi.org/10.1080/01930826.2011.601273.
5. Jeehyun Yun Davis, "Transforming Technical Services: Evolving Functions in Large Research University Libraries," *Library Resources & Technical Services* 60, no. 1 (January 2016): 63, https://doi.org/10.5860/lrts.60n1.52.
6. Jeanie D. Duck, "Managing Change: The Art of Balancing," in *Harvard Business Review on Change*, Harvard Business Review Paperback Series (Boston: Harvard Business School Press, 1998), 64.

7. Sheila S. Intner, "Evaluating Technical Services," *Technicalities* 36, no. 5 (October 9, 2016): 6.

8. *Framework for Strategic Action, 2015–2021*, adopted December 7, 2015, University of Illinois at Urbana-Champaign Library, https://www.library.illinois.edu/staff/wp-content/uploads/sites/24/2017/10/ADOPTEDFramework_for_Strategic_Action.pdf.

CHAPTER 11

A Framework for Addressing the Psychological Aspects of Relocating Technical Services Off-Site

Christine Korytnyk Dulaney

ABSTRACT

This chapter utilizes the experiences of the American University technical services department to address the psychological aspects of moving a technical services department to an off-site location. A literature review exposes both the increasing popularity of this decision as well as the difficulties associated with such a move. The chapter outlines how staff emotions can be managed using the principles of transition management. This framework outlines three stages: pre-event, transition, and post-move. For each stage, the author describes the actions taken to ensure a successful move-in day as well as post-move staff transformation. Several lessons were learned during the move, including the importance of communication, planning, and organization as well as consideration of the psychological aspects for staff. A move that results in transforming staff productivity and efficiency requires not only logistical support and project management but consideration of the emotional aspects as well.

INTRODUCTION

As libraries struggle to find additional spaces to accommodate needs for new types of learning spaces and expanded services, library administrators increasingly decide that moving the technical services department out of the library building is a cost-effective way to reclaim needed square footage. While successful relocation of technical services to a remote location requires project management, planning, and communication, these technical skills must be coupled with an understanding of the psychological aspects of such a relocation. Using the framework of transition rather than change allows us to understand and address the psychological aspects of such a move. This chapter uses the relocation of the technical services department at American University to describe the framework of transition, how the move was executed, and the lessons learned.

THE PSYCHOLOGICAL CHALLENGE OF A RELOCATION

Viewing the relocation of a department to a remote location as solely a logistical problem fails to address the human side of this experience. As Mahlon Apgar's research shows, "from an early age, we learn how to live in organizations at particular locations."[1] Many librarians and library staff derive professional identify from their work in a library, their direct or indirect relationship with library users, and their role in users' success in using the library's resources and services. This identity is strengthened by the physical environment—including the library building, the library stacks, and the library users—which all create a sense of place. Even when not directly interacting with library users, library staff understand how their work enables access to resources or furthers successful information seeking and discovery. The best library workers take pride in their role in the success of their library. But when library staff are relocated to a location outside of the library or off campus, this sense of professional identity as defined by place is threatened. The challenge when relocating technical services staff to a remote location is to reframe their identity with the physical library setting. As Apgar writes, "In the alternative workplace, we have to learn to be in and of the organization while not being at it."[2]

Relocating library technical services departments to an off-campus location to increase space for additional student study and user services spaces is not a new trend. Relocation and reorganization of technical services have been common themes in the literature for the past 15 or so years. Primarily, however, the library literature emphasizes that comfortable and efficient workspaces optimizes workflows and productivity. Lihong Zhu's survey of technical services librarians and staff in Association of Research Libraries (ARL) librarians exemplifies this theme. This survey confirms the importance of designing an effective office layout, conducting a cost- benefit analysis, allowing for future growth, permitting customization of workspaces, and involving employees.[3] Zhu concludes that productivity and innovation are byproducts of good office workspaces.

More recently, the literature provides descriptions of how libraries implement a technical services relocation either to another part of the main library or to a remote or off-campus location. In her 2007 ASERL presentation, Deborah Jakubs describes the process used at Duke University to relocate technical services. Her presentation provides a roadmap of the steps followed and the goals Duke hoped to achieve for a successful move. She emphasizes the importance of listening, communicating, holding meetings, having the right team, and respecting emotional distress.[4] Similarly, Pricilla Williams and colleagues describe the relocation of technical services as part of a library-wide reorganization. Their experiences also highlight the difficulty of dealing with staff dissatisfaction with the relocation and the importance of communication and staff participation in decision-making as critical to mitigating staff distress.[5]

The difficulties of relocating technical services to a remote location are well-documented. Melanie McGurr's 2011 survey collects information on various solutions that address these challenges. Her results again emphasize the importance of communication, planning, and engaging staff participation in decision-making. In terms of assessing the impact of a remote location, McGurr's respondents reported that the physical location influenced their workflow and created obstacles to productivity. Most respondents also reported that the physical location impacted job satisfaction. They prefer to be in the main library rather than in a remote location. After relocation, respondents emphasized staying focused on the significance of their work to the main library and on maintaining high-quality work. McGurr's analysis indicates that although a relocation may enable the library to fulfill library strategic goals, off-site technical services does not benefit technical services overall. For most respondents, a central location remains optimal.[6]

THE FRAMEWORK FOR TRANSITION MANAGEMENT

A useful framework for addressing the psychological aspects of a relocation is provided by Steve Carter. In his overview of relocation, Carter emphasizes the fundamental difference between managing change and managing transition. A relocation handled as a change rather than a transition misses the emotional impact of the relocation. Understanding and supporting the fundamental shifts in the way the employees think about the organization, its business, and how it is managed is critical to ensuring a successful relocation. Carter asserts that in contrast to a change, a transition involves a series of mental shifts within individuals as they process the relocation through a sequence of pre-event, event and post-event stages. Ignoring these mental shifts creates a negative impact on an employee's level of engagement and leads to low morale and ultimately a negative work culture.[7]

The first stage of transition management, the pre-event, is characterized by the realization that change is coming and that the old ways of working must be discontinued. The primary psychological response to this phase is a sense of loss as staff process what they perceive as an ending. This sense of loss expresses itself in either passive or active resistance. If the relocation is not desired and is not obviously a gain, this calculation can become negative quickly. Depending on the individual and their past experiences, the psychological response may be understood as an indictment of the workers and their work and value to the organization. Left unchecked, the loss recognized in this stage can quickly lead to low morale, anger, and disengagement.

In successful transition management, the second stage is a period of change when critical psychological realignments and repatterning take place regarding the event itself. This phase is characterized by employees appraising or taking stock of the relocation—how will this affect them? What are the losses? What are the gains? Employees make determinations about the effect of the relocation on them personally and on their future. During this phase, library managers need to empathize and address the loss employees feel when leaving the old ways behind. Simultaneously, enthusiasm and optimism for new ways of working in a new location must develop to replace the loss. Communication about the relocation and its impact on the work and their status should be plentiful and support the transition from the old to the new.

The final stage is the post-event. This stage represents the end of the transition and the emergence of a new beginning. The most important post-event outcome is the development of a new professional identity based on a new beginning.[8]

RELOCATING THE AMERICAN UNIVERSITY LIBRARY TECHNICAL SERVICES DEPARTMENT

At American University, the discussion about relocating technical services had been ongoing for many years but became a reality in the fall of 2013 when two opportunities arose. First, the university appropriated funds for a renovation of the American University Library (the main library). Second, the American University Washington School of Law moved to a new location and the former law school building—located off-campus and renamed the Spring Valley Building (SVB)—became available. An early goal was to move all non-student-facing departments off the main quad. The original vision for the SVB was as an administrative building bringing together departments that were dispersed in off-campus commercial spaces. Additionally, some academic departments were scattered over multiple spaces, and SVB was an opportunity to bring these units together into a single space. Ultimately, SVB's occupants are a combination of academic and administrative schools and divisions as well as classrooms.

For the American University Library, funding for a renovation and the availability of off-campus space in SVB created an opportunity to repurpose staff and stacks space for students in the main library. The library determined that it needed additional student study areas and an expanded research commons area. Further, the front of the building facing the main quad was occupied by librarian offices and a library conference room. These spaces were unlit at night, creating a dark and uninviting façade on the quad after sunset. To improve the appearance of the quad and the library building, the librarians would be moved to offices within the library's interior and the front of the building devoted to student study space. Also, approximately

200,000 volumes were removed from the library stacks and sent to the consortial shared collections facility in suburban Maryland.

The library relocated three units to SVB. The technical services department was the largest, with 19 full-time equivalents (FTE) and three units—acquisitions, electronic resources, and resource description. The library's archives and special collections also moved, including 3 FTE and closed stacks of compact shelving, as well as a classroom, reading room, and exhibit space. Because SVB has classrooms, academic technology included one unit of 2 FTE to attend to technology needs in the classrooms. And because the School of Education was relocated to SVB, the library decided to move the curriculum materials collection (CMC)—a collection of juvenile and young adult resources, teaching space plus a circulation desk with 1 FTE staff comprised of students to oversee the collection and circulation functions and maintain the collection.

STAGE ONE: THE PRE-EVENT

At American University, the pre-event phase was marked by a report that confirmed prior multiyear discussions about moving technical services off campus. The long period between the decision to relocate and the actual move date further complicated the situation. The decision to move technical services and archives was announced in the fall of 2013, although the actual move did not occur for technical services until spring 2017—three and a half years later. During project delays, the vacuum was filled with rumors about the move or unrealistic expectations that the relocation would never happen. Both narratives were counterproductive with regard to staff morale, and in general this extended time frame proved challenging.

When the years of theoretical discussion about relocating became real, the staff reacted with expressions of fear and anger. They took great pride in the high-quality services and products they produced, and some staff believed that the relocation would prevent them from being able to maintain this high standard because the geographic distance would create inefficiencies and obstacles. If they wouldn't be able to maintain their usual high level of quality and speed, then their performance ratings would drop. If their performance rating was diminished, then jobs would be threatened. For some staff, this relocation was perceived as a setup for failure and the first step in a slippery slope that would lead to the dissolution of the department.

Other staff were concerned that the off-campus location would render them out of sight, out of mind, and therefore less relevant. The technical services unit heads had spent many years prioritizing the breakdown of silos both within the department and with other library departments such as public services. The staff worried that geographic distance would make the spontaneous communications they had enjoyed with coworkers in other departments more difficult. Without the easy collegiality and information sharing that occurs among colleagues who work nearby, staff worried that the department would be left out of major library initiatives and decision-making. As Ben Waber and colleagues describe, research has shown that this challenge is real: geographic distance does affect communication. From measurements of the strong negative correlation between physical distance and frequency of communication, Thomas J. Allen developed the Allen curve, which estimates that employees are four times as likely to communicate regularly with someone sitting six feet away and that employees communicate more infrequently with colleagues on separate floors or in separate buildings. Distance-shrinking technologies do not break the Allen curve. Ben Waber further describes how colocated coworkers e-mailed four times as frequently as colleagues in different locations.[9]

Ultimately, beneath the relocated staff's anger was a fear of loss.[10] Although anger and resentment diminish with time, these emotions rose sporadically and sometimes without warning. Each staff member had his or her own trigger points that could rekindle the anger over the relocation. The best antidote to these expressions of loss and fear was communication and participation. Project managers and supervisors were required to practice empathic listening, acknowledge anxious emotions, and redirect staff toward the positive aspects of the move. As Williams and colleagues point out, one cannot overcommunicate decisions, changes, and time frames during a relocation.[11]

At American University, to reduce staff anxiety and deescalate this emotional negativity, the department committed to transparent decision-making. To the extent possible, a rationale would be applied to each decision. Consequently, four principles were established to guide decision-making. First, all decisions would be user-focused. Because meeting the needs of library users is a core value, all decisions regarding the move were designed to focus on the user. Second, since we had a long time to prepare for the move, we initially considered revising our workflows prior to the move. But ultimately we decided that during this period it was more important to minimize disruptions. Only workflow changes critical to the relocation would be made during this period. Third, any new workflows or changed processes would have to be defined in relation to solving an existing problem. We agreed to suspend any experimentation. Fourth, every decision would balance efficiency with quality. As we considered how work would change because of the move, we rejected the notion of perfection in exchange for determining an acceptable rate of error. Ultimately, we wanted to leave unnecessary workflows behind but retain the excellence that was a source of pride for the department.

Despite efforts to create various channels for two-way information flow, communication remained the single biggest challenge throughout the project at American University. Determining how much information to communicate, defining information channels, and maintaining consistent two-way communication flows was a challenge at all levels. Although the library could control internal communication, information from external offices was outside the library's control. At the university level, the project manager position turned over several times. With each new project manager, past decisions needed to be revisited and clarified. This reiteration rekindled relocation-related anxiety. When effective communication was achieved, however, negative emotions diminished and staff felt supported as they entered stage two.

STAGE TWO: THE TRANSITION

As described by Steve Carter, stage two marks the transition from the old to the new and occurs in two parts. In the first part, staff identify and release old ways of working. The second part revolves around imagining and creating new workflows and work habits.[12] As the technical services department at American University identified the activities and workflows affected by the relocation and brainstormed alternative ways to accomplish these tasks, the staff created a new vision for the department. Staff participation in the planning and organizing of the move proved to be the best technique for encouraging and supporting this transition to a new perception of the value of their work and how that work can be completed. Central to enabling this type of transition and for ensuring a successful relocation is having the right people in leadership roles and creating teams that encourage and support staff participation.

Creating Successful Teams

A successful transition requires a team with clearly defined roles, responsibilities, and authority. Team members should be various levels of stakeholders. As Jakubs points out, a relocation like this one needs a project manager who is organized, flexible, skilled with communications and empathic listening, and has authority not just in the library but also in dealing with offices external to the library.[13] Depending on the size of the staff and complexity of the project, the project manager and the department head should work in partnership. The project manager handles the external university communications with architects, space planners, university administrative services units, and so forth. The department head manages the staff who are moving, understands their needs, deals with their concerns, and supports the emotional aspects of the move. Achieving this ideal working relationship is a challenge. The individuals in these roles must share a mutual understanding of their respective contributions to maximize the effectiveness of the team.

At American University, staff concerns centered on a cluster of work-related questions. How is the move going to happen? How will workflow be affected? How will materials be moved between buildings? How will the library continue to provide services to an off-site location? How will technical services maintain communications with other library units? Based on these concerns and mirroring the staff committee structure at Duke University,[14] five teams were created to address a topic of concern. Each team was charged with identifying all issues and stakeholders for a category. As Williams and colleagues point out, staff participation provides a greater sense of control and a vested interest in a successful outcome.[15] Each member of technical services was required to volunteer for a team, and a unit manager was assigned to lead each committee.

The move committee was charged with ensuring a smooth day of move. The committee was required to work with the project manager to develop a process for how the actual move would take place. The committee also was responsible for coordinating the move of community-owned items. They would ensure that all supplies and enough boxes were available for the move. This team also determined which book trucks would move and which would stay.

The workflow committee was charged with reviewing issues surrounding various formats of materials and how they would be handled post-move. For example, the library's media department has special handling requirements in terms of speed. The music library also has complex workflows due to its location and its expensive and unique resources. The committee reviewed workflows for transport of newly ordered print books and journals, materials requiring binding or repair, and special handling needs of rush books and interlibrary loan materials.

Because technical services at the main library is responsible for managing the library's loading dock, including receipt and distribution of all incoming and outgoing packages, the staff were concerned about a smooth transfer of responsibilities after the relocation. Technical services also realized the importance of loading dock management for the successful transfer of library resources from SVB after the relocation. Consequently, a loading dock committee was formed and charged with identifying all issues regarding the loading dock and transportation of library resources at Bender and at SVB. This committee further worked out the details of maintaining inventory control for items in transport.

The administration committee was charged with identifying the administrative needs currently being handled by some other library department that would have to be reassigned or reviewed to accommodate the off-site location. These needs included ordering office supplies, maintaining copiers, and managing building maintenance requests, including problems with furniture, lighting, heat/cooling, and so forth. This team also worked with the technology support desk to determine how problems with computers, software, and telephones would be handled. Of concern was the willingness of staff from other library departments to travel to the off-site location to provide support and services.

The communication and hoteling committee's charge was to develop strategies for maintaining communications with other library units. In addition, technical services staff were fortunate to have provisions made for hoteling workstations in the main library for their use as needed. This committee's tasks included developing a strategy for implementing the hoteling workstations as well as preparing guidelines for managing reservations and equipment for each one.

Each committee was required to prepare a report outlining the issues, concerns, and possible solutions the team had brainstormed. In addition, each committee developed a list of stakeholders for its area of responsibility. This information was used to develop a timeline for the relocation and a schedule of meetings with other departments or stakeholders. From these meetings, departments who believed that the relocation did not affect them, or that it was too soon to discuss the move, suddenly became aware of the impact of the move on their work. Gaps in responsibilities became apparent as services provided by technical services would no longer be possible post-relocation. More importantly, having others engage with technical services in revising workflows and brainstorming solutions created a community of sympathetic partners for technical services staff.

Although there were five staff teams brainstorming problems and solutions, several questions predominated the work of each group. First, how are our current workflows impacted? Second, how will resources and people move between buildings? Third, how can we maintain our connection to the main library? Fourth, is there money to pay for what is needed to make the relocation successful? Each of these broad categories—workflow, transportation, hoteling, and budget—required a holistic, cross-team departmental approach for resolution.

Workflow

A clear understanding of workflows proved critical at various points in the transition stage. Having annual statistics on what moves through the department, how much of each type, how often, and who handles what is useful for a variety of purposes. An analysis of workflow statistics provides the data that explains and justifies space needs to either library or university administration more effectively than a well-worded memo. Knowing the formats, quantities, and frequencies as measures of work, and space required to complete the work, justified shelving needs as well. This data is critical for designing the new space and laying out workstations and shelving units.

In addition to statistical data, visualized workflows can show how people use space to complete their work. At American University, the technical services department used workflow visualizations to justify requesting more than the average amount of space between workstations or between a workstation and a wall. Technical services staff understood that those who work with physical resources (books, print journals, media, scores) require space for book trucks around their workstation. In addition, technical services staff understood that their work is collaborative both between each other and between other library departments. For example, selectors work closely with acquisitions staff to review and confirm new resources. Catalogers work collaboratively with acquisitions staff to resolve bibliographic questions. However, university administrators did not inherently understand this work in the same way, and technical services needed a way to describe their workflows that would illustrate the need for space to move resources from one person to another as well as to enable collaboration.

To visualize workflows we used business process mapping.[16] This technique was developed for use in the corporate world to define what an entity does, who is responsible, and how success is defined. Processing mapping is a mechanism for creating workflow charts using a standardized system of symbols and graphics. Each process is broken down into its component parts, each step in the process is represented symbolically, and a defining line of authority is established between each step. This visualization uncovers problems or inconsistencies in the workflow as well as decision points and bottlenecks.

Process maps can also be used to represent space needs at different points in a workflow. In justifying space requirements to university administration, the process maps visualized the importance of collaboration and the need to move materials along with people. Our goal was to get a large enough space so that we could create areas for working in small groups or conferring with individual colleagues as well as retain private spaces for quiet work. We wanted the university administration to understand how different library resources and responsibilities require different work approaches. We provided several process maps to the university administration that visualized how the workflow requires a certain amount and type of space. As a result, the university provided additional square footage for the department.

Transportation

Along with workflow-related concerns, questions about transporting materials between buildings proved equally stressful for technical services staff. Is there a shuttle for people to travel to the main library? How often does it run? How will the resources move? Will the university provide a truck and a driver? Will the library maintain responsibility for them? Can we use mail services or a library-contracted truck and driver? How will the distance between buildings impact rush deliveries? How many pickups per day?

We reviewed statistics that enumerated the number of new physical pieces completed each day as well as the number of rush requests, and based on that data we decided that we needed two pickups—one in the morning and one in the afternoon. This schedule ensured minimal delays, especially in transporting rush materials. The library purchased special shipping bins that can be closed and fastened to minimize spilling of or damage to the contents. We purchased separate shipping bins for media materials as well as shipping bags for individual items that require special handling. Because of concerns about loss of materials in transit, we developed a system of check-in and checkout of materials in transit in collaboration with the main library.

Although the university initially planned to provide a truck and driver, this decision was reversed due to the expense. Instead, the university added the twice-daily movement of resources to the existing university mail contract. Through this process we learned the importance of identifying and communicating with the appropriate person on campus who has the authority to make decisions. After the move, the contact person who had initially agreed to this arrangement rescinded his approval. Apparently, he was not authorized to make this decision. Instead, the mail services contract needed to be renegotiated, and all mail services were discontinued for two weeks until the new contract was in place. Fortunately this mail delivery complication occurred during the summer when demand for new materials was low. Anxiety about the relocation was temporarily reignited, but staff relaxed again once the problem was resolved.

Hoteling

Relocation planning should also acknowledge that connections with the main library need to be maintained. We were fortunate that space was allocated to technical services in the renovated American University Library's staff area for hoteling. These hoteling workstations enabled technical services to have a place in the main library to work if there was a need to come to the library. Hoteling space also allows technical services to work on various collections projects without having books or resources transported to SVB.

To plan for other hoteling uses, each person identified how they anticipated using the hoteling space. All concerns and desires were considered. Some ideas presented were that it would serve as a place to hold office hours and ETD consultations, work on personal scholarship, complete bindery prep, perform book or bibliographic record error cleanup, catalog partner collections, check stacks, work between meetings in American University Library, or merely get a change of scenery. These discussions uncovered additional costs in terms of computer needs since not all staff have a laptop. Furthermore, the hoteling spaces needed coat racks, locks for personal items, access to printers, and to be stocked with supplies.

The technical services managers came up with some options for how to use this space to retain a presence in the main library and address workflow needs or options. Several scenarios were developed for analyzing how best to accomplish this goal. Four possible scenarios were outlined. The first scenario represented the smallest presence of technical services staff in the main library. The technical services staff would relinquish all responsibilities for the library loading dock, all print materials would be mailed directly to SVB, all bindery prep would be sent to SVB, and staff would sign up for one of four hoteling workstations. The scenario with the greatest presence of technical services staff included all print resources continuing to be delivered to Bender; all receipts, processing, and copy-cataloging would be done in Bender; and technical services staff would be permanently assigned to work in Bender. Ultimately, the decision was determined by the amount of space allocated for hoteling. Because Bender space was maximized for students, technical services was only able to retain four hoteling workstations. Consequently, all materials were mailed directly to SVB and hoteling was reserved for ad hoc use.

Budget

A budget that not only identifies expenditures but also defines responsibility for funding is critical in determining if and how to relocate technical services to a remote location. Even if the university is responsible for providing resources to pay for infrastructure expenses, including all aspects of the facility and facility maintenance, the library should also have an opportunity to review how the funding is allocated and understand what is and is not funded by the university. For our move, American University funded all expenses related to the building's infrastructure and furniture. However, technical services' relocation involved setting up services and facilities in the new space that had been shared in the library. All shared equipment and services had to be replicated, including book trucks and shelves. The implications for the budget were not insignificant.

These new services—transfer of loading dock duties, need for dedicated transportation of resources, hoteling spaces, a staff lounge—all required resources. To alleviate cost concerns, the technical services staff developed a spreadsheet of items that had been purchased collaboratively with others but now needed to be purchased independently. The spreadsheet listed five categories of expenses. Furniture included shelving, receiving room furniture, lockers, shared file cabinets and storage cabinets, bulletin boards, white boards, guest chairs, coat racks, wall clocks, recycling and garbage receptacles, and easels. Transportation costs included totes, dollies, and costs associated with an extra consortial truck stop. Administrative costs included an initial stock of office supplies, extra book trucks, recycling containers, staff lounge items such as a microwave, refrigerator, and sink, and equipment needs—copier, scanner, shredder. IT needs included laptops, headsets for Skype and conference calls, conference room equipment including a monitor, conference call telephone, microphone, white board, and so forth. A separate staff lounge and a conference room large enough to accommodate the entire department were factored into the space requirements and costs, including equipment for teleconferences such as a wall-mounted monitor and a conference phone. Peripheral purchases included white boards, calendars, bulletin boards, and clocks.

The Event: Move Day

Although every library's move day will depend on requirements from the company hired to move the boxes and equipment, several decisions we made enabled us to enjoy a smooth, stress-free day. First, a time was arranged prior to move day for the staff to meet with the moving company to get instructions on how to pack and label boxes and label equipment. Second, staff were assigned responsibility for labeling and preparing all shared equipment, book trucks, and so forth. The shared equipment would move along with each assigned staff member's items. Third, one staff member was responsible for the move out of the building, while a second was responsible for the move into the new space. These two staff members worked with the department head and other senior staff to become well-versed on what was moving and what was staying and to have a clear idea of the planned usage and configuration of the new space. Everyone else was given a day of administrative leave.

STAGE THREE: POST-MOVE

In the third stage of Carter's successful transition management, staff fully embrace the new ways of working. For the technical services staff, however, the transition remains a work in progress. Some of the expected advantages did not materialize for us. For instance, in some cases, individual workspace was diminished, with smaller workstations and no windows or access to natural light. The physical plant is an ongoing challenge in an older building without a dedicated building manager. The technical services staff also remain acutely aware of the challenges of being in a remote location. Not only do they continue to worry that being out of sight means they are out of mind, but the librarians and other staff who remain at Bender must also transition to including SVB staff when planning meetings, events, and other activities.

The transition management process, however, illustrated that important aspects of the relocation are fully under our control. The staff have embraced and refined new procedures that allow them to retain pride in their work. In establishing new workflows to replace old processes, the transition enabled us to identify and affirmatively state our work values. Most importantly, our department has realized that we can control the culture for the new space. These values include a commitment to maintain a high standard of quality in our work, to appreciate and respect our work relationships, and to create a work culture that enables us to achieve goals that reflect these values. Rather than perceiving the relocation as a change that disrupts and creates obstacles to getting the work done, the relocation enabled us to rewrite our workflows and create a new work culture. This successful transformation would not be possible without addressing the emotional and psychological aspects of the relocation.

LESSONS LEARNED

The technical services department at American University learned several critical lessons through our relocation project. First, open, iterative, and regular communication is critical to the success of a relocation and to dealing effectively with the inevitable anxiety and fears a relocation like this generates. University and library administration must be willing to listen to concerns and share information, while keeping in mind that varied communication tools are required to accommodate the different ways people process and understand information. The entire library should be brought together to support the relocating department. Library colleagues can become allies not only in dealing with the emotions related to the move but also in brainstorming solutions.

Second, good planning and organization is imperative. Roles for team members should be clearly defined and the leadership team empowered to make decisions. Staff participation in planning is critical for a successful transition.

Finally, acknowledging the sense of loss and disruption as well as addressing anxiety and fears will further diminish staff resistance. Empathic listening and leadership enable staff to transition to a new identity and work culture that leverages the benefits of the move. Ultimately, success is measured by the group's ability to replace old ways of working with new workflows, policies, and work culture.

FURTHER RESEARCH NEEDED

Although initial work to address the psychological impact of a technical services relocation has been conducted, further research is needed to understand the full implications for the workforce and the work product. As McGurr concludes from her survey's respondents, "no matter how content respondents were with their current situation, overall, they still thought a central location was best."[17] Library administrators need to understand the opportunity costs inherent in maintaining a suboptimal physical environment. If an off-site location makes collaboration more difficult, what is the impact on library innovation? If employees in a remote location feel isolated and disengaged, what is the impact on library services?

In contrast, libraries such as Georgia Tech embrace a contrasting vision and priority: "Only by physically housing the Library's employees in one building is the Library able to provide one-stop shop support, turning internal efficiency into more effective deployment of services and greater productivity and improved practices of the Georgia Tech community as a whole."[18]

In reimaging libraries to meet the evolving and expanding needs of library users, various approaches to library design must be studied and analyzed to make the best decisions for the future. An area of further research is whether the size of the library and its academic institution impacts staff perception of an off-site move. Are staff in smaller libraries impacted to a greater degree than staff in larger libraries? Does the number of staff moved make a difference? Does moving more than one department lessen the impact?

CONCLUSION

Moving technical services to an off-site location is a pragmatic solution to the space problem faced by many libraries. This relocation can be implemented with the appropriate project management tools and skills; however its success depends on a strong commitment to understanding and addressing the psychological aspects of a relocation.

NOTES

1. Mahlon Apgar, IV, "The Alternative Workplace: Changing Where and How People Work," *Harvard Business Review* (May–June 1998):

135, https://hbr.org/1998/05/the-alternative-workplace-changing -where-and-how-people-work.

2. Apgar, "The Alternative Workplace," 135.

3. Lihong Zhu, "The Physical Office Environment in Technical Services in ARL Libraries," *Library Collections, Acquisitions & Technical Services* 37, no. 1–2, 54, https://doi.org/10.1016/j.lcats.2013.09.001.

4. Deborah Jakubs, "Technical Services on the Move" (fall 2007 membership meeting presentation slides, New Orleans, LA, November 27, 2007), 15.

5. Priscilla R. Williams et al., "Relocation or Dislocation: Optimizing Change in Technical Services," *Technical Services Quarterly* 20, no. 1 (2002): 24, https://doi.org/10.1300/J124v20n01_02.

6. Melanie J. McGurr, "Remote Locations for Technical Services: An Exploratory Survey," *Technical Services Quarterly* 28, no. 3 (2011): 293–97, https://doi.org/10.1080/07317131.2011.571596.

7. Steve Carter, "Office Relocation: Managing People in a Workplace Transition," *Work Design Magazine*, August 26, 2013, accessed December 21, 2017, https://workdesign.com/2013/are-you-managing -change-or-managing-transition/.

8. Ibid.

9. Ben Waber, Jennifer Magnolfi, and Greg Lindsay, "Workspaces That Move People," *Harvard Business Review* 92, no. 10 (2014): 73, https://hbr.org/2014/10/workspaces-that-move-people.

10. Carter, "Office Relocation."

11. Williams et al., "Relocation," 24.

12. Carter, "Office Relocation," 3.

13. Jakubs, "Technical Services," 5.

14. Ibid., 8.

15. Williams et al., "Relocation," 14.

16. Dina Tbaishat, "Using Business Process Modelling to Examine Academic Library Activities for Periodicals," *Library Management* 31, no. 7 (2010): 484, https://doi.org/10.1108/01435121011071184.

17. McGurr, "Remote Locations," 296.

18. Charlie Bennett et al., Reimaging the Georgia Tech Library, Georgia Tech Library, 2014, accessed December 21, 2017, https://smartech .gatech.edu/bitstream/handle/1853/51712/reimagining_the_georgia _tech_library_1.pdf.

CHAPTER 12

Building an Infrastructure: Integrating Access and Technical Services for Improved Service Quality Utilizing a Supply Chain Model

Karen Glover, Elizabeth Winter, and Emy Nelson Decker

ABSTRACT

This chapter explores the philosophy and vision behind the Library Next initiative (the Georgia Tech Library renewal project) and its impact on services and describes the ways in which service quality has been improved upon by using a supply chain model that encompasses both the internal library infrastructure (formerly access and technical services) and the point of delivery (known as the Library Store). It will trace the steps taken to transfer processing tasks (traditionally performed by access services) from the public-facing Library Store to the supporting infrastructure unit to create an environment of efficiency and improved customer service. The innovations discussed in this chapter offer an exciting possibility and a potential roadmap for institutions wishing to undertake a similar approach to the changing academic library environment.

INTRODUCTION

The Georgia Institute of Technology (Georgia Tech) is a STEM-focused four-year public university that has just under 30,000 students enrolled and is a member of the University System of Georgia. The Georgia Tech Library, which has around 90 faculty and staff members, has recently looked to effective business practices to help support the

Library Next initiative. Library Next encompasses a complete renovation of the library's physical spaces and a reimagining of the services housed therein, designed to meet and exceed the needs of the 21st-century library user. In addition to exploring practices such as Lean Six Sigma, the library has worked to implement a supply chain model toward goals of improved processes and efficiency and enhanced customer service.

Decreases in print book circulation, the dizzying increase in electronic formats of scholarly resources, budget constraints, and changing views and roles of libraries and librarians have imperiled the traditional roles of access services and technical services positions in academic libraries. Recognizing these changes, the Georgia Tech Library saw an opportunity to reenvision library workflows to create a more streamlined library user experience and more efficient delivery of library resources and services to the Georgia Tech user community. In addition, by realizing that even as print needs decrease, the skills, abilities, and knowledge sets of librarians and staff are transferrable and can be enhanced as service and support roles to facilitate the new mission and goals of the 21st-century library.

This chapter will explore the philosophy and vision behind the Library Next initiative (the Georgia Tech Library renewal project) and its impact on services and describe the ways in which service quality has been improved using a supply chain model that encompasses both the internal library infrastructure (formerly access and technical services) and the point of delivery (the Library Store). It will trace the steps taken to transfer processing tasks traditionally performed by access services from the public-facing Library Store to the supporting infrastructure unit to create an environment of efficiency and improved customer service. The innovations discussed here offer an exciting possibility and roadmap for institutions wishing to undertake a similar new approach to the changing academic library environment.

LIBRARY NEXT

Library Next is in support of the mission to "define the technological research library of the 21st century" and encompasses many different projects, but it is centrally driven by the overwhelming demand for electronic resources and research solutions and is fueled by the dramatic decline of overall print circulations. Library Next initially started as the Library 2020 Plan. The 2020 Plan was the primary tool used to convince campus leaders that a complete renovation of the two adjoining library buildings (Price Gilbert Library, 1953, and Crosland Tower, 1968) was not only necessary because of very out-dated facilities, health and safety concerns, and a too-small power grid but also a great opportunity to clean out the space and make room for new services and programs that support a leading research university. The hope was to set an example for what a modern research library could become without the constraints of managing physical collections. The foundation for the 2020 Plan revolved around three key drivers: moving the physical collections off-site, a full renovation of the two library buildings, and introducing new services while also changing traditional library service models. All three initiatives are interdependent and happening in tandem but rely on the ability to move physical collections off-site while still maintaining the highest level of service and quality.

To maintain that high level of service delivery, it became necessary to look outside the Georgia Tech community and take advantage of collaborative partnerships. Georgia Tech and Emory University have engaged in collaborative efforts throughout the years, particularly in joint programs in biomedical engineering. New campus leadership at both institutions afforded the opportunity to enhance the relation-ship between the two institutions and the collaboration between the libraries became a shared collection initiative. The Georgia Tech and Emory Libraries are a perfect pairing; their areas of focus complement each other nicely. The collaboration also represents a unique initiative between a public (Georgia Tech) and a private (Emory) university. Georgia Tech's collection is heavy in the engineering and sciences while Emory houses a vast collection in the humanities and medicine. Both institutions can supplement their own collections in the areas in which they are the weakest. This allows them to continue to use their financial resources on collections that are the most appropriate to their academic disciplines while still being able to supply the needed resources to other areas of interest and research for their campus. The collaboration enhanced an already existing partnership between the two libraries to allow equal access to physical materials from both institutions and paved the way for future electronic access collaborations. Georgia Tech and Emory had a shared interest in an off-site facility and the symbiotic relationship would afford the opportunity to implement access initiatives between the two libraries.

THE LIBRARY SERVICE CENTER

The library service center (LSC) opened in the spring of 2016 and is jointly owned and managed by Georgia Tech and Emory. The LSC is a state-of-the-art high-density storage facility that houses about 2,000,000 items. It has capacity for 4,000,000 volumes and room to add another module when necessary, and it is climate controlled with the goal of long-term preservation in mind. The LSC houses archival collections as well as circulating collections from both institutions. Emory contributed items previously housed in a separate storage location to the LSC and consider these items low-use, while Georgia Tech took a more dramatic approach and relocated over 95% of its overall circulating collection. Housing such a large percentage of the collection off-site created many challenges for Georgia Tech; there was not only the need to deliver items to users in a timely manner but also the need to change the processing and management of physical materials. To make it even more challenging, the Georgia Tech Library migrated to a new library management system mere months before ingesting materials into the new facility. Emory also migrated to the same library management system—in advance of Georgia Tech—which afforded both institutions the technology to support the shared access to the collections for the respective user groups. However, implementing so many new programs in unison and in such a short amount of time made it difficult to set standard work procedures and meet high data standards, particularly in technical services.

LIBRARY RENEWAL

In 2013 a design plan was approved for Crosland Tower to be completed in 2019 and Price Gilbert Library by 2020. Crosland Tower

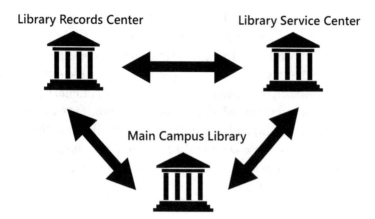

Figure 12.1 Supply chain.

originally held most the library's physical collections and closed in 2016 to prepare for the move of the collections to the LSC. Technical services, librarian offices, and administrative offices also resided in Crosland Tower and, with very little space in the Price Gilbert building, it was necessary to look outside the library for workspaces. The subject librarians and administrators were relocated temporarily to spaces on campus while technical services were relocated to a facility off-site but near campus. This facility, known as the library records center (LRC), already housed campus records as well as some pre-1980 journal holdings. The warehouse was renovated with funds provided by the institute to include an open office workspace for technical services and records management, as well as meeting spaces and offices for librarians and managers. This created an interesting dichotomy for the library, with a physical distance between three locations with units that must work together to meet the customers' needs. This relationship between the locations is now referred to as the supply chain, as shown in figure 12.1.

SUPPLY CHAIN

The supply chain refers to the process of meeting customer demands through cross-training, collaboration, and continuous process improvement across all library locations. Before a transition to the supply chain service model could be achieved, though, the services performed in public areas of the main library needed to be reinvented and enhanced; while services considered to be processing needed to be moved to the LRC, the LSC, or logistics within in the main library. Those processes or, what many would consider traditional library services, were moved either off-site or out of the public eye to highlight more of the nontraditional and innovative programs that the library provides. In effect, these actions put more emphasis on research and learning support and less on more transactional tasks.

NEW SERVICES

This repositioning of traditional library services granted the opportunity to make room for new services and, with the help of a consulting firm, several new programs were envisioned in conjunction with both renovated spaces and the reinvention of current services. This is particularly true with the change from the library services desk to the Library Store. In preparation for the future openings of the renovated buildings, pilot projects and endeavors in areas such as visualization, innovation and ideation, and digital scholarship are already in the design and implementation phases. All of these services and projects make up the library's portfolio and, with the help of a portfolio manager, a systematic approach to managing projects was adopted using Lean Six Sigma principles. Lean Six Sigma is a way of leveraging teamwork to improve performance by removing waste and lessening variation in methodology. Included in the portfolio are projects related to the supply chain, Library Store, and continuous process improvement. While significant progress has been made toward our changing service models, continuous change is understood as being the new standard for operations.

SUPPLY CHAIN AND INFRASTRUCTURE

As part of Georgia Tech Library's Library Next initiative, redefining the way that work in technical and support service areas takes place is a critical goal and a cornerstone of the plan for how the library will conduct business in the coming years. This will better enable the delivery of scholarly content to users in all locations and improve the efficiency of these internal operations.

The library has undertaken a multi-phased series of projects to transform technical services, access services, and support services into the library infrastructure supply chain. The Library Next portfolio management process has provided the project management tools, processes, and empowerment needed to move these plans to fruition. The new operational model for the infrastructure is built on the following key elements.

- Unify processes and staff from seven formerly separate work units to maximize efficiency. Library functional areas include acquisitions, electronic resource management, cataloging, interlibrary loan, course reserves, archives support, account management, scholarly communication services, and records management.
- Seek to enhance service, with customer satisfaction as a key performance indicator.
- Develop standard work to ensure bench strength and prevent single-point failures.
- Continuously improve operations for better customer service and efficiency.
- Work collaboratively with other parts of the library and the Georgia Tech-Emory LSC to ensure deliveries of library materials and services on time and with high quality.
- Improve transparency and accountability in staffing, work processes, communication, and productivity.
- Learn from challenges and mistakes.
- Celebrate and build on successes.
- Focus on the future and embrace innovation to define the research library of the 21st century.

The first phase of the infrastructure supply chain project, undertaken in 2015–2016, sought to understand the current state for all library support and technical services processes. Working with an external business process consultant, project leaders conducted in-depth interviews with nearly 50 library employees to document their work processes. Processes were then mapped with Microsoft Visio to allow us to better understand and represent them visually. By reviewing the detailed process maps and considering the processes comprehensively, similarities among work emerged, as did the knowledge required to complete it. Opportunities for reducing redundancies and inefficiencies within and between the various processes began to appear as well. Using a supply chain model, subject matter experts in each functional area worked together to craft a set of more unified processes, representing a draft future state.

During the summer 2016 project phase, participants revised the future state processes draft and created deliverables toward defining a staffing model aimed at bench strength, with staff cross-trained to work in multiple functional areas (acquisitions, cataloging, electronic resources, interlibrary loan, archives support, records management, and institutional repository support) for efficiency. A team of subject matter experts from the various functional areas worked together to develop checklists of tasks and skills needed to perform the work in all functional areas, in service of gaining a fuller picture of what a comprehensive cross-training plan might look like. All impacted staff then performed a baseline self-assessment to report their individual competency levels vis-à-vis these tasks and skills. This enabled the unique mix of areas of strength and areas in which to focus cross-training efforts to come into scope (for example, training cataloging staff on electronic resource management and interlibrary loan).

Concurrently in 2016, another Library Next portfolio project enabled the renovation of 3,500-plus square feet of off-site space at the LRC and provided a new work environment for the library infrastructure team. At a cost of $1.4 million and with significant support from the institute, the library completed the LRC construction project in fall 2016. Staff moved in September 2016 and have been enjoying the state-of-the-art, flexible open workspace conducive to agile and innovative operations of the library supply chain. As with any organizational change and major relocation, there existed significant apprehension among impacted staff. The project team made every effort to communicate plans and update the team as changes in timeline and details took place. Library leadership provided support for morale with library-wide mindfulness training, and departmental leadership offered a resilience workshop to facilitate candid discussion about managing change and coping with uncertainty.

After the physical move, during the third phase of the project (fall 2016 through spring 2017), the project team refined the future state process maps, documented new staff roles and responsibilities, and developed standardized procedures and work instructions as a foundation for the transition to the library infrastructure supply chain. Requirements for a comprehensive technology solution to enable management of workflows, fulfillment of customer requests, allocation of resources, and tracking of service and success metrics came into focus during this time as well.

The subsequent phase of the project (completed in fall 2017) was focused on training and implementation. This phase involved finalizing standard work, creating training materials, and training staff on the knowledge and skills needed to work across all functional areas. This is where the investment of significant efforts paid off as the new operational model came into play. Goals for this phase were to have the process efficiencies implemented and to have all staff cross-trained and beginning to work within the new model.

The library's infrastructure team, responsible for the technical and support services described above, were working actively to become as a single team. The commitment was to ensure that each employee owned responsibility for successful delivery of services to Georgia Tech Library users and the Georgia Tech community. With the implementation of the infrastructure supply chain plans came the recognition of the significant amount of progress already made. Considered as a checklist, the following steps have been completed. Processes and skills sets have been analyzed and documented. New roles and standard work for each role and process (for example, how to efficiently unify the intake, triage, customer interaction, and fulfillment of requests for everything from a new e-book purchase to an interlibrary loan to a review of specific campus records) are in place. Workspaces that inspire efficiency and innovation have come to fruition. A training model that will build bench strength and overall knowledge continues to grow and evolve.

Beyond fall 2017, the goals are to capture metrics to monitor and assess process improvements against established key performance indicators, move forward with continuous improvement to refine work processes, implement a technology solution to manage the infrastructure supply chain service model, and identify new library services that the team can support. The Georgia Tech community and leadership have given feedback in a variety of forums, confirming this direction and this path toward improved productivity, efficiency, and customer service through the infrastructure supply chain.

THE LIBRARY STORE—THE PHYSICAL POINT OF FULFILLMENT

The Library Next initiative also includes a services program, which is subdivided into three equal parts. Within the enticement and inspiration services section of the program resides the project for the creation and development of the Library Store. In the supply chain model employed by the Georgia Tech Library, the Library Store is the user's point of final fulfillment. In other words, this is the place where a user would expect to retrieve an interlibrary loan book, borrow a reserve book, try out a technology gadget, and ask a staff member for assistance, as well as the place for other traditional circulation-related activities. The store evolved directly from the services traditionally performed in the public services department, in the access services department, and at the library services desk area. The Library Store, which is currently in its beta test phase, is in the pre-renovated Price Gilbert Library building. Once the building renovations are complete, the store area will span a space about the size of a football field between the two buildings that make up the Georgia Tech Library: Price-Gilbert and Crosland Tower. The store represents a new way of meeting and exceeding user needs; it is a space reimagined to address changing user needs and to efficiently serve as the place of fulfillment for circulating items.

As the contemporary academic library on most campuses experiences pressures from other venues such as the student center and even local or on-campus coffee shops, the Library Store redoubled its efforts to emphasize the contributions of expert staff. While other venues may boast attractive study spaces, the Library Store offers a forthcoming physical space renovation and, more importantly, the undivided attention of expert staff. The ethos of Library Next requires a steadfast commitment to bolstering those elements that set the library apart from other potential venues and emphasizing the expertise of library staff.

Members of the public services department staff the Library Store. While some of them possess MLIS degrees, all of them are classified as library staff. Subject liaison librarians are classified as faculty and belong to the campus engagement and scholarly outreach department. Librarians are available for consultation on an appointment basis. There are 18 full time-staff members in the public services department, 9 to 11 part-time student workers (depending upon the semester), and the Library Store is open 24 hours a day, 7 days per week. The Library Store area previously housed the library services desk. In May 2017, the library undertook a project to remove the desk as it was understood, through qualitative student feedback, to sometimes thwart student engagement with library staff. The desk, which some users perceived as being a physical and relational barrier, often deterred them from approaching staff. By removing the desk, this barrier to communication would also be theoretically removed.

The desk removal was a major change, and some members of the public services team felt some trepidation in seeing it disappear. To prepare for this change, public services staff members started developing their roving mobile customer service model as early as May 2016. Roving staff offer excellent customer service by proactively engaging users in their place of need on the multiple floors of the Price Gilbert Library. While other academic institutions have used a hybridized model of roving that includes a library services desk in addition to roving staff, the Georgia Tech Library uses only a roving model. Roving staff at the Georgia Tech Library have had the opportunity to customize roving to fit their users' needs. During the year May 2016 to May 2017, public services staff used Microsoft Surface tablets, carried a GT-labeled satchel and wore name badges to identify them as rovers, and made their way through the four floors of the Price Gilbert Library to engage users and perfect their own methods of offering this mobile customer service. Efficacy of roving is assessed via a brief survey that rovers present to users to complete on their Surface tablets after an interaction with a user. Students qualitatively report that they enjoy having staff come to them instead of having to pack their belongings and walk down to the first floor desk when they have a question, like they did prior to the roving service.

Now with the desk removed and roving staff working around the 24-hour clock, activities in the public services department include time spent assisting users in the Library Store area, answering virtual service inquiries from chat and email and answering phone calls, and spending time roving on the upper floors of the library. All these activities are customer service oriented and are based on the actions of requests for fulfillment. There is no longer any processing work that takes place in the public services department under the Library Store paradigm.

Prior to the creation of the Library Store, with its focus on customer service, the public services department was responsible for numerous processing tasks. The processing of interlibrary loan books and the scanning of sections of requested books historically took place in the department and was assigned to the third shift (overnight) staff when foot traffic to the library services desk was at a low ebb. Also, DVDs were inspected for their condition and updated in the catalog accordingly. The dean of the library wanted a complete separation between the processing side of operations and the fulfillment, or in this case customer service, activities, so these processing operations moved to the LSC and/or LRC as required by the action.

These tasks, traditionally undertaken by public services staff, were moved to the infrastructure side of the Library Next operation. As is understandable, these changes caused stress for some members of the public services team. Several of these individuals had worked in the department for upward of 20 years, and these changes ushered in concerns of job sustainability for them. Also, while processing tasks are not always thought of as being exciting work given their repetitive nature, other people understand it as satisfying work with clearly defined and measurable outcomes. For example, statistics capture the number of items processed more clearly than one can evaluate the efficacy of a customer service interaction. This aspect also gave rise to concerns about how job performance would be evaluated under the new Library Store paradigm.

To combat the uncertainty about new roles in the store that did not include processing, management took steps to train public services team members in the fine art of offering excellent customer service. Members of the team who had previous experience working in retail provided information about working the room. Strategies such as walking figure eight–shaped paths on the upper floors of the library to catch the eye of a user in need helped team members frame what they needed to do while roving. Georgia Tech's human resources department offered formal, free-of-charge training on the tenets of excellent customer service. As staff members developed their own strategies for roving, they gave demonstrations to their fellow team members to create a veritable repository of roving tips and tricks that would eventually be codified into a work instruction document as part of the Library Next portfolio.

Understandably, once the library services desk was removed and the roving method of customer service was in full swing, several staff members decided to leave their positions because they determined that this was no longer a library environment that they recognized. Interestingly, new candidates for these open positions were increasingly evaluated—and often selected—based upon their previous customer service experience. This new hiring criteria represented a strict departure from the library experience the previous generation of staff would have been sought and hired for having. Changing needs in the supply chain and, specifically, at the point of fulfillment required these different skill sets of new team members. Outgoing, engaging, almost salesperson-like personalities often provide the best customer service within the store and with roving.

During the summer of 2017, the Library Store received its first shipment of furniture, understood to be a beta test for what the area required. While it was necessary to have some type of seating options in the store area, traditional chairs were not necessarily the most appropriate choice. Stools and more perch-like seating options allowed store staff to catch a break for their legs. Not having traditional chairs also encouraged the upright, greeter-type stance desired for Library Store staff. Another consideration was that the store needed to avoid furniture that would come across as barrier-like, while still providing staff the support they needed for their work-related accessories. Library Store staff needed a place to set their Surface tablets, book scanners, and general office supplies. The furniture addition further promoted the customer service experience for users in the store and was used to determine what would be best for the future version of the Library Store in the renovated Price Gilbert building.

CONCLUSION

The academic library will continue to need to adapt to meet the changing needs of users. The Georgia Tech Library has experienced success by borrowing from the business world and bridging processes such as project management and the supply chain. In so doing, it has paved the way for an enhanced understanding of customer service: one that is measurable, trackable, and adaptable enough to provide a clear vision for access and technical services in the current epoch of the academic library. This model offers one method of approaching the change by reinventing, reimagining, and ultimately recreating the way in which the library offers service to its users. While the supply chain model has not been without its difficulties, this method has, by and large, resulted in an enhanced user experience at the Georgia Tech Library. For example, despite the volumes being housed off-site, users receive their requested materials within a 24-hour period. It is rare indeed that an item is misplaced or delayed even with the vagaries of physical transportation (weather, traffic, etc.). Many staff members in the public services department have benefited from the roving model, and some even track their steps with Fitbits and other such fitness devices. This, too, was an unintended and fun consequence of our roving model of customer service. The supply chain model at the Georgia Tech Library is still in its infancy despite many years of planning and beta testing. Assessment is critical to improved service and will continue to inform and shape the destiny of the future as we move forward.

CHALLENGE FOUR

Staffing Technical Services

CHAPTER 13

Diversity, Inclusion, and Social Justice in Library Technical Services

Rhonda Y. Kauffman and Martina S. Anderson

ABSTRACT

The Massachusetts Institute of Technology (MIT) Libraries recently embraced a large-scale initiative to incorporate the values of diversity, inclusion, and social justice (DISJ) into library practices. In early 2017, the MIT collections directorate task force on DISJ released a report with recommendations for embedding DISJ values into the daily work of archives, technical services, preservation, scholarly communications, and collections strategy staff. This chapter focuses on the challenges and opportunities in undertaking a sustained effort to achieve DISJ specifically within technical services. The authors highlight how technical services staff can use their unique position within libraries to dismantle existing structures of inequity and privilege by providing access to information and shifting resources to underrepresented groups. This chapter presents the historical context of DISJ within the library profession and the MIT Libraries, discusses implications of this paradigm shift for library technical services departments, and presents cataloging and acquisitions job profiles to help readers envision the practical significance for library staff of the imperative to incorporate DISJ values into the regular practice of their work.

INTRODUCTION

The values of DISJ are widely embraced among members of the library profession. Indeed, in our current context, it is not particularly controversial among library professionals to assert that libraries should play a role among other social institutions in ensuring that all members of our communities have opportunities for full participation in society.[1] At the same time, it can be challenging for some people working in libraries to envision precisely how their daily work activities within libraries must change if these values are to be fully realized. That challenge is especially acute for technical services professionals, for whom job competence is generally measured through the lens of values such as productivity and efficiency.

The purpose of this chapter is to address this challenge directly by discussing in concrete terms how the jobs of technical services library staff can be described and undertaken to ensure that DISJ values are consistently advanced by libraries and library staff of all kinds. We begin by providing accounts of two contexts that together create the backdrop for this conversation: how the library profession has responded to questions of DISJ in a society long characterized by inequality and discrimination and how one library, the MIT Libraries, is seeking to remake itself to support DISJ. We then turn to a specific discussion of the role of technical services library staff in advancing DISJ. We lay the foundation for that discussion by presenting three job descriptions for standard technical services roles and then offering suggestions for how these staff members can support the library's DISJ mission through their job activities. Our central purpose is to enable library workers to engage in focused, practical discussions of how to move DISJ forward by enlisting the capacities of everyone working in libraries.

BACKGROUND

Discussions of DISJ in libraries are often met with confusion. Libraries are often considered sites of intellectual freedom in which the equal dignity of all is recognized and in which the right of all people to find the information they want and need according to their own judgment is enabled by library workers. After all, the mission of the American Library Association (ALA) is "to enhance learning and ensure access to information for all,"[2] and ALA articulates the core values of librarianship as "access, confidentiality/privacy, democracy, diversity, education and lifelong learning, intellectual freedom, preservation, the public good, professionalism, service, social responsibility, and sustainability."[3] Like so many institutions in the United States, however, libraries and the library profession have a complex history with respect to diversity, equity, and inclusion.[4] Idealized visions of the library profession's altruism[5] tend to mask the library's role in reproducing and perpetuating dominant social structures that affect people in unequal ways based on their race, gender, religion, sexual orientation, gender expression, class, and ability.[6] As ShinJoung Yeo and James R. Jacobs argue, "Despite the dominant notion that librarianship at its core is neutral . . . the library as a social, educational and cultural institution has never been isolated from its political and social climate or historical context."[7]

As in so many contexts, moving the library profession forward requires looking back in order to participate fully in a trajectory of change. That backward look reveals that while attention to issues of equity and inclusion is on the rise in the library profession (as evidenced by the recent adoption and/or reaffirmation of diversity and inclusion statements by many library professional organizations[8]), we are nonetheless still engaged in a process of overcoming systemic inequities. It is no secret that "[the] librarian profession suffers from a persistent lack of racial and ethnic diversity that shows few signs of abating."[9] In 2017, the U.S. Department of Labor's Bureau of Labor Statistics reported that 86.3%[10] of librarians were not Hispanic or Latino whites (compared with 60.7% of the U.S. population[11]), with 6.4% of librarians black or African American, 10.4% Hispanic or Latino, and 5.2% Asian.[12] In 2019, the percentage of librarians who were not Hispanic or Latino whites increased to 87.8%, with 6% of librarians black or African American, 9.8 % Hispanic or Latino, and 3.2% Asian.[13] The reasons for this persistence of whiteness in the library profession are myriad and not straightforward, but reckoning with the present necessitates honest accounting of the past. For example, ALA tolerated segregated state associations that denied membership to African American librarians until 1964.[14] Consider, also, that in 1977, the ALA's Intellectual Freedom Committee recommended rescinding a resolution to combat racism and sexism in the profession, which had passed unanimously during the 1976 centennial conference, because, in the view of committee members, it conflicted with the Library Bill of

Rights. (It was not withdrawn.)[15] Much more recently, differing opinions and reactions from libraries regarding the Black Lives Matter movement demonstrate a continued struggle with issues of racial injustice within librarianship.[16]

How does the library profession's history affect day-to-day activities in the present? Although it may be difficult to attribute specific phenomena in the present to legacies of the past, those legacies shine through as reminders that they have always been there. For example, Library of Congress classification reflects historical and socially embedded structures of privilege and power.[17] In the D class for World History in the LC Classification Outline, Western history consists of classes D through DR, with entire subclasses of DA, DD, and DF allotted to Great Britain, Germany, and Greece, respectively, while the entire continents of Africa and Asia (more than 100 countries altogether) are represented only by DS and DT, respectively. The way library resources are categorized communicates biases—or those of our predecessors that we continue to tolerate—to users, and it limits the accessibility of information. Similar unconscious or unrecognized biases affect how vendors categorize books, how selectors evaluate new resources, and how library staff decide to acquire or retain specific materials.[18] Challenging such embedded inequality requires actively reenvisioning our work in the present and future.

LOCAL CONTEXT

The following section provides a closer look at the MIT community and the MIT Libraries. The MIT student population is made up of 11,520 students (4,530 or 39% undergraduates and 6,990 or 61% graduate students). Forty-seven percent (47%) of undergraduate students are women, and 51% are members of U.S. minority groups. Thirty-six percent (36%) of graduate students are women, and 19% are members of U.S. minority groups. Of international students, 3,331 are enrolled in degree programs, including 10% of undergraduate students and 41% of graduate students, with 53% of international students coming from Asia.[19]

More than 12,800 faculty and staff support the MIT community, including 2,015 teaching staff.[20] The MIT Libraries employs 91 FTE (full-time equivalent) professional staff, 66 FTE support staff, and 15 student assistants.

The MIT Libraries holds 2.2 million print volumes across five libraries (humanities and sciences, engineering, architecture and planning, management and social sciences, and music), the archives and special collections, and off-site storage facilities. The MIT Libraries' structure consists of three directorates: research and learning, digital library services, and collections. The MIT Libraries' technical services department is part of the collections directorate.

The MIT Libraries recently refocused its vision and mission toward one committed to the values of DISJ. At the forefront of this initiative was the work of MIT Libraries associate director for collections Gregory Eow in his sponsorship of the MIT collections directorate DISJ task force in 2016.[21] The task force, comprising members from all departments (acquisitions, cataloging, preservation, digital collections and reformatting, archives, scholarly communications, and collections strategy) and professional levels within the collections directorate, authored a 30-page white paper examining themes related to and making recommendations for incorporating DISJ values into the daily work of library staff.[22] Eow initiated the task force shortly after his arrival at the MIT Libraries to foreground his leadership priorities. He stated, "By structuring the task force the way we did—including many functional areas, bringing together librarians and archivists, administrative and support staff, my intention was to signal that we as an entire collections directorate would work together to advance DISJ values."[23] The intentional inclusion of social justice within the framework of the report is particularly worth noting. Whereas previous discussions within the MIT Libraries and more broadly at MIT had focused on issues of diversity and inclusion, the task force saw a necessity in identifying, confronting, and working to dismantle the systemic structures of inequity within which libraries and archives and librarians and archivists operate, while still embracing the values upon which the profession is built. Eow said, "I believe the term 'social justice' emboldens librarians and archivists to revisit their professional first principles and values (democracy, access, public good) and to fight for them."[24]

The MIT Libraries' director, Chris Bourg, is also a strong advocate for the advancement of social justice values. The task force used the following quotation from an article co-written by Bourg to guide its work: "[The] future of academic libraries [is] where librarians confront and creatively address the lack of racial and ethnic diversity within our profession and actively pursue a social justice agenda within our libraries and in the communities we serve. This future requires that we acknowledge that many of our current practices reinforce existing structures of inequity and privilege, and that we leverage our services and resources to support, document, and encourage diversity and social justice efforts within librarianship and society."[25]

To inform their work, task force members conducted literature reviews, interviewed staff, and held forums for all collections directorate staff. With an understanding of the issues in the contexts of both the global scholarly realm and the local community, the task force developed the following definitions. Each definition builds on and sharpens the previous one; they should be considered always in relation to one another; focusing on any one of them without considering the others does not fully account for the societal and institutional dimensions of these issues.

- **Diversity** simply means difference. It is the heterogeneity found in the composition of the workforce, our collections, and community.
- **Inclusion** means creating and actively sustaining an organization and community in which all can participate fully, be respected, and be treated in an equitable manner.
- **Social justice** is a commitment to recognizing, addressing, and correcting systemic power imbalances that privilege one group at the expense of another. It is based on the premise that all people are of equal and incalculable value. The work of social justice includes individual and collective action to disrupt the patterns and structures of power in our community, organization, culture, and society.[26]

These definitions were subsequently adopted by an MIT Libraries-wide task force that created a resource manual to support a new required component of the annual performance review that sets staff goals that demonstrate organizational values of diversity and inclusion. The *DISJ Resource Manual for MIT Libraries Staff* acknowledges historical, systemic imbalances and urges staff to work to dismantle these structures, empowering staff across the MIT Libraries to embrace these values: "DISJ should be a focus throughout the library—in every department, at every level, pertinent to every job and every staff member. DISJ is a core part of the MIT Libraries' mission—not an 'add-on' to what we already do—but an essential part of every job. To change systemic imbalances and honor the various voices in our community, we must work together collectively."[27]

At the beginning of the 2017–2018 academic year, the MIT Libraries adopted new vision, mission, and values statements that specifically affirm our commitment to these values: "The MIT Libraries aspires to advance knowledge by providing a trusted foundation for the generation, dissemination, use, creative engagement with, and preservation of information, in support of the MIT mission and so that it can be brought to bear on the world's great challenges and in the cause of social justice" and specifies a value in which "MIT Libraries contribute to a better world . . . by pursuing social justice and an ethic of care."[28]

APPLYING THE DISJ FRAMEWORK TO TECHNICAL SERVICES

While the foregoing statements from MIT Libraries are impactful and visionary, they are also broad and abstract. Because the connections between broad values and practical work are not always evident, technical services staff may reject the idea that their daily work relates to the lofty mission and values of the library profession. Working in a production-oriented, behind-the-scenes environment, technical services staff can have difficulty seeing how their work is impacted by and has an impact on DISJ issues.

We resist the notion that visionary big picture thinking has little to do with the practical day-to-day activities of staff working in technical services. It is this context that led us to seek to provide concrete examples for how technical services staff can apply these visionary ideas to their daily job activities. This application is crucial if we are to advance real change. As the earlier example of biases embedded in Library of Congress classifications suggests, we are often unaware, as we implement systems and processes, of our role in reinforcing or reproducing privilege and inequality. Embracing a DISJ mindset involves developing habits that tend toward increasing equity even in situations where the connections between specific actions and more equitable outcomes are not readily visible. The practical application of DISJ values involves not only concrete reconfigurations of work activities but also "continuous, reflexive, professional engagement on the part of library workers to be more inquisitive, idealistic, engaged and attentive."[29] For that engagement to be fully realized, all libraries staff must also feel valued and heard within the organization.[30]

Interestingly, the technical services landscape already shows some signs of shifting.[31] In early 2016, the authors of the MIT collections directorate DISJ task force report noted that despite librarians increasingly embracing DISJ values as essential to our profession, a systematic reenvisioning of daily work through the lens of DISJ was "unusual and perhaps unique in academic libraries."[32] In addition to MIT collections directorate DISJ task force members presenting on their work in various forums,[33] several Association for Library Collections and Technical Services (ALCTS) activities specifically centered on integrating diversity and inclusion into the work of library technical services. To provide just a few examples: the focus of the ALCTS 2017 Midwinter Symposium was "Equity, Diversity, and Inclusion: Creating a New Future for Library Collections," and later that spring, ALCTS members shared strategies for integrating equity, diversity, and inclusion into technical services work in libraries during a two-day e-forum.[34] Additionally, in May 2017, a session in the ALCTS Exchange entitled "A Technical Services Toolkit: A Guide for New and Emerging Leaders" was in part "designed to address the ALA key action area of incorporating equity, diversity, and inclusion into technical services workflows."[35]

Building on these burgeoning discussions, we suggest that library staff approach their work with an open mind and take time to think critically and creatively about possible impacts that existing workflows, software, vendors, and decision-making processes may have on the greater marketplace and community. To ground that critical thinking, we turn to the MIT collection directorate's DISJ task force's identification of four broad areas in which DISJ values could be advanced:

1. **The scholarly publishing and academic library marketplace:** exploring ways in which our actions can effect changes on the academic library marketplace that has increasingly seen intrusions of market and corporate values that are at conflict with library missions and goals of advancing equitable access to knowledge and social justice.

2. **Representation of marginalized perspectives:** exploring ways in which libraries and archives can expand the breadth of information resources to include voices that have been historically marginalized.

3. **Community inclusion and outreach:** exploring ways to more accurately reflect the diversity of and connect more genuinely with the communities we serve.

4. **Building organizational infrastructure for diversity, inclusion, and social justice:** exploring ways in which library staff at all levels, and especially administrators, must allow time and provide support to effectively shift to a DISJ framework.[36]

Within these broad areas, technical services staff can begin asking questions such as the following:

- Do my current workflows favor one ethnic group, perspective, language, or type of resource over another? How might I change the current workflows to give equal attention to my resources?

- Do my current vendors represent large, monopolistic corporate entities? Can I use vendors that represent local, smaller, family-, minority- or women-owned businesses?

- What impacts do my current vendors have on the environment? Can I suggest the use of recyclable materials to them or change to a vendor that is geographically closer?

- What steps can be taken to negotiate ADA compliance into contracts and licenses?

- Am I accurately describing my resource using language used within the group being described? How might I add access that would make this resource discoverable using within-group language? What is the historical context of the creation and construction of the resource? What adjustments can I make to address historical inequities?

- What do my library's policies related to organizational structure look like through the lens of DISJ? Do policies related to hiring (including temporary employees), onboarding, benefits, workflows, decision trees, training, and advancement seek to treat people equally and address social inequities?

Acquisitions and cataloging staff are in a unique position to directly affect the marketplace and community and to make resources discoverable in their daily work. An empowered acquisitions staff can make decisions about the vendors they use and ways to interact with local communities to donate and acquire materials. A cataloger with a critical eye can enhance access to materials and suggest changes to existing vocabularies and policies. These are just a few examples of ways staff at all levels can realize the work of DISJ in technical services.

THE DAILY WORK OF LIBRARY TECHNICAL SERVICES

To demonstrate ways to incorporate DISJ values into the regular practice of this work, we thought it would be useful to present job descriptions for staff in both supervisor and assistant capacities in technical services. Because we ourselves work in acquisitions and cataloging, we have focused on those work areas but hope others can see parallels in their own workflows and responsibilities.

The descriptions and roles of the technical services manager and acquisitions and cataloging assistants detailed below were created after conducting a brief internet search for job postings at 22 libraries at four- and two-year U.S. universities and colleges. The profiles reflect an aggregate job description based on similar significant duties described in the job postings. We acknowledge that actual duties of these positions vary widely, and the following are merely examples of activities that staff members acting in these roles may perform on the job. Each job description is followed by suggestions for how to think about these activities through a DISJ lens.

Cataloging and Metadata Specialists

Broadly, cataloging and metadata specialists perform duties that are key to making library collections accessible and discoverable. Specifically, the cataloger creates surrogate records in the catalog for the materials held by the library, whether physical or electronic. The surrogate record provides details about the resource (metadata) to describe the resource, contents, format, and location of the materials so library users can decide if this surrogate represents the information they seek. A cataloger's duties include the following:

- Conducting original, complex, and/or copy cataloging for a variety of materials, such as monographs, serials, electronic publications, visual resource materials (e.g., digital images), theses, government documents, locally created documents, audiovisual materials (e.g., DVDs, audiobooks, and CDs), music scores, and maps
- Updating and maintaining bibliographic and authority records
- Maintaining technical documentation for metadata creation and workflows
- Adhering to cataloging standards and classification schema, including Resource Description and Access (RDA), MARC bibliographic standards, Library of Congress Subject Headings (LCSH), and Library of Congress Classification (LCC) and Dewey Decimal Classification (DDC)
- Troubleshooting technical errors and collaborating with other technical services staff

Catalogers hold powerful roles in facilitating access to library resources. The information they provide—or fail to provide—affects how and whether resources are retrieved by users searching the library discovery systems. Catalogers must acknowledge the historical context in which the vocabularies they use were created—that the thesaurus and classification systems created by the Library of Congress both reflect and favor the viewpoints of those writing the stories, specifically white, Christian, straight men.[37] Providing additional access through terms created by members of marginalized communities is one way to alleviate some bias in the catalog.

For terms associated with subcultures or non-majority voices, catalogers working through a DISJ lens should assess whether the subject headings reflect the terms used by the groups being described. For example, for the title *Queer Game Studies*, shown in figure 13.1, there are no established LCSH for "Queer gaming" or "Queer games." In this example, the cataloger took time to create a contents note (MARC field 505) of the titles of the book chapters, which include terms used within the queer gaming community, such as "Queergaming," "Queer(ing)," "Queering game play," and "Queerness in games." These terms have not yet been established in LCSH; in fact, a quick keyword search in classificationweb.net yields only five references for the term "queer," with only two containing the term "queer" in the heading.[38]

Catalogers can also seek non–Library of Congress (LC) vocabularies to add to their catalog records. Examples of non-LC vocabularies include the Getty thesauri: The Art & Architecture Thesaurus (AAT), Cultural Objects Name Authority (CONA), Getty Thesaurus of Geographic Names (TGN), and Union List of Artist Names (ULAN), as well as many controlled vocabularies listed by LC[39] and the Open Metadata Registry.[40] An example of an alternative controlled

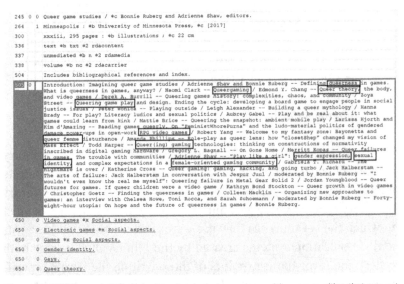

Figure 13.1 Enhanced 505 contents notes include words used by communities that are not represented by LCSH (highlights added). Contents notes can be searched by many online public access catalogs.

vocabulary is the Anchor Archive Subject Thesaurus, which includes many terms used in subcultures (and has seven headings that contain "queer," including "queer," "queer identity," and "queer history"). Terms can be added to a MARC field 6XX_7 with a subfield $2 to indicate the source of the term. There are many sources other than the Library of Congress. Look around; added terms provide additional access to and recognition of often marginalized communities. And if you gather enough evidence, you can also suggest new or changes to existing LCSH.[41]

Non–English language resources in libraries may often be marginalized because they are subject to different workflows than English language resources or because they receive less attention and expertise due to a lack of language specialization on staff. We suggest that cataloging staff examine existing workflows through the DISJ lens and consider corrective approaches. Do non–English language materials sit separately on a shelf to be cataloged, making them easy to forget or avoid? Make efforts to process these materials alongside English titles or create a regular process for cataloging them. Create a list of staff members' language expertise and enlist their help with cataloging when needed. Hold special cataloging training sessions on how to use diacritics and/or non–Roman language alphabets in your cataloging systems.

In everyday work, consider the student assistants and temporary labor with which you work. Rather than looking to hire from the outside, could you have a potential cataloging superstar in your midst? Take a moment to check in with these staff; you may be able to help shape the future of library cataloging at both the professional and local levels.

Cataloging staff are also in a unique position because many items that end up on the shelves must cross their desks first. Could cataloging staff be used in selecting items for leisure collections or curating other highlighted collections? Including cataloging staff in decision-making processes could broaden perspectives showcased on the stacks and empower staff to feel more connected to the collections they support.

Acquisitions Assistants

Acquisitions assistants perform tasks associated with ordering, receiving, and maintaining all new tangible and electronic resources (e.g., books, periodicals, databases, visual and audio materials, musical scores, maps), including the following:

- Ordering materials/resources from vendors and publishers, including selecting appropriate vendors, researching titles for purchasing information, consulting with selectors, providing licensing support, and paying invoices
- Using the integrated library system (ILS) to maintain accurate records of expenditures and resources ordered and received
- Processing renewals and cancellations for periodicals and databases, including tracking cessations and format, title, publisher, and platform changes
- Working with vendors, publishers, interface providers, and library technology staff to establish and maintain access to electronic resources
- Contributing to the development of workflow and procedure documentation
- Implementing retention guidelines for tangible formats, including weeding and preparation of journals for binding

While acquisitions staff do not typically select library materials and resources, they are, as the staff who receive and process materials, in a unique position to be aware of what is being purchased throughout the library. This positioning allows them to see the consequences of choices and provides opportunities to create and expand awareness of DISJ values and can provide value in the decision-making process. For instance, when receiving, processing, and/or shelving newspapers and magazines/journals to which the library subscribes, an acquisitions assistant can ask critical questions: Are marginalized voices represented? Do the materials reflect the full diversity of your student body and of communities in which the campus is embedded, both local and global? Tangible formats create visual landscapes in ways that electronic resources do not. Tour your library. Is shelf space allocated equitably to the full range of voices and viewpoints? What do your library's book displays look like? While you may not have the power to change subscriptions, select monographs, or reconfigure space, you can make suggestions based on your critical observations.

Such suggestions can cut through the power of routine and habit and alert colleagues to the ways that legacies of inequality can be hidden in apparently neutral practices.

Similarly, acquisitions staff are well-positioned to notice the consequences of participating in publisher e-book and journal packages. What are the drawbacks of ceding collection-building to commercial entities? Approaching acquisitions through the lens of DISJ values rather than purely efficiency-based values may reveal pathways for providing new options for acquiring materials. As the staff who are placing orders, canceling subscriptions, and tracking cessations, acquisitions staff see the titles that are moving in and out of publishers' packages and title lists. What do you notice when looking at publisher price lists? What are the content distinctions between packages that publishers offer? Similar questions arise when looking at monograph approval plans from the point of view of unconsciously biased profiling and the exclusion of small presses. As an acquisitions staff member, have you identified alternative publication outlets for materials by self- and independently published authors? Have you engaged vendors in a discussion of your findings? So-called big name institutions (those with prestige, privilege, and power) should consider ways to pave the way to make industry-wide change. For instance, members of MIT collections strategy staff are collaborating with a vendor on ways to expand their approval plan profiles to include awards, subject terms, and reviews from marginalized perspectives, thus hoping to make a global change to the product from which all subscribers can benefit. Institutions that feel they may not be heard as an individual voice may consider approaching vendors as a group or consortium.

Marginalized groups have not always had equal access to traditional publishing streams. As an acquisitions staff member, you can ensure that the format of materials does not create unnecessary barriers to their acquisition and preservation by working with others to create viable solutions for housing unusual formats, such as posters, zines, postcards, and artists' books. What criteria drive the decisions regarding which materials your library retains to bind and which get discarded? Have selectors shared these criteria with you? Are library staff weeding materials based on, for example, circulation statistics, which may result in materials by or about underrepresented groups being stored off-site or withdrawn at a disproportionate rate when compared with materials by or about majority groups? In libraries where acquisitions and collections activities are carried out by different staff members, conversations among staff that contextualize decisions about materials can foster shifts in the ways we work and the ways we think about our work.

Acquisitions staff can also use their positions to promote open access and to make open access and/or free materials discoverable through their library catalogs. In an equitable world, people in communities across the globe would have meaningful access to information. For example, people who live and study in developing countries have limited access to most articles published in scholarly journals due to the high cost of subscriptions. Open access publishing models contribute to lifting barriers to social empowerment by making information resources more widely accessible. Acquisitions staff can make the time to establish criteria and workflows that highlight open access materials in their online public access catalog.

Technical Services Managers

Technical services managers are responsible for planning, managing, supervising, and evaluating the library's technical services functions, including budgeting, acquisitions, cataloging, and collection maintenance. Duties include but are not limited to the following:

- Overseeing and coordinating daily activities of the technical services department
- Providing leadership for the formulation, revision, and implementation of policies and procedures related to ordering and receiving of materials
- Implementing new and providing oversight to existing systems and technologies
- Assuming responsibility for securing and facilitating effective relations with vendors, including reviewing current and prospective vendors to assess service and pricing
- Monitoring and providing expertise on cataloging and metadata standards, policies, and procedures
- Supervising, hiring, and training staff

- Participating in cross-departmental and library-wide committees and working groups and representing the library on external committees and within professional organizations
- Participating in developing long-term goals, objectives, and strategic directions for the library

It is important for technical services managers to empower and trust their staff and to establish pathways for staff to explore, critique, and suggest changes to current practices, strategies, and workflows. Ask staff to work alone or in groups to reexamine workflows and/or policies to see if they could incorporate more DISJ-positive actions. Are you incorporating staff from all levels, backgrounds, and genders in your committees and working groups? In meetings, are you making space for typically quiet staff to talk or encouraging talkative staff to take a step back and let others share ideas?

Think about how you are contributing to the local and professional library community. Examine the committees and working groups you currently serve. Instead of volunteering on the boards of large professional organizations, consider sharing your expertise by serving on the boards or committees of smaller associations, professional groups, or nonprofit community organizations.

Embracing DISJ values as a manager necessitates a reexamination of the culture of technical services. It requires reevaluating the implications and impacts that business decisions have on other institutions, the local community, the marketplace, and the environment. The staff in traditional production-oriented technical services environments will need extra time and mental space to allow for intentional reflection and DISJ work. Using new vendors may add time to adjust to new software and to incorporate its use alongside current systems. Are you allowing cushion in production statistics for catalogers to add additional access for marginalized perspectives? The additional time for slower production also requires communication to other departments affected by your department.

Supervisors and staff need to be willing to participate in (sometimes uncomfortable) conversations and must acknowledge that discussing and adjusting work to incorporate DISJ values is not easy work. It may be harder on some than others; DISJ work can take a significant emotional toll, specifically on members from underrepresented groups. Provide a safe place to talk and create mechanisms for staff to address the emotional and psychological toll that DISJ work can entail. Scaffold professional development and educational opportunities for staff you supervise so they can see how different DISJ learning opportunities relate to each other.[42] Discussions and conversations about DISJ in general and specifically in daily duties help to keep the topic in the forefront of everyone's mind. Recommend readings about DISJ in libraries and discuss them at department or team meetings. Compare professional associations' statements and definitions of DISJ and discuss them as a group. Don't be afraid to share your experiences with others (e.g., other managers, other libraries); this is new territory for many people and hearing about a variety of experiences benefits others.

CONCLUSION

Successfully creating a workplace in which staff actively seek to manifest DISJ values requires an organizational infrastructure that allows staff the space to do so. While commitment to this work among senior administrators is essential, discussion of the definitions and values of DISJ must occur at all levels in order to develop shared understandings of the contexts and structures within which libraries operate and how DISJ work aims to create a more equitable and equal arena for all voices and perspectives. Staff should be encouraged to be compassionate, forgiving, and supportive of one another while conducting DISJ work.

Locally at MIT, the Libraries has experienced a significant paradigm shift in its work since the introduction of a DISJ focus. This shift began with thought leadership from administrators who provided a foundation for growth and learning around DISJ. Anecdotally, we have observed open discussions of DISJ at many technical services staff meetings, whether on the agenda or not, wherein managers have taken time to actively listen and moderate discussions. Staff have felt empowered to experiment with grassroots activities aligned with DISJ work, such as creating a LibGuide for social justice in music, archiving student activism posters, and hosting zine-making workshops. The MIT Libraries has worked on meeting in the middle in a top-down and bottom-up exploration and application of DISJ values to our work to advance a library-wide cultural change.

The reality of persistent inequality demands action. But efforts to root out systems of injustice will never be all rainbows and unicorns; MIT's effort has had its share of missteps and injuries. Staff from dominant groups—at all levels throughout the Libraries—have had trouble leaning into their discomfort. Many staff members of color found it emotionally exhausting to be thrust on a regular basis into discussions of painful issues of race and exclusion in the workplace. Staff knowledge and understanding of the structures of inequity and DISJ values varies significantly, and establishing a shared baseline takes a long time and a lot of iterative hard work. For some, change has been too fast; for others too slow. DISJ work does not progress along a straight line with a consistently positive slope; the inevitable blunders take a disproportionate emotional toll on people of color. Before embarking on inherently disruptive DISJ efforts, senior leaders should evaluate their own readiness to confront these questions and to support staff members of color so that the injustice that motivates change is not compounded. The future success and effectiveness of libraries and their staff members relies on a commitment to continually develop awareness of race, gender, religion, sexual orientation, gender expression, class, and ability bias in the production, distribution, and accessibility of information. With an open mind, serious commitment, and a lot of patience, libraries may begin to see the benefits of working toward a social justice mindset.

NOTES

1. For instance, the Association of Research Libraries states: "It is the Association's position that a firm commitment to diversity, equity, and inclusion is necessary to ensure equitable access to economic and social prosperity, and full participation in society." See "Diversity, Equity & Inclusion," Association of Research Libraries, https://arl.secure.nonprofitsoapbox.com/focus-areas/diversity -equity-and-inclusion.

2. "About ALA," American Library Association, accessed October 21, 2017, http://www.ala.org/aboutala/.

3. "Core Values of Librarianship," American Library Association, adopted January 2019, http://www.ala.org/advocacy/intfreedom /corevalues.

4. An in-depth discussion of this history is outside the scope of this chapter, but readers are encouraged to seek out E. J. Josey, ed., *The Black Librarian in America* (Metuchen, NJ: Scarecrow Press, 1970); E. J. Josey, ed., *What Black Librarians Are Saying* (Metuchen, NJ: Scarecrow Press, 1972); Dennis Thomison, *A History of the American Library Association: 1876–1972* (Chicago: American Library Association, 1978); E. J. Josey, ed., *The Black Librarian in America: Revisited* (Metuchen, NJ: Scarecrow Press, 1994); Andrew P. Jackson, Julius Jefferson, Jr., and Akilah S. Nosakhere, eds., *The 21st-Century Black Librarian in America: Issues and Challenges* (Lanham, MD: Scarecrow Press, 2012).

5. For a related discussion of libraries, librarians, and altruism, see Fobazi Ettarh, "Vocational Awe and Librarianship: The Lies We Tell Ourselves," *In the Library With the Lead Pipe*, January 10, 2018, http://www.inthelibrarywiththeleadpipe.org/2018/vocational-awe.

6. For an analysis of the legacy of racial discourses within the field of library and information science, see Todd Honma, "Trippin' Over the Color Line: The Invisibility of Race in Library and Information Studies," *InterActions: UCLA Journal of Education and Information Studies* 1, no. 2 (June 2005), https://escholarship .org/uc/item/4njow1mp.

7. ShinJoung Yeo and James R. Jacobs, "Diversity Matters? Rethinking Diversity in Libraries," *Counterpoise* 9, no. 2 (2006): 5–8.

8. A few examples: In late 2016, the Association of Research Libraries (ARL) reaffirmed its long-standing commitment to diversity, inclusion, equity, and social justice: "Diversity and Inclusion Highlighted in ARL's Research Library Issues 286," http://www .arl.org/focus-areas/diversity-and-inclusion#.WhIbNbQ-cgo. At its 2017 Midwinter Meeting, the ALA Council approved "Equity, Diversity, and Inclusion" as a strategic direction for the following 3–5 years: *American Library Association Strategic Directions*, http://www.ala.org/aboutala/sites/ala.org.aboutala/files/content /governance/StrategicPlan/Strategic%20Directions%202017 _Update.pdf. The Association for Library Collections and Technical

Services (ALCTS) adopted its diversity statement in June 2017, asserting the importance of open discussions about equity, diversity, inclusion, bias, and social responsibility across collections and technical services in all types of libraries: "About Us," http://www.ala.org/alcts/about. The Association of College and Research Libraries (ACRL) and Society of American Archivists (SAA) have made similar commitments: "Advocacy & Issues," http://www.ala.org/acrl/issues; "SAA Statement Reaffirming Our Commitment to the Importance of Diversity and Inclusion," https://www2.archivists.org/statements/saa-statement-reaffirming-our-commitment-to-the-importance-of-diversity-and-inclusion.

9. *Library Professionals: Facts & Figures*, DPE-AFL-CIO Fact Sheet 2019, Department for Professional Employees (AFL-CIO), accessed April 19, 2020, https://www.dpeaflcio.org/factsheets/library-professionals-facts-and-figures.

10. "Labor Force Statistics From the Current Population Survey" (2017), U.S. Department of Labor, Bureau of Labor Statistics, accessed February 28, 2020, https://www.bls.gov/cps/cps_aa2017.htm.

11. "QuickFacts: United States" (2017), United States Census Bureau, accessed November 12, 2018, https://www.census.gov/quickfacts/fact/table/US/PST045217.

12. "Labor Force Statistics From the Current Population Survey."

13. "Household Data Annual Averages" (2019), U.S. Department of Labor, Bureau of Labor Statistics, accessed February 28, 2020, https://www.bls.gov/cps/cpsaat11.pdf.

14. E. J. Josey and Ismail Abdullahi, "Why Diversity in American Libraries," *Library Management* 23, no. 1/2 (2002): 10–16, https://doi.org/10.1108/01435120210413544.

15. "To Be Black and a Librarian: Talking With E. J. Josey," *American Libraries* 31, no. 1 (2000): 80–82.

16. Amelia N. Gibson et al., "Libraries on the Frontlines: Neutrality and Social Justice," *Equality, Diversity and Inclusion: An International Journal* 36, no. 8 (2017): 751–66, https://doi.org/10.1108/EDI-11-2016-0100.

17. Emily Drabinski, "Teaching the Radical Catalog," in *Radical Cataloging: Essays at the Front*, edited by K. R. Roberto (Jefferson, NC: McFarland & Co., 2008), 198–205.

18. Nina De Jesus, "Locating the Library in Institutional Oppression," *In the Library With the Lead Pipe* (September 24, 2014): 1–30, http://www.inthelibrarywiththeleadpipe.org/2014/locating-the -library-in-institutional-oppression/.

19. "MIT Facts 2020: Enrollments 2019–2020," http://web.mit.edu /facts/enrollment.html.

20. "MIT Facts 2020: Faculty and Staff," http://web.mit.edu/facts/faculty .html.

21. Gregory Eow was appointed president of the Center for Research Libraries, effective August 1, 2019.

22. Michelle Baildon et al., *Creating a Social Justice Mindset: Diversity, Inclusion, and Social Justice in the Collections Directorate of the MIT Libraries* (Report of the Collections Directorate Task Force on Diversity Inclusion and Social Justice; Cambridge, MA: MIT Libraries Research Collection, 2017), 3, http://hdl.handle.net/1721 .1/108771.

23. Greg Eow, personal email communication, January 31, 2018.

24. Ibid.

25. Myrna Morales, Em Claire Knowles, and Chris Bourg, "Diversity, Social Justice, and the Future of Libraries," *Portal: Libraries and the Academy* 14, no. 3 (2014): 439, https://doi.org/10.1353/pla .2014.0017.

26. Michelle Baildon et al., *Creating a Social Justice Mindset*, 8.

27. Diversity and Inclusion Resource Development Group, *Diversity, Inclusion, and Social Justice Resource Manual for MIT Libraries Staff*, May 24, 2017, https://libguides.mit.edu/ld.php?content_id =32359042.

28. "Vision, Mission, and Values," MIT Libraries, adopted September 2017, https://libraries.mit.edu/about/vision/vision-mission-values/.

29. Ryan A. Gage, "Henry Giroux's *Abandoned Generation* & Critical Librarianship: A Review Article," *Progressive Librarian* 23 (2004): 70, http://www.progressivelibrariansguild.org/PL/PL23/065.pdf.

30. Michelle Baildon et al., *Creating a Social Justice Mindset*, 18.

31. It should be noted that bias in cataloging has been an actively contested issue in the library profession since at least the early 1970s. The current shift that we are identifying is a more comprehensive shift across all the functions within library technical services.

32. Michelle Baildon et al., *Creating a Social Justice Mindset*, 18.

33. MIT Collections Directorate DISJ task force members presented at ALCTS Exchange, May 11, 2017; ACRL New England's Annual Conference, May 12, 2017; and ALA's Annual Conference, June 22–27, 2017 (in a program cosponsored by ALCTS, the American Indian Library Association, and the Public Library Association entitled "Diversity, Inclusion, and Social Justice in Technical Services"). Michelle Baildon and Rhonda Kauffman also presented an OCLC Works in Progress Webinar, "Diversity, Inclusion, and Social Justice Work in the MIT Libraries' Collections Directorate," September 19, 2017.

34. The ALCTS e-forum, held February 28–March 1, 2017, was entitled "Equity, Diversity, and Inclusion in Library Technical Services" and was led by Emily Drabinski, Paolo P. Guijilde, and Harrison W. Inefuku.

35. Speakers for this ALCTS Exchange session, held May 16, 2017, were Kimberly DeRosa and Melissa Cantrell.

36. Michelle Baildon et al., *Creating a Social Justice Mindset*, 10.

37. Sanford Berman, *Prejudices and Antipathies: A Tract on the LC Subject Heads Concerning People* (Jefferson, NC: McFarland & Co., 1993); Drabinski, "Teaching the Radical Catalog"; Sandra Littletree and Cheryl A. Metoyer, "Knowledge Organization From an Indigenous Perspective: The Mashantucket Pequot Thesaurus of American Indian Terminology Project," *Cataloging & Classification Quarterly* 53, no. 5–6 (2015): 640–57, https://doi.org/10.1080 /01639374.2015.1010113; Morales, Knowles, and Bourg, "Diversity, Social Justice, and the Future of Libraries."

38. Classificationweb.net is a subscription-based cataloging tool for LC subject headings and classification; the two headings for queer are Queer theory and Queer theology, with references under the headings Gender identity, Third-wave feminism, and Sexual minority community.

39. See "Subject Heading and Term Source Codes," Library of Congress Network Development & MARC Standards Office, http://www .loc.gov/standards/sourcelist/subject.html.

40. See www.metadataregistry.org.

41. See "Process for adding and revising Library of Congress Subject Headings," https://www.loc.gov/aba/cataloging/subject/lcsh -process.html.

42. Harrison W. Inefuku made this suggestion in the February 28–March 1, 2017, ALCTS e-forum. He proposed a model with three tracks of educational opportunities: Identity (learning about our identity and the identities of others), Interpersonal (learning how to interact with individuals with differing identities), and Diversity in Libraries and Archives (direct application to library and archival work).

CHAPTER 14

Creative Solutions to Technical Services Staffing Challenges in an Academic Library

Meghan Banach Bergin and Sally Krash

ABSTRACT

This chapter discusses staffing challenges faced by the information resources management (IRM) department at the University of Massachusetts Amherst Libraries and how they were solved. The IRM department (acquisitions unit, discovery and resource management systems unit, metadata unit, and materials management unit) has experienced significant changes in the last few years and recently engaged in several initiatives aimed at assessing and revising staffing and workflows to adapt to these changes. In 2014 the dean of the libraries and the Libraries' administration team commissioned an IRM department workflow review task force and charged the group with writing a report that included an environmental scan of peer institutions, survey results from internal staff surveys, and recommendations on how to move the department forward. In 2016 the IRM department built on the work of the task force by developing and engaging in several new processes. This chapter will explain in detail how the department successfully dealt with staffing issues such as retirements and changing job duties. The department is now better able to manage its workload and has even been able to take on some important new tasks, including doing internal outreach to the Libraries' administration team and other departments in the Libraries to raise awareness about the important work done in the IRM department.

BACKGROUND

The UMass Amherst Libraries' dean and administration team commissioned the information resources management (IRM) workflow review task force in 2014 to look at the ways technical services workflows were changing and make recommendations on how best to respond to the evolving nature of the work. The task force was charged with conducting an environmental scan of technical services operations at peer libraries that explored functions and responsibilities, reporting lines, and workflows other libraries have eliminated, changed, or added. The task force found that while each library organized its staff in a slightly different way, they are all trying to deal with the same shift from managing physical materials to managing licensed electronic resources, local digital collections, and open access materials. They found that priorities in technical services units at other academic libraries mirrored many of the UMass Amherst Libraries' and the IRM department's own priorities, such as discovery and access, electronic resources management, institutional repositories, non-MARC metadata, and batch loading and batch editing vendor records for e-resources. The task force also found that many academic libraries had experienced reorganizations, loss of staff, and changes in functions in their technical services departments. In addition to the environmental scan, the task force gathered feedback from UMass Amherst libraries staff in general and the IRM department staff in particular. The feedback they received about what IRM does well included responding to users' needs and managing an overwhelming amount of information. Several IRM staff mentioned communication and training as areas in which they could improve, and staff outside of IRM said that linking to electronic resources was sometimes a problem. Feedback from IRM staff about what new positions they needed included a new department head (the current department head was planning to retire soon), more staff to manage electronic resources, and at least one additional professional cataloger/metadata librarian. To better meet the needs of users regarding discovery and access to the Libraries' information resources, the IRM workflow review task force recommended that the department do the following:

- Shift our organization to focus more on managing electronic resources and less on managing physical collections
- Continually look for ways to streamline processes and create more efficient workflows
- Standardize procedures to make more processes routine
- Distribute responsibility more broadly and equitably through the department
- Empower decision-making at the lowest possible level
- Establish clear priorities for the work that is done in the department
- Consider implementing a comprehensive library software platform that embraces the concept of a shared community record
- Consider implementing CORAL as an electronic resources management (ERM) tool
- Hire a new IRM department head
- Hire additional electronic resources management staff (one librarian and one classified staff position)
- Hire a metadata librarian
- Hire a user experience librarian who could conduct user studies and help design, improve, and support the Libraries' primary user interfaces, including the website, the catalog, the discovery system, and digital library collections

DEVELOPING AN ACTION PLAN

When the new head of the information resources department was hired, her first order of business in moving the recommendations of the task force report forward was to develop an action plan with a timeline detailing each step required to accomplish the reorganization. The IRM leadership team, consisting of the four unit coordinators and new department head, began looking at what needed to happen to move toward a more efficient 21st-century technical services operation. An action plan was developed, reviewed, revised, and established. Details of the action plan can be found can be found on the IRM wiki.[1] The action plan included the following elements: (1) a review and discussion of the proposed action plan at every level of the department leading to finalization of the plan, (2) documenting and reviewing current workflows, (3) conducting an in-depth analysis of workflows, (4) facilitating a card sort activity by all staff to group like things together as the basis for an evolved departmental model, (5) analyzing of the results of the card sort activity, (6) identifying possible models for the departmental reorganization, (7) conducting pre-implementation work by reviewing and revising job descriptions and determining how training would occur, and (8) implementing the plan. The entire reorganization process was expected to take 14 months and be in place by the end of the 2017 fiscal year.

The action plan was developed in January and February of 2016 then presented to staff in March at a department meeting. Staff reviewed and discussed the plan in individual unit meetings. Some adjustments were made as a result of those meetings, and the final plan was presented to staff at the end of April. At the April meeting, workflows were discussed and worksheets were made available for staff to assist with workflow analysis.

REVIEW OF CURRENT WORKFLOWS

With the change from collecting and supporting (primarily) print resources to collecting and providing access primarily to e-resources, the focus of IRM has changed significantly in recent years. However, some current workflows include legacy processes that either are no longer necessary or need to be revised. Additionally, there are work-flow processes (such as usability testing for e-resources) that need to be added into their workflows. This is necessary to support the Libraries' campus user community moving forward.

The first major phase of the action plan was to list all the workflows in each of the units (metadata, acquisitions, materials manage-ment, and discovery and resource management systems). Each staff member in the department took responsibility for documenting the workflows they did on a regular basis. Staff also tried to identify workflows they thought the department could let go of doing and decided that print serials binding could be eliminated, the number of microfilms they were ordering could be reduced, book plating gift books could cease, and LOCKSS journal preservation processing could be discontinued.

The current workflows analyzed in each unit are listed below.

Acquisitions unit
Manage acquisitions budget
Manage demand-driven acquisitions plans
Manage approval plans
Manage subscription resources (renew, cancel, etc.)
Negotiate license agreements
Acquisitions order processing
Acquisitions invoice processing
Electronic resource management system records
Administer database trials
E-resources outreach and publicity
E-resources access troubleshooting
Compiling usage statistics for e-resources
Proxy server management
Discovery platform management
LOCKSS preservation processing
Link resolver records management

Materials management unit
Physical processing/labeling (all formats)
Book plating
Bindery operations
Book repair
Transfer processing (depository, OCA, etc.)
Records linking
Withdrawals

Metadata unit
Metadata creation/transformation
Name authority records creation and editing
Copy cataloging (all formats)
Original cataloging (all formats)
Serials records management
Reinstatements

Replacements
Withdrawals
Shelf-ready book receiving
Non-shelf-ready book receiving
DVD receiving
Records linking
Transfer processing (depository, OCA, etc.)
Batch loading and editing e-resources records

Discovery and resource management systems unit
Aleph client configuration and installation
Aleph support for Five Colleges (Amherst College, Hampshire College, Mount Holyoke College, Smith College, and University of Massachusetts Amherst)
Batch loading and editing e-resources records
Create and monitor computerized processes
NCIP patron record loads for commonwealth catalog
Support desk ticket system administration
Maintain Oracle tables configuration
Specialty database creation
Managing HathiTrust records
OCLC and RAPID holdings batch updates
Generating reports out of the Aleph Reporting Center
EBSCO GOBI Electronic Order Confirmation Records loading

One of the main goals of this process was to redistribute the work among the units more evenly. Some units like metadata and acquisitions had more work than they could handle, but in other units such as materials management the work was decreasing. Ultimately, both workflows and staff were reorganized among the units to meet this goal. This was achieved through an iterative process, which involved a card sort activity at a departmental staff retreat and subsequent discussions in meetings following the retreat.

CARD SORT ACTIVITY

After evaluating existing workflows and analyzing what needed to be discontinued, changed, or added, the department needed to move forward to determine a new organizational structure. The newly hired head of the IRM department contacted the UMass workplace learning and development (WL&D) office to discuss its availability to assist with developing options for the new structure. WL&D provides programs and services that support organizational growth and staff development. WL&D staff were able to facilitate a departmental retreat that included a card sort activity and affinity diagram exercise. Card sorting is generally used to help design and develop online platforms. In this activity users of the platform sort like things together to inform the architecture for a new or reimagined user experience. The goal is to create a viable usable structure. There are many examples of card sorting available online, including YouTube videos. Affinity diagrams are similar in that they show categories of large amounts of data organized into natural relationships.

The purpose of planning this retreat was to provide staff with the opportunity to express their thoughts and opinions about the connections of current workflows and to share feedback on how workflows within the department could be realigned. The goal for this activity was to develop a framework for a new organizational structure.

First, the head of the IRM department met with a representative from WL&D to review needs and expectations. A meeting agenda was planned that included the following activity:

1. Create cards—one for each major workflow (full pack for each group)
2. Divide department personnel into four to six groups for this activity
3. Each group will sort like workflows into separate categories
   a. For existing workflows
   b. For how workflows should be grouped going forward
4. Record the results from each group
5. Provide typed notes and the results from each group to the IRM department

There were several communications to develop and finalize an agenda for the retreat, which included a 30-minute introduction to card sorting and affinity diagrams, a 1-hour card sort activity, and 1½ hours for analysis and development of affinity diagrams. The activity was conducted in the allotted time, included all IRM staff (no one was out that day), and took the entire 3 hours designated.

When participants entered the room, they pulled a card from a grab bag and sat at one of four tables labeled the same as their card (A–D). This provided random groups, although one table had mostly cataloging staff so some shuffling was done. Besides facilitating the retreat, WL&D provided sticky notes (the cards), markers, and easel pad paper for each of the four groups.

After learning the details of card sorting and affinity diagrams, participants at each table started categorizing their sticky note workflows on the easel pad paper adhered to the wall next to their table. They were instructed to first put up their sticky notes without talking, then after all notes were in place they could discuss and move workflows. It was interesting to watch the group dynamics: some staff had a hard time keeping silent; some moved a workflow to a particular category, only to have someone else move it elsewhere, followed by the original staff member moving it back (sometimes this went on for a while); and some identified processes that they initially failed to include in their workflow listing. (See figure 14.1.)

After the session concluded, everyone walked away feeling engaged in the process of developing a final organizational structure, but also a bit overwhelmed by it. They discussed what they had learned and what they thought needed to happen as they awaited final deliverables from WL&D.

Final deliverables included workflow affinity diagrams for each of the four groups (images and typed-up lists) as well as overall notes on workflow designs: similarities, differences, and processes not included in the initial list of workflows. Analysis of the card sorting activity included looking at the four main categories that corresponded to existing units: acquisitions, discovery and resource management, materials management, and metadata. For each category, any function that was identified by two or more groups was labeled "common among groups." Any workflow that was only selected by one group was labeled "unique."

Each group identified an acquisitions category. There were no surprises among workflows that were common among groups. Some groups did not know where to put things like troubleshooting electronic resources and loading records, and those were placed in the unique label. (See figure 14.2.)

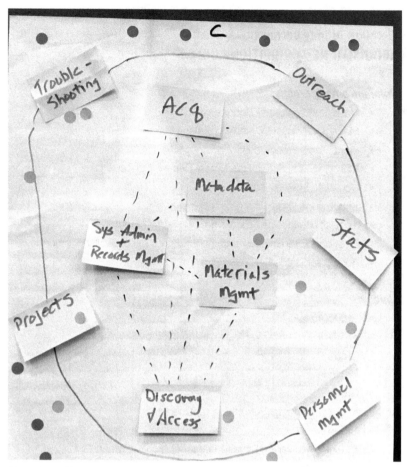

Figure 14.1 Affinity diagram example.

Each group identified a systems category. There were many overlapping workflows in this category, but most dealt with systems, Oracle administration, and various aspects of records management. Each group identified a cataloging/metadata category. There were few surprises here, with many overlapping records management workflows with other units. The physical management category was the most interesting. Many workflows were questioned, like book plating and bindery operations. It was generally believed that this unit had the most flexibility in being dismantled and moved into other areas of the department. Records management functions spanned all units but fell primarily under metadata and discovery and resource management systems functions. (See figure 14.3.)

Workflow Affinity Document
ACQUISITIONS/ACQUISITIONS UNIT

Common among groups:
- Manage Acquisitions Budget
- Manage Demand Driven Acquisitions Plans
- Manage Approval Plans
- Manage Subscription Resources (Renew, Cancel, etc.)
- Negotiate License Agreements
- Acquisitions Order Processing
- Acquisitions Invoice Processing
- Electronic Resource Management System Records Management
- Administer Database Trials

Unique:
- Group A:
  - EDI Invoice Loading (currently handled by DRMS Unit)
- Group B:
  - None
- Group C:
  - Replacements (Purchasing replacements)
- Group D:
  - Link Resolver Records Management (currently handled by DRMS Unit)
  - Usability Testing (proposed that DRMS Unit take the lead)
  - Electronic Resources Outreach (currently handled by Acquisitions Unit)
  - Electronic Resources Access Troubleshooting (Acquisitions Unit and DRMS Unit?)
  - Compile COUNTER and non-COUTNER Statistics (currently handled by Acquisitions Unit)

Workflow - 1

Figure 14.2 Acquisitions category with notes.

Workflow Affinity Document

PHYSICAL/MATERIALS MANAGEMENT UNIT

Common among groups:

- Bookplating
- Physical Processing (all formats)
- Bindery Operations
- Physical Material Maintenance
- Transfer Processing (Depository, OCA, etc.)
- SCUA Preservation
- Preservation Outreach
- Records Linking
  - Withdrawals (MU and MMT)
  - Shelf Ready Books Receiving (2 out of the 4 groups thought this should stay in cataloging)

Unique:

- Group A:
  - None
- Group B:
  - None
- Group C:
  - Withdrawals (MU and MMT)
- Group D:
  - Reinstatements (decided in MU/MMT meeting to keep this in MU Unit)
  - Replacements (decided in MU/MMT meeting to keep this in MU Unit—purchases handled by Acquisitions Unit)
  - DVD Receiving (currently in MMT)
  - Non-shelf Ready Book Receiving (currently in MU)

Workflow - 4

Figure 14.3 Physical category with notes.

Several categories spanned the entire department and were labeled "halo" categories. Those were viewed as categories that could not be subsumed by just one unit. In drawing out possible reorganization strategies, those workflows were kept on the periphery of possible new organizational structures in the affinity diagrams.

DEPARTMENT ORGANIZATIONAL MODELS

During the analysis piece, each group presented their diagram and discussed how they arrived at each category and what they had added that had been left out. The next step was to reconvene as groups and develop affinity diagrams based on their findings. The facilitator then put the diagrams next to each other at the front of the room and staff voted by placing colored dots on the diagrams they liked most and least. There was one diagram that got significantly more votes than any other, so they looked more closely at that diagram. The facilitator drilled down into the workflow categories on that diagram, looking for similarities and differences.

All interactions were captured and documented by the facilitator and provided as a follow-up to the activity. Documents were then shared and discussed at both unit and department-wide meetings. In reviewing the documentation, staff combined needs, discards, and shifts to come up with two possible models for reorganization. The first model was very similar to the existing departmental structure and included the existing four units with some overlap and changes. The second model eliminated the materials management unit and consolidated much of the systems maintenance and bulk records management activities into the discovery and resource management systems unit.

Final discussion about the new organizational structure occurred at the November 2016 IRM department meeting. The second model was selected, which meant that the materials management team would be subsumed into the acquisitions unit. Two staff members from the former materials management unit moved into the acquisitions unit to help with e-resources management as bindery work and physical materials processing decreased. Some workflows that were originally done in the acquisitions unit were moved into the discovery and resource management systems unit, such as proxy server management, discovery platform management, and link resolver records management. Two staff members from the acquisitions unit moved into the discovery and resource management systems unit to help with these workflows. And finally, shelf-ready book and DVD receiving were moved from the metadata unit to staff in the acquisitions unit.

The leadership team then started reviewing and updating job descriptions. As staff were moved into different units and took on new responsibilities, it was necessary to rewrite job descriptions and provide training. A shared spreadsheet workbook was created, showing each of the three major units (one unit per tab). The job descriptions for each staff member were transferred into the workbook on the corresponding unit tab. To remove classism from the new departmental structure, job titles were streamlined and renamed. All paraprofessional staff members became specialists. For example, cataloging assistants became metadata specialists. The unit coordinators felt the job title "specialist" more accurately represented the high level of expertise the paraprofessionals possess. They often perform similar job duties to professional librarians or possess advanced technical skills. Job duties were aligned, showing which duties were shared among all staff working in each unit. Using the metadata specialist as an example, each staff member had about 10 main job duties. Seven of those duties were aligned with the same language for each staff member. Each staff member also had 2 to 4 job duties that were unique. Along with those unique duties, backup functionality was incorporated so that for each unique duty, there was a person who could perform backup whenever the main staff member was out. Seeing all the job descriptions lined up side by side in a spreadsheet made it much easier for the head of library human resources to see the similarities in job duties between each staff member. Because of this easy comparison and the fact that some staff took on more complex job duties, the Libraries' administration team was able to justify several staff having their positions upgraded. Training was done in-house using a peer-to-peer training model, and all staff are now successfully working with their new job duties.

The following list shows how units and workflows changed after the card sort activity.

Acquisitions unit

Manage acquisitions budget
Manage demand-driven acquisitions plans
Manage approval plans

Manage subscription resources (renew, cancel, etc.)
Negotiate license agreements
Acquisitions order processing
Acquisitions invoice processing
Administer database trials
E-resources outreach and publicity
E-resources access troubleshooting
Compiling usage statistics for e-resources
LOCKSS preservation processing (eliminated)
Physical processing/labeling (subsumed into acquisitions unit from former materials management unit)
Transfer processing to off-site storage facilities (subsumed into acquisitions unit from former materials management unit)
Records linking/barcoding (subsumed into acquisitions unit from former materials management unit)
Processing discarded material (subsumed into acquisitions unit from former materials management unit)
*Shelf-ready book receiving (moved from metadata unit)
*DVD receiving (moved from metadata unit)
*Book plating (eliminated)
*Bindery operations (drastically reduced)
*Book repair (moved into special collections and university archives)

Metadata unit
Metadata creation/transformation
Name authority records creation and editing
Copy cataloging (all formats)
Original cataloging (all formats)
Serials records management
Reinstatements
Replacements
Withdrawals
Non-shelf-ready book receiving
Records linking/barcoding troubleshooting
*Batch vendor records loading (shared with discovery and resource management systems unit)

Discovery and resource management systems unit

Aleph client configuration and installation

Aleph support for Five Colleges (Amherst College, Hampshire College, Mount Holyoke College, Smith College, and University of Massachusetts Amherst)

*Batch vendor records loading (shared with metadata unit)

Create and monitor computerized processes

NCIP patron record loads for commonwealth catalog

Support desk ticket system administration

Maintain Oracle tables configuration

Specialty database creation

Managing HathiTrust records

OCLC and RAPID holdings batch updates

Generating reports out of the Aleph Reporting Center

EBSCO GOBI Electronic Order Confirmation Records loading

*CORAL Electronic resource management system maintenance (moved from acquisitions unit)

*Proxy server management (moved from acquisitions unit)

*Discovery platform management (moved from acquisitions unit)

*Link resolver records management (moved from acquisitions unit)

CONCLUSION

The IRM department's staffing, workflow review, and reorganization process was thorough, well thought out, and iterative. The effort was led by the head of the IRM department and the three IRM unit coordinators, with support from the dean of libraries and the Libraries administration team. There was good communication throughout the whole process, and staff were given many opportunities for input. Everyone in the IRM department was involved in the decision-making process, and there was ample time to discuss changes and answer questions. Some staff got raises and others voluntarily moved into other units or took on new job duties. No one was forced to make changes before they were ready or without proper training. As a result, there was strong buy-in, and staff adapted well to the changes that were made.

The department was able to streamline or eliminate several workflows, which allowed staff and financial resources to be devoted to new initiatives such as usability testing for the newly implemented EBSCO discovery system or to higher-priority work such as cataloging hidden collections. Staff were able to cut down on the time spent reviewing catalog records for shelf-ready books by outsourcing via the OCLC Cataloging Plus service. This also allowed staff to batch receive books an entire invoice at a time rather than receiving books one by one and having to review each catalog record individually as they used to do. The department cut back on binding and purchasing microfilm and devoted more staff to e-resource management, updated job descriptions, and provided training for staff who used to spend most of their time working with print materials.

Another benefit of this process was that it brought positive attention to the IRM department at a time when staff were looking to highlight all the important work they do behind the scenes. The Libraries' director for human resources and the dean of the libraries were supportive of the department's efforts to revise job descriptions and upgrade staff positions, because the department had suffered the loss of so many staff due to retirements and because they understood that the nature of the work was changing. The university's central human resources office was also supportive because the Libraries' director of human resources was able to show that upgrades were justified due to staff members taking on higher-level job duties. The library administration team is now interested in using the IRM workflow review process as a model for reviewing staffing, workflows, and organization in other departments in the UMass Amherst Libraries.

NOTE

1. "IRM Evolving Workflows," UMass Amherst Libraries: Information Resources Management Staff Wiki, August 25, 2017, accessed January 16, 2018. https://www.library.umass.edu/wikis/acp/doku .php?id=evolving_workflows_-_2016.

CHAPTER 15

Auraria Library: One Technical Services Department, Three Institutions

Sommer Browning

ABSTRACT

The Auraria Library is the library for three unique institutions of higher education: the University of Colorado Denver (CU Denver), Metropolitan State University of Denver (MSU Denver), and the Community College of Denver (CCD). The library's technical services division is responsible for creating and maintaining access for nearly 50,000 on- and off-campus users while purchasing and managing learning materials for programs as varied as the associate of applied science degree in dental hygiene, bachelor of science degree in cybersecurity, and PhD in civil engineering. All technical services departments must be creative and flexible when it comes to managing their work, but because of Auraria Library's tri-institutional nature, unique issues arise concerning electronic resources licensing, off-campus access, and assessment. This chapter explores the strategies Auraria's technical services division employs to address these issues and how these strategies reflect the changing nature of technical services in 21st-century libraries.

INTRODUCTION

Technical services departments are meeting the needs of the 21st-century library through consortial purchasing, new acquisitions models, reevaluating workflows to streamline electronic resources access, and myriad other innovations. The Auraria Library is no exception, but it does this for three institutions of higher education with very different programs, students, and faculty. The Auraria Library is the library for the University of Colorado Denver (CU Denver), Metropolitan State University of Denver (MSU Denver), and the Community College of Denver (CCD). The library and all three higher education centers are located on the 150-acre Auraria campus in downtown Denver, Colorado. The library is committed to providing support to all three institutions, and this takes the form of equal access to all library services, spaces, and collections for any Auraria student, faculty, or staff member. Supporting three institutions is a daunting task for every division of the library. The researcher support services department continually assesses the needs of three separate faculty, the education and outreach department customizes instruction courses for three discrete student bodies, and the technical services (TS) division creates and maintains access for nearly 50,000 on- and off-campus users while purchasing and managing learning materials for programs as varied as the associate of applied science degree in dental hygiene, bachelor of science degree in cyber security, and PhD in civil engineering.

Auraria Library's TS division comprises the discovery and metadata department, the collections strategies department, and systems administration. The discovery and metadata department and the collections strategies department work together to manage the library's learning materials. The collections strategies department oversees and expends the $3.6 million learning materials budget, licenses electronic resources, provides interlibrary loan services, maintains the physical stacks, and assesses the usage of the collection. The discovery and metadata department catalogs learning materials in all formats, manages the various access points to the library's learning materials, including the discovery layer, customizes and maintains vendor platforms, oversees the purchase-to-discovery internal workflow of learning materials, leads the troubleshooting team that resolves electronic resource access problems, and administers the off-campus authentication software (EZproxy). The systems administration team is a two-person unit that oversees the library's integrated library system (ILS), Sierra, which is hosted on a server within the library.

Technical services divisions must be creative and flexible when it comes to managing their work, but because of Auraria Library's tri-institutional nature, unique issues arise concerning electronic resources licensing, off-campus access, and assessment. This chapter explores the strategies Auraria's TS division employs to address these issues and how these strategies reflect the changing nature of technical services in 21st-century libraries.

ABOUT AURARIA LIBRARY

The Auraria campus is located on the site of Denver's oldest neighborhood; in fact, Auraria predates the founding of Denver. Auraria and what was then known as Denver City (founded a few weeks after Auraria) merged in 1860 to become the city of Denver. Auraria was a distinctly working class, immigrant neighborhood through the 1960s. In its early days the immigrants were Central and Eastern European, but after the turn of the century the origin of the residents began to shift. By the 1940s most of Auraria's residents were of Hispanic origin, moving to Auraria from southern Colorado, New Mexico, and Mexico. In 1965 floodwaters devastated much of Auraria. The city, aided by a bond measure approved by a narrow majority of Denver voters, began a comprehensive redevelopment plan of Auraria that included displacing Auraria residents to make room for the Auraria campus. Despite attempts to overturn the bond measure and keep their homes, Auraria residents were removed from their neighborhood and forced to relocate.[1] The Auraria campus, founded in 1976, was conceived as a shared campus to create efficiencies and to encourage students to pursue their entire higher education in one location. Students could begin their studies at the community college, transfer to Metropolitan State College of Denver (in 2012 it attained university status), and then pursue graduate work at CU Denver. The campus was designed so that students, faculty, and staff of any institution could share academic buildings, and the administration of four central services was split up. MSU Denver administers the health center and a shared campus recreation center, the Tivoli Student Union is administered by the Auraria Higher Education Center (AHEC), a fourth campus entity and a kind of landlord for the campus, and CU Denver administers the Auraria Library. Since Auraria's founding, however, the institutions have increasingly separated themselves. Each school has created its own "neighborhood" with buildings designated for use by its students and faculty only. However, those central services mentioned above are still shared and administered similarly.

The library employs approximately 50 full-time permanent staff (classified state employees, university staff, and a mixture of tenure-track and non-tenure-track faculty librarians) and over 50 student workers. The library consists of three divisions: digital and scholarly services, education and public services, and TS. With a general operating budget of $10 million, a third of which is dedicated to learning materials, the library provides library instruction, research tutoring services, off-campus access to a myriad of learning materials, and other services to about 50,000 students, faculty, and staff.

Each library division faces different and interesting challenges in meeting the needs of three distinct institutions of higher education. In some cases the challenge is simple and merely requires some multiplication. For instance, if the library's hours change, the communications coordinator must communicate the change with CU Denver's, MSU Denver's, and CCD's communication offices rather than just one office. But mostly the challenges are not simple because the needs, missions, student experience, academic programs, and strategic plans of the three institutions are unique. The library has navigated this environment for over 40 years with the explicit aim to serve all three institutions as best and equally as it can. This means that the library offers all students, faculty, and staff the same library services and materials regardless of institution. The library's computers, printers, specialty software and technology, instruction sessions, research tutoring, and special collections, as well as the entirety of its learning materials, are available to any Auraria campus affiliate. This certainly poses specific challenges for each division tasked with these services, and it is no different for the TS division. For the sake of organization and clarity, this chapter focuses on three major TS areas that are affected by Auraria's tri-institutional nature: access, acquisitions, and assessment.

ACCESS CHALLENGES

Over 90% of the library's $3.6 million learning materials budget is spent on electronic resources. The "Start My Research" search box on the library's homepage accesses the library's discovery layer (Summon). In 2017, it received over 1.5 million searches. The library's electronic resources are by far the most utilized service the library offers. Access to these resources is vital to the mission of the library and the missions of the three schools it serves. Most campus affiliates will never come into the library building but will use the library remotely. This is likely true of any modern academic institution, but with three institutions, access to and usability of these resources is more complicated. Some of these complications include managing many internet protocol (IP) ranges, communicating with three separate information technology (IT) departments, and identifying and serving many special user categories beyond the traditional, student, faculty, staff, and alumni, such as dual-enrollment students, international campus students, and others.

IP ranges are notoriously difficult to keep up with. At Auraria, any user coming from a campus IP can access library materials without having to sign in to their campus portals using their institutional credentials, while users who are off campus must log in through their campus portals. This is a decision that was made long ago, and it periodically gets cursorily revisited. While the bulk of campus IP ranges has remained constant, occasionally each institution adds a new one. When this happens, library staff must contact every single vendor to update the library's IPs. For Auraria, with over 300 vendors, this process takes several months. While this process is familiar to all university libraries, in Auraria's case it is a volume and multiplication problem (×3). However, private networks are becoming more and more common, and oftentimes the university or college IT departments are not even aware that someone has created a private IP in a university building. The library often finds out through problem reports—for instance, a faculty member suddenly must sign in as if they were off campus when, in fact, they are in their office. The library can only add these IPs when they know about them. Also, because of the number of Auraria's vendors and limited library staff, updating IPs with vendors for every private network is not possible. As of now, the policy is to not add these private IPs. However, TS staff who resolve access issues must be aware that private networks could be the reason for problems. Resolving issues like these requires communication about why that user must sign in to the library though they are on campus. As these private networks grow, so does the case for asking all users to authenticate no matter where they are. This would unify the user experience and alleviate the problems that changing IPs and private network access issues have on Auraria's TS staff.

The increase of special user groups or categories is an interesting phenomenon. The Auraria institutions, like many others, are focused on increasing their enrollment. They are constantly creating new, innovative programs that reach out to potential students who are not enrolled in the traditional way. There are pipeline programs, dual enrollment programs, certificates offered through community centers, international programs, collaborative degrees such as the program with the Detroit Institute of Music Education (DIME) and MSU Denver, and others. The library often learns of these programs when a student or faculty member is having a problem accessing materials. In these cases, there is always some investigation to be done on the part of library staff to uncover the problem, track down the sponsor of the program, understand the nature of the program and what their students need from the library, and then either contact the registrar to get these students into the student enrollment system or hand-enter these students into the library's patron files. This is a time-consuming process that is usually reactive rather than proactive even though library staff keep up with these user categories as best as they can.

That said, there are several processes and procedures library staff have developed to keep better track of these programs. In the case of affiliate scholars and researchers, library staff created a form for the sponsors of these users to fill out on behalf of their researcher and a process by which affiliate users are purged from the system every year. If these users still need access, their campus sponsor must again fill out the form. In this way, the library stays within the license agreements it signs with vendors and the library records for these users are kept up to date. Special programs that seem to catch the library by surprise, such as the DIME program, are identified and recorded so that the library can reach out to the appropriate office before a new cohort of students arrives.

In the summer of 2017, Auraria Library migrated from the Sierra web access management (WAM) authentication method to EZproxy. EZproxy is an authentication and access software product sold by OCLC. The project was started nearly 10 months before summer 2017 because of the communication and assistance the library needed from three separate IT departments across the three schools. Communicating the library's special situation to EZproxy also was challenging. The library had to act as the translator between OCLC and each institution's IT staff. While MSU Denver and CU Denver have their IT departments located on Auraria campus, CCD has a satellite office on campus. CCD is administered by a larger consortium of regional community colleges, the Colorado Community College System (CCCS). In this case, the coordination of communication was especially difficult because an IT department that was not on campus had to understand the library's needs and work with an outside vendor (OCLC). While challenging, this transition was a success in many ways. Not only did it improve the user experience of off-campus access to library materials, but it created opportunities to streamline communication with the IT departments across campus and the library. Keeping in regular contact with these IT departments, and not just when there are problems, makes collaboration easier for future projects. Indeed, so much of the challenge of serving three schools stems from communication, both from the library and to the library. Since the library is administered by CU Denver, library staff are employees of CU Denver and so receive regular communications from CU Denver IT, upper administration, student support services, various university offices, and CU Denver schools and colleges. This is not the case with MSU Denver or CCD. Network outages, planned maintenance of their registrar systems or campus portals—even administrative reorganizations, campus events, and new hires at the other two institutions—are not easily communicated to the library. Oftentimes these communications go out only to students, faculty, and staff that have institutional email addresses. Since library staff have CU Denver email addresses, this makes some communication impossible. Different email addresses are barriers to signing up for these kinds of communications. Of course, this complicated communication makes troubleshooting and identifying systemic issues concerning access for students, faculty, and staff at these institutions very difficult at times. Conversely, communicating library software outages and system downtime to each institution equally is problematic. Library staff are constantly aware of this challenge and continually try to improve communication. Staff ask to receive newsletters, press releases, and administrative communiques, as well as, read as much local news about the other institutions as they can, and visit their websites frequently. However, nothing can take the place of being an employee of the university and all the communication channels that offers.

ACQUISITIONS CHALLENGES

Auraria faces licensing issues and vendor confusion because of its tri-institutional nature. For the most part, good communication and language skills are ways TS addresses these acquisitions challenges. Technical services work is complicated and detailed to begin with; adding the challenge of clearly describing the funding structure of Auraria Library seems to truly confuse some vendors.

When working with new vendors, and sometimes even established ones, library staff must clearly explain that Auraria is not three separate institutions, it is not exactly three separate campuses either, nor is it a consortium negotiating on behalf of three schools. It is a separate entity altogether. TS negotiates for pricing structure based on Auraria's full-time equivalent (FTE) of all three institutions together. Auraria's tri-institutional nature is easily misunderstood, and that can mean extra emails, phone calls, and web meetings to explain things.

This confusion not only pertains to communicating with vendors and publishers but translates into issues with the software companies with which the library works. Recently it was discovered that WorldCat had seven listings for Auraria under various incarnations of the schools' and library's names. Users had trouble choosing their institution and deciphering the library's holdings. It took some weeks to clear this up, and even now, because of some limitations on the part of WorldCat, if one enters Community College of Denver or Metropolitan State University of Denver in the "Find a library near you" search box, Auraria Library's holdings do not appear. However, if one enters University of Colorado Denver, Auraria Library does appear in the search results. This does a disservice to MSU Denver and CCD, though the library has not received any problem reports about it.

Further, because Auraria is oftentimes forced to choose an institution because of vendor and software limitations, the default is often CU Denver (since that is who administers the library and where the bank account is kept). This makes branding databases and electronic resources difficult, as the "Brought to you by" text often says University of Colorado Denver. As far as student experience goes, this can be confusing and alienating for a student from MSU Denver or CCD, who may think they are logged in incorrectly or have made a mistake. Chasing after branding on these vendor sites is an ongoing and time-intensive process that often falls to the bottom of the staff's to-do list as it is not as important as paying invoices and resolving access issues.

Certainly, prioritizing work is very important for technical services staff at all academic libraries. There is always more work than staff to do it. However, it seems particularly true for TS staff at Auraria. Because of the library's unique nature, it is generally known that staff will have to spend more time with vendors and software companies during negotiations and licensing and spend more time resolving access issues since staff do not always know which institution a report is coming from. This requires patience and flexibility, as well as skills at prioritizing. In general, issues that affect immediate user needs are prioritized over something like keeping up with database branding.

ASSESSMENT CHALLENGES

When providing library resources for three different institutions, it is also challenging to perform consistent and comprehensive assessments of learning materials and access point usage. Understanding learning material usage by each institution, analyzing electronic resources problem reports to look for systemic issues unique to an institution, and conducting user experience assessments concerning off-campus access and the functionality of the discovery layer can require complicated approaches when surveying three institutions.

The TS division regularly assesses the use of its learning materials, collecting COUNTER statistics and other similar usage reports for databases, e-books, and e-journals and circulation statistics for physical materials. The division collates these statistics and offers them to the selectors (collection development librarians) to inform renewal decisions. However, how do librarians know who is using which resource? At a library that serves one university, the question is not even posed. At Auraria, it is a challenge, and in many cases impossible, to separate out usage by institution—a data point that could be helpful for a variety of reasons. For instance, it would be interesting to know if our e-books on dental hygiene were used by students other than those enrolled at CCD, the only institution on the Auraria campus that offers a bachelor of applied science in dental hygiene. If the library noticed an increase in usage from MSU Denver, this could mean that a new program was created of which the library was unaware (not uncommon). Usage statistics according to institution could help selectors assess their purchases differently and inform their outreach to faculty across campus, among other benefits. This kind of usage data at the resource level is currently technologically impossible for the library to gather and would be very time-consuming for library staff even if it were possible. And, of course, even more granular data, for instance at the individual user level, would be completely undesirable from a privacy perspective.

However, larger institutional trends and data would be useful and can be (mostly) gathered—with a bit of gymnastics. There are a few ways the library can attempt to estimate the number of users coming from each institution, but none of the numbers would be exact or easily obtained. Data from EZproxy and the discovery layer could be used together to get a general sense of how much traffic comes from each institution; however, anyone using a guest IP range (guest Wi-Fi is offered by each of the three institutions) would be anonymous as far as affiliation. Another method, which has not been attempted, is to work with each institutional IT department to see if they could supply statistics on portal logins coming from the library's website. While this information might be too general to make specific decisions regarding learning materials, it could be useful in other ways. Knowing these larger numbers or trends could lead to a better understanding of the search behavior of students. It could assist library staff in potentially customizing outreach efforts or library instruction courses for a school. This kind of usage data also informs funding requests from each school's administration and could help to personalize the story of how Auraria supports student success.

The inability to know which institution our users are affiliated with also causes issues when troubleshooting electronic resources problems. For the most part, when the library receives a problem report, it can resolve it in less than 24 hours. In most cases the cause of the problem resides with the library, the vendor, or the user. However, larger systemic issues that might be related to a user's institutional portal, outages with their university's identity management system, or a newly added campus IP range are much harder to identify when the library does not know with which school the user is affiliated. Because of this unknown variable, it takes longer to resolve user problems, and this, of course, can negatively impact user experience.

Assessing the experience of accessing learning materials from a myriad of access points is a complicated task for any library, and only more so when a library serves three institutions. Do students from MSU Denver use the database list more or differently than students from CCD? Which citation management software should the discovery layer incorporate: EndNote because of CU Denver's institutional subscription, RefWorks because it is already integrated in the library's discovery layer, or the citation management software supported by MSU Denver? If it is all three, does the library have the capacity to support all three? Do students need the discovery layer translated into Spanish? Perhaps that makes sense for MSU Denver, which received the Hispanic-Serving Institution (HSI) designation in the spring of 2019. But do the other schools have different language needs? How can the library find that out? And how can it accommodate that? Certainly, user surveys and focus groups could help answer some of these questions, and Auraria utilizes these methods. It just requires a bit more forethought and effort because Auraria must make sure to gather input from a larger number of user groups. (The library participated in LibQual in spring 2018 and analysis of the results proved more complicated with three different institutions. One example is that some majors are grouped differently in different institutions—for instance, history is considered in the humanities at one school and the social sciences at another.) When implementing EZproxy the library asked its student employees from all three institutions to assist with testing the new authentication method to compare their experiences with each other, and this was relatively easy. But for more complicated studies such as assessing user behavior when using the library's discovery layer, organizing surveys and focus groups is complicated. Indeed, that is just the first step because after the results come in, how does one decide which customizations or adjustments to make if the results contradict each other? Because of this, changes to the discovery layer are more generalized than library staff may want; they are changes and upgrades that the library feels would positively impact student experience across all of the institutions.

CONCLUSION

There are other libraries that serve multiple entities and have many kinds of partnerships, such as the Front Range Community College Westminster campus and the Westminster Public Library, and San Jose State University and San Jose Public Library. An analysis of these partnerships might be helpful to libraries involved in these kinds of collaborations or libraries that are looking to maximize efficiencies and cost savings and broaden the resources and services they offer their users. How are other libraries, in partnerships, providing access to their users? Do they make distinctions between their users to assess cost per use of learning materials, for instance? How do they manage the fiscal aspects of their respective budgets when they share materials, services, and/or infrastructure? The answers to these questions are all worth answering and sharing with libraries involved in similar relationships. The nature of Auraria's mission, to serve three academic institutions equally, may be unique, but many of the challenges the library faces and overcomes are common to most academic libraries, whether in partnerships or not. Questions and concerns about access, acquisitions, and assessment are the focus of many technical services departments as they all contend with flat or cut budgets, new acquisitions models, changes in technology, and evolving student needs.

Auraria's future will involve more consortial collaboration, in not only the acquisition of learning materials but likely the purchasing of software and sharing of services. This will require continual monitoring of communication methods, both internal and external. The library's future is inextricably linked to the missions and goals of its three institutions and so it must remain flexible and ready to adapt to changes in those missions. The challenges and collaborative opportunities at Auraria, though more complicated in their details, reflect the challenges at any academic library today.

NOTE

1. "Auraria Neighborhood History," Denver Public Library, https://history .denverlibrary.org/auraria-neighborhood.

CHAPTER 16

Redefining the Pie: Doing More With Less in Technical Services

Monika Glowacka-Musial, Ellen Bosman, and John Sandstrom

ABSTRACT

New Mexico State University is a land-grant institution, a NASA Space Grant College, and a Hispanic-Serving Institution (HSI). NMSU Library has been substantially contributing to the fulfillment of the mission of the university by offering a range of information services, including a variety of research materials, collections, learning tools, and spaces to study. In this chapter we examine various strategies used by the technical services department to support the NMSU operations while absorbing the loss of 50% of its faculty and staff positions over the past 13 years. As the remaining staff members strive to accommodate the ongoing changes in the department, library, institution, and industry, we continue offering quality services. To do so, we have transitioned from strictly defined units and positions to more flexible definitions that allow for multiple roles and responsibilities within the technical services department as well as within the library. This transition to "doing more with less" involves a combination of the department's continuous readjustments at all levels while redefining the roles of the departmental administration as well as redefining job requirements and positions.

REDEFINING THE PIE

Since time immemorial, or at least since the publication of William Playfair's *Statistical Breviary* in 1801,[1] the pie chart has been used to represent and compare various types of quantifiable data. The pie chart has entered modern culture through such sayings as "a bigger

■ Acquisitions   ▪ Cataloging   ▪ Department head

Figure 16.1 Technical services then (2003).

■ Acquisitions   ▪ Cataloging   ▪ Department head   ▪Metadata

Figure 16.2 Technical services today (2020).

piece of the pie," "the whole pie," "cut the pie thinner." In this chapter we describe how we have redefined and reallocated the technical services pie considering current and future challenges in library resource management (see figures 16.1 and 16.2).

INSTITUTIONAL OVERVIEW

New Mexico State University was founded in 1888 as Las Cruces College. In 1889 the territorial legislature established the land-grant

Agricultural College and Experiment Station. During its first full academic year, the nascent institution became known as the New Mexico College of Agriculture and Mechanic Arts. In 1960, recognizing the growth of the institution's population and programs, it was renamed New Mexico State University by amendment of the state constitution.[2] At the time of this study, NMSU is fully accredited[3] with a Carnegie Classification of R2—Doctoral Universities: High Research Activity.[4] Classed as a Hispanic-Serving Institution by the Department of Education,[5] NMSU prides itself on its commitment to discovery, excellence in teaching, celebrating diversity, leadership in research, cooperative extension service, and serving through outreach, as reflected in its mission statement.

> The mission of the New Mexico State University system is to serve the diverse needs of the state through comprehensive programs of education, research, extension and outreach, and public service. As the state's land-grant and space-grant university, and as a Hispanic-Serving Institution, NMSU fosters learning, inquiry, diversity and inclusion, social mobility, and service to the broader community."[6]

The vision is that "by 2025, the NMSU system will excel in student success and social mobility for our diverse student populations, achieve the highest Carnegie research status (R1), and maintain our Carnegie Community Engagement classification."[7]

The most recent official information available shows that NMSU enrolls more than 14,250 undergraduate and graduate students[8] in 204 degree programs.[9] These students come from 50 states and 71 foreign countries.[10] NMSU is a diverse institution with 54.4% of the students being classed as Hispanic, 28.7% classed as white, 7.2% as nonresident alien, and 9.7% as other minority or unknown, which includes American Indian, Asian American, black, Hawaiian Pacific, and multiracial.[11] Women outnumber men 54.9% to 45.1%.[12]

NMSU is funded through several streams, including state appropriations, governmental grants and contracts, private gifts, grants and contracts, sales and services, indirect cost recovery, tuition and fees, federal appropriations, and local government appropriations.[13] Governance of NMSU is through an "autonomous Board of Regents appointed by the Governor of the State and confirmed by the State Senate. The Board delegates authority for the internal management of the institution to the NMSU system chancellor. The faculty elects a Faculty Senate which has legislative jurisdiction over policies affecting the academic mission of the university."[14]

NMSU is currently facing the same challenges many institutions of higher education are facing. Enrollment is flat or trending downward,[15] costs are trending upward,[16] and the state appropriation continues to decrease.[17] These challenges result in an environment in which it is very difficult to develop and implement new programs or even sustain the current ones.

NMSU LIBRARY

NMSU Library is made up of five departments in two buildings. Zuhl Library houses access services, reference and research services, and administration. The Branson Library serves as the home for systems, archives and special collections, and technical services. The reference collection, reserves, interlibrary loan, document delivery, and the A–PZ collection are shelved in the Zuhl Library, while Q–Z, government documents, current periodicals, audiovisual materials, and archives and special collections are in the Branson Library. Both libraries have instructional labs, computers for student and public use, and circulation desks.

Librarians have faculty status, and most are on the tenure track. Two library faculty positions are considered nontenured or college faculty. The department heads are administrative faculty and the associate dean and dean are both considered administrators. Because of institutional issues and turnover, the library has not had a full faculty for several years. This has resulted in some duties being passed around, many faculty wearing multiple hats, and a general loss of institutional memory.[18]

Even as the library has been losing or unable to fill faculty positions, the same has been true of staff positions. Again, this has resulted in duties being passed around, staff covering multiple jobs, and loss of institutional memory as it is seen in the faculty. More and more responsibilities are being pushed to the student assistants, who are, by definition, temporary employees. All these add to the challenge of maintaining a fully functioning technical services department, where the critical component is staffing. There are two primary areas of concern here: staff size and staff skills.

CHANGES IN STAFF SIZE AT NMSU LIBRARY

Over the last decade and a half, publicly funded academic libraries have faced substantial budget challenges. Hunter and Bruning note that the share of academic libraries' university budgets has declined from 3.0% to 2.2%.[19] Oder reports "the economic crisis, coupled with demands on libraries for traditional services . . . portends significant, perhaps permanent, realignment regarding library spending."[20] Universities have used a variety of methods to address these challenges. One such method involves reductions in staff.

Little recent research addressing personnel reductions in U.S. academic libraries is available. One study, however, is very informative on this issue. Regazzi studied library spending, staffing, and utilization between 2008 and 2010 and compared the results to 1998 and 2008. His original findings indicated that staff sizes were declining in all sizes of academic libraries.[21] This trend has continued but at a quicker pace than in 1998–2008. Aside from this study, most information on the topic is based on reports of specific libraries, such as the 2009 decision of Five Colleges Inc. (which consists of University of Massachusetts Amherst, Amherst College, Hampshire College, Mount Holyoke College, and Smith College), to consolidate its technical services functions and eliminate, at least at Mount Holyoke, paraprofessional staff.[22] NMSU is no exception to this trend.

In 2003 NMSU's technical services department had 5 faculty, including the department head, 3 catalogers, and 1 acquisitions librarian. There were 24 paraprofessionals. Today (17 years later), the department has 3 tenure-track and 1 non-tenure-track faculty and 7 paraprofessionals, or a 54% decrease in personnel. The personnel reductions are the result of several factors. Some duties and their positions were transferred to other departments, such as those associated with the mail room and gifts. Attrition and retirements led to vacancies, and some of these positions were recaptured by central administration and redistributed elsewhere in the library. Financial difficulties at the university level also led to position turnover and eliminations. Hiring freezes have also contributed to the problem, with some positions vacant for up to two years. The consequences have been spread across all units and include a backlog of original cataloging, cessation of approval plans, and personnel continually assuming additional tasks.

The duties of the department have also changed. In 2003 the department was responsible for acquisitions, cataloging, gifts, binding, labeling and mending, and mail room, and supplies. Today the department is responsible for many of the same functions, excluding gifts, mail room, and supplies, and has assumed responsibility for electronic journal maintenance and metadata creation for digital objects. Within these units the most affected by the personnel reductions has been cataloging, which now consists of 1 staff and 1 faculty, whereas in 2003 there were 3 faculty and 15 staff. Despite these reductions, the department has tried to keep up with trends.

Redistributing the workload is challenging because of union regulations that require that work associated with a higher classification level not be assigned to a lower classification level. Consequently, some work associated with unionized positions was assigned to student workers. The department has nine student workers distributed among the three units. Student supervision is centralized under one full-time staff member, which is a change from each unit having a student supervisor. The students are cross-trained to meet the needs of each unit and can be deployed to whichever unit has the most critical need. Students mostly perform routine tasks such as journal check-in and mending. However, some students are doing the work previously associated with a full-time position. For example, two students are creating preliminary metadata and one student now works in cataloging performing withdrawals and transcribing abstracts for theses and dissertations. Using student labor presents several challenges. Academic schedules make it difficult for the department to arrange a plan that works for both the department and the student, and the high turnover in student employees translates to repeated time spent hiring and training.

Another challenge has been the faculty's nine-month contract, which is essentially an eight-month contract once holidays are included. The consequences of this arrangement are twofold: work is not performed during the four months the faculty are off contract, or the work gets pushed up to the department head. One task automatically pushed up to the department head is personnel supervision. In terms of other work, the department head has limited discretion regarding which work they will take on. For example, if a project has a deadline in the summer, the department head will assume the responsibility. Work that can wait until a faculty member returns may or may not be taken on by the department head.

The direct effect of personnel reductions has been a decrease in the tasks performed by the department. The department no longer assigns subject headings to theses and dissertations and has ceased authority control and e-book cataloging. Another result is a reduction in the cataloging of selected formats, especially maps and music. More crucial than a reduction in tasks is the loss of institutional and functional knowledge. While personnel are cross-trained, the sheer number of positions eliminated and the union restrictions means that the expertise associated with certain tasks has been lost. For example, the department previously created collection management reports, but with the elimination of the correlating position, technical services now relies on the IT department to produce reports.

Despite these difficulties, the department does its best to implement new tools and tasks. For example, it has launched an electronic management system, deployed the Resource Description and Access (RDA) standard, created a metadata unit, and transitioned to a new integrated library system. To carry out these changes, personnel went through retraining, and positions shifted from one unit to another. Onboarding and training of new faculty has also been readjusted.

CHANGES IN STAFF SKILLS, ONBOARDING, AND CROSS-TRAINING

The process of bringing new library personnel on board at NMSU (often entry-level employees) includes numerous campus-wide orientations, library-specific workshops, and departmental trainings. In fact, a new faculty member must complete 51 main tasks within the first 30 days. For example, one of these tasks is the mandatory Compliance Certification Program for all employees that consists of several online training modules, including Family Educational Rights and Privacy Act (FERPA), Preventing Discrimination/Civil Rights, Computer and Data

Security, Employee Safety and Loss Control: Emergency Preparedness, Drug-Free Workplace, Family and Medical Leave Act (FMLA), Title IX: NMSU, A Caring Community, and Conflict of Interest. In addition, the NMSU Teaching Academy prompts new faculty to join its campus-wide mentoring program, as well as encourages them to participate in a variety of sessions on teaching, research, writing, publishing, and developing a tenure-track portfolio. This rapid immersion in the campus culture continues for many weeks. The sheer amount of information that a new employee must digest in a relatively short period of time is enormous and can prove challenging for these individuals. Very quickly time management becomes the first challenge as newcomers try to satisfy all onboarding requirements. While absorbing university policies and procedures, new personnel are also expected to learn and perform their regular job duties. Balancing this experience with additional mandated tasks can be a barrier to a newcomer's ability to learn how to do their job. At the NMSU Library this tension is compounded due to a hiring freeze, which makes the traditional master-apprentice model to learning one's job duties difficult. Presently, a newcomer learns by consulting several colleagues who either have been cross-trained or assigned to cover specific areas of another's position, used to have the same job, or are somehow involved in shared projects. While these coworkers often teach newcomers how to perform their basic tasks, they also encourage them to continue exploring software tools, programs, and available documentation on their own.

Simply reviewing documentation either provided by vendors or left by one's predecessors can be another challenge. Commonly, such documentation is not meant for newcomers. Internal working documents tend to be rather sketchy and fragmented, having been written for the insiders who share common practice and have no need for basic instructions and detailed explanations. As a result, it is not easy for a new person to adopt or apply inherited project specifications. The process of familiarizing oneself with project design, workflows, best practices, and reports becomes quite puzzling, and it tends to be very time-consuming. To make things worse, the time investment in learning one's job may be wasted if the institution changes critical features such as software or other technological aspects. Best practices and workflows developed for one system inevitably become obsolete as soon as the library changes its primary software.

Now, how do we effectively train new faculty and staff members despite their busy onboarding schedules, diffused expertise, and fragmented documentation? How do we get ready for a new system with limited staff and resources available? One answer would be to approach these challenges as an opportunity for improving communication and cooperation within and among library departments and units.

A possibility for increased cooperation that has considerable advantages is to bring newcomers and experienced librarians together in regular workshops. A major advantage of having such meetings is a comprehensive, hands-on learning experience directly connected to specific job duties. NMSU Library early on established regular workshops on how to utilize current software and popular digital tools. Using PowerPoint presentations and guided practical exercises, senior librarians share their expertise with newcomers and those faculty and staff members who want to refresh their skills. A second advantage of organizing such mixed workshops is forging professional partnerships among librarians across units and departments. To this end, senior librarians make themselves available for newcomers, who in turn may now seek consultation and advice daily either in person or via email.

Another initiative established to increase cooperation and collegiality was reviewing best practices within departments and units. For instance, the metadata unit in the technical services department organized weekly "meta-reviews" based on current and emerging standards. Since the unit needed to accommodate a new faculty and a new staff member, both having different professional backgrounds, we used a textbook, *Metadata for Digital Collections* by Steven J. Miller,[23] as a starting point for our discussions. The main purpose of utilizing this manual was to develop common terminology along with common understanding of metadata purpose, schemas, elements, workflows, and the importance of thorough documentation. Such documentation not only ensures smooth day-to-day operations of the technical services units but also provides comprehensive training material. [24] The next step in our meta-review involved the entire unit team revising legacy digital project specifications with reference to the standards examined earlier. This process helped us in clarifying basic steps and filling information gaps in our workflows. For example, we documented rationales for decisions made regarding the selection of metadata properties and values. Similarly, we included background information about specific digital collections, with attention paid to their origins and reasons for making them accessible online. Such systematic documentation of digital collections has become easy to read and follow by both insiders and newcomers alike.

Working together on a project's specifications has allowed the metadata unit faculty and staff to share individual experiences and challenges related to their specific tasks. As a result, we have not only learned about our daily duties and helped each other solve technical problems but also forged a sense of partnership and mutual responsibility for the quality of work done within the unit.

We took a similar approach to learning a new integrated library system. Again, we scheduled regular meetings for all units within the technical services department. During these meetings we watched video tutorials together and discussed related issues and concerns. One of the outcomes was a list of questions to be addressed by our new vendor.

The next step in our transition to the new system, which is ongoing, involves exploring the online sandbox of the new system along with extensive documentation. Again, we have decided to do it together. This strategy allows us to pool our diverse talents and limited resources and use them for our mutual advantage and growth. The old documentation and the process of learning the former system helped us define our expectations for the new one. Without our foregoing experiences we would not be able to customize our new digital tools and know which of their functionalities we would really like to utilize. Our experience has become an essential learning resource.

Along the same lines, the latest initiative originated in the technical services department is the NMSU Library oral histories project. It aims to collect and preserve knowledge and experiences of senior librarians who have worked at the institution for more than 10 years. Initially we selected 10 librarians for individual audio-recorded interviews designed around a brief set of open-ended questions. The questions were primarily focused on learning, developing, and documenting best practices as appropriate for different tasks and duties associated with specific faculty and staff positions, such as "How do you capture your learning experiences?" "How do you share your knowledge with others?" "What is your unique contribution to the operation of this library?" Such questions invited senior librarians to think about the significance of their regular practices, and they also highlighted the current need for the proper documentation of these practices. Such documentation, in turn, can be utilized for several purposes, including quick self-reference, faculty and staff cross-training, succession plan development, and institutional socialization. We think that creating an easily searchable digital collection featuring audio recordings of the interviews, along with the word-for-word transcripts and indexes, could serve well in addressing these various needs.

In short, the growing collection of personal accounts on various aspects of academic librarianship may then be viewed as a unique reference collection, or perhaps as an introduction to the NMSU Library, its history, its day-to-day operations, and recent developments. The stories told by librarians include descriptions of their own documentation practices that are meant to preserve their legacy of quality librarianship, scholarship, and service. We hope that these stories will inspire new librarians to carry on their legacy.

CONCLUSION

In this chapter we have tried to show how technical services departments are affected by changes in resource availability and allocation; how we at the NMSU Library are working together as a department to ensure that the library continues to provide the best service possible to our students, faculty, staff, and community; and how we continue to plan for the future. We are working to maintain the flexibility to continue providing traditional services while eliminating services that are no longer needed and adding new services as they develop.

Although the technical services pie is changing, the resources going into it decreasing, and the individual slices getting smaller, we are still a critical, vibrant part of the academic library.

NOTES

1. William Playfair, *The Statistical Breviary: Shewing the Resources of Every State and Kingdom in Europe* (London: J. Wallis, 1801), https://books.google.com/books?id=Y4wBAAAAQAAJ.

2. "Our Heritage," About NMSU, New Mexico State University, accessed March 2, 2020, https://home-p.nmsu.edu/about_nmsu/Our%20 Heritage%20.html.

3. "Statement of Accreditation Status: New Mexico State University," Higher Learning Commission, accessed March 2, 2020, https://www .hlcommission.org/component/directory/?Itemid=&Action=Show Basic&instid=1504.

4. "Institution Lookup," The Carnegie Classification of Institutions of Higher Education, Indiana University, accessed March 2, 2020, http://carnegieclassifications.iu.edu/lookup/lookup.php.

5. "Points of Pride," About NMSU, New Mexico State University, accessed March 2, 2020, https://www.nmsu.edu/about_nmsu /universal-page.html.

6. "Be Bold. Shape the Future," About NMSU, New Mexico State University, accessed March 2, 2020, https://www.nmsu.edu/about .html.

7. "NMSU Leads 2025," About NMSU, New Mexico State University, accessed March 2, 2020, https://nmsu.edu/about_nmsu/index.html.

8. New Mexico State University, *New Mexico State University Quick Facts*, 1, accessed February 19, 2020, https://oia.nmsu.edu/files /2019/11/Quick-Facts-2019-20.pdf

9. Ibid.

10. "Factbook 2017," 2, New Mexico State University, accessed February 19, 2020, https://oia.nmsu.edu/data-reports/factbooks/.

11. Ibid, 2.

12. Ibid., 3.

13. Ibid., 1.4.

14. Ibid., 1.

15. Christian Tizon, "Current Term Enrollment Estimates—Spring 2016," *National Student Clearinghouse Research Center* (blog), May 23, 2016, 4, https://nscresearchcenter.org/currenttermenrollment estimate-spring2016/.

16. Commonfund Higher Education Price Index, 2016 Update, Commonfund Institute, 2, accessed March 2, 2020, https://www .commonfund.org/wp-content/uploads/2016/10/2016-HEPI-Report .pdf.

17. "State Map: Funding Down, Tuition Up," Center on Budget and Policy Priorities, accessed March 2, 2020, https://www.cbpp.org/research /state-budget-and-tax/state-map-funding-down-tuition-up.

18. Christopher Pollitt, "Institutional Amnesia: A Paradox of the 'Information Age'?" *Prometheus* 18, no. 1 (2000): 5–16, https://doi .org/10.1080/08109020050000627.

19. Karen Hunter and Robert Bruning, "The Global Economic Crisis: What Libraries and Publishers Can Do and Are Doing," *Serials Librarian* 59, no. 2 (2010): 150, https://doi.org/10.1080/03615261003623161.

20. Norman Oder, "Permanent Shift?: Library Budgets 2010," *Library Journal* 135, no. 1 (2010): 44–46.

21. John J. Regazzi, "U.S. Academic Library Spending, Staffing and Utilization During the Great Recession 2008–2010," *Journal of Academic Librarianship* 39, no. 3 (2013): 217–22, https://doi.org/10 .1016/j.acalib.2012.12.002.

22. L. Kniffel, "Tech Services Consolidation Looms Over Massachusetts' Five Colleges," *American Libraries* 40, no. 12 (2009): 26–27.

23. Steven J. Miller, *Metadata for Digital Collections: A How-to-Do-It Manual*, How-to-Do-It Manuals, no. 179 (New York: Neal-Schuman Publishers, 2011).

24. Roger Brisson, "Online Documentation in Library Technical Services," *Technical Services Quarterly* 16, no. 3 (1999): 1–19, https://doi .org/10.1300/J124v16n03_01; Hollie C. White, "Documentation in Technical Services," *Serials Librarian* 49, no. 3 (2006): 47–55, https://doi.org/10.1300/J123v49n03_04; Laura McCann, "Conservation Documentation in Research Libraries," *Library Resources & Technical Services* 57, no. 1 (2013): 30–50, https://doi .org/10.5860/lrts.57n1.30; John Sandstrom and Liz Miller, *Fundamentals of Technical Services*. ALA Fundamentals Series. (Chicago: Neal-Schuman, an imprint of the American Library Association, 2015); Kara Long et al., "The 'Wicked Problem' of Neutral Description: Toward a Documentation Approach to Metadata Standards," *Cataloging & Classification Quarterly* 55, no. 3 (2017): 107–28, https://doi.org/10.1080/01639374.2016.1278419.

CHAPTER 17

Crossing Conventional Lines: Innovative Staffing and Cross-Training in Technical Services

Lisa Kallman Hopkins

ABSTRACT

The technical services department at the Texas A&M University-Central Texas University Library has effectively implemented creative staffing solutions to stretch its limited personnel resources while at the same time responding to the demands of the university's special community. A&M-Central Texas is an upper-level university located near Fort Hood, one of the largest military installations in the United States. This proximity gives rise to an unusual student body, largely made up of older students who face possible deployment at any time and who may be using their GI Bill to pay for their education. To meet this population's unique demands and fulfill the university's emphasis on community engagement, the technical services team has embraced opportunities for some innovative and unorthodox solutions, requiring versatility and flexibility, sometimes significantly beyond the practices taught in traditional MLS programs. Capitalizing on their strengths and experiences, the technical services team has successfully initiated unusual collaboration and outreach, resulting in valuable and sustaining relationships throughout the university campus as well as the local Killeen community. These relationships and successful initiatives have demonstrated and solidified the department's value in a time when technical services departments nationwide are being downsized and outsourced.

INTRODUCTION

Texas A&M University-Central Texas is a nonresidential institution located in Killeen, Texas, home of Fort Hood, "the largest active duty armored post in the U.S. Armed Forces,"[1] where close to 40,000 soldiers are stationed. A&M-Central Texas was established as the newest university in the Texas A&M University System in May of 2009 and is one of the nation's few upper-level universities, offering only junior- and senior-level coursework and graduate degrees. Its proximity to Fort Hood has a profound impact on both the composition of the student body and delivery of course instruction and library services. More than half of the 2,575 students are over 30, and approximately 50% are military-affiliated, including active or retired military personnel and their families.[2] To accommodate our unique and nontraditional students—many of whom work full time or are unable to physically attend classes on campus for varied reasons—most degrees are also offered online.

The two-story University Library was designed to anticipate and meet the needs of this distinctive population, providing such accommodations as group technology spaces, a student lounge, and a family study area situated near an unusually large children's book selection that serves to welcome students with young children as well as provide material to support the robust education program. Prior to the university archives moving into the newest building on campus in January 2019, archives and special collections were located in two converted classrooms in a separate building from the library. In addition to its attractive and inviting physical space that spans two floors of a four-story classroom building, the library has created a robust virtual presence, with an emphasis on prioritizing electronic resources over print and making bibliographic instruction and services completely accessible online as well as in person.

The library currently employs 13.5 full-time equivalent (FTE) staff. In addition to the dean of the library and the business coordinator, the library's public service department consists of three full-time and three part-time reference librarians, two full-time and three part-time circulation paraprofessionals, and four student workers. The technical services department consists of three librarians—head of technical services, the collection development and acquisitions librarian, and the archivist—along with a full-time paraprofessional copy cataloger, a part-time paraprofessional technical services specialist, and a student worker.

Despite the relatively small number of staff, the University Library has large aspirations: our long-term goal is to become the research library for our Central Texas region. The librarians and paraprofessionals are hired to fill positions, but they often end up filling multiple roles and wearing many hats. We are a flexible, adaptable bunch, open to trying new things and taking on new projects. The library dean encourages library staff to think big and try new things, expanding our services and our reach. Roles are always shifting as staff members gravitate to duties in which they unexpectedly excel, while others fill the gaps they leave behind. These roles often ignore library boundaries that traditionally separate public services from technical services.

Nationally, universities and their libraries are facing shrinking budgets and ever-shifting priorities; yet the six-person technical services team at A&M-Central Texas has proven its relevance in a climate where many other universities' technical services staff have been outsourced. We have made ourselves indispensable by injecting ourselves into every aspect of the library and concurrently becoming an integral part of the broader university community.

SETTING THE SCENE

Before delving into an introduction of the current team members and the many ways our department has broken out of the traditional technical services mold, I will describe briefly how we found ourselves in this situation. I was hired as the cataloging and acquisitions librarian in 2014, just after the library broke away from Central Texas College, a local community college with which it had previously shared resources and space. Additionally, the library was migrating from the integrated library system Evergreen to Innovative Interface's Sierra and Encore Duet. I worked within a newly formed technical services team that also included a technical services manager, who oversaw the system migration and was responsible for establishing guidelines and procedures for the department; a part-time cataloging librarian; a technical services specialist who did the copy-cataloging full time; and a part-time clerk who received and processed books. Our mission and assigned duties focused primarily on purchasing material—with an emphasis on electronic resources—and ensuring that all users could locate and access that material.

Two years after I was hired, the technical services manager left to pursue another job and I was promoted into her position and assumed the title head of technical services. The part-time cataloging librarian moved into my former position, but with the new title of acquisitions and cataloging librarian to recognize and reflect a new emphasis for the position. In 2020, this position changed names once again to collection development and acquisitions librarian after the former head of reference retired. It made sense to align collection development duties with acquisitions. Due to Sierra's efficiency regarding its acquisitions and cataloging functions, the newly unfilled part-time cataloger position was converted to a part-time archivist position whose role would be to organize and manage the university's permanent records collection. Both technical services specialists and the student worker continued in their original roles.

On its face, the technical services team appears to inhabit traditional job titles and descriptions. However, over the past several years each one of us has crossed boundaries and divisions within the library, within the university, and even within technical services itself. Having undertaken so many extra duties—both out of necessity due to a small library staff and in response to appeals for more challenging assignments—the team has leveraged individuals' expertise and past experiences in ways that augment each team member's strengths, as well as enhanced the value of the department. Below I will discuss who we are four years after I became head of technical services and how we have individually crossed invisible lines to increase the value and worth of our department and, inevitably, that of the library. Then I will discuss ways the department has joined in some innovative projects that reach from the library into the university and local community.

BREAKING THROUGH JOB DESCRIPTION BOUNDARIES

As head of technical services, I supervise five other individuals within the department, maintain and update the guidelines and procedures my predecessor established, and oversee a multitude of technical services activities. I oversee all e-resources, the library services platform, the discovery system, the link resolver, and database maintenance. Additionally, I am the liaison between the library and the university IT department, as well as the subject specialist for assigned academic departments. Along with these expected roles, my talent for and previous training in editing and writing has allowed me to step outside of the traditional librarian's role. With the support of the library dean and university administrators, I became a copy editor for university publications and one of eight faculty authors for the Quality Enhancement Plan (QEP), one of the documents required for reaffirmation of accreditation. In addition, I agreed to be the university copyright specialist and have taken numerous classes to equip me for this role. As the copyright specialist, I work with all departments and members of faculty and staff concerning issues from the use of popular music in promotional videos created by the marketing and communications department to faculty concerns over their rights when publishing scholarly achievements. Additionally, I clear all documents for copyright compliance before they are posted in the e-reserves system, maintain an informational subject guide on copyright, and conduct annual workshops for university constituents.

As expected, the collection development and acquisitions librarian orders all library material that the subject liaisons select and faculty members request, both print and electronic monographs and serials. She chooses the vendors and strives to maintain excellent, collaborative relationships. She oversees the library's gifts-in-kind donations. She creates all original cataloging and uses MarcEdit—a batch MARC editing application developed in 1999 by Terry Reese at Oregon State University[3]—to catalog all purchased and subscription e-books, streaming media, and serials. She also purchases some very unorthodox material, the circumstances of which I will detail later.

Recently, this supremely adaptable librarian inherited a crucial role previously filled by the retired head of reference, that of managing and developing the university's many collections. It is logical and appropriate for the individual with intimate knowledge of the collections budget through spending and communication with subject liaisons, university faculty, vendors, and donors to manage the collection itself.

In addition to filling the roles implied by her apt title, the collection development and acquisitions librarian has assumed the responsibilities—previously practiced by the circulation staff—of coordinating the ongoing inventory for the entire 80,000-volume collection, as well as managing the tracking and replacing of billed, lost, and missing books. It made sense for technical services to assume these duties, since issues revealed during inventory can be resolved easily within the department—for example, mis-shelved books can be re-shelved, resolving many missing book issues; incorrect or incomplete call numbers can be remedied by the copy cataloger; and books found to be damaged can be repaired by the technical services specialist. Likewise, it made sense for the acquisitions librarian to generate a report of so-called billed items (books overdue by 45 days or more) on a weekly basis. Those items can then be evaluated for replacement, assigned a replacement value, and ordered immediately (they are marked "lost" in Sierra once a patron pays for them), avoiding a messy chain of messages between departments.

The archivist oversees both the university archives and special collections. In her short but effective tenure with us, she has made strides toward establishing a digital archive within Vital, the digital repository solution we purchase from Innovative, which is built upon and adds to the open source repository platform Fedora.[4] She has been digitizing documents from the university's history, as well as a collection of documents donated by one of Fort Hood's celebrated four-star generals.

The archivist's situation bears closer examination as it is unconventional, the result of resourceful and out-of-the-box thinking. The University Library was committed to transforming the part-time professional archivist position into a full-time library faculty position but lacked the funds to do so. When the library dean discovered that the College of Arts and Sciences had lost its primary history researcher, she contacted the college dean and brokered a deal that would benefit both departments in a year when steep budget cuts university-wide would have prohibited any new hires. It was a natural progression to add to her duties the responsibility of digitizing and processing a large and significant donation and helping to establish what the history department hopes will be a military history center.

In addition, the archivist's role expanded to include that of scholarly communications officer with the University Thesis Office, working with the director of the Graduate School to guide graduate students through the process of researching, writing, and preparing their theses for evaluation and final submission into ProQuest Dissertations & Theses Global database and the university's digital archives. Though she has no formal training in this area, she inherited the role not only because theses will ultimately reside in the digital repository but also because it fills a growing need in the Graduate School. The director of the Graduate School is providing training, and together they are creating a thesis manual that will be distributed to all graduate students. In summary, leveraging an unorthodox but effective strategy, three university units—the Graduate School, the College of Arts and Sciences, and the University Library—are all working together to fully fund this one full-time library faculty position.

The technical services specialist was originally hired as a copy cataloger, but her duties have expanded as her hidden talents have surfaced and the library's needs continue to grow. As the circulation staff turned their focus more to outreach programs and expanded customer service needs, many of their former duties migrated to technical services. The specialist was the recipient of many of those duties, the most significant of which was the management of course reserves. One of the University Library's most appreciated services is acquiring and then making available to students a copy of every textbook adopted in all university courses every semester—in fact, approximately 15% of the materials budget is spent on textbooks. The monumental task of tracking which textbooks are being adopted and determining which are owned and which need to be purchased has fallen to the technical services specialist. Working closely with the university bookstore manager, she compiles a list of titles to be ordered and relays the information to the collection development and acquisitions librarian. Each semester she switches out all the textbooks, both in Sierra's course reserve system and on the reserve shelf. The latest inventory report revealed a breathtaking amount of textbook theft from main stacks, so the specialist responded by suggesting that we create a closed stacks collection for textbooks between rotating course adoptions. In addition to designing a label to identify and track textbooks, she manages the closed stacks conveniently housed in her large, shelf-lined office. These books are marked available in the catalog, but rather than being located in main stacks they must be requested at the circulation desk.

The specialist, in addition to copy cataloging and course reserves, performs the multiple duties that many individuals are hired to perform in larger departments at other universities, taking charge of discarding material that has been marked for weeding, performing all book repairs, and training the student workers in processing physical material.

Our second, part-time technical services specialist, in addition to the duties for which she was originally hired—specifically, assisting the collection development and acquisitions librarian with preorder bibliographic verification, duplicate checking, and receiving materials—inherited the brand new and tremendously successful e-reserve program. The library employs the E-Reserves and Document Management add-on module in LibGuides to house electronic course reserves[5] and provide an easy-to-navigate platform for students and faculty. The part-time specialist intercepts all new requests that come in both via email and through an online form embedded on our website. She then processes those requests, which sometimes entails setting up a link to an article, e-book, or streaming film from one of our databases or media platforms, but often involves scanning a chapter or section from a text. The Texas A&M University System demands absolute compliance with Section 508 of the Rehabilitation Act, amended in 1998 to require all federal agencies to make their electronic and information technology (EIT) accessible to people with disabilities,[6] so anything posted online must be made accessible. To this end, several staff within technical services have been trained to utilize software to render digital documents accessible—namely, Abbyy Finereader (to perform optical character recognition, or OCR) and Adobe Acrobat DC Pro (to verify and perform accessibility checks and create alternative text for figures and tables). Much of the specialist's 20-hour week is spent digitizing documents and making them accessible before they can be uploaded into the e-reserves system. The university's new director of access and inclusion has looked to the library technical services department for help making textbooks and readings accessible for visually impaired students who contact his department for assistance, and the part-time specialist is the primary contact for this ongoing project.

Student workers in every department at A&M-Central Texas are given more responsibility than those at a typical four-year university. Our students are either upper-level or graduate students, having completed their first years of college prior to their arrival, and that gives them a certain gravitas and maturity. Many of our students are military-affiliated, and a significant number are over 30 years of age. As such, the students tend to be more stable, staying with a department for at least 2 years, and most are seamlessly integrated with the budgeted staff. In fact, many of the university's student workers apply for and successfully fill permanent positions within the university after they graduate. The library employs five student workers, four in circulation and one in technical services. The student worker in technical services assists with receiving and processing physical materials, duplicate-checking as part of the acquisitions preorder process, inventorying the collection, weeding and de-processing, scanning for e-reserves, and tracking inventory of the department's supplies, which is an impressive collection of accomplishments for someone who only works 15 hours a week.

All three of the technical services librarians cross the conventional public-technical services line to staff the reference desk five hours a week. In a role once reserved for the reference librarians, we serve as liaisons for academic departments, which entails selecting material in that discipline for purchase, serving as embedded librarians in courses within that discipline when the faculty request that service, and establishing communication with the department faculty members to ensure their scholarly needs are met and students remain supported.

REACHING ACROSS THE UNIVERSITY

Our regular outreach to other university departments has led to some unusual endeavors for library staff and has amplified the library's value, solidified its reputation as a department that engages in collaboration and support within the institution, and ultimately ensured its continued generous funding by the university. We have made friends across campus who will serve as advocates and defenders. When the Texas legislature imposed unprecedented cuts on education spending a few years ago, the university administrators protected the library budget.

I will describe a few specific examples of how we began collaborating with other departments and how each instance originated organically out of a problem, scarcity, or unique situation that provided the opening for creative solutions and partnerships.

Campus libraries often find themselves at odds with information technology departments, but our ability to provide a service to the technology enhanced learning (TEL) on our campus has resulted in an enhanced and valuable give-and-take partnership between the library and TEL. This mutually beneficial opportunity arose when a faculty member submitted an e-reserve request for a streaming film for which no closed-captioning was available. Recognizing that, per A&M System rules and regulations, without closed-captioning this film could not be shared, and due to the prohibitive cost of outsourcing this service and the fact that TEL department was too short-staffed to accomplish it in-house, three library technical services staff members took a crash course in the application of closed-captioning. With the acquisition of this valuable skill, the library can assist in future closed-captioning projects and solidify our positive relationship with IT and TEL.

Capitalizing on similar opportunities, the collection development and acquisitions librarian and technical services specialist established a positive relationship with the university bookstore while also providing one of the library's most popular services, acquiring and then lending a copy of every adopted textbook. Our reach extended to the marketing and communications department to monitor and educate staff about copyright to ensure the legality and enhanced quality of university promotional material. Likewise, members of the technical services staff secured the goodwill and esteem of the institutional research and assessment department when we agreed to edit the *University Catalog*, strategic plan, and accreditation documents. The technical services EIT accessibility experts were able to work with the accessibility and inclusion office to assist them with rendering texts accessible for visually impaired students on campus, which has made it possible for the university to expand limited resources in this area and allow students to succeed and excel. The dean of the library, herself a resourceful, ambitious leader, encourages all library staff to take advantage of opportunities as they present themselves. While we sometimes find ourselves "voluntold" to take part in unconventional partnerships, it is usually the case that individuals initiate the collaborations themselves.

REACHING INTO THE LARGER COMMUNITY

In addition to individual team members taking on a smorgasbord of unorthodox work, the technical services department as a unit has developed partnerships or leadership roles within the library, university, and the community, which expands its reach and augments its ability to provide valuable services that are foreign to the typical technical services department. In 2016 the library dean, education librarian, and outreach and instruction librarian applied for and were awarded a significant grant through the Texas State Library and Archives Commission (TSLAC). The funding allows the University Library to support "'Library Programming for Multiple Intelligences' targeting children with disabilities. Components of this project include offering library programming for Oak Creek Academy, a local nonprofit private school for grades Pre-K-12; working with [A&M-Central Texas] education students to use innovative resources in the classroom; and providing workshops and training for families, educators, and librarians in the local community."[7]

This grant award had a profound impact on the University Library and shaped many of the staff members' duties and priorities. One of the biggest impacts within technical services was $20,000 designated for the purchase of educational books, manipulatives, and furniture. The onus of this task fell on the collection development and acquisitions librarian, who had approximately six months to select, purchase, and create original cataloging for manipulatives, which included a wide range of educational toys, tools, and materials within each of the traditional school subjects (reading, mathematics, sciences, social studies)—for example, puppets, puzzles, chemistry sets, teaching cash registers, counters, phonics sets, literacy word-building tiles, et cetera.

The technical services specialist worked closely with the collection development and acquisitions librarian to devise appropriate housing for the manipulatives—in some instances, they had to get very creative, such as when they used luggage tags to attach barcodes and call numbers to puppets, audiobook cases to house language cards, and plastic shoeboxes to contain games and items with many pieces. Most of the technical services staff are called on twice a month to assist with children's programming when students from the local Oak Creek Academy visit the library, or when the education librarian performs pop-up presentations at neighboring Killeen Independent School District schools or in-house training for community educators.

Another massive undertaking associated with the TSLAC grant is the creation of the library at Oak Creek Academy. A&M-Central Texas technical services staff researched the most appropriate and cost-effective school cataloging software for the school, facilitated the purchase and installation of the software, and then initiated the cataloging of the collection. Additionally, our staff evaluated, organized, and arranged the collection, labeling the shelves and establishing best practice for the school's needs. We made weekly trips to the library, cataloging and processing all the nonfiction material. At the end of six months, the technical services specialist created an illustrated, step-by-step, easy-to-follow manual to enable Oak Creek employees or volunteers to take over the cataloging and maintenance of their library.

CAPITALIZING ON STRENGTHS AND EXPERIENCES

Prior to joining our team, the collection development and acquisitions librarian was the assistant director of the Killeen Public Library, and she brings a wealth of knowledge about collaboration and teamwork. She helped establish a partnership with Killeen Public Library, whereby we serve as a satellite branch for them. Rather than discard their duplicate best sellers and children's books, as well as aging but still relevant material, we have agreed to house those items in our collection, demarcated with a yellow piece of tape over the call number. When those items are checked out, we share those statistics with Killeen Public Library, increasing circulation at both libraries. In addition, she has encouraged annual community reading events with the area public libraries to expose community members to our program and to empower and enrich the local community with scholarly events.

The QEP that will be implemented in 2018 is a "Writing in the Disciplines" initiative that includes an extensive library component. Not only was a member of the technical services department one of the eight authors on the document, but all the library's professional staff will be deeply involved in the resulting plan. The plan envisions the University Writing Center and University Library in partnership to provide an embedded librarian and embedded writing tutor for every single writing-intensive class, at least one of which will in turn be required of every student who graduates from the university. When this program reaches its peak, every librarian from every area (public and technical services) will serve as an embedded librarian in these classes.

THE VALUE OF PLASTICITY FOR SUCCESS AND INNOVATION

Because of its members' open-door attitudes and collaborative spirit, the technical services department is perceived in a very positive light both within the library and within the university. The culture and climate of A&M-Central Texas—in part because it is a young university—inspires innovation, multitasking, hard work, experimentation, and outreach to promote the university brand. Such a climate provides fertile ground for our department to flourish and evolve. Everybody in the university wears many hats, and the University Library technical services department is no different. Personnel are given freedom to try new things. Talent is recognized and valued, and those individuals are prized and rewarded. This university promotes and encourages cross-training and cross-university partnerships more than any other with which I have been involved.

These changes in duties have occurred because of an emphasis on discovering and employing talents when they are found in innovative ways that break free from the confines of job descriptions and traditional tasks, and even institutional divisions and boundaries. Success at this has been augmented by creative and continued effort to capitalize on grant opportunities and other extra-institutional initiatives. Our library staff think outside the box, both in terms of traditional job categories and boundaries and in terms of connecting to the larger academic and nonacademic communities.

Technical services departments nationwide are being outsourced, downsized, and challenged. One way to combat the threat of extinction and instead become indispensable and essential is to become more agile, be proponents of teamwork, and develop deep partnerships within the department, within the library, across the university, and even within the local community. In my university, the members of technical services have proven to be resourceful team players. Cross-training is paramount—cross-training within the department, so that there is support for overcommitted team members during the crunch times, such as semester beginnings when textbooks and e-reserve requests are flooding in; and cross-training within the library, so that technical services staff can jump onto the circulation desk when needed. Beyond the obvious benefit of fostering cooperation within the library, providing opportunities for technical services staff to take shifts on the public service desks enhances their work behind the scenes. Being broadly knowledgeable about procedures in both public services and technical services represents technical services staff as the obvious go-to source for answers. Further, our direct communication with vendors and intimate knowledge about library systems and technology give us an edge when problem-solving.

Another key factor is collaboration, which involves listening closely to what is happening across campus, and when an opening is discovered, communicating individual strengths and the department's services to the university community. Collaboration also means watching for opportunities to deliver expertise and services to the local community outside of the university—not only enhancing the department's reputation but benefiting the university from increased exposure. Ultimately, the key to establishing any library department as indispensable is to share your services—as individuals and as a team—within your department, library, university, and community.

NOTES

1. "History," U.S. Army Fort Hood, last modified March 8, 2019, https://home.army.mil/hood/index.php/about/history.
2. Paul Turcotte, Director of Office of Institutional Research and Assessment, email message to author, November 29, 2017.

3. "About MarcEdit," MarcEdit Development, accessed October 25, 2018, https://marcedit.reeset.net/about-marcedit.

4. Fedora is an open source repository system for managing digital content. For more information on this platform, see "About Fedora," Duraspace, https://duraspace.org/fedora/about/.

5. LibGuides, a content management system supported by SpringShare, is nearly ubiquitous in libraries. Our library web page and all research guides are built using the LibGuides platform. For more information on this content management system, see "LibGuides," SpringShare, https://www.springshare.com/libguides/.

6. "IT Accessibility Laws and Policies," GSA Section 508, reviewed/ updated July 2018, https://www.section508.gov/manage/laws-and -policies.

7. "Library Receives Special Project Grant Funding," Texas A&M University-Central Texas news release, October 21, 2016, https:// news.tamuct.edu/library-receives-special-project-grant-funding/.

CHAPTER 18

Challenging the Status Quo: Collaboration and Creativity in Small Academic Libraries

Susanne Markgren

ABSTRACT

Technical services departments have experienced more than their fair share of change in the past 20 years, but have they changed enough or are they mired in the immutable status quo, complacent with the tradition of how things have always been done? Small libraries offer additional challenges of reduced staff, resources, and budgets, which can lead to creative solutions and more holistic environments. This chapter addresses the challenges that affect technical services departments, primarily in small academic libraries, from the point of view of a new technical services manager and offers ideas on how to employ creativity, enhance productivity, and encourage change.

INTRODUCTION

Not much has changed in technical services departments in the past 20 years. Materials are acquired, classified, processed, and made accessible to patrons. Catalogs and databases are built and managed and migrated. Licenses and renewals and invoices are reviewed and retained. And statistics and data are harvested and assessed. So . . . 20 years of status quo, right? Well, not exactly. Lots of things have changed (of course)—like systems, software, processes, formats, classification schemes, vendors, workflows, purchasing models, publishing models, patron expectations, and academic culture, to name just a few. But, have the roles and work of the staff, librarians, and departments changed at the same pace? Have libraries embraced change in public-facing areas, while succumbing to the status quo in other, not-so-public, areas? Have they become so complacent in the status quo that they are blind to the changes going on all around—changes that can affect daily routines and changes that are enmeshed with the attitudes and ideology of the current world climate?

This chapter addresses some of the challenges that affect technical services departments—primarily in small academic libraries—and those who work in them and offers ideas on how to collaborate and employ creativity in order to enhance productivity and change, while emphasizing the importance of advocacy, transparency, communication, and support as crucial pillars for the future success and sustained existence of technical services roles and departments.

BACKGROUND

As someone who has recently moved into an administrative role in a technical services department of a small academic library, and someone who has worked in academic libraries for more than 20 years, I've experienced change on many levels—in different libraries, in different departments, and in different roles. And now, in my current position as the head of technical services, I am excited to be able to help transform and rethink roles, functions, and processes and to protect an area that is becoming increasingly endangered. Currently I work in a small private college in the Bronx with a full-time equivalent (FTE) of approximately 4,000 students (undergraduates and graduates combined), with 8 librarians and a staff of 25, in both full- and part-time positions. I am the only librarian in technical services. My department handles acquisitions, serials, cataloging, electronic resources, systems, and interlibrary loan with a staff of 7 (5 full-time, 2 part-time) and me.

Through a combination of choice, chance, and external circumstances, I have worked in small libraries for most of my professional career. Small libraries have given me more freedom to be involved with decision-making for the library, more freedom to take on projects that I think are important, more freedom to explore and try out different roles and learn new skills, and more freedom to test out alternative ideas, processes, and tools with less administrative baggage. Small libraries come with many rewards and opportunities, and just as many roadblocks and challenges. They typically have smaller collections, fewer staff members, less space, smaller budgets, and fewer resources. Due to many of these constraints, smaller libraries often need to reduce services, disperse resources, and forgo specialization among staff and librarians in lieu of a more generalist and holistic approach.[1] But constraints tend to force us to think more creatively, more out-of-the-box, and can lead to more collaboration, more crossover, less hierarchy, and fewer silos—or divisions—within the library. These, along with planning for the constants of employee attrition, generational divides, and technological change, can help to transform departments and libraries into more dynamic and sustainable institutions that challenge the status quo.

Once growing and thriving, with the advent of online catalogs, online resources, and integrated library systems, many technical services departments are now being downsized: staff members are not replaced when they leave, functions and processes have been outsourced, and all too often, they've been left without vision and leadership, which can lead to a lack of innovation and motivation. A 1998 article in *The Journal of Academic Librarianship*, prescribes that

> innovation is essential for the survival of libraries in the rapidly changing information world. In particular, technical services will be expected to acquire and process material more quickly than ever before and with fewer human resources. The economic environment and the speed of technological change demands and provides new alternatives. Changing patron expectations have accelerated the need for rapid evaluation, selection, and implementation of these new alternatives. The choices available from vendors will continue to proliferate. As a result, strong, competent technical services managers are an essential component to this process. These managers must continue to envision the future, to think intuitively and creatively, and to implement innovation effectively.[2]

Not only are these accurate predictions, they are spot-on 20 years later. Libraries are still dealing with changing technology and patron expectations, an unending onslaught of new resources and vendors, and fewer staff members to perform necessary functions. And, if anything has been learned from the past 20 years, it is that these things will continue to change, and libraries will need to continue to change with them and seek out effective ways to cope and thrive, while being mindful of the larger picture, of what's happening outside offices and departments and libraries and institutions. If they remain in oblivious isolation, mired in the traditions of how things were once done, librarians and staff may become not just out of touch but irrelevant.

In many smaller libraries, there is a disconcerting absence of structure, hierarchy, and leadership within technical services departments. As people retire, their positions either are not filled or are moved to other, more public-facing, areas of the library. And positions of leadership and management (e.g., department heads and librarian positions) are often not filled, and many departments have been essentially flattened out, left on the fringe, or entirely outsourced. Leadership can, perhaps, be found in other places, and from staff members and librarians outside of the department, but a lack of hierarchy and vision within the department itself can lead to disengagement and a sense of isolation from the rest of the library. Staff members are left to their own devices to stay current with systems and technology.

Outsourcing and downsizing are not always bad decisions, and may be necessary for some libraries, but these decisions should be based on evidence and supported and understood by all those affected. Outsourcing key roles can be detrimental to workflow if no one on staff understands enough to troubleshoot problems and edit/import/export on the fly. And, no matter how small or depleted, technical services departments need competent managers. Who else will fight for the future of the department, for staff training and retention, for technical enhancements and innovations? Who better to understand how to utilize various skill sets, work with a variety of critical library systems, collaborate with other departments, and help to redefine roles to meet the current, and ever-changing, needs of the library and its patrons?

BEYOND TRADITION

The word *tradition* is often tossed around when one starts a new position, and statements like, "This is how things have traditionally been done," are common. For a newly hired individual, this usually means don't mess with the status quo. The word (or idea of) tradition seems to connote the opposite of progress or change, the amnesia to what's happening around us. We forget to change when we hold on too tightly to our traditions. It's fine and good to look at our past, to revisit where we came from and how we got here. But tradition in the disguise of nostalgia can be dangerous to our future. To focus on a traditional role or function of libraries—or how things were done in the past—is to press the pause button on a singular moment in time, taken out of context, that rarely captures the true nature and purpose of libraries: to serve the reader (or researcher or seeker).

So how do we get past our traditions and move toward change? How do we disrupt the status quo while maintaining cohesion and productivity? Any kind of change, small or large, can be disruptive, stressful, unnerving, and scary. Many people will resist, or shut down, when confronted with it. Many people prefer to continue in their traditional roles and workflows. And they may (perhaps rightfully so) fear for the security of their positions. But much of this resistance and fear can be alleviated with observation, communication, empathy, and time. From personal experience, I can offer the following: Before implementing change, watch and learn how the staff interact with one another, and with the rest of the library. Understand the various workflows and procedures and—most importantly—ask questions. Meet with others, both informally and formally. Learn the history, the when and the why, of the way things are traditionally done. And, if you are in a position of authority, or a position to create change, ask staff and librarians for input into their own roles and duties, and for ideas on how to help them, whether that means being more efficient, learning new skills, working with different people, or sharing knowledge. As a manager, it is important to understand the emotions and reactions that people must change, and to garner support and ideas in order to optimize buy-in for potential new workflows, systems, and processes, and be responsive to any concerns that may arise.[3]

Like the phases of the moon, our roles can wax and wane. A couple of members of my staff found their roles in print serials and media—which used to keep them busy—waning over the past few years. We've been cutting print periodicals in lieu of online ones, and the media center, which once housed thousands of VHS, DVDs, CDs, and microforms, has become a computer lab. Also over the past few years we have subscribed to a new interlibrary loan system (a big upgrade to what we previously had) and made improvements to our website, our e-journal holdings, and our OpenURL resolver, which has caused our borrowing numbers to rise dramatically. To help sustain the need in this one, waxing area, we approached the two staff members to see if they would be interested in working part-time in interlibrary loan. They were thrilled to learn something new, and even more thrilled to be needed and busy once again.

Our roles and processes and institutional structures are dynamic and evolving. At times, we may need to be reminded of this. It can be helpful to occasionally look to the past, to figure out how and why things were done a certain way, and to learn from our successes and our failures. But we shouldn't dwell too long on things we used to do, or place too much importance on the way things were done, which can slow us down in the present and prohibit progress.

CREATE YOUR TEAMS

Beyond our daily routine work, much of what we do in libraries is project-based. In smaller libraries, a lot of the bigger projects, ones that may be written into the normal workflow at larger institutions, are done only when there are enough people to do them and those people have enough time to start them. Time that isn't taken up with other daily tasks and interruptions. In academia, this usually means that these projects are put off until intercession or summer. In previous positions, I was often asked to take on large-scale projects because someone thought I had the skills and know-how to do it myself. This was flattering at first, but it quickly became overwhelming. I would eventually come to the realization that I did not possess all the skills or tools or time needed to complete the project, and I had no one to ask for help. Or, alternatively, I felt paralyzed to move forward at any given step because I didn't feel like I was capable, or should have been capable, of making certain decisions on my own. After plenty of frustrating starts and stops, I learned that to combat this lonely ritual I needed to create my own teams, to recruit people I want to work with and convince them that these projects are bigger than just one of us. All it takes is a discussion to get others interested in a project. The next steps involve setting up meetings and creating objectives, timelines, and deadlines. Communication (to stimulate accountability) is a key part of the process. With a team, no one person is seen as being in charge—we all have different tasks working toward a singular goal, we are all equals, and we are working together in the most efficient way possible to benefit the library. In an article focused on creating solutions, Gibson discusses teams as part of the process: "Moving away from strictly defined job functions to a more general purpose and direction can combine like-minded functions rather than maintaining clearly defined silos. . . . It is a concerted effort of looking at the organization and determining the skills necessary for innovation and discovery."[4]

We would be nothing without collaboration. Or, more precisely, we would get nothing done. In smaller libraries, especially, collaboration and team-building are critical to survival. Many technical services librarians do their work alone, or in tiny departments. Technical services departments themselves can often become compartmentalized (silos within a silo) because people do perform specialized functions, in different systems, with little if any overlap. But our goal is simple and shared: make our collections discoverable and accessible. I consider my department to be my primary team. My goal is to create a supportive and sharing environment and to implement a structure of reinforcement for us to support one another with backup if someone is out, and to understand each other's roles so we can dismantle the silos within the department.

What we do in technical services ultimately affects how public services staff work, and how our users interact with our resources. In a recent study on cross-perceptions of technical services and public services librarians, the authors concluded that "the key solution is to enhance institutional communication and understanding and to build a trusting team culture." They go on to say that "management and leadership play a critical role in cultivating a trusting team environment."[5] I regularly team up with people outside of my department to work on various projects, such as collection and weeding projects, space reorganization projects, and reclassification projects. We utilize people, both librarians and staff members, who understand the work, who have needed skills or expertise, and who are interested in a specific project. Recently, we were tasked with building a new library website. We constructed a team of five people, two from technical services, and three from public services. We designed and created the website in working meetings, held in a computer lab, that lasted anywhere from two to six hours. We worked on different components of the website and made decisions as a team, and we completed it within a tight time frame. Teaming up with others provides camaraderie and accountability as well as more visibility for technical services functions and staff. Working across departments utilizes our combined strengths to accomplish projects (that are bigger than just one of us) and learn from one another. And, perhaps most importantly, it makes the work so much more fun.

Another way to support staff and encourage them to share their own skills and interest is to offer hands-on training sessions, taught by librarians and staff members, on certain resources, tools, and software. Not only does this help in team building, it provides a sense of professional purpose and pride for those who attend and those who develop them. And ultimately, this is our job as managers and leaders: to encourage growth and engagement. Our constraints—lack of budgets, resources, staffing, time—can spur creativity and incite action. All staff members should be allowed to connect their personal interests with available workplace options to stimulate engagement and learning.[6] Technical services librarians and staff need to step outside their roles, their walls, and their comfort zones and work on projects that interest them. They should be encouraged to share ideas, to be creative, and to utilize their own skills and passions within the workplace.

FIND YOUR CREW

Internal collaboration and working with teams are important, but seeking collaborators and mentors outside of one's workplace can be equally as essential for professional growth and satisfaction. At times we may feel like we are an island unto ourselves, or a tiny silo, especially if we work in smaller libraries and we are the only person in the library who does what we do, or if we have to take on many roles and cannot afford the luxury of specialization in one particular area (electronic resources, systems, interlibrary loan, serials, acquisitions, cataloging). Getting involved in associations and consortia can provide access to like-minded librarians and staff who may work in the same role as us but in a different library or organization. These connections can offer a wealth of resources and knowledge to tap into when we have a question, need assistance, or want advice. These people can become our allies if we are feeling misunderstood or undervalued in our own library, and they can become our collaborators on projects. I've met some of the most amazing, insightful, and inspiring people when I've gotten out of my library to attend meetings and discussion groups, and when I have volunteered to work on committees. And, in turn, I feel more engaged in my work when I can bring back the energy and ideas that I get from meeting with my crew.

I've been involved with the WALDO (Westchester Academic Library Director's Organization) consortium for many years. Its primary role is to support member institutions with the procurement and administration of electronic resources. Along with an executive board, it consists of committees that meet regularly to discuss various aspects of librarianship and to share information with local librarians. As a member of the collection services committee, I meet with my peers in other institutions, where we discuss the broader concept of collections and narrower facets that fall within our scope of duties, such as metadata, discovery, pricing, usage, e-books, open access, and new resources and interfaces. We also talk about best practices, vendor relations, administrative issues, staffing woes, and access problems. Discussions are loosely structured and mostly organic, and meeting topics are gleaned from the group members. Meetings are both in-person and virtual, using Zoom[7] to facilitate discussion and sharing of information, as well as the occasional vendor webinar. Members are from small and large libraries, public and private, staff and librarians. Together we are stronger and more empowered to make suggestions (or demands) of publishers, vendors, and the consortium itself. And they are more apt to listen. The more we share with one another, the more informed and energized we become.

It can be difficult to get away from work to attend meetings or discussion groups, but communication and collaboration can be found from online groups as well. ALCTS[8] (Association for Library Collections and Technical Services) offers free moderated e-forums and webinars on a variety of relevant and timely topics. Finding your crew may take some time and effort, but it is so worth it. In the larger library world we are not islands unto ourselves—we are a community. Seek out discussion groups or start your own. Get involved in local, regional, or national associations. Find online groups and forums and consider partnering with people in other libraries or institutions to collaborate on presentations or writing projects and to share your knowledge and ideas with the rest of us.

ADVOCACY AND COMPASSION

One of the biggest challenges for those who work in technical services is a lack of understanding—even among librarians—of what we do, how we do it, and how important it is to the health and advancement of the library and the institution. Charles Sicignano, in a chapter for *Rethinking Technical Services*, writes that

> many academic librarians who are in technical services find themselves in an awkward position. Technical services librarians juggle many responsibilities, much of which happens out of view. This can make it difficult to explain or prove that what happens within the department is important and can have a real effect on the university's overall curriculum.[9]

When we are out of view, we are out of touch with our colleagues, administrators, and campus communities. This can and does lead to stereotyping, which is especially harmful when we do it to ourselves and can ultimately be harmful to our profession. We've all heard it before—technical services people are introverts, prone to obsessing over proper categorization and formatting. We work in dark basements, our desks are meticulously organized, and we don't interact with others, especially not patrons. We are socially inept, bitter, and territorial. While some of this may be slightly true to a certain extent, it is somewhat troublesome that this stereotype still exists within our profession. We are not the opposite of public service librarians. We don't exist in the upside down.[10] We are not averse to interacting, or collaborating, with colleagues or patrons. Technical services staff must be skilled at, and properly trained in, using advanced systems and tools for cataloging, serials management, acquisitions, budgeting, website development, interlibrary loan, and data analysis. We also need to be aware of changes occurring around us, such as updates with software and systems, security issues, and access problems. And we need to effectively communicate with colleagues in other departments and patrons who need assistance.

So, how do we educate others about what we do? How can we let them know what we can do for them? And how can we be more transparent with our processes and projects? This can be as simple as sending out emails to our colleagues and administrators with collection statistics or details on completed or ongoing projects. It can involve an open house event where colleagues and others can visit the department and ask questions, and we can showcase the technology and systems we use. It can involve teaching colleagues, student workers, and interns about our fundamental roles within the library and working with others to help build, promote, and maintain the collections. It can involve speaking up at meetings and asking for the equipment and resources that we need. It can involve sharing our data with those who can benefit from it. It can involve writing and presenting and committee work. It can involve sharing on social media outlets. It can involve self-promotion and telling our stories to those who will listen. And, it should involve compassion for our colleagues and for ourselves. We do not like being in the dark (even though some of our departments may be in windowless basements), and the work we do shouldn't be shrouded in darkness.

FINAL THOUGHTS

Twenty years can seem like an eternity, but it goes by in the blink of the eye. And 20 years from now we will—almost certainly—be discussing the same things we are now and lamenting the status quo. We need to believe that technical services can influence and lead innovation and progress for the rest of the library, as Michael Gorman explores in his 1998 book:

> Technical services are as important in libraries today as they have always been. The imaginative use of technology to enhance and expand library services and resources has, to a great extent,

stemmed from innovation in technical services areas. The technical services librarian is uniquely placed to have a rewarding career in service to humankind—the ultimate purpose of all libraries and librarians.[11]

There is much work to be done in technical services. It is, in fact, endless and exciting and in constant motion; therefore we should never be in fear of extinction. But we cannot be complacent and immutable, confined in our traditions, and accepting of the status quo. We need to make sure that those around us, both inside and outside the library, understand our importance and value our skills. We need to have a clear vision of our individual roles and our departmental goals and be able to communicate them passionately and effectively. We need to be our own advocates. We need to be able to adapt to the dynamic environment around us and transition and update our skills and roles when necessary. We need to use our imagination and creativity to break our constraints and battle our fears. We need to keep our eyes open and be aware of the changes going on around us. And we need to create our own teams, seek out leadership if we don't have it, and continue to learn and grow and teach.

NOTES

1. Brian Doherty and Alison Piper, "Creating a New Organizational Structure for a Small Academic Library: The Merging of Technical Services and Access Services," *Technical Services Quarterly* 32 (2014): 161, https://doi.org/10.1080/07317131.2015.998466.
2. Carol Pitts Diedrichs, "Using Automation in Technical Services to Foster Innovation," *Journal of Academic Librarianship* 24, no. 2 (1998): 119–20, https://doi.org/10.1016/S0099-1333(98)90171-9.
3. Wyoma VanDuinkerken and Pixey Anne Mosley, *The Challenge of Library Management: Leading With Emotional Engagement* (Chicago: American Library Association, 2011), 45.
4. Sally Gibson, "Creating Solutions Instead of Solving Problems: Emerging Roles for Technical Services Departments," *Technical Services Quarterly* 33, no. 2. (2016): 150, https://doi.org/10.1080/07317131.2016.1134998.

5. Cathy Weng and Erin Ackerman, "Towards a Sustainable Partnership: Examining Cross Perceptions of Public and Technical Services Academic Librarians," *Library Resources & Technical Services* 61, no. 4. (2017): 207.

6. Tom Kelley and David Kelley, *Creative Confidence: Unleashing the Creative Potential Within Us All* (London: William Collins, 2015).

7. Zoom Video Communications (https://www.zoom.us/) provides remote conferencing services using cloud computing.

8. See "Online Learning," ALCTS, http://www.ala.org/alcts/confevents.

9. Charles Sicignano, "Emerging Roles and Opportunities for the Technical Services Manager," in *Rethinking Technical Services: New Frameworks, New Skill Sets, New Tools, New Roles*, edited by Bradford Lee Eden (Lanham, MD: Rowman & Littlefield, 2016), 44.

10. The "upside down" is a reference from the popular Netflix series Stranger Things, first released on July 15, 2016.

11. Michael Gorman, *Technical Services Today and Tomorrow* (Englewood, CO: Libraries Unlimited, 1998), 6.

CHAPTER 19

Out From the Shadows: Transforming Technical Services During an Academic Library's Reorganization

Courtney McAllister

ABSTRACT

Within academic libraries, technical services departments can be marginalized due to a variety of tensions and misperceptions. However, a library-wide reorganization represents an ideal opportunity to challenge assumptions and reposition technical services as a vital and innovative component of library services and operations. When The Citadel's Daniel Library launched its comprehensive reorganization in October 2015, technical services played a multifaceted role that demonstrated the department's leadership potential, strategic planning skills, and collaborative culture. The process helped chip away at the preexisting schism between reference ("front stage") and technical services ("backstage"). As a result, technical services personnel have become integrated into interdepartmental teams and projects, which facilitates meaningful cross-pollination and shifts narratives about the value of technical services' roles and responsibilities. Although the reorganization's recent impact is still reverberating throughout the library, technical services has become more thoroughly embedded in the library's strategic planning and daily operations. To some extent, the department is transitioning into the role of the library's internal reference service. Personnel from elsewhere in the organization are more actively seeking advice and guidance from technical services, now that we have emerged from the shadows. The next step may involve integrating technical services into formal instruction and liaison assignments.

INTRODUCTION

Technical services (TS) librarians and paraprofessionals are essential to a library's daily operations and adaptive, collaborative culture. Without dedicated, resourceful personnel assessing and improving processes involved in acquisitions, cataloging, print and electronic resource management, and collection assessment, meeting patrons' information and research needs would be an exercise in futility. Despite this inherent symbiosis, TS department personnel are not typically recognized in academia as being change-positive or innovative. Rather, the default characterization is that they prefer to reside in the "back room"[1] and tend to be secretive, antisocial, inflexible, and overly attached to rules and structure.[2]

These perceptions are difficult to dispel once they become ingrained in a library's culture. Even the addition of new personnel, and the physical modification of workspaces, will not automatically disrupt the mythology of the back room and its denizens. In some instances, a comprehensive cultural overhaul, like a library-wide reorganization, is needed to introduce new mental models,[3] deconstruct inherited silos, and create opportunities for change and growth that benefit technical services, the library, and its patrons. These organizational changes must be implemented with care and concern for both short-term disruptions and long-term, sustainable transformation. The library reorganization that took place during 2015–2016 at The Citadel's Daniel Library excelled in some respects but left the organization with lingering growing pains and opportunities for future improvement.

ENVIRONMENTAL CONTEXT

The Daniel Library serves the students, faculty, and staff affiliated with The Citadel, The Military College of South Carolina, as well as members of the PASCAL (Partnership Among South Carolina Academic Libraries) consortium and the local community. Founded in 1842, The Citadel is a public liberal arts college located in Charleston, South Carolina. As a military college, The Citadel's iconography and culture are heavily influenced by military discipline and hierarchies.

Most of the 3,600-student body is part of the Corps of Cadets. These 2,349 undergraduate students reside in barracks rather than dorms, wear military uniforms, and follow a highly regimented schedule that combines academics with leadership training and rigorous physical demands. Commission into the armed forces is voluntary; however, roughly 30% choose to enlist after completing their degree. Other graduates pursue careers in government, law enforcement, business, and engineering.

In addition to maintaining its solid undergraduate base, The Citadel has expanded its graduate programs and online course offerings to attract a wider range of students and bolster enrollment without expanding the campus's physical footprint. The Citadel is especially attractive to veterans since their military service is valued and many of the customs embedded in campus life evoke or emulate military culture. Enrollment has grown in recent years, though state funding has declined. Because of the accelerated rate of change and increased financial pressures at the campus level, the Daniel Library began to methodically assess its operations, services, and staffing in 2015. This analysis eventually catalyzed a library-wide reorganization to enable the library to better serve the campus community and provide more 21st-century information services.

DANIEL LIBRARY, PRE-REORGANIZATION

The Daniel Library, which was constructed in the 1960s, also houses The Citadel Archives and The Citadel Museum. Prior to the reorganization project, the library's organizational structure revolved around the following departments and associated tasks:

Library administration: The library director (librarian) and administrative assistant (paraprofessional) managed personnel, facilities, and budgetary issues.

Circulation: The circulation manager (paraprofessional) and four direct reports (paraprofessionals) coordinated basic circulation functions, interacted with patrons at the circulation desk, and managed print and electronic course reserves, interlibrary loan services, and stacks maintenance.

Technical services: Two librarians, two paraprofessionals, and
one part-time temporary employee shared responsibility
for acquisitions, cataloging, integrated library systems (ILS)
management, government documents, collection development, and the management of print and electronic serials,
e-books, and databases.

Research and instruction: Four librarians were responsible for
providing research assistance at the reference desk, teaching
information literacy (IL) classes, serving as departmental
liaisons, managing the library's website, supporting library
systems and technology, and conducting archival research.

The organization of the seven librarians and eight full-time paraprofessionals that made up the Daniel Library's staff had not been
reevaluated for decades. The distribution of personnel and skills
was not only out of step with the shifting needs of a contemporary
academic library and its patrons but also placed a tremendous supervisory burden on the library director, who had eight full-time direct
reports. As a result, the library director, who was hired in 2012, had
insufficient time to provide visionary leadership for the library, The
Citadel Archives, and The Citadel Museum, let alone pursue development opportunities for all three.

REORGANIZATION INSPIRATION AND GOALS

The pre-reorganization allocation of responsibilities and personnel
revolved around obsolete patterns and bygone needs. Staffing both
a circulation and a reference desk, for example, did not reflect the
decreased volume of circulation transactions, nor the variety of communication channels patrons utilize to obtain information assistance,
such as chat, email, and text. Having a paraprofessional position
almost exclusively dedicated to print serials was also incongruous with
the transition to e-journals. In addition to these inefficiencies, there
were cultural schisms that needed to be ameliorated.

Although silos are often discussed in the context of large,
bureaucratic institutions, even small organizations can succumb to
fragmentation and unhealthy subcultures. At the Daniel Library,

the inherited organizational structure had created silos among circulation, research and instruction, and technical services. The public-facing side of the house seemed to have very little understanding of, or appreciation for, the contributions made by technical services, which undermined the morale and sense of communal rapport in TS. The dynamic between librarians and paraprofessionals was also strained. To some extent, the campus economy of status and military authority had predisposed the library to problematic hierarchies. At The Citadel, librarians and other members of the faculty wear army uniforms, while most staff are in civilian attire, creating a symbolic asymmetry that, if left unchecked, can lead to divisiveness and tension. For example, on The Citadel's campus, uniformed personnel exchange salutes and military courtesies with cadets and other uniformed colleagues. Those in civilian attire are not included in these rituals. In addition to sabotaging collaboration and collegial communication, these patterns were diametrically opposed to the library's mission, vision, and egalitarian values. A library-wide reorganization emerged as the best option to disrupt these kinds of patterns and realign the library's structure and operations with its mission and vision.

Reorganizations have become common for libraries at both the departmental and organizational level. Libraries reorganize for many reasons, including economic pressures, building or facilities changes, the adoption of new technologies or workflows, and/or changes in a library's upper management or executive leadership.[4] Although the reorganization impulse may be a familiar landmark in the library landscape, its goals and desired outcomes are determined by the individual library's needs, challenges, and environmental context.

For the Daniel Library, there were many practical and ideological goals informing the decision to reorganize and shaping its eventual outcomes. In addition to realigning the library's structure and culture to better support its mission and advance toward its vision, reorganizing the library was intended to stimulate the development of more contemporary skills like technology competencies, make assigned duties more congruous with individual strengths and interests, and create more consistency in position descriptions that were written over multiple decades by various managers. The reorganization was also designed to stimulate peer-to-peer knowledge-sharing and demystify areas of library operations, such as cataloging, that most personnel were either uncomfortable with or oblivious to.

The macro-level inspiration for the reorganization was to make the Daniel Library more of a learning organization, which Peter Senge defines as

> organizations where people continually expand their capacity to create results they truly desire, where new and expansive patterns of thinking are nurtured, where collective aspiration is set free, and where people are continually learning how to learn together. [5]

This would involve changing staff roles and responsibilities, shifting cultural attitudes, placing a greater emphasis on collaboration and teamwork, and methodically dismantling thoroughly naturalized operational and social silos.

THE REORGANIZATION PROCESS

The library director began to articulate the general need to reorganize in fall 2015. Several librarians and paraprofessionals were early advocates for the process and helped refine the concept and develop preliminary planning documents, such as the project charter and timeline. Prior to the project's formal launch, the acquisitions librarian was selected to serve as project manager. Putting a technical services librarian in this role was unexpected. However, the acquisitions librarian possessed many skills suited to the task, and the appointment worked as a powerful gesture that foreshadowed subsequent changes.

When the library director first introduced the reorganization, the project was characterized as focused and compressed, with a tentative timeline of October 2015 to January 2016. The reorganization was socialized as an intense, but necessary, endeavor that would only succeed if all library personnel were engaged on some level. Some expressed enthusiastic buy-in, but others were resistant. During the formal project launch meeting, where all library personnel assembled to discuss the project and its outcomes, it became clear that substantive cultural changes would need to be pursued more delicately to keep tensions at a manageable simmer instead of a toxic roar. Anxieties were not localized; rather, they affected all departments, librarians and paraprofessionals, and newer hires as well as senior personnel. Based on the expressions of discomfort that emerged during the project launch, the reorganization process shifted slightly. Most importantly, the timeline was extended to allow more time to socialize ideas of change and give personnel opportunities to process the reorganization on conceptual and emotional levels.

The decision-making process was also modified, from radically inclusive to a more traditional team dynamic. Several research and instruction librarians, the acquisitions librarian, and the head of technical services joined the director and administrative assistant to form the executive committee. A month later, the interlibrary loan coordinator (circulation) and cataloging manager (TS) were invited to join the executive committee. This interdepartmental group of librarians and paraprofessionals worked together to assess library services and operations and make recommendations for departmental changes, position revisions, and long-term skill development. The group reported to the entire library during open management meetings, which took place at least twice a month. Minutes were dutifully recorded and made available to all personnel, which was particularly helpful for those who wanted to refer to the documentation later or were unable to attend in person.

Periodically, library-wide meetings were organized to give personnel reorganization-specific updates and invite feedback or questions. This allowed the reorganization to maintain transparency, while still preserving momentum and focus. Although the executive committee's role restructured the project manager's responsibilities, the value of collective discussion and agile decision-making made the adjustment worthwhile. The acquisitions librarian continued to work closely with the director to keep the project on track and frequently reported on the reorganization project during management meetings.

THE REORGANIZATION AND TECHNICAL SERVICES

The reorganization process drew on the expertise and problem-solving abilities of several TS personnel. This contribution instigated cultural changes that would eventually be infused throughout the entire library. During executive committee meetings, representatives from circulation, administration, and research and instruction were directly exposed to the talents and contributions of technical services. In addition to performing more traditional TS tasks, such as running reports and gathering collection and usage statistics to inform data-driven decisions, TS personnel engaged in conceptual and theoretical work throughout the reorganization process. While many had operated under the assumption that the back room lacked big-picture thinking, or, at the very least, was more committed to nitpicky details than broad issues and trends, the discussions among the executive committee gestured toward a very different reality.[6] The discussion of specific workflows and services further helped refine the committee's collective appreciation of their colleagues' versatile skills and perspectives.

Seeing TS personnel take on leadership roles and demonstrate strategic thinking stretched the mental models of those from other library departments, which was an important first step in dismantling inherited silos and cultural cliques. The formal rebranding of technical services helped to further revitalize the department's role and perception among library personnel.

Early in the reorganization process, the names and responsibilities of the library's existing departments were evaluated.[7] In addition to reconceptualizing services, this led to the discontinuation of some obsolete terminology. "Circulation" seemed meaningless to younger staff members, as well as patrons. "Reference" was deemed to be similarly dated, while "technical services" came across as cryptic and vaguely intimidating. To better capture the work of each department, the library was reorganized around the following departments:

> *Support and collection services* (SCS) was formed around existing TS responsibilities, such as acquisitions, cataloging, collection management, and government documents. Print and electronic course reserves were moved from circulation to SCS due to the inherent overlap between acquisitions and cataloging. Interlibrary loan was also incorporated into SCS to enhance synergies between acquisitions, resource sharing, e-resource troubleshooting, and subscription assessment.

Learning services (LS) was formed around information services provided at the circulation and reference desks, which were consolidated into a joint service point named the information service desk. Learning services also incorporated instruction support, stacks maintenance, and some involvement with library technologies and marketing.

Information services (IS) integrated information literacy instruction, liaison activities, faculty outreach, and support of library technologies.

Library administration was not renamed but was modified to incorporate programming and student outreach into existing responsibilities related to budgeting, personnel, and facilities management.

Replacing the term "technical services" with "support and collection services" contemporized the department's identity and involvement with the library. The term "support" represents the underlying role TS plays in enabling a wide range of library services, such as instruction, circulation, and access. Including a specific reference to "collection services" also served to remind both library personnel and patrons that many of the resources they utilize are selected, processed, made discoverable, and maintained by TS. Without being overly didactic or aggressive, transforming technical services into support and collection services helped the department better manage its image and emphasize both its openness (support) and its vital contributions to the entire library and campus community (collections).

Perceptions and attitudes can be difficult to quantify and assess, but the reorganization also led to more concrete consequences for TS. To reduce the supervisory burden on the director and diversify upper management, a deputy director position was created. The acquisitions librarian was appointed to serve in that capacity, further cementing the association between TS and formal leadership.

Personnel from the newly created support and collection services department also assumed prominent roles in library teams and projects. The cataloging manager was appointed to lead an interdepartmental project devoted to assessing the print collection and reimagining the library's physical footprint. SCS staff were also embedded in the library's assessment team and made significant contributions to the creation and ongoing support of The Citadel Makerspace, which opened in spring 2017.

To further deconstruct perceived boundaries between public-facing and back room activities, many SCS staff members were cross-trained to work at the information services desk, with two librarians becoming regularly scheduled (at least one shift a week), in addition to providing backup or emergency coverage. Embedding SCS personnel in this central service point opened channels of communication between departments and among librarians and paraprofessionals, which enabled all personnel to deepen their understanding of other operational areas and acquire new skills and knowledge. Being more fully integrated with frontline service also helped broaden SCS's awareness of patron needs and common stumbling blocks, which subsequently improved acquisitions decision-making, cataloging practices, and the configuration of the library's web-scale discovery layer.

The enhanced visibility of support and collection services also encouraged other library personnel to recognize their soft skills and inherent approachability. Misperceptions about back room aloofness and antisocial tendencies began to be replaced as a result of more open communication and knowledge sharing among personnel throughout the library. Working alongside SCS representatives in team and project environments further reiterated their important role in strategic planning, project implementation, and inventive problem solving.

To some extent the library reorganization rebranded technical services as the library's internal reference service. Questions about catalog records, missing items, holdings errors, broken links, and a variety of other issues are now brought to the attention of SCS personnel without fanfare. SCS has also led several library-wide training sessions to help elucidate services like interlibrary loan and course reserves. SCS personnel are also becoming more involved in larger professional conversations by representing the library at conferences and then disseminating industry news and insights at the local level.

FUTURE GOALS

The formal reorganization project may have concluded, but the work of maintaining a dynamic, collegial library culture takes persistence and perpetual vigilance. In many ways, the library reorganization helped the Daniel Library advance toward the lofty goal of becoming a true learning organization. Interdepartmental teams and projects support substantive communication and collaboration, while the consolidated information service desk provides valuable opportunities to work together to serve library patrons. A more egalitarian interpersonal dynamic has replaced rigid silos.

The rejuvenation of technical services has created more leadership opportunities and general recognition of acquisitions, resource sharing, cataloging, and collection management. However, there are still underutilized opportunities to create meaningful cross-pollination between information services and support and collection services. Incorporating the two SCS librarians into the liaison and faculty outreach efforts could help the current liaisons improve their understanding of collections management, especially subscription assessment and acquisitions decision-making, while expanding communication channels between nonlibrary faculty and the SCS personnel who are often instrumental in helping with program accreditation and other administrative academic procedures.

Creating more involvement between SCS and the information literacy curriculum could also be advantageous. Much of a one-shot IL session revolves around teaching students how to navigate the facets and functionality of the library's web-scale discovery layer. However, the SCS personnel who maintain that discovery layer, and make decisions about default settings and other variables, are not embedded in the classroom. Dismantling this lingering silo could enhance the overall usability of the discovery tool and expand SCS's understanding of patrons' needs, preferences, and expectations. Although still in a protean state, the library's new usability team might bridge this gap. This interdepartmental team, led by an SCS librarian, focuses on optimizing the processes of discovery and access for all patrons. The library-wide discussions involved in this assessment could synchronize how collections, access, and discovery are being taught in IL with the SCS department's policies, procedures, and priorities.

CONCLUSION

A library reorganization reflects a specific library's needs and cultural landscape, but a unique case study can still have relevance and resonance for other institutions. Even though The Citadel is a distinctive institution, and its accompanying challenges might not affect other libraries in the same way, the Daniel Library's reorganization can be used to identify possible solutions to systemic and broad issues, such as communication barriers, inherited inefficiencies, and the anxiety and fear radical change can inadvertently instigate.[8]

Prior to the reorganization, Daniel Library's technical services department contained an abundance of underutilized skills and potential. The assumptions about the back room and the supposed unapproachable or uncooperative nature of its personnel had become internalized, producing silos and communication barriers. This is not a unique situation, especially within academic libraries. Revitalizing technical services is challenging because of the need to balance specialized skills with more visible, discrete signifiers of value that are more salient to other library personnel. Ensuring TS representation in upper management, library teams, projects, and trainings proved effective for the Daniel Library, but other libraries, especially larger institutions, might not see the same results. One alternative approach could involve TS personnel becoming internal liaisons to library colleagues in other departments to advocate for TS and share their substantial tacit knowledge in a peer-to-peer environment. Another strategy might be to reevaluate the onboarding or training process of new library hires, so each new member of the team spends some time learning both public-facing and back room roles and responsibilities, regardless of their official departmental affiliation. Cultivating this multifaceted frame of reference from the outset can build interdepartmental relationships and perpetuate an open and collaborative library culture.

Regardless of the instigating forces motivating a specific library's reorganization, the prospect of change will invariably catalyze some form of resistance or anxiety. In some instances, familiar inefficiencies may seem preferable to unknown enhancements. The "that's how we've always done it" mantra can bring even the most sophisticated reorganization process to a standstill. Having a governing goal or vision can help improve buy-in, but it is not a panacea. At the Daniel Library, the prospect of becoming more like a learning organization was attractive to many personnel and helped contextualize their temporary discomfort within a greater sense of purpose. However, this philosophical goal was also accompanied by more concrete, material benefits. While evaluating the inherited organizational structure, the executive committee looked for ways to recognize skills and justify promotions, where appropriate. The director worked with human resources to update position descriptions, coordinate promotions, and pursue commensurate raises. This process bolstered short-term morale, while the ideals of a learning organization generated more sustainable, cultural changes. In general, a reorganization process must deftly navigate a complex interplay of immediate needs and long-term growth.

Determining the success of a reorganization can be a complex and daunting process. There will always be a plethora of subjective interpretations of what changes worked and which were problematic. However, an increase in leadership opportunities, improved communication practices, and more effective collegial collaboration all gesture toward overall success. For the Daniel Library, the TS department's contributions to the reorganization project instigated positive shifts. The newly formed SCS department is poised to perpetuate that momentum by maintaining an active, multifaceted role in the library's progress toward the ideals of a learning organization.

NOTES

1. Laura Turner and Alejandra Naan, "Venturing From the 'Back Room': Do Technical Services Librarians Have a Role in Information Literacy?" *Charleston Conference Proceedings* (2013), https://doi.org/10.5703/1288284315293.

2. Cathy Weng and Erin Ackerman, "Towards Sustainable Partnership: Examining Cross Perceptions of Public and Technical Services Academic Librarians," *Library Resources & Technical Services* 61, no. 4 (2017): 198–211.

3. Peter Senge, *The Fifth Discipline: The Art and Practice of the Learning Organization* (New York: Doubleday Currency, 1990), 8.

4. John Novak and Annette Day, "The Libraries They Are A-Changin': How Libraries Reorganize." *College & Undergraduate Libraries* 22, no. 3–4 (2015): 364, https://doi.org/10.1080/10691316.2015.1067663.

5. Senge, *The Fifth Discipline*, 3.

6. Sally Gibson, "From Problem Solvers to Solution Creators: Shifting Roles of Technical Services," in *Creating Sustainable Community: The Proceedings of the ACRL Conference* (2015): 290–93 , http://www.ala.org/acrl/sites/ala.org.acrl/files/content/conferences/confs andpreconfs/2015/Gibson.pdf.

7. Brian Doherty and Alison Piper, "Creating a New Organizational Structure for a Small Academic Library: The Merging of Technical Services and Access Services," *Technical Services Quarterly* 32 (2015): 160–72.

8. John Kotter, *Leading Change* (Boston: Harvard Business Review Press, 2012), 4.

CHAPTER 20

Technical Metamorphosis by Design

Maaike Oldemans and Jennifer Kronenbitter

ABSTRACT

Libraries are dynamic organizations, always striving to improve services to their patrons. Technical service departments strive to meet the informational needs of internal and external patrons by continuing to adjust workflows and processes. At State University of New York (SUNY) Cortland Memorial Library, processes regularly carried out in bibliographic services were performed in two different departments on two different floors. The two departments operated separately and independently of one other with the staff of these two units reporting to different supervisors. To improve services to the library community, SUNY Cortland Memorial Library undertook a workflow review and reorganization. This chapter explains the history of how the services were separated, the goals set for the reorganization, and the steps used to implement the change. The outcome was a merging of services into a new technical services department, the relocation of the archives, and, ultimately, streamlined workflows that benefited the library community.

INTRODUCTION

Academic libraries are dynamic organizations, always responding and adjusting their services to environmental, technological, and sociological changes in our society. These changes ensure that the libraries succeed in providing quality services to their patrons. Changes in technology and evolving ideas about library organization and personnel retirements have led to new opportunities in technical services.[1]

At State University of New York (SUNY) Cortland Memorial Library, processes regularly performed in bibliographic services—including acquisitions, cataloging, processing materials, periodicals, stack management, binding and preservation, collection maintenance, and interlibrary loan—were carried out in two different departments: bibliographic services and collection support services. To better serve SUNY Cortland's library community, Memorial Library undertook a workflow review and reorganization.

In this chapter we discuss how the reorganization impacted our workflows and transformed disconnected services into a functioning department that responds to both the public's and the staff's needs. In addition, we describe our experiences and choices as well as the process of implanting the transformation.

BACKGROUND

SUNY College at Cortland is a founding member of the State University of New York (SUNY), the nation's largest comprehensive public university system, established in 1948.[2] SUNY comprises 64 schools: 29 state-operated campuses; 5 statutory colleges consisting of research universities, liberal arts colleges, specialized and technical colleges, health science centers, and land-grant colleges; and 30 community colleges. In contrast to other SUNY institutions, the Memorial Library is a department within the college's division of information resources, under the associate provost for information resources. The mission of information resources is to support the college community by providing information services and technology environments that enable the teaching, learning, scholarly creation, and operational goals of SUNY Cortland's diverse constituencies.

Information resources consists of the following departments: administrative computing, campus technology services, Memorial Library, networking and telecommunications services, and system administration and web services. The collaboration among the different departments within information resources creates technological advantages for the library. Further, Memorial Library has an integrated help desk and circulation services. The Help Center, located on the main floor, is a one-stop service point for patrons who require assistance with library needs, including course reserves and technical issues.

The mission of the library is to foster individual and collaborative research, learning, teaching, and scholarly creation and to enable our college community members to navigate the worlds of information and knowledge. The technical services department employs two academic librarians, two adjunct assistant librarians, six full-time staff, and five student assistants and currently consists of the following sections: acquisitions, cataloging, processing materials, periodicals, stack management, binding and preservation, course reserves, collection maintenance, interlibrary loan, and archives.

THE HISTORY OF BIBLIOGRAPHIC SERVICES AT MEMORIAL LIBRARY

For 25 years bibliographic processes at SUNY Cortland Memorial Library were dispersed between two different departments, bibliographic services and collection support services, housed on two different floors. Staff responsible for acquisitions, cataloging, and physical processing were part of bibliographic services and reported to the technical services librarian. Staff responsible for interlibrary loan, stack management, binding and preservation, and periodicals were part of collection support services and reported to the collection services librarian. In addition, the college archives were being housed in the bibliographic services area. (Over the years, the archives had been moved around within the library. Maintained by a SUNY Cortland retired librarian archivist, archival material was only accessible to patrons through appointment one day a week.)

Technological advances and budget cuts led us to rethink our processes and workflows. While retirements over the past 10 to 15 years were the main reason that the number of staff working in bibliographic services and collection support services was reduced, positions had not always filled after the retirement of staff, mostly because of technological advances. Electronic formats are often preferred over print. The use of electronic tools as well as electronically available methods from vendors like EBSCO's GOBI Library Solutions and Amazon has made acquisition and collection development more efficient.

Technology has also changed cataloging processes: the availability of OCLC MARC records and increased opportunities to rely on copy-cataloging decreased the need for original cataloging. Additionally, the broad availability of electronic resources has simplified the processes for resource sharing through interlibrary loan.

IMPLEMENTING ORGANIZATIONAL CHANGE

To improve our library services, we established the following four goals: (1) balance traditional library services and emerging technologies to best serve the needs of students, faculty, staff, and community; (2) collaborate with all departments within the library to ensure the seamless integration of services along with smooth communication; (3) continue to develop standards for cataloging, acquisitions, and preservation of materials across the unit to include streamlined workflows; and (4) increase reliance on and establishment of collaborative work across the library.

As we researched the literature on models of change in library technical services to help us with our implementation, we found that Karen Calhoun from Cornell University Library discusses how the five different stages of Beckhard and Harris's model for management of transformational change can guide change in organizations.[3] After some consideration, we decided to use Beckhard and Harris's model[4] for our departmental shift.

To reach the four goals we established to improve our library services, we adapted the following five steps outlined in Beckhard and Harris's model: (1) envision the future organizational structure; (2) diagnose the current organizational structure; (3) determine the organizational needs; (4) identify the stakeholders, and (5) identify the necessary steps to ensure that the change occurs and endures.[5] Our implementation process is described below.

Step One: Envisioning the Future Organizational Structure

Casey Stengel, the great baseball manager, said, "If you don't know where you're going, you might end up somewhere else."[6] This advice shared by Beckhard and Harris was used to envision our future organizational structure.

The director, associate directors, librarians, and staff collaborated to create vision and mission statements for the library that would be relevant and complement and reflect the vision and mission of the college:

> Memorial Library is an integral part of the SUNY Cortland academic community and supports the vision of diverse learning experiences by expanding the classroom experience with information, resources, technology and assistance in community oriented spaces. . . . The mission of Memorial Library is to foster individual and collaborative research, learning, teaching, and scholarly creation, and to enable our college community members to navigate the worlds of information and knowledge.[7]

A strategic plan was then created for Memorial Library.[8]

Step Two: Diagnosing Our Current Organizational Structure

Diagnosing our current organizational structure and obtaining a clear view of the functionality of the different departments before making an action plan for achieving the goals was step two from Beckhard's and Harris model.[9] The library management team examined the functionality of the processes in bibliographic services, collection support services, and circulation. As we anticipated, this review helped define the need for change. Workflows, staff office space, and the work environment in the different units were reviewed. Results indicated that processes were inefficient in the different units due to a lack of communication and lack of information-sharing. This inefficiency was compounded by disorganized and disconnected work areas, which contributed to the forming of silos. Kowalski describes silos as "workplace constructs and mindsets that isolate departments from one another through bureaucracy or rigid hierarchies" and asserts that "silos act as barriers to progress" while also dividing the library into groups that compete against each other instead of working together as teams.[10] Although there was an atmosphere of collaboration among staff in bibliographic services, their work area was not efficient. A chaotic arrangement of individual working areas, grown naturally through the building of walls using filing cabinets, bookcases, partitions, and desks, contributed to the disorganized work environment.

Step Three: Determining Our Organizational Needs

We needed to create a workplace where teamwork, information-sharing, and showing appreciation for each other's contributions would be valued and encouraged. The silos that had formed because of staff personalities and the challenges of the physical environment needed to be addressed. The inefficiency of the cluttered workspace within bibliographic services needed to be reviewed. Identifying those areas that needed to become more efficient would assist in adjusting work-flows as well as provide an understanding of where the skills of our staff needed to be updated. By identifying those areas, also, it was clear that we needed to review our policies and procedures while also considering the needs of our patrons. Workflows and processes in the different areas were all related and focused on the mission and vision of the library, and it made sense that they should be performed in one area. Merging the two areas of bibliographic services and collection support services into one area might improve the team-building. The library director and the associate director realized there would be resistance from staff in both areas. However, to make the merge possible the physical space in bibliographic services needed to be decluttered to create a more efficient workspace to accommodate staff from both divisions. In addition, the supervision of these areas needed to be consolidated.

In addition, the physical location of the college archives needed to be addressed. As the archives might become more relevant for the college in the future, a more permanent space within the library needed to be found. In addition, archive accessibility, both online and in-person, needed to be considered.

With the merging of bibliographic services and collection support services, the name for the newly formed department was changed to technical services.

Step Four: Identifying the Stakeholders Critical to Reaching Our Goal

To ensure successful implementation of our goals and needs, the stake-holders needed to be identified. The stakeholders included current staff from the different departments affected by the changes, supervisors in bibliographic services, circulation, and collection support services, the library director, and the associate provost of information resources. The library director and the associate director met with all stakeholders to discuss the future of our services, workflows, and workspace and how to best reach our goals. Staff were involved in discussions around the reallocation plan to ensure the best chance of success. While some of our staff were reluctant to embrace the proposed changes, open discussions and the promise that they could choose their own cubicle made them more receptive to change. One of the biggest challenges was tackling the silo created by the two departments working independently from one another. The goal was to change the silo culture into a culture where staff would be motivated to collaborate and engage in the process.

Step Five: Identifying the Steps to Ensure That the Change Occurs and Endures

Considerable effort was spent merging, defining, and redefining workflows and the expectations of the 10 staff members involved in the merger. Overcoming interpersonal dynamics heightened by physically merging staff into one location and reorganizing the reporting structure to be more responsive to staff needs was top priority.

Circulation services was merged with the help desk, resulting in the Help Center. Since staff in bibliographic services had more experience with processing library items, the processing of reserves moved from circulation to bibliographic services, leading to a more streamlined course reserve process.

To ensure that the transformation we envisioned would occur and be successful, several options to adjust the physical environment of bibliographic services for the merging divisions, while also aiming to make the workspace more efficient, were researched. Once individual cubicles with identical furniture for all staff were constructed, the collection support services staff would be merged into the new bibliographic services area. In order to ensure that the different cultures from both areas would blend while working together in one space, cross-training, workflow improvements, and assistance to staff who were transitioning into a new work area with new tasks was implemented. With the integration of the two departments into the space originally assigned to bibliographic services, the relocation of the college archives from the bibliographic services area to a temporary location within the library needed to be reviewed.

Workflows in the areas that had merged into the existing bibliographic services, as well as staffing needs in the new environment, needed to be reviewed and adjusted. Attention needed to be focused on improving efficiencies in course reserves, stack management, binding, and interlibrary loan areas. Course reserves procedures needed to be updated to ensure copyright compliance with the new reserve system in Blackboard. An existing staff member would focus on reserves as well as on the maintenance of our print collection, including small book repairs and other binding activities. The creation of a dedicated stack management staff position would ensure efficient access for our patrons to our print collection. Over the years, interlibrary loan services had been moved to various areas within the library. Having been part of the circulation area before becoming part of collection support services, interlibrary loan would now become part of the bibliographic services area. Procedures needed to be reviewed to make the interlibrary loan service as efficient as possible. The merging of staff and services from collections support services, as well as the change in workflows, led to a change in the existing reporting structure. Staff from acquisitions, cataloging, physical processing, course reserves, periodicals, stack management, and collection maintenance would report to the technical services librarian, with the interlibrary loan staff reporting to a librarian under the technical services librarian.

To ensure a successful transition of staff and services, five phases were identified to be implemented as soon the college archives were moved to the third floor of the library: (1) integration of course reserves services into the bibliographic services, (2) integration of stack management, (3) integration of interlibrary loan, (4) integration of periodicals, and (5) the integration of binding and preservation. Through the phased transition and integration, staff could easily adjust to the different tasks. To better reflect the current processes of the merged bibliographic and collection support services, this newly formed department became the technical services department.

LESSONS LEARNED

When instituting change, both structurally and organizationally, it is important to have support from every level within the organization. Our change was immediately supported by upper-level administration and the library director. Staff needed more time to see the value to themselves and the library and also needed to be able to express their concerns and ideas. To meet this need, informational sessions and one-on-one meetings were held. Breaking down the silos had been crucial for the success of the merge of the two departments into one technical services department. The merge of acquisitions, cataloging, processing materials, interlibrary loan, periodicals, stack management, collection management, archives, and binding and preservation into one technical services department has led to a more efficient workflow and a technical services unit that can better meet the needs of the patrons. Instead of competing, staff now communicate and collaborate while working in teams, which has improved the workplace atmosphere.

The key factors to a successful change are the involvement and willingness of the participants in the organization to be a part of the change. While technology might trigger the need for change, it does not necessarily guarantee its success. Technical services departments need to keep adjusting their workflows and processes to ensure that the informational needs of patrons are being met.

NOTES

1. Michael Gorman, "Technical Services Today and Tomorrow," in *Technical Services Today and Tomorrow,* ed. Michael Gorman. (Englewood: Libraries Unlimited, 1998).
2. "History of SUNY," State University of New York, accessed March 18, 2018, https://www.suny.edu/about/history/.
3. Karen Calhoun, "Technology, Productivity and Change in Library Technical Services," *Library Collections, Acquisitions, & Technical Services* 27 (2003): 285, https://doi.org/10.1016/S1464-9055(03)00068-X.
4. Richard Beckhard and Reuben T. Harris, *Organizational Transitions: Managing Complex Change* (Reading, Massachusetts: Addison-Wesley, 1987).
5. Ibid., 45–70.
6. Ibid., 45.
7. "Memorial Library," State University of New York College at Cortland, accessed March 18, 2018, http://www2.cortland.edu/library/about/.

8. Beckhard and Harris, 46.

9. Ibid., 57.

10. Meghan Kowalski, "Breaking Down Silo Walls: Successful Collaboration Across Library Departments," *Library Leadership and Management* 31, no. 2 (February 2017): 1.

CHAPTER 21

Responding to Evolutionary Workflow Challenges Through Staffing Adaptation: A Play in Five Acts

Kimberly W. Stevens, Mary Bevis, Bethany Latham, and Jodi Poe

ABSTRACT

The technical services department at Jacksonville State University's Houston Cole Library has had to adapt to changes in workflow as technology has impacted operations. From migrating print journals to online access to the library's focus on digitization projects to competing with other university departments for space in the library, the technical services unit at JSU has had to be flexible in addressing these challenges. This chapter describes the steps the unit took to evolve its workflows, starting with reevaluating job titles and position descriptions to better reflect the work being done by the staff, reallocating staff time to new initiatives, and partnering with other departments in the library to effectively work on projects. By showing flexibility and enhancing skill sets, technical services personnel have been able to position themselves as key players in the library's performance on the university's stage.

INTRODUCTION

Jacksonville State University (JSU) is a medium-sized institution, a regional university nestled in the foothills of the Appalachian Mountains in northeast Alabama. The Houston Cole Library (HCL), a 13-story building that houses a collection of over 800,000 titles, serves as the hub of this campus, providing resources to support the curriculum at the undergraduate, masters, and doctoral levels. The views from the 12th-floor observation deck are stunning, yet seldom enjoyed by technical services personnel, who are housed in the building's windowless basement. The structure of HCL's technical services department includes acquisitions and serials, cataloging, electronic resources, and government documents.

New technologies, resources, formats, and goals have necessitated a rethinking of traditional technical services workflows, and, as these workflows have evolved, challenges have arisen that can only be addressed through the flexibility and adaptation of technical services personnel. This chapter will address the types of challenges that have been encountered and offer examples of how job responsibilities and staffing have been adapted to further technical services goals in an evolving environment.

DRAMATIS PERSONAE

HCL's technical services personnel include both professional librarians who are tenure-track faculty and paraprofessionals. Thus, in addition to publication, service, and the other requisites of faculty status, as well as the daily workload, three of the five HCL technical services librarians also supervise paraprofessional staff—including training, performance evaluation, and so forth. They are unique in this status, not only in comparison with their teaching faculty colleagues, but also with HCL's public services librarians, who have no supervisory responsibilities. The head of public services supervises the supervisor of user services, a paraprofessional position, who supervises circulation personnel. The technical services department head receives a stipend for supervising faculty; technical services librarian faculty receive no additional remuneration for their supervision of paraprofessionals.

Table 21.1 shows the breakdown of technical services personnel.

While the authors freely admit that, as humble players, mathematics is not their forte, it is readily apparent that the numbers do not add up to the actual number of personnel working in the technical services department (which is, for the record, five library faculty and seven paraprofessionals). The reasons for this will soon become clear but can be stated in a nutshell as that most dramatic of costuming choices: multiple hat wearing.

Table 21.1 Technical Services Personnel

Area	Number of Library Faculty	Number of Paraprofessionals
Acquisitions and serials	1	2
Cataloging	2	2
Electronic resources	2	2
Government documents	1	1

THE PLOT: ENUMERATING THE CHALLENGES

HCL's technical services personnel have seen their job duties and departmental goals shift, primarily due to the introduction and continual evolution of various forms of technology and the proliferation of electronic resources. In the realm of library administration, some institutions have seen a corollary shift in ideology, questioning whether traditional technical services positions are necessary in-house. Some of these institutions, to divert resources to other areas, have made the decision to outsource certain technical services functions. HCL is not among them, but it is typical in that institutions that do not outsource often expect the same number of personnel to shoulder an increasing volume of work, as well as adapt to changing types of work, with autodidacticism the principal method of acquiring the skills necessary to perform on this redressed stage.

ACT I: HYBRIDIZATION OF PROFESSIONAL POSITIONS

The first step taken by the technical services department toward meeting these challenges was hybridization of position responsibilities, with a focus on shifting as many people as possible toward the management of electronic resources. HCL technical services faculty often have three-slash titles—e.g., professor/electronic resources/documents or professor/acquisitions/serials. These reflect the hybridization of job duties, and this hybridization extends even to the department head, who is heavily involved in electronic resources.

The job titles can be deceptive given the amalgamation of position responsibilities that have occurred. The electronic resources/documents librarian, for example, was originally a position that oversaw HCL's participation in the Federal Depository Library Program, ensuring compliance with the federal regulation this entails. This librarian performs selection, acquisition, cataloging, assessment, and management of a government information collection of over 40,000 titles, in addition to fielding government information reference queries and performing outreach regarding this collection (though the position is classified in technical rather than public services). As tangible federal documents have increasingly shifted into the digital realm, a corresponding shift in position responsibilities has occurred. The electronic resources section of the title was added chiefly to address government-related electronic resources (e-books, websites, databases, et al.), but management of the library's web presence via the university's content management system and LibGuides, position responsibilities also shared by the head of technical services, was later added. When the HCL began digitizing its archival collections, digital project management, administration of the library's ContentDM instance, creation of metadata for digital objects, and the like joined the list since HCL has no archivist.

When it comes to the tangible realm, the acquisitions assistant and a graduate assistant handle the print book ordering and receiving, which is generally straightforward. Staff download MARC records from OCLC into the acquisitions client, assign a predetermined fund code, and mark the vendor's site for ordering. Upon receipt, the cataloging unit completes the processing and validates the catalog record content.

The introduction of e-books into the acquisitions process, however, has taken procedures in a different direction. The current position of acquisitions/serials librarian, which was originally two separate professional positions of acquisitions and serials, incurred the responsibilities for e-book ordering primarily because of the decisions that go into the process. These include selecting the appropriate MARC record and choosing the preferred platform and number of users. The library has approximately 55,000 e-book titles in the catalog, which represents a combination of demand-driven acquisitions (DDA) titles, collection purchases, open access, and individual orders. Because of limited staff, there is minimal cleanup on the MARC records for DDA and collection titles; records for individually ordered e-book titles receive more scrutiny. Since e-books are not forwarded to the cataloging unit for processing, the modification and cleanup of the catalog records to meet the library's standards has also been assumed by the acquisitions/serials librarian (excluding authority validation, which is still completed by the senior catalog librarian). Plans are to transfer some of this process to the acquisitions assistant, with supervision and proofing by the acquisitions/serials librarian. The acquisitions/serials librarian also liaises with the head of technical services to provide access to these resources. The head of technical services finalizes catalog access through local practices: adding an additional 246 field with a gathering code, as well as addressing some subject heading issues specific to electronic resources and adding the proxy information for the 856 to provide public access. The head of technical services also works closely with the acquisitions/serials librarian to ensure the accuracy of e-journal holdings information in EBSCO's Full Text Finder, a goal that requires updating coverage information, adding/removing proxy information, and removing incorrectly activated titles. As will be apparent in a cursory look at these players, neither digital nor archival nor e-journals nor web services (et al. ad infinitum) appears anywhere in the job title for the positions. Neither do these types of responsibilities feature in the position duties as enumerated in job descriptions held by JSU's human resources department. Yet these types of responsibilities are now integral parts of the workload and fall under that catchall "other duties as assigned." Other duties as assigned implies that these types of hybridization are the result of planned assignment, but this is seldom the case. Instead, they often occur organically—brought on by outside factors and what individuals are willing to take on to address library needs. This hybridization is not limited to library faculty but also includes the paraprofessional staff, who have repeatedly risen to the challenge, as explicated in Act II.

ACT II: RISING TO THE CHALLENGE THROUGH STAFF REALLOCATION

At JSU, teaching faculty are often given additional remuneration when they are required to update their skill sets to perform position responsibilities (e.g., being paid more to teach courses online or for duties considered "overload"), or that additional responsibility is shunted off entirely to another (new) position (e.g., instructional designers are hired to create online course content for faculty). Library faculty are not afforded these opportunities, yet they must rise to meet the challenge of new library priorities, and this involves retraining and enhancing skill sets not only for technical services faculty but also for paraprofessionals, who play a key role in adaptation to shifting workflows.

One example is HCL's digitization initiatives. These initiatives had their genesis in consortia participation (dramatized in Act IV), but the central takeaway is that technical services personnel were asked to digitize a collection and make it publicly accessible without any additional equipment, training, or financial resources. To achieve this goal, both faculty and paraprofessionals had to update their skill sets (through a combination of on-the-job learning, webinars, and vendor training) to deal with a variety of new technologies. Examples include setup and ongoing administration of ContentDM and other systems for digital asset management, a variety of programs for manipulation of images and other digital files (e.g., Adobe's Creative Suite), and running/correcting optical character recognition (OCR). This also resulted in a substantial, entirely new workflow. (Many libraries have designated digital projects personnel; the HCL did not.) Another example is the adoption of HCL's discovery tool (EBSCO's Discovery). At the time that various discovery options were reviewed, and an option selected, the library was without a systems administrator so the management of this system fell to the head of technical services and has remained there, despite the later acquisition of a systems administrator (who now reports to the information technology department, not the library, as was formerly the case).

These are far from the only areas of technical services that have required creative restructuring to further departmental goals. They are but the latest iteration of an ongoing, historical pattern. One professional librarian, with the help of two paraprofessional staff (one assigned to monographs, the other to serials) and one part-time graduate assistant, heads HCL's serials and acquisitions responsibilities, which were combined into a single unit within technical services. In the 1970s, HCL began preparing for automation by banking its machine-readable cataloging with OCLC, while still ordering printed cards. Over the next decade HCL methodically, and at a timely pace, became fully automated with its first integrated library system (ILS), NOTIS, followed 10 years later by Voyager. Retrospective conversion and smart barcode projects were completed, all the while addressing the countless problems that came with the exceptions. This progression logically included major workflow changes which HCL put in place at that time (documented by Mary Bevis and Sonja McAbee in "NOTIS as an Impetus for Change in Technical Services Departmental Staffing").[1] These changes naturally were adapted and altered as needed to streamline the process.

As this period of adjustment neared its end and the library upgraded its ILS to Voyager, the focus of automation turned to the migration of library resources from print to electronic format in both monographs and serials. At HCL this transformation has, as expected, affected both areas, but more so serials. As individual subscriptions changed from print to online or were canceled due to inclusion in subscribed aggregator databases, the duties of the serials assistant were significantly reduced. The reasons for this are process-related: a reduction in mail sorting and distribution, fewer individual check-ins, fewer claims, a decrease in catalog maintenance (barcoding, holdings maintenance, etc.), less shelf maintenance, and considerably fewer binding responsibilities.

The serials assistant exclaimed more than once, as he was given a list of canceled titles, "You're canceling me out of a job!" Since his character's backstory included being named Employee of the Year for the university, job obsolescence wasn't a proper plot twist. Technology was taking duties away, but, fortunately, technology would also bestow new opportunities for different responsibilities that would enhance the library's collection in innovative ways.

The purchase of electronic journal archive collections from JSTOR has been an impetus for extensive periodicals deselection projects, both bound and microfilm, freeing up much needed shelf space. Logically, this task was assigned to the serials assistant, including removal of volumes from the shelves, deleting barcodes from the catalog, sending lists to vendors for possible sales (no one really wants them these days, but occasionally someone does), and preparing volumes for recycling. Other occasional duties acquired by the serials assistant include gift books (distributing books to appropriate subject specialists for review and sending thank-you letters), inventory verification, updating holdings and item records, and other nonrecurring issues that need attention.

With HCL's digitization projects in full swing and the serials assistant's traditional duties shifting, the extra time that this paraprofessional could now devote to digital projects was much needed and welcomed. As is the case with most of these newly introduced duties, all training was done in-house. The government documents assistant, a university Employee of the Month, was experiencing a similar situation, though to a lesser degree—as tangible documents dwindled, she volunteered the time this freed up to help with digitization initiatives. The government documents assistant, having essentially trained herself in the use of OCR software (she read the manual, had her first attempts checked by her supervisor, and then sallied forth in earnest), was now happy to train the serials assistant. They threw themselves into these new duties and now pursue them daily, as time from their primary duties permits.

The serials assistant and the government documents assistant were joined in their work on digital projects when two other paraprofessional positions were reallocated. Originally classified as cataloging assistants, these two positions opened through the retirement of long-time technical services personnel. Discussion among the library faculty, especially the senior catalog librarian and the head of technical services, about demonstrated needs and the opportunities to address them resulted in these positions being reallocated to electronic resources/digitization. With staff from multiple sections of technical services (serials, government documents, electronic resources) now working together on digitization projects, the head of technical services asked the individuals involved to detail their workflows to aid in improvement of those workflows and prioritization of projects. While the paraprofessionals still directly report to library faculty for their primary job duties (i.e., acquisitions, serials, cataloging, or government documents), the department head provides top-level supervision for digital projects to oversee the diverse units working together on these initiatives.

None of these initiatives, nor the achievement of departmental goals, would be possible without the paraprofessional staff, who have demonstrated extraordinary flexibility and exhibited a cheerful willingness to expand their competencies and take on new responsibilities.

ACT III: STAGE FIGHTING

In a 13-story building (a structure that, incidentally, holds the record for tallest academic building in Alabama), one might assume that lack of space would be one dramatic conflict not placed between the players and their denouement. There are certain actualities, however, that belie this assumption. The building is somewhat idiosyncratic in its design, and outside of the collection itself (i.e., shelving) and study space, a great deal of space is also lost to elevators, stairwells, a coffee shop, a conference center, and so on. The conference center and coffee shop illustrate an ongoing trend that is proving to be an increasing challenge: the conquest of space by oppositional forces—food services, higher-level administrators, retired faculty, and most recently and relevantly to technical services, the information technology department.

These "land grabs," as they have come to be less-than-affectionately known, have negatively impacted the living space necessary for effective pursuit of some technical services goals. It is particularly unhelpful in that once something has been annexed, it is often difficult, if not impossible, for the library to reacquire that space, even if the original usurper relinquishes it. These villains often do not notify, much less consult with, library administration before launching expeditions of acquisition. Land grabs usually first appear in the plotting when library personnel inadvertently encounter hostile scouting parties surreptitiously measuring floor space, resulting in crossed swords and delicious dramatic tension.

Though examples are myriad, they can be found especially in areas that affect digitization projects. One current, ongoing project involves scanning of deteriorating photographic negatives, some 120,000 of them. This collection requires a good deal of space to process for several reasons. The fumes the film stock emits preclude these negatives from being stored in technical services office space (or around any being that breathes regularly). As part of the preservation process, some of the materials must be soaked in baths and hung to dry. All of this, along with large-format scanning equipment and workstations, takes up more space than is found in technical services' basement allocation. A nonlibrary unit that remediates students in English and math occupies one entire side of the basement. There is also another audiovisual-related unit—originally a part of the library but absorbed over a year ago by another division. This division has assimilated the unit's budget and supposedly plans to move the personnel, but no such firm directive has yet been forthcoming. Accordingly, space on the library's third and ninth floors had already been blocked out for digital projects and had been in use for this purpose for some time. The space is far from ideal ("closet" would be an accurate descriptor), but even this is endangered.

Exposition: A Quality Enhancement Plan (QEP) pursued as part of JSU's reaccreditation involved distributing iPads to all freshman students. This plan was administered by the Office of Institutional Research and Assessment, a department outside the library in a different division. Office space was required for storage and management of the devices, and the personnel; this was created by enclosing space on the library's ninth floor, staffed by individuals whose positions were grant-funded (thus, theoretically, temporary). The library was to reacquire the space, slated to be used as group study space, when the QEP had run its course. Yet when the QEP ended, not only did the personnel remain, but also these individuals were moved underneath the information technology department, which relocated more of its personnel into the space and reallocated it as a technology center. This directly affects the digitization space on that floor, since information technology also evinced plans to exponentially expand that space (engulfing the digitization space, along with entire ranges of bound periodicals, which support a doctoral-level program). The space taken up by the audiovisual unit in the basement offered an alternative, at least for the technical services dilemma—if the AV unit moved and was housed with its new division, then that space could be reallocated to the displaced digitization workspace. However, it soon became apparent that information technology (who reports to the division of finance and administration, outside the library) had designs on this space as well, for more personnel, offices, an imaging lab, ad nauseum.

While the library is yet unaware of the causative factors (Russian winter, alien virus, English longbow), the advance on this front has stalled—at least for now. The permanency of this reprieve is far from assured, however, and this may be a challenge that reasserts itself in the future and will have to be addressed.

ACT IV: PLAYING WELL WITH OTHERS

As mentioned in Act II, the library's digital projects had their origins in consortium participation—an Institute of Museum and Library Services (IMLS) grant was used to begin a statewide digitization project for Alabama-related materials, and part of HCL's participation involved acquiring a free instance of OCLC's ContentDM product to input the materials contributed to the consortial project. The library saw no IMLS grant funds itself, but the desire to participate in such programs—to play well with others—and further digitization of HCL's own unique collections resulted in seeking out other players willing to participate in the library's drama. One such player was found in the university's photographic services department. The collection of negatives mentioned above was acquired from photographic services, which had the financial resources and equipment, but not the personnel, to pursue digitization of this project. In exchange for the library's work on digitizing the negatives, photographic services donated the workstation, scanner, backup storage, and other props necessary to open the library's debut digitization projects to a wider audience—garnering praise as Best Supporting Actor.

A vital part of playing well with others, of the well-oiled technical services machine, are its 7 paraprofessionals. The serials and government document assistants mentioned above are the rule rather than the exception—over the years, many of these library employees have received the university's Employee of the Month recognition, and two have been chosen university Employee of the Year at an institution that employs over 1,100 people. This illustrates that the value of their work and accomplishments are recognized by entities external to the library.

Technical services paraprofessionals have proven to be much like Shakespearean actors who change their costumes to assume multiple roles within the same play. They collaborate among themselves, offering support within the department when needed. Extra hands have pitched in to help the acquisitions assistant unbox a deluge of books arriving for the library's textbook adoption area. Paraprofessionals have worked with each other to mend items and build boxes to house fragile books. Some have even worked as set designers, painting the long-neglected walls in technical services when no satisfaction could be found from other quarters within the university.

Not only do the paraprofessionals work seamlessly within the technical services department, they also work and play well with others outside the department. Although they are cast as technical services departmental players, they at times help in the public services venue. As just one example, some volunteer for the late-night shifts during the library's extended hours during final exam weeks. In this capacity, they bag and take out trash filled at an alarming rate by thirsty and hungry patrons; they patrol floors, keeping an ever-wary eye out for restless students building book forts in the stacks; they round up stragglers reluctant to leave the building at closing time in the wee hours of the morning. At other times, they are integral players in the library's annual autumn "tailgate" open house. At this event they fill numerous roles, including decorating the building, welcoming students, and serving food. Some have even put their creativity to use by building a prize wheel for door prizes.

The technical services paraprofessionals have also assisted in other departments on campus. When there was a staff shortage in the financial aid office, an emergency call from the university administration for help with scholarship applications went out to the deans, and library paraprofessionals were some of those tapped to answer the request. They have even become a traveling troupe, taking their talents beyond the university walls and into the community. A recent instance occurred when they helped the overwhelmed media specialist at the city's new elementary school unbox, relabel, and shelve around 10,000 books over the course of two days, just in time for the opening day of school.

Like chameleons, the technical services paraprofessionals blend seamlessly into other work areas, while never neglecting their primary duties. It bears stressing that they fill all these extra roles without any lapse in the quality of their own work—or anything remotely resembling merit raises, which were discontinued by the university several years ago.

ACT V: DENOUEMENT

In examining the acts above, it becomes apparent that there are certain factors that could be controlled (or, at least addressed) by technical services personnel, and others that could not. There were no financial resources to expend on additional positions—no deus ex machina to descend from on high and provide—so creative solutions had to be employed to use the existing number of technical services staff to address expanding responsibilities. Fortunately, the library's organizational culture is such that permission was afforded to shift the roles of these positions as needed without question or administrative interference.

That same culture has ensured that the technical services department has enjoyed little turnover in either faculty or staff over the past several years—the few departures have been due to retirement of long-standing personnel. Contrary to the adage "familiarity breeds contempt," the close acquaintance of the personnel with one another has smoothed what could otherwise have been choppy waves occasioned by the changing workflows within the department. The members of the HCL technical services staff are flexible, congenial, and creative. Their willingness to take on different roles has made tackling the changing environment so much easier than it would have been with recalcitrant or entrenched employees. Technical services personnel, both faculty and paraprofessional, have readily adapted to the changing environment and risen to the new challenges with good grace, a spirit of teamwork, and no small measure of humor.

The enhancement of skill sets and the flexibility displayed have not only promoted technical services but also the library as a unit—a great many unique digital objects from the library's archival and other collections (photographs, oral histories, university and other historical items, and much more) are now publicly accessible, seeing far greater use than when these collections languished under lock and key in the library's closed stacks. These collections, as well as the furtherance of access through other types of electronic resources (e.g., e-books, e-journals, EBSCO's Discovery) made possible by the willingness of technical services staff to adapt themselves, have a noticeable benefit to library users, and to the university. Technical services personnel often wait in the wings or man the catwalk; end users are unaware of the specifics of technical services' contributions to library performance—but these contributions greatly affect the level of service end users receive. Technical services department players have risen to the challenges of a changing environment and proven themselves resilient.

There is no doubt that they are well poised to take on any new roles when the casting call goes out, and they will continue to play their part in making HCL a shining star on the university's stage.

NOTE

1. Mary D. Bevis and Sonja L. McAbee, "NOTIS as an Impetus for Change in Technical Services Departmental Staffing," *Technical Services Quarterly* 12, no. 2 (1994): 29–43.

CHALLENGE FIVE

Government Documents Collections in a Digital Era

CHAPTER 22

Using CRDP to Manage Cataloging in a Federal Depository Library

Edith K. Beckett

ABSTRACT

The New Jersey State Library has been a federal depository library since 1895. Prior to 2009, staffing limitations in the library meant that only 60% to 70% of the materials received from the Government Publishing Office were added to the library's catalog. The library also had no effective practices for cataloging the growing number of digital documents in its federal depository library collection. In March of 2010, the New Jersey State Library began participating in the Government Publishing Office's Cataloging Record Distribution Program (CRDP). Through this program, MARCIVE, a U.S.-based library services company, supplies the library with MARC formatted bibliographic records for all the new titles published by agencies in the library's depository profile. As a result, all the materials received through the depository library program since 2010, including those in digital format, are routinely added to the library's catalog.

INTRODUCTION

The New Jersey State Library (NJSL), in operation since 1796, is one of the oldest state library agencies in the United States. Located in Trenton, New Jersey, NJSL provides a full range of library-related services to state government and the citizens of the state. The technical services department at NJSL has a staff of seven full-time employees, three of which are full-time catalogers. This department is responsible for all copy and original cataloging for the general book collection and nine special collections. The technical services department is also responsible for library acquisitions, management of NJSL's Horizon integrated library system (ILS), including the database authority files, and bindery and preservation activities. NJSL is also a depository library for state and federal government publications. This chapter will describe NJSL's efforts to provide catalog access to its tangible and electronic federal government documents using records provided by MARCIVE Inc. as a part of the Cataloging Records Distribution Program (CRDP).

ORGANIZATION BACKGROUND

The services offered by NJSL fall into three broad categories: services for state government, services for public libraries, and services for the public. Services for state government include access to on-site research collections, including extensive law, state and federal documents, and genealogy collections. The library also provides comprehensive reference and research support, including access to approximately 227 databases, interlibrary loan services, and a collection of more than 1,000,000 books, documents, and journals. State government workers are also provided services through branch libraries located in the Department of Banking and Insurance, the Department of Environmental Protection, and the Department of Transportation. The library at the state Attorney General's Office, while not a branch library, shares NJSL's ILS and catalog.

Services for public libraries include the provision of broadband connectivity and related services, a statewide interlibrary loan system, and training for public library trustees and new public library directors. NJSL also administers New Jersey library laws and the per capita state aid program for libraries. The public is provided on-site access to all the collections, and New Jersey residents are permitted borrowing privileges from the circulating collections. Services are also provided to people with print disabilities through the Talking Book and Braille Center. In July 1996, NJSL became an affiliate of Thomas Edison State College, now Thomas Edison State University. Under this arrangement the university provides administrative oversight to NJSL, but NJSL's operations are primarily funded by appropriations through the state budget. In FY 2017 the direct funding for NJSL was $5.3 million.[1]

SETTING THE STAGE

The Government Publishing Office (GPO) was established in 1861 as the primary printer for U.S. government publications. "All printing for the Congress, the Executive Office, and the Judiciary—except for the Supreme Court of the United States—and for every executive department, independent office, and establishment of the government is required to be done at or contracted by GPO."[2] GPO "is also responsible for the acquisition, classification, dissemination, and bibliographic control of tangible and electronic government information products."[3] In December 2014, the Government Printing Office officially became the Government Publishing Office in recognition of the fact that dissemination of digital content continues to be a significant part of the organization's efforts.[4] These information products are distributed by the superintendent of documents through a nationwide system of depository libraries, through govinfo.gov, and through distribution centers in Laurel, Maryland, and Pueblo, Colorado.[5]

As one of the world's largest content creators, the United States government uses the GPO and the Federal Depository Library Program (FDLP) to distribute "certain classes of Government documents free of cost to designated libraries throughout the United States and its territories. These libraries are known as federal depository libraries. Federal depository libraries must offer free, public access to their federal collections."[6] Federal depository libraries can be either a regional depository library that receives every publication distributed by the GPO or a selective depository library that receives publications in self-selected categories. NJSL has been a selective federal depository library since 1895. As a selective depository, the library receives materials that support its primary mission of providing support for the work of New Jersey's executive, legislative, and judicial branches of government. Most of the materials received through the FDLP are a part of the U.S. documents collection; however, appropriate titles are also added to the law collection. The federal depository library materials come in a variety of formats, including print, microform, and video. There are also computer files on various media ranging from 3.5-inch floppy disks to DVDs. Most of the materials received by NJSL are in the areas of law, health, education, and the environment. There is also an extensive collection of U.S. Census materials, some of which date from the 1790s, and congressional reports and documents dating from 1776–1889 and 1921 to the present.

Providing bibliographic access to government documents has long been a concern of libraries. Government documents can be "bibliographically complex entities" due to the changeable nature of the government entities responsible for their production.[7] In their 1987 study, researchers Turner and Latta found that a majority of the research libraries reported that many of the federal publications in their collections were "uncatalogued and housed in a centralized document collection . . . [and] anticipated use, subject, and anticipated research or permanent value [were] prominent criteria used to determine the level of bibliographic control for an individual government publication."[8] Lynch and Lasater suggest that while government publications are valuable sources of information, working with them in large numbers often means that they seldom receive the full cataloging afforded to other library materials.[9] The experiences at NJSL conform to these reported findings. While the goal of the technical services department has always been to have all of the materials in all of the library's collections represented in the catalog, the sheer volume of materials received through the FDLP has meant that the staff has been only moderately successful with regard to the depository library materials. NJSL's experiences have been much like those reported by Western Kentucky University, where this "goal" would be more accurately described as "a heartfelt commitment" rather than an achievable goal.[10]

Cataloging duties for materials received through the federal depository libraries program are currently allotted one-quarter to one-third FTE (full-time equivalent) of staff time. In the past, NJSL catalogers focused primarily on cataloging documents that were sent to the technical services department by the librarian responsible for the management of the federal depository collection. Most of these were documents in print and VHS/CD-ROM/DVD formats. Selected microform materials were also cataloged, but most of the materials in this format remained uncatalogued. NJSL is an OCLC member,[11] and the catalogers would search the OCLC database for records that matched each document sent for cataloging. Once an appropriate record was found, catalogers would make edits following local practice guidelines, then export the record into the library catalog. On average, it took about 15 to 20 minutes of staff time to get an item cataloged and ready to circulate. According to the librarian managing the federal depository documents collection, 30% to 40% of this collection was still uncatalogued as of 2009. The number of uncatalogued federal documents in the collection continued to increase as GPO began distributing more and more publications in digital formats. Absent specific policies or guidelines, these digital documents were treated in the same manner as microfiche documents—that is, some of them were selected for cataloging, but many of them were not. The current budget environment meant that adding additional staff to address the growing influx of federal documents was not a viable option; this problem had to be addressed using existing staff. Without significant changes in cataloging practices, it seemed very likely that the uncatalogued portions of NJSL's federal depository library collection would continue to rapidly increase.

THE CATALOGING RECORDS DISTRIBUTION PROGRAM (CRDP)

In 2009, the librarian managing the federal depository documents collection suggested that NJSL could benefit from participation in a new program being piloted by the FDLP. This program, originally called the cataloging record distribution project, would provide participating depository libraries with MARC records for federal materials free of charge. The provided records would be created by GPO and would be distributed to participants by MARCIVE Inc. MARCIVE is a U.S.-based library services company, established in 1981, that specializes in supplying MARC bibliographic and authority record services to libraries.[12] The entry for CRDP in the FDLP *News & Events* blog provides detailed information about the program.[13] This blog posting lists the following advantages to participants:

- The service is available at no cost to participants.
- The service provides monthly delivery of quality bibliographic records.
- Bibliographic records match participants' FDLP item selection profiles, and the delivered records can easily be adjusted to accommodate changes in the profile.
- Records can be easily acquired by the participants.
- Participation in the program will reduce staff cataloging time.
- Participants can request community support from other CRDP-participating libraries.

The program is open to all federal depository libraries on a first come, first served basis. Libraries usually join at the beginning of the federal fiscal year, but if a "program vacancy arises during the fiscal year, the next library on the waiting list is able to join the program at that time." The program has expanded every year, and as of May 2017, was providing bibliographic records to 165 federal depository libraries.[14]

To remain an active participant, libraries are required to do the following:

- Maintain CRDP point(s) of contact with both GPO and MARCIVE Inc.
- Retrieve, review, and load the records on a timely basis.
- Set profile to receive at least 10 records each month, on average.
- Complete an annual GPO survey about the CRDP.
- Have an ILS system that supports Resource Description and Access (RDA) bibliographic records.[15]

Participating libraries are also expected to make all records available in their ILS/OPAC. Libraries may edit bibliographic records according to local protocols, and there are limited provisions that allow libraries to request that MARCIVE repost records if staff at the library fail to retrieve records within the designated one-month window. Each participant may choose to receive either all newly created bibliographic records or all newly created and changed bibliographic records. In addition, libraries can add Historic Shelflist[16] records to their selections, or they can elect to receive only Historic Shelflist records.

IMPLEMENTATION

In 2010, NJSL began participating in CRDP. Staff at NJSL elected to receive both newly created and changed bibliographic records. The new records would be edited, if needed, to make them compliant with cataloging standards, which are currently RDA, and all would contain Library of Congress Subject Headings. Catalogers would add the newly created records to the library's catalog and update OCLC to indicate that NJSL held the titles.

Many of the modifications to the records in the changed record file did not appear to affect the access points for the bibliographic items. There was also concern that batch loading the changed record files would overlay existing records and wipe out any local record modifications. This overlay problem could be eliminated by having cataloging staff review the file, but there was insufficient cataloger time to review both the new and changed record files. After some discussion, it was decided that the federal depository collection librarian would review the changed records to see if any of the changes were significant enough to require replacement of the existing NJSL catalog records. Those records with significant changes would be flagged for the cataloger, who would edit the records to meet local specifications and upload them into the library's catalog. NJSL elected not to receive the records for the Historic Shelflist. The rationale for this decision was that there was not enough staff time to process new records, review changed records, *and* deal with the records from the Historic Shelflist. NJSL's participation in the CRDP pilot project began in March 2010 with the download of two batches of test records. The first batch of actual records, downloaded from the MARCIVE website on March 30, 2010, consisted of records for 172 tangible (print/microform/CD-ROM/DVD) titles and 466 digital titles.

The new records for NJSL are uploaded to the MARCIVE website each month as a series of four files, each containing varying numbers of records. The number of records in each file is determined by the documents cataloged or modified by GPO each month that fit NJSL's depository selection profile. There are new and changed record files for items issued in tangible formats, and the same for items issued in digital format. All the digital records have persistent uniform resource locators, or PURLs. "The FDLP uses persistent uniform resource locators (PURLs) to provide stable URLs to online federal information. When a user clicks on a PURL, the request is routed to the federal publication. As federal agencies redesign and remove information from their sites, GPO staff reroute PURL entries to the appropriate location."[17]

The records for items in tangible formats do not have PURLs, but many have fields indicating that the title was issued in additional formats. Staff at NJSL decided that adding PURLs to the records for tangible items would be beneficial to users. It was also decided that to facilitate resource sharing, our OCLC holdings would be updated for all the records added to our local catalog. Once NJSL staff decided how they wanted to use the records, understood how the records were structured on the MARCIVE website, and worked out the procedures for retrieving and storing the records, the next steps in the process were figuring out the most effective way to edit and process the records.

CREATING AN EFFECTIVE WORKFLOW

One of the earliest decisions faced by the staff was how to edit the records supplied by MARCIVE to conform to NJSL local protocols. Staff decided to use the MarcEdit software, and batch editing to process the records. MarcEdit is a MARC editing utility designed to support all MARC formats, including MARCXML. It is available as open source software and was developed by Terry Reese at Oregon State University.[18] Several members of the technical services staff had attended a MarcEdit training workshop in 2009 and so were familiar with the basic functions of the software. Additional training was provided by online tutorials.

The cataloger uses the program's *MarcBreaker* to convert the records downloaded from MARCIVE into a human-readable mnemonic format. Then, the *MarcEditor* is used to review the records and perform batch and individual edits. Next, the *MarcValidator* is used to check the structure of the records and alert the catalogers to issues with field/subfield structure that could cause problems when the records are imported into the library catalog. Then, the edited and validated records are converted back into the MARC format using *MarcMaker*.[19] Finally, OCLC holdings are updated for each record using batch processing, and batch import functions are used to add the edited records to the library's catalog.

CRDP was NJSL's first experience using batch uploads of vendor-supplied records. Prior to CRDP, every record added to the catalog was created or selected by a cataloger, and selected records were individually reviewed or edited prior to being uploaded into the catalog. NJSL management wanted to retain this level of quality control, so the decision was made to review and, if needed edit, every CRDP record prior to upload. This decision created a couple of initial challenges. First, the sheer volume of records, an average of 600 records each month, meant that the cataloger for the federal depository collection would have to devote significant time to this process. Since only one-quarter to one-third FTE of cataloger time was allotted for this collection, an extremely efficient process would have to be put in place to meet these editing needs. Working at this level of intensity also made cataloger fatigue a real possibility. Since a single person needed to review and edit all the CRDP records, procedures had to be developed to guard against cataloger burnout, assess the quality of the uploaded records, and reduce errors caused by cataloger fatigue. The solution implemented by NJSL staff involved several parts: working with small batches of records, working in short editing sessions, and keeping a written log to track the process.

After some trial and error, it was determined that 15 records were the optimal batch size. This means that larger files are easily divided into workable units using MarcEdit's *MarcSplit* function—for example, the 662 e-docs records from the November 2016 download were processed as 44 15-record files and a single 2-record file. These smaller files are then edited over the course of a month. Files of records for tangible items are generally smaller—for example, the November 2016 download contained 25 records. The cataloger typically spends eight hours each week editing records. This usually results in an average of 360 records edited each week. The editing sessions are usually no longer than two hours, and an average of six files, of 15 records each, are edited during each session. Staff has found this amount of time at this pace sufficient to keep up with the flow of records without creating undue fatigue.

Staff at NJSL decided that, when available, PURLs would be added to the records for tangible items. This decision was taken to support user access by ensuring that whenever possible, users have direct access to documents through the catalog. This step requires the cataloger to locate the OCLC record for the electronic version of the tangible item and copy the PURL into the record being edited. This process is aided by the GPO catalogers' decision to include MARC field 776 in many of the records. This field indicates what additional formats are available (e.g., microform, online, and so forth) and gives some descriptive information about that additional format, including the OCLC control number of a bibliographic record for that related format. Approximately 95% of the tangible items selected by NJSL have PURLs that are added to the appropriate bibliographic records.

The cataloger for the federal depository collection also uses a written log to track progress through each batch of records. The cataloger records the OCLC control number for each record edited, whether there is an electronic version and a PURL available for tangible items, whether OCLC has been updated to indicate NJSL holdings, and whether the record has been added to the Horizon ILS. This written log provides a mechanism to maintain workflow consistency over multiple files and over many working sessions. The log easily allows the cataloger to see what batch is currently being edited (the latest entry in the log), and what processing has been completed on the files. The log also facilitates OCLC batch processing by providing a list of OCLC control numbers that have been edited. The OCLC control numbers from the log are also used for random quality assurance spot-checks in the Horizon catalog. The written logs are created from standard five-subject college-ruled spiral notebooks, with hand-ruled columns to track the work completed on each batch of records.

IMPORTING CRDP RECORDS

Once the editing process was established, the next challenges were related to getting the records into the Horizon catalog. NJSL uses import profiles to automatically create item records for each newly added bibliographic record. For other collections, catalogers generally work with smaller batches of 10 to 30 individually selected records. Once these small batches have been imported into the library's catalog, each automatically created item is manually modified with specific barcode and collection information. This was impractical for the hundreds of records in the CRDP batch imports, so two record import profiles were created to minimize the processing work for the CRDP records. The import profile for electronic records automatically indicates that the item is in electronic format, is available in the U.S. Documents collection, and assigns "online" as the item's location.

The import profile for tangible item records was a little more challenging. In cases where the item had already been cataloged, and the CRDP used the same OCLC record as NJSL catalogers, the imported CRDP record would simply overlay the existing catalog record, and no additional staff intervention was needed. However, quite a few of the tangible records were for titles that had never been cataloged. Since these records could be matched with physical items in the library's collection, the initial plan was to retrieve these items and update the catalog records with the appropriate barcodes and locations. This required an overwhelming amount of staff time to retrieve, process, and reshelve these items. The final implemented solution uses the import profile to designate that the items are available in the collection. The result is that existing items and their barcodes remain unchanged when the new CRDP bibliographic record is imported to overlay an existing bibliographic record, but if there are no previously existing items/bibliographic records, new items are created with a status of "Ask Librarian." Reference and access services staff have received training to know that if someone looks for an item with this status, it is most likely on the shelves filed under the Superintendent of Documents classification number. If the item is needed for circulation, a barcode is added to the record. However, if the item is only used in-house, it generally remains un-barcoded. Resolving this issue removed the last implementation hurdle, and the cataloger for the federal depository collection began to successfully add hundreds of records for documents to the catalog each month.

QUALITY CONTROL, BOTH BEFORE AND AFTER IMPORT

One of the biggest concerns for NJSL management was ensuring that the vendor-supplied records met the library's quality benchmarks. These previously established benchmarks require full-level descriptive catalog records, created in accordance with current cataloging standards (RDA) that have at least one name or subject access point and contain only subject access points based on valid Library of Congress Subject Headings (LCSH). The records should not contain locally excluded subfields and should include only name access points created in accordance with Library of Congress Name Authority Cooperative Program's (NACO's) rules and recommendations. Staff at NJSL ensures that the CRDP records meet these benchmarks with multiple levels of staff review. The first level of review is performed by the cataloger who examines each record and edits them as needed to meet the desired benchmarks. The second level of review occurs when other technical services staff look specifically at the new name and subject authority records generated by the record imports. Once the records have been imported into the library's catalog, the third level of review is conducted by the depository collection cataloger and the librarian who manages the federal depository collection. These librarians randomly select records from each month's imports for review.

CRDP AND LOCAL AUTHORITY RECORDS

The primary challenge related to CRDP participation is local authority control for the new records. NJSL maintains local authority files for its Horizon catalog, and batch imports of hundreds of records can often generate hundreds of new authority records. For example, a recent import of 120 bibliographic records generated 45 new name authority records and 141 new subject authority records. Technical services staff checks each new authority record to verify that it is not an alternative form of a name access point already represented in the catalog, or to confirm that the subject is a validly constructed LCSH access point. New authority records are generated by all catalogers, so the CRDP generated authority records are often supplemented by an additional 10 to 50 records added during a typical day. Checking hundreds of authority records each day proved to be an overwhelming task. After some discussion, it was decided to limit the number of records in each CRDP import batch to no more than 120, and to limit the large imports to no more than twice each week. Breaking the editing and processing into stages, and tracking progress on the stages, allows many independent editing/upload sessions. This reduces cataloger fatigue, minimizes the chances of error, and allows gradual integration of large numbers of bibliographic records and their related authority files into the library catalog.

CRDP BENEFITS FOR TECHNICAL SERVICES

Work with CRDP has helped raise the profile of the technical services department within the library. Working closely with the federal depository collection librarian has become a model for the way that catalogers interact with the librarians who manage the other special collections. As an example, catalogers now routinely send lists of titles to the special collection managers when new materials are cataloged for their collections. This is beneficial because there can be a significant lag between placing an order for materials and the receipt of those materials for cataloging. Sending the notifications lets the collection managers know that the ordered materials are now available, provides another level of review of the records, and makes the work of technical services much more visible to library colleagues outside of the department. Catalogers have also become more aware of the relationship between their work as catalogers and the functionality of the library catalog authority files. This results in fewer name and subject heading errors in the bibliographic records. Catalogers have also begun work on cataloging and preserving legacy materials in the federal depository collection. This was enabled in part because NJSL now receives primarily electronic documents in this collection, and no additional processing is required beyond the work with CRDP. In addition to the increased productivity from participating in CRDP, the technical services department has also benefited from the expertise that has developed because catalogers are consistently working with large numbers of good quality catalog records.

CRDP was NJSL's first experience using large batches of vendor-supplied bibliographic records. One of the unanticipated benefits of participation in CRDP is a willingness to use vendor-supplied bibliographic records for other collections. Most notably, cataloging staff used MarcEdit and vendor-suppled bibliographic records to eliminate a cataloging backlog of approximately 4,000 records for the general e-book collection. Currently, catalog records for all new titles added to the general e-book collection, as well as some titles in the reference collection, are created using vendor-supplied records.

NJSL plans to continue participation in CRDP for the foreseeable future. Some future plans include developing facility with regular expressions to further streamline some editing tasks in MarcEdit. It would also be useful to collect data to see if there is empirical evidence of increased use of federal depository materials. Staff may also explore whether adding fee-based services from MARCIVE (e.g., purchasing authority records) could further streamline implementation.

CONCLUSION

CRDP implementation has been extremely beneficial for the New Jersey State Library. Table 22.1 shows the number of federal depository documents cataloged by year during the first seven years of NJSL's participation in the program. Given the available staff, it is extremely unlikely that cataloging many of these 48,607 records could have been completed without CRDP. In 2013, physical space constraints prompted the decision to increase the number of federal

Table 22.1 Federal Depository Documents Cataloged Each Year of CRDP Participation

Year	Number of Records Cataloged
2010	7,081
2011*	5,230
2012	7,289
2013	7,257
2014	6,344
2015	7,062
2016	8,344

*The lower number of records cataloged in 2011 is a reflection of staffing changes and staff time spent away from cataloging working on special projects.

depository library program documents received in digital formats; receipt of catalog records through CRDP was a major factor in support of this decision. CRDP implementation has resolved many of the cataloging issues for this collection, but NJSL will need to assess the impacts of this change and develop strategies to preserve and provide access to this digital content.[20] For NJSL, participation in CRDP, along with the use of MarcEdit and OCLC's batch processing, has resulted in significantly more records for federal depository materials in the collection, getting us closer to that elusive goal of having all of the materials in all of the collections represented in the library catalog. It has also resulted in improved service by the technical services department to both library staff and the users that they service.

NOTES

1. Chris Christie and Kim Guadagno, *The Governor's FY 2017 Budget*, State of New Jersey, accessed September 15, 2017, https://nj.gov /treasury/omb/publications/17budget/pdf/FY17BudgetBook .pdf, D-291.

2. United States General Accounting Office, *Electronic Dissemination of Government Publications* (Report to Congressional Committees, report no. GAO-01-428; Washington, DC: United States General Accounting Office, 2001), 4.

3. Ibid.

4. "GPO Is Now the Government Publishing Office," *FDLP News & Events* (blog), last updated December 17, 2014, accessed October 10, 2017, https://www.fdlp.gov/news-and-events/2153-gpo-is-now-the -government-publishing-office.

5. "Mission, Vision, and Goals: Keeping America Informed," United States Government Publishing Office, accessed February 27, 2020, https://www.gpo.gov/who-we-are/our-agency/mission-vision -and-goals.

6. "About the FDLP," Federal Depository Library Program, accessed July 20, 2017, https://www.fdlp.gov/about-the-fdlp/ federal-depository-libraries.

7. Carol Turner and Ann Latta, *Current Approaches to Improving Access to Government Documents: An OMS Occasional Paper Produced as Part of the Collaborative Research-Writing Program*

(Washington, DC: Association of Research Libraries, Office of Management Studies, 1987), 18.

8. Ibid., 19.

9. Frances H. Lynch and Mary Charles Lasater, "Government Documents and the Online Catalog," *Bulletin of the Medical Library Association* 78, no. 1 (January 1990): 23.

10. Rosemary L. Meszaros, "Western Kentucky University and the CRDP," *FDLP Connection* 6, no. 4 (2016), last updated August 25, 2016, https://www.fdlp.gov/all-newsletters/community-insights/2670 -western-kentucky-university-and-the-crdp-under-community-nsights.

11. OCLC is a global library cooperative that provides shared technology services, original research and community programs to thousands of libraries around the world. (OCLC home page, accessed August 2, 2017, https://www.oclc.org/en/home.html.)

12. "MARCIVE Company History," accessed July 21, 2017, http://home .marcive.com/history.

13. "Cataloging Record Distribution Program," *FDLP News & Events* (blog), entry updated November 27, 2019, accessed February 27, 2020, https://www.fdlp.gov/news-and-events/23-about/projects/125-crdp.

14. "Cataloging Record Distribution Program," last updated November 27, 2019, accessed February 27, 2020, https://www.fdlp.gov/project-list /cataloging-record-distribution-program.

15. Ibid.

16. The GPO Historic Shelflist is the GPO's historic card catalog of over one million 3 × 5 cards arranged in Superintendent of Documents (SuDoc) order. ("GPO Historic Shelflist," October 25, 2012, last updated July 23, 2014, https://www.fdlp.gov/project-list/gpo-historic-shelflist.)

17. "Federal Depository Library," Federal Depository Library Program, persistent URL home page, accessed August 2, 2017, https://purl .fdlp.gov/.

18. MarcEdit Development home page, accessed August 2, 2017, http:// marcedit.reeset.net/.

19. "Features," MarcEdit Development, accessed August 8, 2017, http:// marcedit.reeset.net/features.

20. Atifa Rawan, Cheryl Knott Malone, and Laura J. Bender, "Assessing the Virtual Depository Program: The Arizona Experience," Journal of Government Information 30 (2004), 710–26, https://doi.org/10 .1016/j.jgi.2004.11.004.

CHAPTER 23

Bridging Functions: Government Publications Librarians as Technical and Public Service Ambassadors

McKinley Sielaff

ABSTRACT

Colorado has a committed group of government information specialists who have worked closely together for decades to weather the
changing needs at their different types of libraries as they work to
acquire, process, and make available key government information.
These librarians have forged strong ties between the enduring regional
library leadership and the 20-odd selective public, military, and public and private academic libraries. This chapter provides examples of
the wide variety of practices the Colorado Government Publications
Group has explored. These practices include piloting ways of working
with others in evaluating how the program is implemented at individual institutions, sharing information and providing tips for effective
administration, and establishing joint policies, agendas, and values for
collections. This has led to multiple benefits for the group members and
their individual institutions. The benefits are numerous and transcend
traditional technical services/public services silos. They range from
inspiring people to engage with others, to fostering dialogue around
trends and regulations, to enabling greater geographical coverage, to
establishing relationships between members of institutions that have
led to other work and projects, and to overall greater collaboration
within the group. It has also helped in providing a network of people
who exchange expertise and knowledge. Working across institutions,
sharing files, sharing digital repositories and remote housing facilities, sharing expertise, sharing processing procedures, sharing catalog

records, sharing best practices, and adapting to trends are all part of the Colorado Federal Library Depository Program Libraries' story.

INTRODUCTION

As the traditional lines between technical and public service areas blur, librarians have had to sharpen their skills and acquire new proficiencies. The case for librarians handling government information through the Federal Library Depository Program (FDLP) is no different in that regard, although it has its own peculiarities and pressures. This chapter will explore how librarians in Colorado have adjusted to innovations in the depository library program while fostering leadership and collaboratively building collections.

The FDLP was established to provide citizens with access to government documents in perpetuity at no cost. In 1813, a congressional joint resolution mandated that certain publications be distributed to libraries outside of the federal government.[1] Subsequent legislation established the Government Printing Office (GPO) as the agency to distribute government information to libraries via a depository program[2] and expanded the distribution list to include executive documents[3] and updated the program to include electronic publications and data.[4] In 2014, GPO was officially renamed the Government Publishing Office to reflect the contemporary nature of its operations.[5] These changes have impacted how libraries manage their collections.

In order to meet FLDP requirements, depository librarians and staff straddle both public and technical services areas. Some government publications departments perform like a special collections or branch library; they have their own technical service staff and offer public services. In other cases, processing tasks and providing access are dispersed throughout the library. There are currently over 1,200 libraries in the United States and its territories with federal depository library collections (FDLC). Twenty of these are in Colorado.

IN PRACTICE

Colorado has a committed group of government information specialists who have worked faithfully together to weather the changing needs of their constituencies. Along with participating in the FDLP, the Colorado Government Publications Interest Group (CoGoPub) and the Alliance Government Publication Committee are two additional vehicles that foster collaboration. These core groups have kept up with new policies, trends, and innovations. They have created a shared retention scheme, pioneered batch loading of MARC records, harvested online data, scanned historic materials, augmented interlibrary loan agreements, strengthened circulation options, launched a reoccurring regional conference, and initiated an Institute of Museum and Library Services (IMLS) grant. A state plan, a feature in a memorandum of understanding signed by library directors in Colorado, underwrites the value of the program. These efforts have strengthened bonds within and between libraries, thus enriching the FDLP vision for citizens in Colorado. They have also eliminated barriers between collecting/processing materials and finding/using them. At the national level, depository librarians have influenced policies and helped shape federal regulations. CoGoPub's endeavors have concentrated on mentoring and collaboration, adapting to innovation, and managing the collection.

MENTORING AND COLLABORATION

The FDLP includes a variety of library types. In Colorado, they have included large and small public libraries, special libraries (including the Supreme Court Library), and a variety of academic libraries (a military academy, a Research I university system, a land-grant university, a school of mines, a teacher's college, private universities, a private liberal arts college, and several state-funded institutions of higher education). In terms of partnerships, CoGoPub has been a venue for collaborations between public and academic libraries for over three decades. Deepening these connections supports the departmental mission of all of the libraries—namely, to nurture lifelong learning through public access to government information.

Mentoring registers high in importance for success in the library environment.[6] The structure of regional and selective libraries creates a local support network that encourages mentoring. Opportunities abound for interacting with others who are currently going (or recently went) through similar developmental stages. Taking on a leadership role within the group offers participants low-risk opportunities and experiences that build resumes and lead to advancement. They have earned promotions to department heads and heads of library branches. As a former depository librarian and library director wrote, "Librarians and library workers who work in the middle play a critical role in the future of organizations."[7]

Mentoring and collaboration have been key components for success for many FDLP staff in Colorado. Documents librarians frequently come from a background in reference or other public service activities rather than technical services. They lack cataloging skills and understanding in how to work with vendors; they have little acquisition and processing experience. Documents librarians report that while on-the-job training is helpful, it did not lead to them to feel effective in their jobs.[8] Along with receiving practical guidance on supervising and fulfilling the requirements of the program, staff in this network of depository libraries feel less isolated, receive encouragement, and gain collaboration experience. Learning more about cataloging issues and understanding MARC fields enables librarians to offer substantial suggestions for improving how records display to the catalog and in conversations with vendors. By sharing practices, providing examples of policies and procedures, and helping one another, these librarians have saved their institutions thousands of dollars in training and consulting fees. By providing pertinent information about the FDLP, they have shaped organizational goals and programs.

Regular meetings promote a mentoring/leadership environment. Rotating locations and offering virtual conferencing ensures varied attendance. It also allows clerical staff and non-depository librarians to attend meetings hosted at their library, thereby extending this network. Tours are on every agenda and provide examples of how to envision and modify workspaces (e.g., workstations configurations, learning commons, compact shelving, off-site storage, and remodeling). This has been extraordinarily expedient in the instances where government information departments have been absorbed into other library units. Training sessions are another agenda item; typically delivered by library staff, sessions have been supplemented with presentations from employees of government entities, non-depository libraries, and museums, further expanding the network of people engaged with government information. This network enables library staff to call on each other for support in dealing with issues involving government publications, as well as for career advice and library initiatives at their respective institutions.

Librarians have shared their expertise by presenting jointly and serving on panels at state and national conferences. CoGoPub also initiated a regional conference in 2001. Programs ranged in content from technical service processes to public outreach. Subsequent biannual conferences have followed with attendance spread across a growing geographic area after it moved to an online platform. In 2005, a small group of librarians obtained an IMLS grant to train approximately 1,000 library staff to be government information specialists. Along with piloting a broad geographic model of networking for training and resource development for multitype libraries, this grant offered a new model for the FDLP, where training and support of non-depository library staff was the primary target. Additionally, it was an excellent opportunity for professional development; some librarians worked on the grant while others served as researchers, developers, experts, leaders, and trainers.

Depository staff have taken on other erstwhile roles. They have served as representatives to national conferences and professional meetings. A librarian from Colorado frequently sits on GPO's Depository Library Council. They have acted as ombudspersons, such as when a public library clerk wrote to the Colorado Legislative Council regarding catalog records and access to publications. Depository staff have also participated jointly in the rulemaking process of governmental agencies giving feedback and comments. Recently this dealt with feedback on changes to Title 44 of the U.S. Code, which establishes the legality of the program.

These examples specify how FDLP staff perform beyond their daily tasks. In addition to building skills and learning practical applications for routine work, they have undertaken leadership roles and acted as ambassadors of the program to their local libraries. The depository libraries network "serve[s] as the local voice of the GPO, providing interpretations, explanations, and updates of policies and regulations. Under the RDL's [regional depository library's] leadership, the Government Publications Interest group present[s] opportunities for depository librarians and staff to exchange ideas, share best practices and knowledge about the collection strengths and areas of expertise."[9]

Institutional benefits of mentoring have served as a mechanism for hiring, retention, and promotion, exposed librarians to multiple organizational cultures, and dispersed leadership throughout library units.

ADAPTING TO INNOVATION

As GPO transformed into a digital information provider, depository staff needed to acquire new competencies in working with electronic and born-digital items as they responded to government agencies experimenting with an array of new technologies to disseminate information. They were at the forefront, being both early adopters of the Internet and creators on the web. They set up email accounts and a listserv to promote communication with colleagues and government entities. As hypertext transfer protocol (http) evolved, members led training sessions and traded code along with instructions for developing wikis, RSS feeds, and blogs. Technical services tasks expanded to include new technologies.

It was not always feasible for each depository library to load and host access to all the software arriving from such diverse agencies as the Forest Service to NASA. Yet starting with the arrival of floppy discs, depositories were obligated to do so. Sharing content, tips on processing, instructions on loading requirements, and the like was crucial. As storage formats changed, migration of information to usable platforms became an issue. Consequently, depository librarians wrote and shared policies for digital preservation. They pioneered the use of emerging technologies such as remote desktop features, social tagging of documents, virtual conferencing software, instant messaging, chat, and texting. Moreover, depository librarians introduced proposals in their libraries regarding Google Books, HathiTrust, open repositories, and public domain publications. They were often innovators, creating standards and procedures as they went. Some libraries carried out web harvesting initiatives. Others undertook scanning and digitization projects. Colorado legislative publications and documents are openly available online due to one such undertaking. Several libraries are GPO preservation stewards.

Through brainstorming sessions, depository staff constructed comprehensive plans for their FDLC and later used that knowledge in working with nongovernment items; an e-book is not conceptually different from a born-digital congressional report. Those staff with computer proficiencies shared in-house programs that tracked URL use by counting the number of click-throughs on links from individual records in the catalog. These data parallel traditional circulation statistics and are used by libraries in statistical reports. Because some FDLCs participated in LOCKSS DOCS, based on Stanford's LOCKSS (Lots of Copies Keeps Stuff Safe) program of preserving electronic journals, they were included in consortia discussions regarding preservation platforms.

By working through issues related to managing the FDLP, staff became authorities in said technologies and shared their expertise in working on other initiatives. Their feedback and input helped shape how new technologies were ingested into routine library work, in terms of not only depository library tasks but those for the rest of the library also.

COLLECTIONS

Managing and developing collections is a large part of library work. Traditional approaches to collection development have been supplemented with new technologies, access methods, and formats. FDLPs have unique considerations that may offer insights into managing libraries' general collections. The government retains ownership of all these materials. Moreover, there are federal requirements for selecting, deselecting, and withdrawing items. It is not solely a library's choice whether to retain an item.

Acquisitions are straightforward. Collections are built through selection profiles based on item numbers. (The item numbering system groups together materials produced by individual government agencies and subagencies.) Regionals receive all items. Selective libraries (selectives) create their profiles by adding and deleting item numbers they determine are important to their local communities and congressional districts. Adding items to the collections is a bit more challenging. GPO distributes tangible items. Usually a library subscribes to a third party to supply matching MARC records. These files of records are batch loaded into the catalog. Staff accustomed to this workflow have lent expertise to cataloging staff for ingesting multiple items at a time and in cataloging non-tangible items.

Withdrawal of federal publications is a joint enterprise. Selective libraries consult with their regionals to get permission to remove items from their collections. Before these items can be discarded, they must be offered to other selectives. By following these requirements, librarians have learned to work together to meet collection goals. Librarians also have learned to balance in-hand versus on-demand as they balanced tangible and born-digital items. As commercial vendors began offering electronic publications, these librarians offered valuable insights into working with online software and platforms.

Another area where FDLP librarians have been of assistance in Colorado is in working on collaborative collection development projects within consortia and multiple library settings. CoGoPub members have worked on the following plans to forecast and document goals and actions connected to shared collections.

- A shared depository collection plan (2002, revised 2015) for the entire state. This plan, initiated by depository staff, opened dialogue between library directors, leading to a memorandum of understanding that pledged to support the FDLP and clarified each library's collection scope and commitment to retain materials.
- A consortia plan (2007) for the board of directors of the Colorado Alliance of Research Libraries (Alliance), who commissioned a committee to create a plan for the future of Alliance depositories. This plan addressed shared collection agreements and building collections cooperatively. It included expanding access to the FDLCs and enhancing interlibrary loan operations.
- A state-focused action plan (2012) for GPO. This plan prioritized three initiatives, one of which is that all depository libraries in Colorado will work collaboratively to share expertise and to provide outreach and training for libraries and users.

Further collaborative collection development projects have been undertaken between libraries and through the Alliance. Pilot projects in acquiring materials across libraries have included librarians who serves as liaisons to academic departments and who manage an

FDLC. Currently the Alliance libraries are discussing a shared paper collection where the government documents plan serves as a model for this next step in collective collection building.

The government document plan highlights several goals of the new initiative: reducing redundancies in collections, distinguishing retention commitments, borrowing and loaning of materials, and the use of off-site facilities.

Ensuring access to documents is another way in which the work of technical services staff undergirds public services. Government publications staff have acted as ombudspersons, as shown in the follow examples.

- Representing library needs with vendors by ensuring access to a state regulatory publication, the Colorado Administrative Code, through the database LexisNexis.
- Evaluating specific proposals, such as when replacing integrated library systems, upgrading to discovery layers, and making consortium database purchases.
- Complying with GPO programs such as inspections and biennial surveys.

Overall, external reviews of work and collections in this one department familiarizes the library with the processes and procedures of external reviews and accreditation visits.

Space concerns and corresponding costs have led library administrators to reconsider their collections. Depository collections, having weathered this concern, offer some solutions. First, depository librarians provided their administrators with information and data regarding the repercussions, costs (both expenses and savings), federal regulations, and processes of relinquishing depository status. Next, there was a review of the program in 2007 by a task force charged with examining shared collection development of FDLCs housed at Alliance member libraries. Library responses to reallocation of labor and space varied (from drastic downsizing to shifting to an electronic collection and transferring all tangible documents to off-site storage to changing depository status). A few libraries did conduct a major downsizing of their collection, resulting in a team of depository librarians conducting on-site visits and making recommendations to assist in the process.

FDCLs with separate government information departments merged with other library departments. As staff were rehoused, they became liaisons between depository and other library divisions and found that other library units welcomed their skills and knowledge. As staff merged and more people began working with the depository items, the depository became less an unknown entity and more normalized as a collection. Overall, merging departments served as a positive model for the repurposing of staff to align with changing and emerging work needs, with the added benefit of sharing knowledge about technical services tasks as well as the collection.

The U.S. government, as the largest publisher in the world for over 150 years, has produced a substantial historic collection of tangible publications. FDLCs are required to have piece-level catalog records for every tangible item. Government publications are tricky to catalog, so this is often a burden for libraries without robust cataloging staff. When trained staff catalog and convert their holdings, they not only provide greater access to the legacy depository collection but in sharing those records they also supply others with MARC records they can copy. By loading these records into a shared catalog, library users and librarians benefit through improved access to and bibliographic control of FLDCs. Benefits to libraries in the state include the following.

- Staff have acquired supplemental cataloging skills, from copy-cataloging to batch loading of records.
- Thousands of electronic government publications records have been added to a shared catalog.
- Hundreds of serial records were added to the Alliance's electronic resource management system.
- The regional library, in a joint project with the National Renewable Energy Lab, upon finding issues with item selection implications, informed GPO so that system-wide corrections could be made at the national level
- Vendor MARC records have been replaced with free records from the Catalog of U.S. Government Publications.
- The government approved a CoGoPub recommendation waiving the annual membership fee for Prospector (a consortia catalog) so that the Colorado State Publications Library could join, thus adding its valuable collection to that catalog.

All of this work has created uniform government publications records that significantly enhance the shared catalog, provided similar treatment of documents across the various libraries, and resulted in more knowledgeable staff within institutions. It ensures that government periodicals are included in coverage in catalogs and for proxy servers. It bridges technical service expertise with the needs of public services staff and library users. Other technical skills and knowledge have further improved access. When depository librarians scan and digitize unique government publications, they also create metadata and finding tools that they share broadly. An example is a joint pilot project with GWLA (Greater Western Library Alliance) to digitize certain federal agencies' technical reports. MARC records and metadata created for those documents was given to GPO. Additionally, several federal agencies posted this digitized information online.

In 2009, an Alliance-initiated task force investigated a consortia purchase of a microform scanner. Once approved, depository librarians helped develop operational procedures and led training sessions. In addition to supporting regional digitization projects, the purchase improved interlibrary loan. It expedited service, enhanced availability, and improved access of government microforms, a format that had never before been available for loan.

FDLP staff, in working with their collections, have contributed to achieving institutional goals in significant ways. Managing an FDLC means those librarians and staff are familiar with working collaboratively. They deal with the constraints of external regulations on how items are accessioned/deaccessioned and inventoried. They are experienced in working with multiple formats, with electronic items and digitizing publications, with harvesting and preserving online publications, with new cataloging processes (such as batch loading), and so on. In managing the FDLC, they have developed traditional technical services skills and implemented them to handle 21st-century library challenges, such as utilizing alternative storage formats and building shared collections to reduce the physical footprint of collections and working collaboratively in shared collection development across institutions. They have then used those skills and knowledge in other aspects of work in their libraries. In taking what they have learned in curating the FDLC, librarians and staff have implemented proven solutions and workflows for similar issues faced by the entire library.

Since depository librarians and staff deal with both the back-of-the-house tasks and frontline services, they bridge the department silos of technical and public services.

CONCLUSION

The FLDP has been operating in the Colorado territory since before it gained statehood. Spread out across the state's 104,185 square miles, Colorado librarians have found advantages in working together. They have forged strong and enduring ties between the regional and the 20-some selective public, military, legal, and public and private academic libraries. Successful projects have set the stage for more collaborations whose outcomes have helped *transcend traditional technical services/public services silos*.

Together librarians in Colorado have mastered new skills and adjusted to an ever-changing, fast-paced information age. They have expanded the definition of what traditional technical services tasks are as they transitioned into a digital world. In doing so, they have developed efficiencies in problem-solving and proficiencies in communication and have engaged in strategic collaborations. These have led to individual professional development and improvements in their home libraries. Mentoring has been a significant motivator for librarians to participate in CoGoPub. These relationships have created trust and fostered intimacy that spans both formal and informal work channels. They have also helped librarians to evolve in their thinking about technical versus public services tasks and encouraged leadership roles within the group, which has led to leadership within institutions extending beyond the FDLP. Confident in their leadership roles, these librarians and staff can extend their reach to regional and national arenas, serving as ambassadors for all aspects of library work in both technical services and public access.

Championing technical services continues with growing exigency. Collecting, organizing, creating access points, and retaining government information is more critical than ever. Escalating amounts of information are created daily, and cataloging and enhancing access to this information is becoming exceedingly important. People need official sources to support their fact-finding activities, in debunking fake news, and in navigating increasingly complex government websites. Librarians must advocate for findability and usability. By pledging ongoing participation in the FDLP with its commitment to technical service activities, the librarians in Colorado will ensure, both individually and communally, that the goal of free, perpetual access to government information endures.

NOTES

1. Federal Depository Library Program, *Designation Handbook for Federal Depository Libraries* (Washington, DC: GPO, 2008), https://www.fdlp.gov/file-repository/about-the-fdlp/5-designation -handbook-for-federal-depository-libraries.
2. An Act Providing for the Public Printing and Binding and the Distribution of Public Documents, Pub. L. No. 502, 28 Stat. 601 (1895).
3. An Act to Revise the Laws Relating to Depository Libraries, Pub. L. 87-579, 76 Stat. 352–356 (1962).
4. An Act to Establish in the Government Printing Office a Means of Enhancing Electronic Public Access to a Wide Range of Federal Electronic Information, Pub. L. 103-40, 107 Stat. 112–114 (1993).
5. Government Publishing Office Act of 2014, 44 U.S.C. 44 §§ 1 et seq. (2014).
6. Lisa K. Hussey and Jennifer Campbell-Meier, "Is There a Mentoring Culture Within the LIS Profession?" *Journal of Library Administration,* 57, no. 5 (2017): 500–516, https://doi.org/10.1080 /01930826.2017.1326723.
7. Maggie Farrell, "Leading From the Middle," *Journal of Library Administration* 54, no. 8 (2014): 699, https://doi.org/10.1080/019 30826.2014.965099.
8. Kathryn Yelinek and Marilou Hincliff, "Accidental Government Documents Librarian: A Review of Experiences and Training Needs of Interim Document Librarians," *Journal of Academic Librarianship,* 35, no. 1 (2009): 46–56.
9. Letter to the dean of libraries at University of Colorado-Boulder from the alliance depository librarians, April 25, 2008. In author's possession.

CHALLENGE SIX

Adapting for the Future

CHAPTER 24

Facing Distance Education Challenges in the Library Through Collaboration Between Technical and Public Services Departments: A Case Study

Katherine Hill and Samantha Harlow

ABSTRACT

Distance learning in higher education has grown extensively over the last few years, with now almost 6,000,000 students enrolled in at least one distance education course. Distance education provides challenges to the idea of the library as physical space, and challenges technical services departments to expand their online presence, both in terms of collections and outreach. This chapter explores using the strategies of instruction, outreach, collaboration, and course integration to more effectively respond to the increase of distance education programs through a case study of the efforts of the University Libraries at University of North Carolina at Greensboro. While numerous avenues are explored, this chapter focuses on ways to improve service to distance students through a joint effort between public and technical services librarians.

INTRODUCTION

Technical services librarians face many challenges when working with distance education programs and students at universities. It is difficult to manage time and outreach strategies, with increasing distance student enrollment, the hiring of adjunct instructors, and the multiplying of online courses and programs offered. Distance education is a trend in American higher education that is rapidly growing. According to the National Center for Education Statistics, as of fall 2017, 6,651,536 higher education students are enrolled in at least one distance education course, including just over 1,000,000 graduate students.[1] Problems do exist: dropout rates are higher in distance education courses and students feel isolated due to a lack of physical contact with instructors.[2] Knowing the isolation that online students can feel, it's important for libraries to work hard to reach out and provide efficient services and resources.

Librarians also must deal with the legal questions and issues of communication that come when class content is developed by instructional technologists who design content without understanding the library's role within the university, resources that are available through the library, or even copyright and fair use laws that govern the online classroom. In addition, when engaging in collection development, librarians face the challenges of aligning purchases and budget with online course needs, while ensuring all material is available globally and conveniently online for students. These two issues can cause many challenges for technical services as librarians attempt to meet collection needs for an online population.

Even though there are many challenges, technical services can still effectively work with university distance education students and programs, especially through collaboration within the library and university. In this chapter, two public university librarians, one from technical services and one from public services, will discuss using strategies of instruction, outreach, collaboration, and course integration to more effectively respond to the increase of distance education programs through the following:

- Partnering with a variety of librarians, such as those in the library's research, outreach, and instruction (ROI) department, to create a smooth system for individual ordering of library materials and to jointly create library guides on distance education services, streaming media, and e-book collections
- Instruction from technical services to professional librarians, library interns, and university faculty and instructors about online materials acquisitions workflows, copyright, open educational resources (OER), accessibility, and more

- Outreach to the rest of campus through marketing resources to distance education faculty and instructors, performing OER workshops, and working and meeting with various University of North Carolina at Greensboro (UNCG) employees and departments outside of the library
- Online course integration through embedding librarians in the university learning management system (LMS) and creating digital content on research

While UNCG implemented many programs and solutions, the thread that they all had in common was intense collaboration between public and technical services librarians, as well as other campus stakeholders in UNCG online education. Though all libraries are different in terms of their own administrative setup, student makeup, and distance education needs, the programs and strategies listed above will be shared in greater detail so that the reader can see how one library dealt with some of the challenges of distance education and potentially be inspired to create their own collaborative solutions.

ABOUT UNCG

The University of North Carolina at Greensboro (UNCG) is one of the 17 campuses in the University of North Carolina system. Located in Greensboro, North Carolina, UNCG currently enrolls over 19,000 students, with approximately 3,600 graduate students. UNCG has a variety of programs and courses that are online and hybrid. Some online programs are designed and run through UNCG Online. UNCG Online designs and runs 8 undergraduate programs, 11 master's programs, and 14 graduate certificate programs, as well as an EdS in educational leadership and an EdD in kinesiology.[3] This does not include the many courses that are run online through face-to-face or hybrid undergraduate and graduate programs. According to one author's discussion with the university registrar, in spring 2020, just under half of all classes for undergraduates were taught online.

The UNCG University Libraries provides online support to all online programs, whether they are fully online, are hybrid, or have some online components.[4] The library employs an electronic resources librarian, housed in its technical services department, and an online learning librarian, housed in the research, outreach, and instruction (ROI) public services department, which manages all of the library academic liaisons, instruction, research, outreach, and reference services.[5] The online learning librarian coordinates online library services through instruction, serves as a liaison to UNCG academic departments, and creates online research tutorials for campus use. The electronic resources librarian works in technical services. At UNCG, technical services cover collection development, cataloging and metadata creation, and acquisitions. As a member of this unit, the electronic resources librarian manages all the online materials that distance students need to complete their coursework and that online faculty need to teach their classes. Management here covers all aspects of the electronic resource life cycle, which is well-described in figure 24.1 by Jill Emery, Graham Stone, and Peter McCracken.

For distance students, this means that the electronic resources librarian does the following:

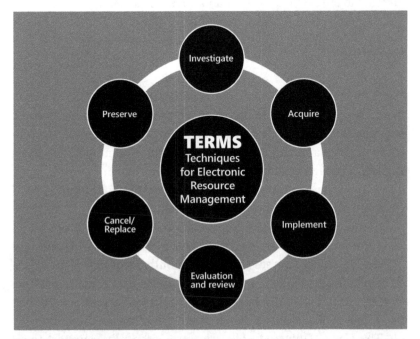

Figure 24.1 TERMS cycle demonstrating the general cycle of electronic resource management. (Image by Jill Emery, Graham Stone, and Peter McCracken. "Getting Back on TERMS 2.0," https://library.hud.ac.uk/blogs/terms/. Reprinted with permission.)

- Works with publishers and other outside parties to ensure that patrons off campus can get the same access to online materials as those on campus
- Integrates online content into the library's discovery systems, catalog, website, and LMS (when appropriate) to ensure the discoverability of said content
- Promotes and markets online materials through collaborations with the online learning librarian and through direct marketing campaigns targeting online faculty
- Ensures access is maintained to all resources so that distance students can get whatever they need, whenever they need it

DEVELOPING PARTNERSHIPS

Technical services librarians need to collaborate across the library and campus to effectively reach distance and online students. UNCG librarians work on a liaison model, where "library liaisons are members of the library faculty who act as contacts and facilitators for the faculty representatives" for each academic department at UNCG.[6] The technical services librarians work with library liaisons to coordinate the ordering of library materials. While this might seem typical, the collaboration here pulls technical services staff into the selection of materials at a high level. Starting in 2011, liaison librarians moved away from a focus on collection development and toward greater outreach and teaching roles. This means that the electronic resources librarian and the head of collection development instead perform most of the material selection. To create greater flexibility for the ever-changing needs of students and faculty, the library also migrated most of its acquiring of materials online and, for individual item purchases, toward an evidence-based (EBM) or patron-driven (PDA) model. EBM and PDA, in this case, refer to systems where many resources from one publisher or vendor are made available to users, but only purchased by the library permanently once that resource has been viewed by users a certain number of times. In PDA collections, this purchase is triggered and occurs without direct library intervention, whereas in EBM, collection librarians examine the resources that get used and select from among them regularly. In this system, the liaison librarian acts as the eyes and ears of the library, gathering information from distance education faculty and students about what types of projects they involve themselves in, what assignments are commonly given, and any upcoming curriculum changes. The liaison librarians then meet with the head of collection development and the electronic resources librarian (either in person or via email) to let them know about unmet library resource needs. Together, the subject liaison and these two librarians decide on how much money to allocate to specific EBM or PDA resources, the percentage of money that should be spent for each department on books versus journals, and whether any new types of resources should and can be added to library collections.

By working closely together and having both public and technical services librarians looking at budgets simultaneously, this allows for greater flexibility when new patron and department needs arise. For example, the geography department recently began offering more online courses on urban planning. The library liaison to geography met with professors, talked to geography online students, and discovered that they needed a specific journal, the *Transportation Research Record*, as well as a product to help them easily find and compare census and population data. Technical services then worked with the liaison and the department to transfer funds from their monographs account to the subscription of the online journal permanently. The technical services department also provided a list of databases to meet geography's data needs to the library liaison, which led to the purchase of SimplyAnalytics.[7] This very close relationship between liaisons and technical services provides distance students and faculty solutions in a short period of time and with little extra expenditure.

Another partnership is the creation of non-course-related SpringShare LibGuides, which are online guides to library services and resources. UNCG uses LibGuides to create research guides by subject for departments and courses.[8] These guides provide a means of promoting databases and library subscriptions to instructors and students based on their courses and programs. The librarians also create and maintain additional, non-course-related guides on a variety of services and resources. Some of these guides include streaming media,[9] e-books,[10] distance learning,[11] open educational resources (OER),[12] and scholarly communication.[13] These guides are created and maintained by a combination of technical services and public services librarians based on the needs of the student or faculty population, spanning beyond majors and programs. Once created, these guides are not forgotten; instead, they are treated as living documents and regularly updated and improved.

A good example of how these documents are organic training tools maintained by collaboration between technical and public services is the streaming media LibGuide. This guide constantly gets updated as technology changes, as new streaming resources are added to the collection, and as new questions arise from patrons. For example, one page on this guide discusses embedding videos in Canvas, UNCG's LMS. This page was created because the electronic resources librarian met regularly with the online learning librarian and with other stakeholders in online education, mainly online course designers and instructional technologists. These conversations made clear that many online instructors struggled with embedding and properly linking streaming videos provided by the library into their online classes. In response, the electronic resources librarian developed step-by-step instructions on how to embed streaming video in Canvas on the streaming media guide.[14] While the electronic resources librarian keeps it up to date, the online learning librarian promotes it across all programs and regularly incorporates it into her consultation and training programs for faculty. This guide currently is the fifth-most used LibGuide at UNCG, which indicates how useful this guide is to the university community.

Lastly, librarians partner across campus to tackle the issues of making library content and purchases accessible and ADA compliant. The online learning librarian creates documentation, gives presentations, and hosts webinars for librarians (at UNCG and beyond) on how to make tutorials and objects more accessible and ADA compliant, as well as creates instructional materials using Universal Design for Learning strategies.[15] Since accessibility has become such an issue in online education, the online learning librarian also works with the University Teaching and Learning Commons (UTLC),[16] UNCG Office of Accessibility Resources & Services (OARS),[17] UNCG Online, course designers, and Information Technology Services (ITS)[18] to create better guides and resources for online students facing accessibility issues. This librarian also is on a committee to hire an accessibility coordinator to help coordinate these efforts. Ultimately, the online learning librarian communicates these issues of accessibility to the electronic resources librarian and all UNCG libraries for purchasing and beyond. For example, the online learning librarian worked with library access services, public services, and library electronic resources and instructional technology (ERIT) to establish a workflow to create accessible, screen-readable pdfs for electronic reserves to be linked to UNCG's LMS Canvas and online courses.

INSTRUCTION

At UNCG, many librarians in public services provide trainings for other librarians to help with professional development. The online learning librarian not only creates tutorials on a variety of databases and services for distance students but also provides monthly scheduled trainings to public and technical services librarians on topics such as using Canvas, WebEx (a virtual meeting tool), creating interactive video, and more.[19] Technical services also is involved with instruction through this professional development training, which regularly includes creating screen-recording videos on library databases and resources for later reference. Creating videos and digital objects is easier than ever, with the availability of a variety of free screen-recording software and tools, which can be used by all librarians with very little training. Figure 24.2 chronicles a comparison table of commonly used screen-recording tools. Screen-recording can be used beyond just creating tutorials; technical services can make quick videos about technical issues in databases to show to vendors, librarians, and more. Lastly, the online learning librarian is available to check accessibility and ADA compliance issues within UNCG University Libraries–created videos.

The electronic resources librarian takes advantage of this public services training model to provide electronic resource troubleshooting cross-training to librarians and interns. Based on reference desk data and meetings with public services librarians, the electronic resources librarian realized that many reference questions arise out of the patron's inability to access library online materials. However, in an internal, informal survey to library staff, she discovered that 75% of UNCG's public services librarians did not feel comfortable performing preliminary troubleshooting. To improve the online patron experience, she developed two trainings, one for reference interns and one for public services staff. These sessions introduced how access is created for electronic resources, pointed out common patron errors and how to recognize them, described what kinds of questions can be asked to help diagnose access problems, and demonstrated how to describe initial troubleshooting in referral emails to the electronic resources librarian. After the trainings, there was an improvement in electronic resource issue referrals, demonstrated by the significant increase in using screenshots, providing greater details in the emails (indicated by email length), and increased reporting of problems by reference interns, as can be seen in Figure 24.3.

Technical services librarians also work with public services librarians to teach online instructors about library resource integration in courses. The online learning librarian participates in faculty development of online course design throughout UNCG, working with a variety of instructional designers to create training and workshops for instructors teaching online. In fall 2017, the online learning librarian collaborated with the UTLC to create a series of webinars on online learning and innovation as well as a library webinar series on research and applications. Some topics covered in these webinars were citation management, using library resources, Canvas tools, and more. And lastly, the online learning librarian worked with the UTLC and public services librarians to create materials and tutorials for an online course in Canvas for instructors teaching online for the first time. In this training, instructors learn how to use the catalog and library databases to search for course materials (including e-books and streaming videos), as well as embed library materials in Canvas.

ONLINE COURSE INTEGRATION

Public services librarians consistently embed within Canvas courses through the liaison model. The online learning librarian works with all liaisons, including the electronic resources librarian, to train them on Canvas. She also communicates and works with ITS about the library having a presence within Canvas and online courses. For example, the online learning librarian worked with ITS to create a librarian role in Canvas. This means that the librarians and archivists can enter

	Microsoft PowerPoint	Keynote	Screencast-O-Matic
URL	https://office.live.com/start/powerpoint.aspx	https://www.apple.com/keynote/	https://screencast-o-matic.com/
Video length	Unlimited	Unlimited	Record up to 15 minutes of video
Costs	Costs money or institutional license	Free with Mac; need to download from Apple App Store	Free; $18 a year for Pro and it comes with many features (editing, no watermark, etc.)
Voiceover & audio input options	Record with voice and internal/external sounds	Record with voice and internal/external sounds	Record with voice and internal/external sounds
Output	WAV, which can be uploaded to YouTube; link through Office 365 Cloud	MOV and iCloud; can be uploaded to YouTube/Canvas	MP4 and to YouTube
Logos & watermarks included	No logo on output	No logo on output	Embedded logo on output
Editing abilities	Yes, within the recording screen; quizzing options	Can edit Keynote as you go and re-record	Limited editing; can trim start and finish times
Downloads	Download PowerPoint through Office 365	Download software from Apple App Store	Download the Screencast-O-Matic launcher; does have Chromebook extension
PC & Mac	PC and Mac	Mac	PC and Mac
Webcam	Can use webcam for face time during recording	No use of webcam for face time during recording	Can use webcam for face time during recording

	TechSmith Capture (Jing)	QuickTime	Screencastify	Camtasia
URL	https://www.techsmith.com/jing-tool.html	https://support.apple.com/quicktime	https://www.screencastify.com/	https://www.techsmith.com/video-editor.html
Video length	Record up to 5 minutes of video	Unlimited	Record up to 10 minutes of video; 50 videos a month	Unlimited
Costs	Free	Free with Mac	Free; need a Google account	Cost money or institutional license
Voiceover & audio input options	Record with voice	Record with voice and internal/external audio	Record with voice and internal/external sounds	Record with voice and internal/external sounds
Output	Own video format (.swf) and to Screencast.com	MOV and can be uploaded to YouTube/Canvas	Direct upload to Google Drive and YouTube; no file output	MP4 and can be uploaded to YouTube
Logos & watermarks included	No logo on output	No logo on output	Embedded logo on output	No logo on output
Editing abilities	No editing	No editing	Limited editing; can annotate in video	Can edit with many different tools and effects; interactive SCORM option
Downloads	Download	QuickTime comes on Mac (preinstalled)	Works through Chrome extension (good for Chromebook)—no downloads	Download software
PC & Mac	PC and Mac	Mac	PC and Mac	PC and Mac (works best on PC)
Webcam	No use of webcam for face time during recording	Can face time through iPhoto during recording	Can use webcam for face time during recording	Can use webcam for face time during recording

Figure 24.2 Screen-recording software and tool comparison chart.

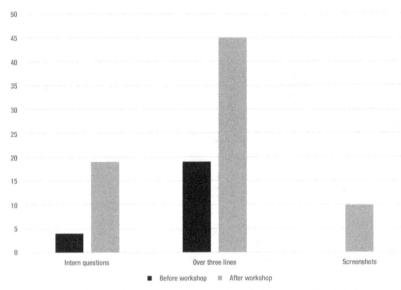

Figure 24.3 Graph taken from data from number of emails before and after technical services training session. The left column in the pair represents the number of emails in each category in the semester before the workshop; the right column represents the number of emails in each category in the semester after the workshop.

Canvas courses to add content, make announcements, and participate in discussions, while the students will see their role as the librarian (instead of an instructor) for the course in Canvas. This helps online students understand the librarian role within Canvas, while learning more about library resources.

Both the electronic resources and online learning librarians are liaisons to academic departments, which provides them hands-on experience embedding in online courses. Because of their ability to take on the role of librarian in classes, the electronic resources librarian and the online learning librarian can work with instructors of online courses to provide stable links to or directly embed library resources in Canvas. This in turn increases the use of library resources in classes and provides a better user experience when using library resources through Canvas.

UNCG University Libraries also runs OER mini-grants for the faculty. UNCG defines open educational resources as "low-cost or free alternatives to expensive course materials; these can include open-access scholarly resources, library-licensed and owned resources, and learning objects and texts that faculty create themselves."[20] OERs are important for all students, but especially for distance students; OERs are often available online and can be easily integrated into the LMS, meaning that distance students do not have to purchase course print materials via either ordering online or finding them at physical, and often faraway, campus bookstores. These grants were started by Beth Bernhardt, the University Libraries assistant dean for collections and scholarly communication and provide an extra $1,000 for faculty to restructure their courses using OER materials.[21] Though it began as a technical services initiative, its success relies on a close partnership between public and technical services. Public services librarians promote this program to their academic departments and advise instructors on how to best incorporate library OERs within Canvas. They also consult with the electronic resources librarian and technical services staff on questions about copyright, resource availability, and licensing that arise. Once grant winners decide on their plan, technical services staff begin to search for the needed OERs, including negotiating with vendors to ensure the materials are appropriate for classroom use (meaning no limits on number of users who can access the resource, ADA compliant, can be downloaded with ease, and can be printed). Library liaisons and the electronic resources librarian then help professors appropriately place these materials into Canvas.

In addition to these grants, the library also recently has begun another OER collaboration that helps fully online students. Working with the bookstore, technical services receives a list of all course textbooks (for both online and in-person classes) slated for the semester. Then two staff members in charge of all book acquisitions goes through this list to see if any of these textbooks are owned by the library or can be purchased under terms that make them acceptable for classroom use. If a course text is owned by the library in a way that is not conducive to online coursework, technical services contacts the vendor to try to remove the restrictions. Once they have found appropriate course materials that allow for no limits on number of users who can access the resource at the same time, technical services staff make a non-course LibGuide listing the semester readings by subject and course and then email the professors about the online availability of these items.[22] Liaisons are also alerted to what books are available for their academic subjects, and they then take charge of promoting the use of these materials. By having this OER service available, the library helps online students get access to needed and free (to students) course materials.

Though these OER efforts and greater integration of librarians into the LMS have helped address some library course integration challenges, issues remain. For example, instructors and course designers are often confused about copyright and legal issues surrounding putting materials in online courses. UNCG Online is a division of UNCG that designs some courses for an online environment and has many questions about copyright and the legality of providing content to online students. This department's designers often have no experience with library content and services from their past jobs and training. To help with this issue, the electronic resources and online learning librarians met with UNCG Online staff in spring 2017 to discuss legal issues with e-reserves, copyright, putting film online, and more. The librarians worked together to create a training document that catered to this group of designers' specific questions. The online learning librarian also serves on the UNCG Online Advisory Committee; hearing about UNCG Online's new initiatives and programs enables technical and public services to better provide and promote services, budgets, and resources before a course is designed. This work has paid off as UNCG Online designers have started contacting the online learning librarian before they develop classes instead of midway through the semester, when it's harder to fix technical issues and purchase e-books and online films quickly.

OUTREACH

For library technical services to properly serve distance students, we must provide effective outreach about our collections. Currently, the electronic resources librarian is spearheading an initiative to more systematically conduct marketing and promotion of library electronic resources to online students and instructors. To do this, she put together a multi-department electronic resources marketing team, including the online learning librarian. This group's charge is to coordinate promotion of electronic resources and look for potential opportunities on campus to conduct library outreach. So far, types of marketing include the following:

- Presenting sessions on available streaming media content to the College of Nursing, the College of Health and Human Services, and UNCG Online
- Incorporating information on e-books and streaming media into every UNCG Online orientation
- Regularly writing announcements concerning new resources to put on the front page of the library's website and in the campus-wide news and events publication, *Campus Weekly*

University Libraries liaisons have been active in promoting library resources, but this example demonstrates how technical services departments are shifting toward a stronger focus on outreach. No longer can collection development and electronic resources librarians buy materials and hope that people use them; with the competition from Google and SciHub, technical services librarians need to promote library collections outside of the library physical space—in classrooms, department meetings, workshops, conferences, and websites.

To provide better outreach to students, we must understand the needs of online students. In fall 2017, the electronic resources and online learning librarians designed and distributed a virtual survey to distance and online students about UNCG University services and resources. Over 700 students filled out the survey, and through it we discovered that students are using UNCG's LMS Canvas the most to learn about new information for school and courses. The survey also showed that that many students have never used virtual library services, such as chatting with a librarian, and that online students listed access to online resources (databases, articles, e-books, streaming films, etc.) as their most important need over tutorials, instruction, consultations, chatting, and interlibrary loan. This survey also brought to light that even though students do use the library for resource discovery, they find the usability of the catalog and the database list lacking. In the end, the survey showed that we need to expand outreach, rethink some of our current methods of resource discovery, and provide more services to online students. Though this means that the library has work to do in terms of outreach, the data from this survey will provide librarians the means to promote the needs of online students, and technical services can use the data and comments from this survey to advocate for better budgets and resources for online students and programs.

FUTURE DIRECTIONS

UNCG University Libraries technical services collaborates throughout UNCG and beyond to provide better services to online students and instructors by creating campus partnerships, integrating in online courses, training librarians and instructors, and promoting materials. While there has been progress, which can be seen in the initiatives discussed in this chapter, there are still many new areas in which technical services can begin to explore and expand in their collaboration. Though UNCG University Libraries has been working on improving our budget flexibility, actual budget allocations for departments have not changed. With the rise in online programs and the greater online student population that follows, there is a need to do a full reexamination and evaluation of library material budgets for each department. The survey that the authors conducted shows that while there has been outreach, there is a lot more work to be done to convince both instructors and students to use library resources in the classroom and to promote them for coursework. This will require even more public-facing work by those in technical services in collaboration and coordination with public services colleagues. The survey also shows students' lack of engagement with library systems, which indicates that the UNCG University Libraries' promotion of online resources might not be as effective as we would hope. Because of this, the online learning librarian and electronic resources librarian have begun regular usability tests on different aspects of the library's online presence, including the Library Database and Journal A-Z List.

In the end, while collaboration both within and outside the library has allowed UNCG to develop innovative programs, better reach online patrons, and navigate a shifting world of online course development, the efforts to evaluate and improve must continue to evolve.

Only through constant communication, assessment, and innovation can librarians hope to keep up with the ever-evolving world of online and distance education within technical services.

NOTES

1. "Fast Facts: Distance Learning," National Center for Education Statistics, Institute of Education Sciences, 2017, https://nces.ed.gov/fastfacts/display.asp?id=80.
2. Doris U. Bollinger and Trey Martindale, "Key Factors for Determining Student Satisfaction in Online Courses," *International Journal of E-Learning* 3, no. 1 (2004): 61–67, https://www.learntechlib.org/p/2226.
3. "UNCG Online," University of North Carolina at Greensboro, https://online.uncg.edu/.
4, "University Libraries," University of North Carolina at Greensboro, https:/library.uncg.edu.
5. "Research, Outreach, and Instruction," University of North Carolina at Greensboro University Libraries, https://library.uncg.edu/info/depts/reference/.
6. "Faculty Representatives and Library Liaisons," University of North Carolina at Greensboro University Libraries, http://library.uncg.edu/info/faculty_liaisons.aspx.
7. "SimplyAnalytics: Analytics for Everyone," SimplyAnalytics Inc., http://simplyanalytics.com/.
8. "Research Guides by Subject," University of North Carolina at Greensboro University Libraries, http://library.uncg.edu/research/guides/.
9. Katherine Hill, "Streaming Media," University of North Carolina at Greensboro University Libraries, http://uncg.libguides.com/streamingfilms.
10. Katherine Hill, "eBooks A-Z," University of North Carolina at Greensboro University Libraries, http://uncg.libguides.com/ebooks.
11. Samantha Harlow, "Distance and Online Learning Guide," University of North Carolina at Greensboro University Libraries, http://uncg.libguides.com/de.

12. Beth Bernhardt, "Open Educational Resources (OER)," University of North Carolina at Greensboro University Libraries, http://uncg .libguides.com/oer.

13. Beth Bernhardt, "Scholarly Communications at UNC Greensboro," University of North Carolina at Greensboro University Libraries, http://uncg.libguides.com/scholarlycomm.

14. Katherine Hill, "Streaming Media: Embedding Streaming Media in Canvas," University of North Carolina at Greensboro University Libraries, http://uncg.libguides.com/streamingfilms/embed.

15. "About Universal Design for Learning," National Center on Universal Design for Learning, accessed April 5, 2020, http://www.udlcenter .org/aboutudl/whatisudl.

16. "University Teaching and Learning Commons," University of North Carolina at Greensboro University, https://utlc.uncg.edu/.

17. "Office of Accessibility Resources & Services," University of North Carolina at Greensboro, https://ods.uncg.edu/.

18. "Information Technology Services," University of North Carolina at Greensboro, https://its.uncg.edu/.

19. Samantha Harlow, "UNCG Instructional Technology Training," University of North Carolina at Greensboro University Libraries, last modified January 9, 2018, https://uncg.libguides.com/lib instructionaltech.

20. Beth Bernhardt, "What are OER," University of North Carolina at Greensboro University Libraries, http://uncg.libguides.com/OER /whatareOER.

21. Beth Bernhardt, "2018 Mini Grants," University of North Carolina at Greensboro University Libraries, http://uncg.libguides.com/c.php ?g=83604&p=4438149.

22. "Course Adopted Texts by Department: UNCG Course Adopted Texts by Subject," University of North Carolina at Greensboro University Libraries, http://uncg.libguides.com/c.php?g=532866&p=5423390.

CHAPTER 25

Evolving Ethos and Etiquette: Why and How We Altered Our Library-Vendor Relationships

Laurel Sammonds Crawford and Allyson Rodriguez

ABSTRACT

In this chapter we discuss a major shift in our mindset regarding vendor interactions and the reasoning behind that change. We provide details about how we evaluate and negotiate for products and how we set boundaries with vendors; these measures allow us to be more productive while remaining fiscally responsible and responsive to the changing library environment. The burden of building an excellent collection that serves the needs of the patrons ultimately rests on the shoulders of librarians, not the vendors who sell the content. Setting good goals, evaluating resources thoroughly, embracing an appropriate mindset, negotiating wisely, and establishing boundaries enables librarians to serve the patrons in the most efficient manner possible. Navigating the tension between budgetary concerns, usability, licensing terms, and vendor demands is difficult. However, our libraries—and patrons—will benefit when we can acknowledge the changes happening in the library environment, recognize the unique type of relationships we have with vendors, and adapt accordingly.

INTRODUCTION

As vendors consolidate and the electronic resources market matures, libraries' relationships with vendors are under pressure. Changes such as unstable funding of public institutions, increasing product complexity, and ever-evolving business models exacerbate the pressures on the library-vendor relationship. To remain relevant, libraries must adapt to the changing information environment. To safeguard the financial health of our institutions and the utility of our collections, technical services librarians must be cognizant of the shifting climate and proactively develop a new mindset. For the University of North Texas (UNT) Libraries, the need to rock the status quo became evident as we experienced major budget cuts and underwent a drastic collection development philosophy change.

The UNT Libraries serve a large, tier-one research university located in Denton, Texas. With 13 different colleges and schools supporting more than 100 bachelor's, 80 master's, and 30 doctoral degrees, the Libraries must serve a wide array of students, faculty, and staff. More than 50 librarians and 90 staff members collaborate to support the research, teaching, and education of more than 38,000 students and 1,000 faculty members. To effectively meet the needs of our users, the collection development department had to realign our thinking and change our practices. The collection development department, housed in the collection management division along with cataloging and metadata services, is the centralized unit that handles evaluation, selection, and ordering of library resources; we do not have individual selectors with individual budgets. The collection development department, led by the head of collection development, consists of a monograph acquisitions unit, an electronic resources unit, a serials unit, and a collection assessment unit. Within each unit there is one faculty librarian and at least one staff member. Members of this department with the most direct vendor contact underwent intensive negotiation training and determined a shift in our thinking was necessary. In this chapter we discuss our changing mindset and the reasoning behind that change, how we evaluate and negotiate for products, and how we set boundaries with vendors, allowing us to be more productive, to be more fiscally responsible, and to adjust to the changing library environment.

THE CHANGING ENVIRONMENT

All library types are experiencing an increasing dependence on electronic resources (any online information resource, including databases, e-books, and journals). Public libraries are seeing the fastest growth in expenditures on e-books, and school libraries are shifting to incorporate more electronic resources.[1] Academic libraries have seen a noticeable shift in their institutions to emphasize online and distance education.[2] Changes in what is requested, required, and suggested by library patrons have forced libraries to acquire different resources and necessitated a change in how those resources are acquired. However, even with these changes, expectations of a high level of service have not changed, leading to possible negative impressions of the library if resources are unavailable.[3]

Libraries have witnessed a great shift in the vendor environment too. Many industries experience consolidation, which can be positive in some respects, but damaging to the consumer in many. Dangers of consolidation include higher prices due to "collegial pricing," or an unofficial price-fixing, loss of product advancement due to lack of competition, and limited opportunity for new competition as larger companies shut down, price out, or acquire smaller ones.[4] In the last decade, library vendors experienced consolidation (see figure 25.1), with varying results. One example of the potential negative effects of consolidation in library vendors is the acquisition of Ravel Law by LexisNexis. Ravel Law typically is a more user-friendly legal resource, while LexisNexis tends to have platforms more useful for expert searchers. There has been discussion that LexisNexis will ingest certain features of Ravel into LexisNexis platforms. While to some this may seem like a positive approach, it could have an impact on users. If LexisNexis maintains its expert-level user focus and the novice user option, Ravel, no longer exists or is not maintained in the same way, what can libraries offer those novice users?

Vendor consolidation examples

- EBSCO: NetLibrary, Learning Express, HW Wilson, and YBP
- ProQuest: RefWorks, ebrary, EBL, Coutts, ExLibris, Alexander Street Press and SIPX
- Elsevier: Mendeley, Knovel, SSRN, Plum Analytics, and bepress
- Baker & Taylor: Bridgeall Libraries, and Blackwell Book Services North America
- Follet: Baker & Taylor, Valore Inc., Advanced Online, and Neebo

---

Figure 25.1 Selected library vendor acquisitions since 2008.

In tandem with this vendor consolidation, libraries are experiencing increasing complexity with the content available and the methods of acquisition. New and inventive content is being packaged and sold to libraries—data and statistical packages, teaching tools for information literacy, unique digitized collections, and much more. Many of these new resources and the more traditional serials and monographs are sold using an ever-evolving variety of terms and models that can be difficult for librarians to analyze. To describe the variety of possible acquisitions processes, vendors use terms such as demand-driven acquisition (DDA), patron-driven acquisition (PDA), evidence-based acquisition (EBA), and token programs, among others. Adding confusion to complexity, these terms are not interchangeable between vendors. Each vendor's DDA, PDA, EBA, or token program can have different implications for the library and can sometimes vary by product for any given vendor. This can lead to confusion within the acquisition process and mean more time that technical services librarians must work to understand what they are purchasing. It can also lead to miscommunications between vendors and libraries. For example, if a librarian uses a term to mean one thing, and the vendor uses the same term to mean something slightly different, there could be issues with invoicing, acquisition, or contract language.

Furthermore, limited library budgets, especially in publicly funded institutions, are causing issues. Since the Great Recession, a study on Association of Research Libraries (ARL) member institutions showed minimal increases in acquisitions budgets, but not enough to return libraries to their prerecession levels.[5] In one study of public libraries, more than 40% of libraries saw decreased or flat budgets over the past three years.[6] With decreasing or flat budgets, libraries are unable to keep up with the increased demand for electronic resources, and their continuously rising costs. Responsible use of library funds while meeting the needs of diverse users in a complicated and ever-changing landscape means that librarians, especially technical services librarians, must change their mindsets and activities.

RELATIONSHIPS—THE END OR THE MEANS?

The attitude with which a librarian approaches vendor interaction can make the difference between a smooth acquisition and a frustrating experience. The recent literature offers a bewildering amount of advice about how best to interact with vendors. Authors consistently identify as important the practice of establishing a relationship with the vendor—but what exactly does that mean, and why is it important? Although we sometimes speak about vendors as "partners" or "colleagues," librarians should remember that, at their most fundamental, vendor interactions constitute a business relationship based on financial transactions. Librarians must examine their own goals and attitudes before entering into such a business transaction.

The relationship between libraries and vendors is often described as interdependent; since vendors have something libraries want, we need to maintain a positive relationship. Arthur and Sieck suggest that librarians are obliged to be non-adversarial with vendors, going so far as to say this is "imperative" to our success.[7] According to Ostergaard and Rossmann, regular interactions and good relationships between librarians and vendors, according to anecdotal reports from librarian respondents, led to better pricing.[8] The following year, Ostergaard and Rossmann conducted a survey of librarians to follow up on the research they had presented in this article. The results of this survey showed that 71% of librarians regard the vendor relationship as one of *partnership*, yet 60% were unhappy with the result of their most recent difficult negotiation.[9] To our knowledge, the correlation between good relationships and lower pricing has not been empirically studied, but Bergstrom and colleagues theorized that *assertive negotiation* on the part of libraries is the cause of lower pricing.[10]

We suggest reexamining the objective: "maintain relationship" should not be the end goal, but a means to an end. The end should be "increase access," "make effective decisions," "improve usability," or "make efficient use of funds." The best approach is to stay focused on benefits to the patrons and to the library. At UNT, we see ourselves as a collaborative client—willing to work with the vendor, while remembering that we are a buyer entitled to excellent goods and services. We maintain the relationship in service to the patron's needs.

We should be wary of believing, without evidence, that vendors and librarians naturally share the same goals and therefore a productive, colleague-like partnership is easy to maintain. Some experts claim vendors' and libraries' goals are aligned.[11] Bates goes so far as to state that vendors and libraries "share the goal of getting critical information to the people who need it."[12] Reality contradicts this rather romantic notion; we should acknowledge that vendors want to increase market share, and librarians want to serve their patrons' needs. When these goals correspond, each party can benefit. However, librarians will inevitably experience conflict at some point as they negotiate with vendors for the best possible deals on behalf of the library and its patrons.

Some writers assert that the vendor-library relationship should build on mutual understanding of each party's obstacles and motivations. However, "understanding" should not prevent librarians from calling attention to poorly designed products or careless customer service. As an example, Remy reported a vendor representative describing to a conference audience a specific obstacle: many vendors are unable to provide consistently timely invoicing because their fulfillment software is not designed to provide this function.[13] It is good for librarians to be aware of this difficulty, but providing on-time and accurate billing is a core function of a business relationship, and librarians should not hesitate to insist on timely invoicing. Another example is that vendors seem to want librarians' frequent attention; this is variously attributed to the need for feedback, a monthly quota for sales contacts, and a harsh sales environment increasing the pressure on representatives.[14] Librarians can acknowledge these possible motivations while still setting boundaries to manage their own workload (more on this later). We should be flexible but firm in demanding both excellent service and products that perform as expected; and ideally, a good relationship will function in service to this goal.

In the end, it is up to the *librarian* to ensure that the library's and patrons' needs are met. As Ostergaard and Rossmann state, "Vendors have their own sets of pressures which may be largely unknown to, unrecognized by, or of no concern to libraries. An inherent tension exists with libraries serving in a service model and as a customer to vendors, while vendors have expectations from the corporate environment, which may be foreign to the academic library world."[15] A wise librarian will keep this in mind when determining when and how to interact with vendors.

EVALUATION

Evaluating electronic resources can be a time-consuming process, but is vital to the acquisitions process, safeguarding the financial health of our institutions, and maintaining the utility of our collections. Librarians must fully understand increasingly complex products, pricing structures, and how new resources overlap with existing content. Library-vendor relationships are essential to this process.

When evaluating a resource, criteria can vary largely by institution. Below are common evaluation criteria, but you should also consider local concerns when evaluating any new electronic resource.

- **Cost.** Often cost is one of the most important factors when evaluating a resource.[16] If a resource is too expensive or exceeds the library budget, there may not be a need to continue evaluating the resource. However, direct costs (like the list price), indirect costs (like maintenance fees), and staff time costs should be taken into consideration as well.[17] It is essential that vendors provide accurate, up-to-date costs and include cost options such as multiyear payments, subscription or purchase options, and hosting fees. UNT has seen success in reducing costs through negotiation and utilizing available consortia deals.
- **Uniqueness.** Duplication of resources is normally not good stewardship of funds. Completing an overlap analysis or evaluating the uniqueness of a resource can help librarians understand whether a new product will fill a collection gap or should not be purchased.[18] For librarians to be able to evaluate this correctly, vendors must provide accurate, up-to-date holdings information for the resource.
- **Licensing or contract language.** Depending on the parent institution, library resource contracts may be subject to applicable law or institutional guidelines.[19] Examples of required or prohibited language may include governing law and venue, indemnification, interlibrary loan ability, cancelation restrictions, or alternative dispute resolution.[20] Vendors must understand that certain clauses or stipulations may be legal deal breakers and you will be required to walk away from a resource if they cannot meet this requirement. UNT has had great success in negotiating license language by educating vendors on our specific legal needs and the reasoning behind them.

- **Accessibility.** Because accessibility is a subset of legal requirements, it is important for libraries to recognize and require accessibility of electronic resources for all users. Law requires any library that receives federal money to adhere to sections 504 and 508 of the Rehabilitation Act.[21] Both librarians and vendors must be aware of the legal requirements and the implications for adherence. Vendors must be willing to work with libraries to ensure compliance and continued subscription.
- **Other considerations.** Depending on the institution, library, and administration, other considerations may come into play. Factors such as compatibility with library systems, relevance to the goals and focus of the parent institution, inflation rates for subscriptions, product reviews, MARC record availability, quality, and cost, anticipated usage, or feedback from a trial of the resource should be taken into consideration as applicable to the resource and the needs of your library and institution.[22]

Many tools and tips can assist librarians in evaluating resources. Saving emails, writing executive summaries of evaluations or transactions, or using checklists or rubrics can help librarians articulate decisions to purchase or not purchase electronic resources. Additionally, using resources like TERMS: Techniques for Electronic Resources Management 2.0 (https://library.hud.ac.uk/blogs/terms/) can provide librarians with best practices and criteria for the entire life cycle of an electronic resource.[23] Finally, librarians must ask probing questions and provide constructive feedback to vendors. Asking analytical questions allows librarians to understand the resource, acquisition process, cost, and other considerations. Providing constructive feedback allows vendors to make improvements and librarians and vendors to have open lines of communication, improving both the relationship and the resources that libraries can offer.[24]

NEGOTIATIONS

Negotiations can be a daunting task for any librarian. However, negotiations are essential to ensure access to important materials and

maintain control over the library's finances. Being prepared, antic-
ipating behaviors and tactics, and practicing appropriate behaviors
and tactics ourselves can improve libraries' negotiation outcomes and
produce win-win situations for libraries and vendors.

Librarian Behaviors

Listed below are some practical tips we have implemented to assist
librarians in negotiating for features, pricing, and contract terms. This
is by no means an exhaustive list but provides a starting point for new
negotiators.

- **Be prepared.** Preparation is key. This means clearly identifying and understanding your needs, knowing your alternatives, and knowing who you are negotiating with.[25] At UNT,
  being prepared has allowed us to articulate our needs and
  stand firm in our requirements and expectations.
- **Stand firm.** Know what is fair and stick to it. This does
  not mean being rude or aggressive, but assertive in the fact
  that you have prepared and are aware of your needs and
  the alternatives. A polite no can be very useful in standing
  firm.[26] In several contract negotiations this allowed UNT to
  work toward a compromise without seeming uncooperative
  or aggressive.
- **Be patient.** Listening first to gather information can head
  off some tactics such as false concessions (see below). You
  should plan to talk no more than 30% to 40% of the time.[27] If
  negotiations stall, do not be afraid to bring in someone new,
  whether from the vendor side or the library side.[28] Bringing
  in a fresh set of eyes or someone who might view issues differently can help move forward a stuck negotiation.
- **Learn and document.** Each new negotiation is an opportunity to learn about the vendor or about yourself as a negotiator.
  Documenting that learning can lead to more successful negotiations in the future.[29] At UNT, we start documentation prior
  to the negotiation and include tactics we have seen in previous negotiations with that vendor, goals for the negotiation,
  alternative resource options, the importance of each issue, and
  our limits.[30] During the negotiation, we document concession
  points, clarifications required, questions, concerns, offers and

counteroffers, and all promises or agreements made. By creating this documentation, we have seen improved outcomes and are better prepared for the next negotiation.

Negotiation Tactics

Listed below are common objectionable tactics used in negotiations. Each tactic is coupled with a successful response that UNT Libraries has used when faced with that tactic. This is not an exhaustive list, nor is it meant to represent every vendor or vendor representative. Some companies or individual representatives may use some, all, or none of these tactics. It is up to the librarian to anticipate, recognize, and respond accordingly.

- **False/padded concessions.** Items that are being portrayed as concessions when they are not.[31] These can be used to make negotiators make concessions of their own. Be aware of this because it can cause you to give up something important without the vendor giving up something they wanted.
  Response: Concede slowly and not too often, too soon, or too much; keep a record of concessions made to try to identify patterns; use trade-offs to get something in return for each concession.[32]
- **Stalling.** Manipulating the timeline to force the other party to make concessions to meet their deadline.[33]
  Response: Continually check in to ensure timelines that you need; bring in other parties as needed to get more traction; start negotiations well in advance of your deadlines.[34]
- **Snow job.** Providing too much information, often about topics irrelevant to this negotiation, to confuse negotiators.[35]
  Response: Ask as many questions as you need to clarify the information; take copious notes to ensure your understanding; redirect the negotiations to focus on relevant resources and topics.[36]
- **Aggressive behavior.** An aggressive tone is used while continuously and repeatedly requesting concessions.[37]
  Response: Ask for a pause in the negotiations to discuss the process itself; point out the interests and needs of each side;

do not respond in kind—an aggressive response to aggressive behavior will only increase the likelihood of a negative negotiation outcome.[38]

SETTING HEALTHY GOALS AND BOUNDARIES

Vendor interactions can become a problem when they grow in scale and intensity. Vendor representatives reach out with requests for meetings, conference event invitations, new product pitches, discount offers, and feedback solicitation and even ask for reasoning for negative decisions. For many libraries, the sheer number of vendors and representatives can make for an overwhelming amount of time-consuming interactions. To do our work effectively, librarians should set both good goals, as discussed above, and healthy boundaries.

Ostergaard and Rossmann use a perfect term to describe a librarian's limited time and energy for vendor interactions: *bandwidth*. "Libraries may find themselves overwhelmed by a perpetual barrage of information, and limited bandwidth and resources with which to devote to vendor relations."[39] At UNT, we have certainly found this to be true. Each person in our department receives dozens of emails and calls from vendors per week: not only alerts and requests as described above, but also important communications about problems, outages, and current negotiations. A sales representative may have one of several objectives at point of contact with a librarian: sale of a product, market research, expansion of territory, retaining an account, or customer service. At UNT, we do business with several hundred vendors; some of the larger companies employ several representatives to work with us on varying products. How can librarians get what we need out of relationships with vendors without becoming overwhelmed? Here we present some ways we set effective, yet collegial, boundaries with vendors.

First, we took some time to examine the problems associated with vendor contacts. We realized we had an overwhelming number of contact requests from vendors, both collectively and in some cases individually; phone calls and visits take time away from other high-priority duties. Who should handle vendor interactions was sometimes unclear; we wasted time when multiple employees were simultaneously working on the same problem. We determined that although we *appreciate* being notified of deals and sales, we are capable of investigating products on our own and do not *require* advertisements to create awareness of the available universe of products.

Next, we created guidelines to make vendor interactions more efficient.

- Generally, we want a once-per-year check-in meeting with our major vendors.
- Other visits to explain or demo new products are appropriate if we initiate the invitation. Unless we are interested in participating, a webinar, visit, or phone call should not be required to obtain a price quote.
- All meetings are scheduled well in advance, with an agenda and a strict time limit. We encourage vendors to bring tutorials and conduct training webinars, but they must be coordinated through a UNT librarian to ensure that timing is appropriate and all interested parties are invited.
- Email communications are *required* for effective documentation and project management. Phone calls are used only in urgent situations and are followed up with email documentation. To facilitate this guideline, we removed phone numbers from our email signatures and screen calls using caller ID and voicemail.
- We politely but firmly decline calls and visits about products we are not interested in.

We also determined an overall vendor communication style. We use a collaborative tone while maintaining the boundaries described above. We proactively provide context for the vendor, like changes that have occurred in our operations, new collection initiatives, general budget predictions, and so forth. We provide both constructive and positive feedback about products and services whenever possible. Because we believe it is the vendor's job to sell the product to us, the library client, we adopted an attitude of persistent inquisitiveness; we ask politely but firmly for more information when presented with confusing price models or anything else we do not understand.

Determining who will handle vendor-related tasks is easily just as important as establishing the guidelines described above. At UNT, we have designated a single person—the electronic resources librarian (ERL)—to be the gatekeeper for all vendor visits and demonstrations. We ask our fellow librarians to likewise alert the ERL to any offers, sales pitches, or demos by vendors. We have found it useful for a single person to monitor and facilitate vendor activities. Because of the sheer volume of requests, this puts a workload burden on the responsible librarian; libraries seeking to implement such a measure should be mindful of the amount of time it takes to properly respond to vendor contacts.

Other librarians have made helpful suggestions too. A useful distinction to make is between two major types of communication: content versus service. News about content (new titles, discounts) is best delivered in writing; communications about support, problem-solving, and answering questions are usually urgent and therefore preferably done over the phone.[40] Do not be pressured into listening to the hard sell if you are not interested—as Stamison, Persing, and Beckett point out, aggressive tactics are a sign of a bad sales representative.[41] In their presentation, Ginanni, McKee, and Wilson suggest responding to a vendor with a firm no and providing a rationale—this can prevent repeated future contacts and will avoid wasting the time of both parties.[42]

CONCLUSION

At the time of this writing, it has been over a year since we implemented the guidelines outlined in this chapter. Since then, UNT library personnel have felt more empowered to ensure that their own time is spent wisely, in support of library operations and the collection itself. The time we can devote to face-to-face meetings with vendors is more focused and is more judiciously spent on mutually beneficial discussions. Our acquisitions are thoroughly vetted and the terms of purchase the best possible.

Collection development librarians report positive effects on their ability to focus appropriately on making purchasing decisions; collectively, we have increased our efficiency in using both personnel time and funding. Since our guidelines apply regardless of setting, our librarians are free to use conference time as they see fit—either meeting with vendors or attending professional development opportunities as they wish. With few exceptions, vendors seem satisfied with the boundaries we have established and adhere to our preferred communication methods. The long-term sustainability of our more structured interactions has benefited both parties. Our closest vendor collaborators (those with whom we do the most business) easily adapted to the slight changes we implemented. Our methodical approach, particularly requiring email for most interactions, has prevented many problems and misunderstandings—something that both parties appreciate. Because we confidently negotiate on price, both parties seem more comfortable with conversations around pricing and terms.

Faculty and librarians outside of collection development have likewise adjusted to the new guidelines. We allow everyone to discuss products with vendors as they wish, but all decisions must be vetted by and negotiations conducted by collection development personnel. This structure not only allows collection development to ensure that products meet the library's rigorous standards but also prevents mistakes on the part of UNT personnel who may not have the entire context for a purchase. In asking the faculty and librarians to involve collection development in vendor interactions, we have successfully framed our requests to save them time.

The burden of building an excellent collection that serves the needs of the patrons ultimately rests on the shoulders of librarians, not the vendors who sell the content. It is up to librarians to identify and serve the needs of our clientele and administrators. Setting good goals, evaluating resources thoroughly, embracing an appropriate mindset, negotiating wisely, and establishing boundaries enables us to serve the patrons in the most efficient manner possible. Navigating the tension between budgetary concerns, usability, licensing terms, and vendor demands is difficult. However, our libraries—and patrons—will benefit when we can acknowledge the changes happening in the library environment, recognize the unique type of relationships we have with vendors, and adapt accordingly.

NOTES

1. Kathy Rosa and Tom Storey, "American Libraries in 2016: Creating Their Future by Connecting, Collaborating and Building Com-

munity," *IFLA Journal* 42, 2 (2016): 97, https://doi.org/10.1177/0340035216646061.

2. Bryna Coonin, Beth Filar Williams, and Heidi Steiner, "Fostering Library as a Place for Distance Students: Best Practices From Two Universities," *Internet Reference Services Quarterly* 16, 4 (2011): 150, https://doi.org/10.1080/10875301.2012.618796.

3. Ibid., 152.

4. James Brock, "Economic Concentration and Economic Power: John Flynn and a Quarter-Century of Mergers," *Antitrust Bulletin* 56, 4 (2011): 724–25, https://doi.org/10.1177/0003603X1105600402.

5. Charles B. Lowry, "ARL Library Budgets After the Great Recession, 2011–13." *Research Library Issues: A Report from ARL, CNI, and SPARC,* no. 282 (2013): 9, https://doi.org/10.29242/rli.282.2.

6. John C. Bertot et al., *2011–2012 Public Library Funding and Technology Access Survey: Survey Findings and Results* (Information & Policy Access Center, University of Maryland, 2012), 55.

7. Michael A. Arthur and Stacy Sieck, "Cooperation is Key: How Publishers and Libraries Are Working Together to Achieve Common Goals," *Against the Grain* 27, 6 (2015): 23, https://doi.org/10.7771/2380-176X.7225.

8. Kirsten Ostergaard and Doralyn Rossmann, "Vendor Relations Strategies for Libraries," *Against the Grain* 27, 6 (2015): 14, https://doi.org/10.7771/2380-176X.7222.

9. Kirsten Ostergaard and Doralyn Rossmann, "There's Work to Be Done: Exploring Library–Vendor Relations," *Technical Services Quarterly* 34, 1 (2017): 15, https://doi.org/10.1080/07317131.2017.1238196.

10. Theodore C. Bergstrom et al., "Evaluating Big Deal Journal Bundles," *Proceedings of the National Academy of Sciences of the United States of America* 111, 26 (2014): 9429–30, https://doi.org/10.1073/pnas.1403006111.

11. Arthur and Sieck, "Cooperation is Key," 23; Mary Ellen Bates, "Learn to Love Your Information Vendor," *Online Searcher* 38, 3 (2014): 80; afry, "Working Together: Tips for Vendors," *ACRLog,* February 28, 2011, https://acrlog.org/2011/02/28/working-together-tips-for-vendors/.

12. Bates, "Learn to Love Your Information Vendor," 80.

13. Charlie Remy, "Libraries Are From Mars and Vendors Are From Venus? Understanding One Another Better to Achieve Common

Goals," *Journal of Electronic Resources Librarianship* 25, 3 (2013): 234, https://doi.org/10.1080/1941126X.2013.813318.

14. Christine Stamison et al., "What they Never Told You About Vendors in Library School," *Serials Librarian* 56, 1–4 (2009): 140–44, https://doi.org/10.1080/03615260802665555.

15. Ostergaard and Rossmann, "There's Work to Be Done," 22.

16. Richard Bleiler and Jill Livingston, *Evaluating E-Resources* (Washington, DC: Association of Research Libraries, 2010), 14, http://publications.arl.org/Evaluating-Eresources-SPEC-Kit-316/; Nathan Hosburgh, "Managing the Electronic Resources Lifecycle: Creating a Comprehensive Checklist Using Techniques for Electronic Resource Management (TERMS)," *Serials Librarian* 66, 1–4 (2014): 214, https://doi.org/10.1080/0361526X.2014.880028; William H. Walters, "Evaluating Online Resources for College and University Libraries: Assessing Value and Cost Based on Academic Needs," *Serials Review* 42, no. 1 (2016): 13, https://doi.org/10.1080/00987913.2015.1131519.

17. Walters, "Evaluating Online Resources," 13.

18. Bleiler and Livingston, *Evaluating E-Resources*, 14; Hosburgh, "Managing the Electronic Resources Lifecycle" 214–15.

19. Bleiler and Livingston, *Evaluating E-Resources*, 15; Hosburgh, "Managing the Electronic Resources Lifecycle," 215.

20. Bleiler and Livingston, *Evaluating E-Resources*, 15.

21. Angela Dresselhaus, "The Americans with Disabilities Act Compliance and Library Acquisitions" (speech, Acquisitions Institute at Timberline Lodge, Oregon, May 20, 2013), https://works.bepress.com/angela_dresselhaus/24/.

22. Bleiler and Livingston, *Evaluating E-Resources*, 14–16; Hosburgh, "Managing the Electronic Resources Lifecycle," 214–18.

23. Jill Emery, Graham Stone, and Peter McCracken, "Getting Back on TERMS (Version 2.0)," *TERMS: Techniques for Electronic Resource Management* (blog), March 2017, https://library.hud.ac.uk/blogs/terms/.

24. Hosburgh, "Managing the Electronic Resources Lifecycle," 217.

25. Janet L. Flowers, "Specific Tips for Negotiations With Library Materials Vendors Depending Upon Acquisitions Method," *Library Collections, Acquisitions, & Technical Services* 28, 4 (2004): 447, https://doi.org/10.1080/14649055.2004.10766015; C. Derrik Hiatt,

Lesley Jackson, and Katherine Hill, "Principles of Negotiation," *Serials Review* 41, 3 (2015): 180–81, https://doi.org/10.1080 /00987913.2015.1064339; Elaine W. Hamner, "Negotiating Strategies and Skills," (presentation, University of North Texas Library, Denton, October 2016).

26. Hamner, "Negotiating Strategies and Skills."
27. Hamner, "Negotiating Strategies and Skills."
28. Hiatt, Jackson, and Hill, "Principles of Negotiation," 182.
29. Hiatt, Jackson, and Hill, "Principles of Negotiation," 182.
30. Hamner, "Negotiating Strategies and Skills."
31. William Baber and Chavi C-Y Fletcher-Chen, *Practical Business Negotiation* (London: Routledge, 2015), 103–4; Hamner, "Negotiating Strategies and Skills."
32. Hamner, "Negotiating Strategies and Skills."
33. Baber and Fletcher-Chen, "Practical Business Negotiation," 105.
34. Hamner, "Negotiating Strategies and Skills."
35. Ibid.
36. Ibid.
37. Ibid.; Baber and Fletcher-Chen, "Practical Business Negotiation," 107.
38. Hamner, "Negotiating Strategies and Skills."
39. Ostergaard and Rossmann, "Vendor Relations Strategies," 14.
40. Ostergaard and Rossmann, "There's Work to Be Done," 20.
41. Stamison et al., "What They Never Told You," 140.
42. Katy Ginanni et al., "Yer Doin' It Wrong: How NOT to Interact With Vendors, Publishers, or Librarians," *Serials Librarian* 68, no. 1–4 (2015): 255, https://doi.org/10.1080/0361526X.2015.1023131.

CHAPTER 26

Adopting Agile: Workflow and Personnel Management in Technical Services at a Small Academic Library

Paromita Biswas

ABSTRACT

In today's library landscape cataloging responsibilities have increased. In addition to traditional cataloging work, catalogers increasingly work to provide metadata for electronic resources and digital collections items. These changes necessitate the need for reassessing cataloging workflows in favor of more streamlined approaches, such as the Scrum project management technique. This chapter discusses Scrum in the context of libraries and presents a case study of its successful adoption within the cataloging unit of a small academic library. It highlights how Scrum increased the unit's productivity and energized and motivated personnel and covers considerations to keep in mind when adopting this management style.

INTRODUCTION

Cataloging units in libraries today are faced with a future in which change is constant. In the not too distant past, replacement of Anglo-American Cataloging Rules, 2nd edition (AACR2), with Resource Description and Access (RDA) standards required catalogers to learn new cataloging rules. Today's catalogers face the prospect of the BIBFRAME (Bibliographic Framework) data model supplanting MARC (Machine-Readable Cataloging) in a linked data universe. At the same time, while shrinking library budgets have often prevented the hiring of new staff, cataloging responsibilities have increased. In addition to traditional cataloging work, catalogers now process an increasing amount of electronic resources, including digital collections. These changes necessitate the need for reassessing cataloging workflows in favor of more streamlined approaches that satisfy user needs. This chapter discusses one such streamlining approach, the Scrum project management technique, by describing the framework, explaining its adaptation in libraries, and highlighting its successful adoption within the cataloging unit of a comparatively small academic library. It showcases Scrum's usefulness in increasing a cataloging unit's productivity while also benefiting its personnel and covers considerations to keep in mind when adopting this management style.

THE SCRUM METHOD

The Scrum project management technique, a component of the Agile project management framework, originated in the software industry and emphasizes interaction, collaboration, simplicity, self-organized teams, continuous improvement, and response to change.[1] In the Scrum project management style, teams work in short iterations (Sprints) toward clearly deliverable goals and favor direct communication over extensive project documentation; these steps minimize risk and allow team members to adapt quickly to changing environments.[2] Each team member brings his or her special set of skills to the team and works in consecutive short Sprints of two to four weeks' duration.[3] The Sprints are time-boxed—that is, they never extend beyond the set date, decided at the beginning regardless of whether the work has been completed or not. At the beginning of each Sprint, all players in Scrum meet to identify a Sprint Goal, which gives the team an idea of the deliverable and allows it to plan accordingly. A Sprint Burndown Chart (either in a spreadsheet or on paper) is used to plot progress toward the Goal. During the Sprint, no new items are added, and team members meet every day to go over progress. At the end of the Sprint, work concluded, or goals achieved, are communicated to the various stakeholders, and feedback is incorporated into the next Sprint.

The Scrum Primer defines three primary roles for those involved in Scrum: Product Owner, Team, and Scrum Master.[4] The Product

Owner is responsible for maximizing return on investment through identifying product features, has profit and loss responsibility for the product, and in some cases is the customer for the product. Team members have no titles assigned to anyone. The Team builds the product indicated by the Product Owner and is self-managing with a high degree of autonomy. The Team decides how many items will be built in each Sprint that incrementally contribute toward building the final product and how best to achieve that Goal. The Scrum Master is the facilitator for the Team, not a leader or a manager assigning tasks to people. He or she supports the Team as it organizes and manages itself. Before starting a Sprint, the group identifies a product backlog with the Product Owner making prioritization decisions that inform the goals set in the Sprints.

While the Scrum Primer is detailed about the procedural aspects of Scrum, what has led to successful adaptation of Scrum by libraries is the understanding that while Scrum involves a concrete set of practices, it is "more importantly . . . a framework that provides transparency, and a mechanism that allows 'inspect and adapt.'"[5] As Campanelli and Parreiras have pointed out, Agile methods are not always used to their fullest extent due to organizational needs and constraints; organizations can adopt Agile practices in different ways depending on their unique goals, culture, and resources.[6]

ADOPTION OF SCRUM BY LIBRARIES

Literature on adoption of Scrum by libraries has largely delved into the use of the Agile framework by relatively large libraries; not much appears to have been written on its applicability within smaller libraries. In their case study on applying the Scrum project management framework to digital collections production at the University of Colorado-Boulder libraries, Dulock and Long note they adopted only those aspects of Scrum that seemed most likely to result in improved outcomes for their digital production workflow; they maintain other aspects of Scrum can be adopted later if the pilot proved successful.[7] Favoring this methodology, while at the same time being not "too rigid in its approach,"[8] resulted in several benefits, including digital collection production work becoming more regular, improved communication, and better cooperation and team spirit among pilot project participants. In addition to publication, librarians from multiple academic institutions have presented at American Library Association conferences on adopting the Scrum framework. Individuals from the libraries of George Washington University, Michigan State University, New York University, North Carolina State University, Yale, and Columbia have presented on adoption of the Scrum framework for facilitating their workflow related to creating access and discovery of digital collections.[9]

CASE STUDY: ADOPTION OF SCRUM BY HUNTER LIBRARY AT WESTERN CAROLINA UNIVERSITY

Western Carolina University (WCU) is located in Cullowhee, North Carolina, near the Great Smoky and Blue Ridge Mountains. WCU is one of the 17 constituent campuses of the University of North Carolina System. The institution is a regional comprehensive university with more than 11,000 students in various undergraduate and graduate fields. WCU serves not only students from North Carolina's western region but students nationally and internationally as well.

As the only library for the university, Hunter Library serves WCU's more than 100 undergraduate and 60 graduate programs. Library collections include print resources, physical media, archives and special collections, electronic resources, and digital collections. Hunter Library's 56 full-time staff members are divided between three departments and administration. The three departments are content organization and management (formerly known as technical services); digital, access, technology, and special collections; and reference and instruction services. The cataloging unit (the focus of this case study), along with the acquisitions, electronic resources, and collection development units, make up the content organization and management department. The cataloging unit is responsible for the creation of access to all of the library's collections and for catalog database maintenance work.

To understand the context for the introduction of the Scrum project management method, it is necessary to understand the composition of the cataloging unit and how its workflow has evolved over time. The metadata librarian heads the cataloging unit and directs four full-time staff catalogers. While the traditional work of this unit entails cataloging of print materials, instructional kits and games, and special formats such as maps, videos, and sound recordings, over the past couple of decades the unit has become increasingly involved in creating metadata for digital collections. An increase in the number of digital collections housed in CONTENTdm, a digital collection management software from OCLC, and the adoption in 2014 of the ArchivesSpace platform to publish special collections finding aids have necessitated these changes. The cataloging unit was responsible for migrating the finding aids from Microsoft Word documents housed on an internal server to ArchivesSpace. This process involved copying and pasting of these documents into ArchivesSpace and creating access points by adding name and subject headings. Furthermore, special collections has decided that all new findings aids, even those created initially in Microsoft Word, will be added to ArchivesSpace, with cataloging responsible for the work of migration and creation of access points.

Although cataloging saw a significant increase in workload related to digital collections, there were no concurrent additions to staff in cataloging who could handle this additional work. Digital collections cataloging work continued to be performed by the metadata librarian and three of the staff catalogers.[10] These staff members were also responsible for MARC cataloging of different formats of materials as well as theses, dissertations, and electronic resources, catalog database maintenance, and ongoing collections weeding projects.

Catalogers were therefore faced with a situation in which they had to balance multiple tasks while prioritizing certain projects depending upon the requirements of involved stakeholders external to the department. These responsibilities accumulated atop ongoing professional development training catalogers undertook to keep abreast of current cataloging rules and standards. While the cataloging unit enjoyed an excellent reputation within the library for its dedication to creating detailed records while adhering to deadlines, unit members felt that processes could improve. The metadata librarian, through conversations with catalogers and through tracking their work, felt that digital collections cataloging—both CONTENTdm and ArchivesSpace items—tended to be neglected in favor of MARC cataloging, especially when no pressing deadlines were attached to the former. Reasons for this likely included MARC cataloging projects being more time-sensitive; cataloger comfort with MARC; digital collections cataloging often not coming with a priority deadline; work related to the ArchivesSpace finding aids project tended to be tedious, with its emphasis on copying and pasting; and correlation between MARC items cataloged and existing personnel productivity measures. Indeed, while cataloging of MARC items could be tracked through the library's integrated library system and tended to play a role in the end-of-year assessments for catalogers, there were no equivalent methods for tracking how many digital collections items were cataloged by each cataloger.

The metadata librarian felt it was important to develop a workflow that would facilitate consistent digital collections cataloging work in CONTENTdm and ArchivesSpace, enable tracking items for each cataloger, and motivate catalogers. The metadata librarian had attended presentations related to adapting the Agile/Scrum methodology to library technical services departments and noted its potential to generate a workflow useful for tackling backlog and facilitating assessment. A review of the literature showing that Scrum could promote cooperation and teamwork among workers and be modified to suit different institutional needs further convinced the metadata librarian of the benefits of adopting the Scrum framework.

Hunter Library's cataloging unit undertook its first Sprint for CONTENTdm items in September 2016. At this time there were 21 digital collections housed in CONTENTdm. The collections mostly comprised digitized photographs, scanned newspapers, yearbooks, theses, and digitized audio recordings (oral histories). The Scrum participants consisted of the metadata librarian and three staff catalogers. In a unit meeting held prior to the start of the Sprint, the metadata librarian explained what the Scrum process would entail and shared Dulock and Long's article about Scrum being used in digital collections cataloging. The Scrum framework's adaptability kept it from seeming too daunting or rigid to the catalogers. Indeed, the Scrum framework adopted by the cataloging unit differed significantly from the Scrum framework outlined in the Scrum Primer.

Unlike Scrum Teams composed of individuals from different backgrounds or skill sets, Hunter Library's Scrum Team consisted entirely of members from the cataloging unit because the unit's aims were to clear a backlog in digital collections cataloging and provide a concrete means of assessment while energizing catalogers to proactively create metadata. The metadata librarian took on the role of the Scrum Master, facilitating the work of the team. There was no official Product Owner responsible for identifying product backlogs; however, the Scrum Team's decision about what items to catalog was often informed by priorities set by the digital initiatives unit of the library responsible for adding the scanned and digitized content into CONTENTdm.[11] Two weeks was decided as the ideal length of each Sprint, with a meeting at the beginning to set Goals, a review meeting in the middle to review progress toward Goals and address concerns, and a meeting at the end of the Sprint to review the work done. As the Scrum Master, the metadata librarian facilitated meetings and discussions and recorded the targets determined and achieved. Though in traditional Scrum the Scrum Master works merely as the facilitator and does not participate in the actual work of the self-functional teams, the metadata librarian also established set Goals and worked toward achieving them in the duration of the Sprint. The metadata librarian felt this would work well in motivating the catalogers and promoting team spirit. Furthermore, while the Scrum Primer does mention that Goals decided at the beginning of the meeting cannot be changed, the Scrum Team at Hunter Library decided that the mid-week review meeting would assess whether modifications needed to be made. Team members knew other projects from different stakeholders might arise that would need to take priority over achieving Sprint Goals.

The cataloging unit's first Sprint was successful. Although the Team had to scale down its initial goal of cataloging 115 items to 76 items during a mid-Sprint review session, the Team achieved this reduced goal. More importantly, the catalogers felt that having a set target to work toward motivated them to catalog digital collections. With this positive feedback, the metadata librarian applied Scrum to cataloging ArchivesSpace finding aids as well. The format of the ArchivesSpace Sprint followed that of the first Sprint. As not all catalogers in the unit worked with ArchivesSpace, only two catalogers participated in the ArchivesSpace Sprints in addition to the metadata librarian.

Since the first Sprint, the cataloging unit has completed nine more Sprints on both CONTENTdm and ArchivesSpace items. There was

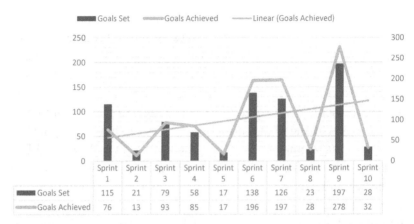

Figure 26.1 Graph showing Goals set and Goals achieved (items catalogued) during each Sprint.

at least a two-week gap between each Sprint; sometimes the gap was a little longer, but it averaged out to be about one Sprint a month. The timing of Sprints depended on the unit's involvement in other projects, everyone's availability, and vacation times (for example, the unit did not have any Sprints in December of 2016). Figure 26.1 shows the steady increase in the number of items cataloged over time in the Sprints for both ArchivesSpace and CONTENTdm. Sprints 2, 5, 8, and 10 focused on cataloging ArchivesSpace items and the remaining on CONTENTdm items. Unlike traditional Burndown Charts, which track progress made each day toward eliminating the Sprint backlog, the graph in figure 26.1 tracks Sprint Goals set at the beginning of each of the 10 Sprints and the Goals achieved by the team.

USEFULNESS OF SCRUM

This simple Scrum framework achieved the objectives envisaged at the beginning.

> **Better evaluation and assessment process:** The framework provided catalogers with a means to accurately record their work in digital collections cataloging through recording their achievements in terms of meeting, failing to meet, or exceeding Goals. This information in turn helped in staff evaluations.

Increased productivity and focus: The Sprint Goals energized catalogers in tackling digital collections cataloging as they gave them focus and targets to work toward. As one cataloger noted, the Goals helped catalogers set aside fixed time during their daily work schedule to devote to working exclusively on digital collections. Prior to using Scrum, digital projects work was not prioritized and was more likely to be the last thing done if there was no MARC cataloging to be done. Furthermore, as H. Frank Cervone has pointed out, because each team member in a Scrum Team is equally responsible for his or her part in the project's completion, ownership of the project is more broad-based and commitment is encouraged, thereby increasing chances for greater productivity.[12] During the Sprints, the catalogers' knowledge of solitary contributions morphed into an understanding of how the group as a whole contributed toward completion of a project. One cataloger noted that they felt like they had "achieved or contributed something" as they achieved their Scrum Goals. Productivity also increased when catalogers set a higher target for themselves in one Sprint if they had not been able to set a high target in the previous one due to work or personal considerations. It was rewarding to see the Goals achieved at the end of each Sprint, and this provided the Team with a sense of accomplishment.

Collaboration and team spirit: The review meetings provided a venue for the catalogers to discuss with each other issues related to cataloging digitized items and learn about the different collections other team members were cataloging. Cataloging is often a solitary enterprise with each cataloger working individually on cataloging items; the Sprint meetings provided a welcome opportunity to break away from this format as they made decisions and resolved questions as a group.

LESSONS LEARNED AND FUTURE CONSIDERATIONS

The Scrum methodology was overall very beneficial for furthering the objective of increased digital collections cataloging. The framework facilitated acknowledgment of the ability of experienced catalogers to function in self-directed teams. The modifiable framework also worked well within the limitations of a smaller cataloging unit whose members might be pulled in different directions to meet urgent needs external to the Sprint. The role of the Scrum Master as a facilitator who at the same time functioned as a horizontal team member further promoted a collaborative work ethic within the team.

Although the cataloging unit's overall experience with the Scrum framework was positive, a few considerations need to be kept in mind when adopting Scrum. The use of Scrum for digital collections cataloging meant that, during the time catalogers were not working in Sprints, digital collections cataloging tended to be overlooked. This omission was especially true for the ArchivesSpace project, an undertaking that catalogers were least familiar with and the most tedious in terms of the work involved. While participation in Scrum helped catalogers devote time exclusively to working on digital collections, it was harder to retain balance between Sprints. This discrepancy can be an area of concern if the Scrum framework is no longer adopted for cataloging workflows.

In addition, though Scrum Teams are meant to be independent and self-directional, the supervisor or unit head had to assume the role of the Scrum Master. While having a nonsupervisory staff member fill the role of the Scrum Master is possible within the egalitarian Scrum framework, staff might be hesitant to take up this role if the supervisor is present. At the same time, the role of Scrum Master is necessary. As one cataloger noted, although the Sprint Goals are set by the team members, without a Scrum Master facilitating, the whole process would become "chaotic." The supervisor, then, needs to be prepared to continue to serve in the role of Scrum Master if Sprints remain a part of the workflow.

Another issue is that, while work done in the Scrum can be an excellent tool to assess performance, the supervisor needs to consider other means of assessing progress when Sprints are not taking place. This concern may not apply in work settings where cataloger output is not used as a performance metric.

Finally, as the Scrum framework was initially adopted to tackle a work backlog, there is the question of whether it is viable to continue holding Sprints indefinitely if backlogs become no longer a concern, as when new staff members join a unit to process the backlog. This is currently the situation of the cataloging unit at Hunter Library. A newly hired cataloger now focuses on digital collections, the source of the backlog. Following the completion of the 10th Sprint in August 2017 and the hiring of this new cataloger two months later, the cataloging unit has not undertaken more Sprints. Before the unit decides to continue with the Scrum framework, it must consider certain questions. Is Scrum still necessary now that there is a position dedicated primarily to working in the area of digital collections cataloging? Or could Scrum be used periodically to address large projects or meet deadlines in areas distinct from digital collections—for example, MARC cataloging or weeding projects? And if Scrum continues in the area of cataloging digital projects, should there be a special role for the digital collections cataloger on the Scrum Team? Might that cataloger assume the role of Scrum Master, and might other catalogers take on the Scrum Master role in Sprints that focus on MARC cataloging and therefore are more closely aligned with their areas of individual expertise?

CONCLUSION

The flexibility of the Scrum project management framework has lent itself to successful adoption by libraries of varying sizes. For the cataloging unit presented in this case study, the Scrum framework will likely be used again for tackling digital collections cataloging backlog. At the time of the writing of this chapter, the cataloging unit was considering starting a Sprint focused on ArchivesSpace. After all, it is not only high-quality deliverables that are the end result of the successful adaptation of Scrum, but the process itself leads to the furtherance of teamwork, communications, and speed,[13] all of which can be goals in and of themselves.

NOTES

1. Amadeu Silveira Campanelli and Fernando Silva Parreiras, "Agile Methods Tailoring—A Systematic Literature Review," *Journal of Systems and Software* 110 (2015): 86, https://doi.org/10.1016/j

.jss.2015.08.035. The origins of the Agile project management method can be traced to a 1986 paper in the *Harvard Business Review* by Hirotaka Takeuchi and Ikujiro Nonaka; the Scrum framework was more fully developed by Ken Schwaber and Jeff Sutherland to help organizations carry out complex projects in software development. See H. Frank Cervone, "Understanding Agile Project Management Methods Using Scrum," *OCLC Systems & Services: International Digital Library Perspectives* 27, no. 1 (2011), https://doi.org/10.1108/10650751111106528.

2. Cervone, "Understanding Agile Project Management," 19.

3. Pete Deemer et al., "The Scrum Primer: A Lightweight Guide to the Theory and Practice of Scrum—Version 2.0," 2012, http://scrumprimer.org/scrumprimer20.pdf.

4. Ibid.

5. Ibid., 16.

6. Campanelli and Parreiras, "Agile Methods Tailoring," 88–89.

7. Michael Dulock and Holley Long, "Digital Collections Are a Sprint, Not a Marathon: Adapting Scrum Project Management Techniques to Library Digital Initiatives," *Information Technology and Libraries* 34, no. 4 (2015): 11, https://doi.org/10.6017/ital.v34i4.5869.

8. Ibid., 14.

9. For example, Hannah Sommers, "Two Weeks at a Time: Applying Agile Frameworks to Library Practice" (presentation, ALA Midwinter Meeting, Atlanta, GA, January 20–24, 2017); Lisa Lorenzo, "Agile and Scrum in the Michigan State University Libraries Digital Repository" (presentation, ALA Annual Conference, Chicago, IL, June 22–27, 2017); Daniel Lovins, "'Agile' as a Key to Collaboration on NYU Digital Collections Discovery Initiative" (presentation, ALA Annual Conference, Orlando, FL, June 23–28, 2016); Maria Collins, "Agile Technical Services: Iterative Strategies to Help, Plan, Merge, and Evolve" (presentation, ALA Annual Conference, Orlando, FL, June 23–28, 2016); Galadriel Chilton, "Using the Scrum Project Management Methodology to Create a Comprehensive Collection Assessment Framework" (presentation, ALA Annual Conference, Orlando, FL, June 23–28, 2016); Kate Harcourt, "Applying Agile Practices to Metadata Workflows: People in Transition" (presentation, ALA Annual Conference, Chicago, IL, June 22–27, 2017).

10. The fourth cataloger was responsible for copy cataloging items with Library of Congress copy and did not work with digital collections.

11. For example, university faculty wanting to use certain digital collections' items in their classes contacted the digital initiatives unit about having those processed on a priority basis or there were grant-funded digital collections that needed cataloging by a certain date as part of grant requirements.

12. Cervone, "Understanding Agile Project Management," 22.

13. "Learn About Scrum," Scrum Alliance, accessed November 2, 2017, https://www.scrumalliance.org/why-scrum.

Glossary

AACR2: Anglo-American Cataloging Rules, 2nd edition
ADA: Americans with Disabilities Act
AFS ET: American Folklore Society's Ethnographic Thesaurus
AHEC: Auraria Higher Education Center
ALCTS: Association for Library Collections and Technical Services
ARL: Association of Research Libraries
ASERL: Association of Southeastern Research Libraries
BIBFRAME: Bibliographic Framework
BTAA: Big Ten Academic Alliance
CCCS: Colorado Community College System
CCD: Community College of Denver
Circa: Circa Wireless Inventory is an Innovative Interfaces Inc. product that enables libraries to update an item record's inventory date and status, as well as compare the stacks against the system's shelf list
CoGoPub: Colorado Government Publications Interest Group
CRDP: Cataloging Record Distribution Program
CRL: Center for Research Libraries
CU Denver: University of Colorado Denver
DAMS: digital asset management systems
DDA: demand-driven acquisitions
DDC: Dewey Decimal Classification
DiSC: digital scholarship center
DPS: digital programs and systems
EAD: Encoded Archival Description
EBA: evidence-based acquisitions
EBM: evidence-based management
EIT: electronic and information technology

431

ERL: electronic resources librarian
ERMS: electronic resource management system
ETD: electronic theses and dissertations
FDLC: federal depository library collection
FDLP: Federal Depository Library Program
FRBR: Functional Requirements for Bibliographic Records
FTE: full-time equivalent
FY: fiscal year
GPO: Government Publishing Office
HCL: Houston Cole Library
HSI: Hispanic-Serving Institution
IFLA: International Federation of Library Associations and Institutions
IFLA LRM: IFLA Library Reference Model
IL: information literacy
ILS: integrated library system
IMLS: Institute of Museum and Library Services
IP: internet protocol
IR: institutional repository
IT: information technology
JSU: Jacksonville State University
LC: Library of Congress
LCSH: Library of Congress Subject Headings
LMS: learning management system
LOCKSS: Lots of Copies Keeps Stuff Safe
LRC: library records center
LSC: library service center
MARC: machine-readable cataloging record
MARCIVE: A U.S.-based library services company specializing in author-
  ities processing, cataloging, and government document processing
MODS: Library of Congress Metadata Object Description Schema
NACO: Library of Congress Name Authority Cooperative Program
NEFLIN: Northeast Florida Library Information Network
NJSL: New Jersey State Library
OCLC: Online Computer Library Center, a U.S.-based, nonprofit
  organization that produces and maintains WorldCat, with the
  help of member libraries
OCR: optical character recognition
OER: open educational resources

OPAC: online public access catalog
ORCID: online researcher ID
PASCAL: Partnership Among South Carolina Academic Libraries
PCC: Program for Cooperative Cataloging
PDA: patron-driven acquisition
PUI: public user interface
PURL: persistent uniform resource locator
QC: quality control
QEP: Quality Enhancement Plan
RA: resource acquisition
RDA: Resource Description and Access
RDMS: resource description and metadata services
RFID: radio frequency identification
RFP: request for proposal
ROTC: Reserve Officer Training Corps
SC&A: Special Collections and Archives
SUNY: State University of New York
TEI: Text Encoding Initiative
TEL: technology enhanced learning
TERMS: Techniques for Electronic Resource Management
TSG: technical services group
TSLAC: Texas State Library and Archives Commission
UNCG: University of North Carolina at Greensboro
UofM Global: distance education offerings of the University of Memphis
URI: uniform resource identifier
WALDO: Westchester Academic Library Director's Organization
WAM: web access management

Bibliography

Abreu, Amelia. "On Cards, Card-Based Systems, and the Material Cultures of Computing." Conference presentation, Systems We Love, San Francisco, CA, December 13, 2016.

afry. "Working Together: Tips for Vendors." *ACRLog*, February 28, 2011. http://acrlog.org/2011/02/28/working-together-tips-for-vendors/.

Alexander, Teri, Pam Draper, Scott Hammel, Darius Jones, Gail Julian, Priscilla Munson, Fredda Owens, Beverly Rainey, Chris Ryan, Eric Shoaf, Chris Vinson, and Derek Wilmott. *Transforming Clemson University Libraries for the 21st Century: Study and Recommendations by the Future Is Now Task Force.* August 9, 2012, p. 2. http://clemson.libguides.com/ld.php?content_id=9028659.

"Always Already Computational—Collections as Data." Accessed November 1, 2017. https://collectionsasdata.github.io/.

American Library Association. "About ALA." Accessed October 21, 2017. http://www.ala.org/aboutala/.

American Library Association. "Core Values of Librarianship." Adopted January 2019. http://www.ala.org/advocacy/intfreedom/corevalues.

Anderson, Rick. *Can't Buy Us Love: The Declining Importance of Library Books and the Rising Importance of Special Collections.* New York: Ithaka S+R, 2013. https://doi.org/10.18665/sr.24613.

Apgar, Mahlon, IV. "The Alternative Workplace: Changing Where and How People Work." *Harvard Business Review* 76, no. 3 (1998): 121–36. https://hbr.org/1998/05/the-alternative-workplace-changing-where-and-how-people-work.

Arthur, Michael A., and Stacy Sieck. "Cooperation Is Key: How Publishers and Libraries Are Working Together to Achieve Common Goals." *Against the Grain* 27, no. 6 (2015): 23. https://doi.org/10.7771/2380-176X.7225.

Association of Research Libraries. "Diversity, Equity & Inclusion." https://arl.secure.nonprofitsoapbox.com/focus-areas/diversity -equity-and-inclusion.

Avram, Henriette D. *MARC: Its History and Implications.* Washington D.C.: Library of Congress, 1975.

Baber, William W., and Chavi C-Y Fletcher-Chen. *Practical Business Negotiation.* London: Routledge, 2015.

Baildon, Michelle, Dana Hamlin, Czeslaw Jankowski, Rhonda Kauffman, Julia Lanigan, Michelle Miller, Jessica Venlet, and Ann Marie Willer. *Creating a Social Justice Mindset: Diversity, Inclusion, and Social Justice in the Collections Directorate of the MIT Libraries.* Report of the Collections Directorate Task Force on Diversity Inclusion and Social Justice. Cambridge, MA, 2017. https://dspace.mit.edu /handle/1721.1/108771.

Bansode, Sadanand Y., and Sanjay K. Desale. "Implementation of RFID Technology in University of Pune Library." *Program-Electronic Library and Information Systems* 43, no. 2 (2009): 202–14. https:// doi.org/10.1108/00330330910954406.

Bates, Mary Ellen. "Learn to Love Your Information Vendor." *Online Searcher* 38, no. 3 (2014): 80.

Beckhard, Richard, and Reuben T. Harris. *Organizational Transitions: Managing Complex Change.* Reading, MA: Addison-Wesley, 1987.

Bennett, Charlie, Wendy Hagenmaier, Lizzy Rolando, Fred Rascoe, Lori Critz, Crystal Renfro, Willie Baer, and Mary Axford. *Reimaging the Georgia Tech Library.* Georgia Tech Library. 2014. Accessed December 21, 2017. https://smartech.gatech.edu/bitstream/handle/1853 /51712/reimagining_the_georgia_tech_library_1.pdf.

Bergstrom, Theodore C., Paul N. Courant, R. P. McAfee, and Michael A. Williams. "Evaluating Big Deal Journal Bundles." *Proceedings of the National Academy of Sciences of the United States of America* 111, no. 26 (2014): 9425–30. https://doi.org/10.1073/pnas.1403006111.

Berman, Sanford. *Prejudices and Antipathies: A Tract on the LC Subject Heads Concerning People.* Jefferson, NC: McFarland & Co., 1993.

Bernhardt, Beth. "Open Educational Resources (OER)." University of North Carolina at Greensboro University Libraries. http://uncg .libguides.com/oer.

Bernhardt, Beth. "Scholarly Communications at UNC Greensboro." University of North Carolina at Greensboro University Libraries. http:// uncg.libguides.com/scholarlycomm.

Bernhardt, Beth. "2018 Mini Grants." University of North Carolina at Greensboro University Libraries. http://uncg.libguides.com/c.php?g=83604&p=4438149.

Bernhardt, Beth. "What Are OER." University of North Carolina at Greensboro University Libraries. http://uncg.libguides.com/OER/whatareOER.

Bertot, John C., Abigail McDermott, Ruth Lincoln, Brian Real, and Kaitlin Peterson. *2011–2012 Public Library Funding and Technology Access Survey: Survey Findings and Results* (2012): 54–60. Information Policy & Access Center, University of Maryland.

Bevis, Mary D., and Sonja L. McAbee. "NOTIS as an Impetus for Change in Technical Services Departmental Staffing." *Technical Services Quarterly* 12, no. 2 (1994): 29–43.

Billey, Amber, Emily Drabinski, and K. R. Roberto. "What's Gender Got to Do With It? A Critique of RDA 9.7." *Cataloging and Classification Quarterly* 52, no. 4 (2014): 412–21. https://doi.org/10.1080/01639374.2014.882465.

Blair, Ann M. *Too Much to Know: Managing Scholarly Information Before the Modern Age.* New Haven: Yale University Press, 2010.

Blakiston, Rebecca. *Usability Testing: A Practical Guide for Librarians.* Lanham, MD: Rowman & Littlefield, 2015.

Bleiler, Richard, and Jill Livingston. *Evaluating e-Resources.* Washington, D.C.: Association of Research Libraries, 2010. http://publications.arl.org/Evaluating-Eresources-SPEC-Kit-316/.

Bollinger, Doris U., and Trey Martindale. "Key Factors for Determining Student Satisfaction in Online Courses." *International Journal of E-Learning* 3, no. 1 (2004): 61–67. https://www.learntechlib.org/p/2226.

Borgman, Christine. *Big Data, Little Data, No Data: Scholarship in the Networked World.* Cambridge: The MIT Press, 2015.

Boyd, Erin E., and Elyssa Gould. "Skills for the Future of Technical Services." In *Rethinking Library Technical Services: Redefining Our Profession for the Future*, edited by Mary Beth Weber, 123–34. Lanham, MD: Rowman & Littlefield, 2015.

Brisson, Roger. "Online Documentation in Library Technical Services." *Technical Services Quarterly* 16, no. 3 (1999): 1–19. https://doi.org/10.1300/J124v16n03_01.

Brock, James W. "Economic Concentration and Economic Power: John Flynn and a Quarter-Century of Mergers." *Antitrust Bulletin* 56,

no. 4 (2011): 683–732. https://doi.org/10.1177/0003603X1105
600402.

Calhoun, Karen. "Technology, Productivity and Change in Library Technical
Services." *Library Collections, Acquisitions, & Technical Services* 27
(2003): 281–89. https://doi.org/10.1016/S1464-9055(03)00068-X.

Caminita, Cristina, and Andrea Hebert. "The Weeding Planner: How
a Research Library Weeded Approximately 2.76 Miles of Print
Materials From Shelves to Repurpose Library Space or Much Ado
About the New Normal." *Against the Grain* 28, no. 4 (2016): 34–36.
https://doi.org/10.7771/2380-176X.7457.

Campanelli, Amadeu Silveira, and Fernando Silva Parreiras. "Agile
Methods Tailoring—A Systematic Literature Review." *Journal of Systems and Software* 110 (2015): 85–100. https://doi.org/10.1016/j
.jss.2015.08.035.

Cannady, Sheryl. "Library Offers Largest Release of Digital Catalog
Records in History." *News From the Library of Congress.* Accessed
May 16, 2017. https://www.loc.gov/item/prn-17-068/.

Carter, Steve. "Office Relocation: Managing People in a Workplace Transition." *Workdesign.com.* August 26, 2013. Accessed December 21,
2017. https://workdesign.com/2013/08/are-you-managing-change
-or-managing-transitions/.

Center on Budget and Policy Priorities. "State Map: Funding Down, Tuition Up." Accessed March 2, 2020, https://www.cbpp.org/research
/state-budget-and-tax/state-map-funding-down-tuition-up.

Cervone, H. Frank. "Understanding Agile Project Management Methods
Using Scrum." *OCLC Systems & Services: International Digital
Library Perspectives* 27, no. 1 (2011): 18–22. https://doi.org/10.1108/
10650751111106528.

Chen, Li, and Yongli Ma. "Library Inventory Using Palm Pilot." *Technical
Services Quarterly* 22, no. 2 (2004): 15–23. https://doi.org/10.1300
/J124v22n02_02.

Chilton, Galadriel. "Using the Scrum Project Management Methodology
to Create a Comprehensive Collection Assessment Framework." Presentation at the ALA Annual Conference, Orlando, FL, June 23–28,
2016.

Christie, Chris, and Kim Guadagno. *The Governor's FY 2017 Budget.*
2017. Accessed September 15, 2017. https://nj.gov/treasury/omb
/publications/17budget/pdf/FY17BudgetBook.pdf.

Colbert, Jessica L. "Patron-Driven Subject Access: How Librarians Can Mitigate That 'Power to Name.'" *In the Library With the Lead Pipe.* November 15, 2017. http://www.inthelibrarywiththeleadpipe .org/2017/patron-driven-subject-access-how-librarians-can-mitigate -that-power-to-name.

Collins, Maria. "Agile Technical Services: Iterative Strategies to Help, Plan, Merge, and Evolve." Presentation at the ALA Annual Conference, Orlando, FL, June 23–28, 2016.

Commonfund Institute. *Commonfund Higher Education Price Index, 2016 Update.* Accessed March 2, 2020. https://www.commonfund .org/wp-content/uploads/2016/10/2016-HEPI-Report.pdf.

Condit Fagan, Jody, Merisa Mandernach, Carl S. Nelson, Jonathan R. Paulo, and Grover Saunders. "Usability Test Results for a Discovery Tool in an Academic Library." *Information Technology and Libraries* 31, no. 1 (March 2012): 83–112. https://doi.org/10.6017/ital.v31i1.1855.

Coonin, Bryna, Beth Filar Williams, and Heidi Steiner. "Fostering Library as a Place for Distance Students: Best Practices from Two Universities." *Internet Reference Services Quarterly* 16, no. 4 (2011): 149–58. https://doi.org/10.1080/10875301.2012.618796.

Coyle, Karen. "The Evolving Catalog: Cataloging Tech From Scrolls to Computers." *American Libraries Magazine.* January 4, 2016. https:// americanlibrariesmagazine.org/2016/01/04/cataloging-evolves/.

Coyle, Karen. *FRBR, Before and After: A Look at Our Bibliographic Models.* Chicago: ALA Editions, 2016.

Coyle, Karen, and Diane Hillman. "Resource Description and Access (RDA): Cataloging Rules for the 20th Century." *D-Lib Magazine* 13, no. 1/2 (January/February 2007). http://dlib.org/dlib/january07 /coyle/01coyle.html.

Cutter, Charles A. *Rules for a Dictionary Catalog.* 4th ed. Washington, D.C.: Government Printing Office, 1904.

Davis, Jeehyun Yun. "Transforming Technical Services: Evolving Functions in Large Research University Libraries." *Library Resources & Technical Services* 60, no. 1 (January 2016): 63. https://doi.org/10 .5860/lrts.60n1.52.

Deemer, Pete, Gabrielle Benefield, Craig Larman, and Bas Vodde. "The Scrum Primer: A Lightweight Guide to the Theory and Practice of Scrum—Version 2.0." 2012. http://scrumprimer.org/scrumprimer 20.pdf.

De Jesus, Nina. "Locating the Library in Institutional Oppression." *In the Library With the Lead Pipe*. September 24, 2014: 1–30. http://www.inthelibrarywiththeleadpipe.org/2014/locating-the-library-in-institutional-oppression/.

Department for Professional Employees (AFL-CIO). *Library Workers: Facts & Figures*. DPE-AFL-CIO Fact Sheet 2018. https://dpeaflcio.org/wp-content/uploads/Library-Workers-Facts-Figures-2018.pdf.

Diedrichs, Carol Pitts. "Using Automation in Technical Services to Foster Innovation." *Journal of Academic Librarianship* 24, no. 2 (1998): 119–20. https://doi.org/10.1016/S0099-1333(98)90171-9.

Dinkins, Debbi. *Technical Services Department Annual Reports 2010–2011, 2011–2012, 2012–2013, 2013–2014*. https://www2.stetson.edu/library/about-us/library-publications/annual-reports/.

Diversity and Inclusion Resource Development Group. *Diversity, Inclusion, and Social Justice Resource Manual for MIT Libraries Staff*. Cambridge, MA, 2017. https://libguides.mit.edu/ld.php?content_id=32359042.

Doherty, Brian, and Alison Piper. "Creating a New Organizational Structure for a Small Academic Library: The Merging of Technical Services and Access Services." *Technical Services Quarterly* 32 (2015): 160–72. https://doi.org/10.1080/07317131.2015.998466.

Drabinski, Emily. "Teaching the Radical Catalog." In *Radical Cataloging: Essays at the Front*, edited by K. R. Roberto, 198–205. Jefferson, NC: McFarland & Co., 2008.

Dresselhaus, Angela. "The Americans with Disabilities Act Compliance and Library Acquisitions." Speech at the Acquisitions Institute at Timberline Lodge, Oregon, May 20, 2013. https://works.bepress.com/angela_dresselhaus/24/.

Duck, Jeanie D. "Managing Change: The Art of Balancing." In *Harvard Business Review on Change*, 55–82. Harvard Business Review Paperback Series. Boston: Harvard Business School Press, 1998.

Dulock, Michael, and Holley Long. "Digital Collections Are a Sprint, Not a Marathon: Adapting Scrum Project Management Techniques to Library Digital Initiatives." *Information Technology and Libraries* 34, no. 4 (2015): 5–17. https://doi.org/10.6017/ital.v34i4.5869.

Dwivedi, Yogesh K., Kawaljeet Kaur Kapoor, Michael D. Williams, and Janet Williams. "RFID Systems in Libraries: An Empirical Examination of Factors Affecting System Use and User Satisfaction."

International Journal of Information Management 33, no. 2 (2013): 367–77, https://doi.org/10.1016/j.ijinfomgt.2012.10.008.

Eden, Bradford Lee. "The New User Environment: The End of Technical Services?" *Information Technology and Libraries* 29, no. 2 (2010): 93–100. https://doi.org/10.6017/ital.v29i2.3148.

Emery, Charles David. "The Use of Portable Barcode Scanners in Collections Inventory." *Collection Management* 13, no. 4 (January 5, 1990): 1–17. https://doi.org/10.1300/J105v13n04_01.

Emery, Jill, Graham Stone, and Peter McCracken. "Getting Back on TERMS (Version 2.0)." *TERMS Techniques for Electronic Resource Management* (blog). March 2017. https://library.hud.ac.uk/blogs/terms/.

Ernick, Linda. "Floating Bibs and Orphan Barcodes: Benefits of an Inventory at a Small College." *Library Resources & Technical Services* 49, no. 3 (2005): 210–16.

Ettarh, Fobazi. "Vocational Awe and Librarianship: The Lies We Tell Ourselves." *In the Library With the Lead Pipe*. January 10, 2018. http://www.inthelibrarywiththeleadpipe.org/2018/vocational-awe.

Farrell, Maggie. "Leading From the Middle." *Journal of Library Administration* 54, no. 8 (2014): 691–99. https://doi.org/10.1080/01930826.2014.965099.

Federal Depository Library Program. "About the FDLP." Accessed July 20, 2017. https://www.fdlp.gov/about-the-fdlp/federal-depository-libraries.

Federal Depository Library Program. "Cataloging Record Distribution Program." *FDLP News & Events* (blog). October 24, 2012. Accessed October 10, 2017. https://www.fdlp.gov/news-and-events/23-about/projects/125-crdp.

Federal Depository Library Program. "Cataloging Record Distribution Program." Last updated November 27, 2019. Accessed February 27, 2020. https://www.fdlp.gov/project-list/cataloging-record-distribution-program.

Federal Depository Library Program. *Designation Handbook for Federal Depository Libraries*. Washington, DC: Government Publishing Office, 2008. https://www.fdlp.gov/file-repository/about-the-fdlp/5-designation-handbook-for-federal-depository-libraries.

Federal Depository Library Program. "Federal Depository Library." Persistent URL home page. Accessed August 2, 2017. https://purl.fdlp.gov/.

Federal Depository Library Program. "GPO Historic Shelflist." October 25, 2012. Last updated July 23, 2014. Accessed July 21, 2017. https://www.fdlp.gov/project-list/gpo-historic-shelflist.

Federal Depository Library Program. "GPO Is Now the Government Publishing Office." *FDLP News & Events* (blog). December 17, 2014. Accessed October 10, 2017. https://www.fdlp.gov/news-and-events/2153-gpo-is-now-the-government-publishing-office.

Feeney, Mary, and Leslie Sult. "Project Management in Practice: Implementing a Process to Ensure Accountability and Success." *Journal of Library Administration* 51, no. 7–8 (October 2011): 745. https://doi.org/10.1080/01930826.2011.601273.

Ferguson, Christine L. "In Favor of Weeding." *Serials Review* 41, no. 4 (2015): 221–23. https://doi.org/10.1080/00987913.2015.1103573.

Flowers, Janet L. "Specific Tips for Negotiations with Library Materials Vendors Depending Upon Acquisitions Method." *Library Collections, Acquisitions, & Technical Services* 28, no. 4 (2004): 433–48. https://doi.org/10.1080/14649055.2004.10766015.

Fons, Ted. "The Tradition of Library Catalogs." *Library Technology Reports* 52, no. 5 (July 2016): 15–19. https://doi.org/10.5860/ltr.52n5.

Gage, Ryan A. "Henry Giroux's *Abandoned Generation* & Critical Librarianship: A Review Article." *Progressive Librarian* 23 (2004): 65–74. http://www.progressivelibrariansguild.org/PL/PL23/065.pdf.

George Mason University. "Fall 2017 Official Census Student Enrollment Master Sheet." Office of Institutional Research and Effectiveness. Accessed December 4, 2017. https://irr2.gmu.edu/New/N_EnrollOff/EnrlSts.cfm.

George Mason University. "Oh Joy Unbounded: A Celebration of Gilbert and Sullivan." Libraries Special Collections Research Center. Accessed December 14, 2017. http://gilbertandsullivan2017.gmu.edu/.

Gibson, Amelia N., Renate L. Chancellor, Nicole A. Cooke, Sarah Park Dahlen, Shari A. Lee, and Yasmeen L Shorish. "Libraries on the Frontlines: Neutrality and Social Justice." *Equality, Diversity and Inclusion: An International Journal* 36, no. 8 (2017): 751–66. https://doi.org/10.1108/EDI-11-2016-0100.

Gibson, Sally. "Creating Solutions Instead of Solving Problems: Emerging Roles for Technical Services Departments." *Technical Services Quarterly* 33, no. 2. (2016): 145–153. https://doi.org/10.1080/07317131.2016.1134998.

Gibson, Sally. "From Problem Solvers to Solution Creators: Shifting Roles of Technical Services." In *Creating Sustainable Community: The Proceedings of the ACRL Conference* (2015): 290–93. http://www. ala.org/acrl/sites/ala.org.acrl/files/content/conferences/confsand preconfs/2015/Gibson.pdf.

Gilliland, Anne J. "Setting the Stage." In *Introduction to Metadata*, ed. 2, edited by Murtha Baca. Los Angeles: Getty Publications, 2008. http:// www.getty.edu/research/publications/electronic_publications /intrometadata/setting.html.

Ginanni, Katy, Anne E. McKee, Jenni Wilson, and Linda A. Brown. "Yer Doin' It Wrong: How NOT to Interact With Vendors, Publishers, or Librarians." *Serials Librarian* 68, no. 1–4 (2015): 255. https://doi .org/10.1080/0361526X.2015.1023131.

Glaser, Robbin. "To Classify or Alphabetize: The Arrangement of Print Periodicals in Academic Libraries." *Serials Review* 33, no. 2 (2007): 91–96. https://doi.org/10.1016/j.serrev.2007.03.002.

Glynn, Tom, and Connie Wu. "New Roles and Opportunities for Academic Library Liaisons: A Survey and Recommendations." *Reference Services Review* 31, no. 2 (2003): 122–28. https://doi.org/10 .1108/00907320310476594.

Gore, Emily, and Mandy Mastrovita. "Collaborative-Centered Digital Curation: A Case Study at Clemson University Libraries." In *Digitization in the Real World: Lessons Learned From Small and Medium-Sized Digitization Projects,* edited by Kwong Bor Ng and Jason Kucsma, 490–502. New York: Metropolitan New York, 2010.

Gorman, Michael, ed. *Technical Services Today and Tomorrow*. Englewood, CO: Libraries Unlimited, 1998.

Gorman, Michael. "Technical Services Today and Tomorrow." In *Technical Services Today and Tomorrow,* edited by Michael Gorman, 1–6. Englewood: Libraries Unlimited, 1998.

Green, Harriet, and Eleanor Dickson. "Expanding the Librarian's Tech Toolbox: The 'Digging Deeper, Reaching Further: Librarians Empowering Users to Mine the HathiTrust Digital Library' Project." *D-Lib Magazine* 23, no. 5/6 (May/June 2017). https://doi.org/10.1045 /may2017-green.

Greenwood, Judy T. "Taking It to the Stacks: An Inventory Project at the University of Mississippi Libraries." *Journal of Access Services* 10, no. 2 (2013): 77–89. https://doi.org/10.1080/15367967.2013 .762266.

Greiner, Tony. *Analyzing Library Collection Use With Excel.* Presentation at the NEFLIN Workshop. Florida Coastal School of Law, Jacksonville, FL, July 8, 2016.

Greiner, Tony, and Bob Cooper. *Analyzing Library Collection Use With Excel.* Chicago: American Library Association, 2007.

Hamner, Elaine W. "Negotiating Strategies and Skills." Presentation at the University of North Texas Library, Denton, October 2016.

Harcourt, Kate. "Applying Agile Practices to Metadata Workflows: People in Transition." Presentation at the ALA Annual Conference, Chicago, IL, June 22–27, 2017.

Harlow, Samantha. "Distance and Online Learning Guide." University of North Carolina at Greensboro University Libraries. http://uncg.libguides.com/de.

Harlow, Samantha. "UNCG Instructional Technology Training." University of North Carolina at Greensboro University Libraries. https://uncg.libguides.com/libinstructionaltech.

Hiatt, C. Derrik, Lesley Jackson, and Katherine Hill, "Principles of Negotiation." *Serials Review* 41, no. 3 (2015): 180–83. https://doi.org/10.1080/00987913.2015.1064339.

Higher Learning Commission. "Statement of Accreditation Status, New Mexico State University." Accessed March 2, 2020. https://www.hlcommission.org/component/directory/?Itemid=&Action=ShowBasic&instid=1504.

Hill, Claire. "The Professional Divide: Examining Workplace Relationships Between Librarians and Library Technicians." *The Australian Library Journal* 63, no. 1 (2013): 23–34. https://doi.org/10.1080/00049670.2014.890020.

Hill, Katherine. "eBooks A-Z." University of North Carolina at Greensboro University Libraries. http://uncg.libguides.com/ebooks.

Hill, Katherine. "Streaming Media." University of North Carolina at Greensboro University Libraries. http://uncg.libguides.com/streamingfilms.

Hill, Katherine. "Streaming Media: Embedding Streaming Media in Canvas." University of North Carolina at Greensboro University Libraries. http://uncg.libguides.com/streamingfilms/embed.

Honma, Todd. "Trippin' Over the Color Line: The Invisibility of Race in Library and Information Studies." *InterActions: UCLA Journal of Education and Information Studies* 1, no. 2 (June 2005). https://escholarship.org/uc/item/4nj0w1mp.

Hosburgh, Nathan. "Managing the Electronic Resources Lifecycle: Creating a Comprehensive Checklist Using Techniques for Electronic Resource Management (TERMS)." *Serials Librarian* 66, no. 1–4 (2014): 212–19. https://doi.org/10.1080/0361526X.2014.880028.

Hunter, Karen, and Robert Bruning. "The Global Economic Crisis: What Libraries and Publishers Can Do and Are Doing." *Serials Librarian* 59, no. 2 (2010): 147–58. https://doi.org/10.1080/03615261003623161.

Hussey, Lisa K., and Jennifer Campbell-Meier. "Is There a Mentoring Culture Within the LIS Profession?" *Journal of Library Administration* 57, no. 5 (2017): 500–16. https://doi.org/10.1080/01930826 .2017.1326723.

Indiana University. "Institution Lookup." The Carnegie Classification of Institutions of Higher Education. Accessed March 2, 2020. http:// carnegieclassifications.iu.edu/lookup/lookup.php.

Institute of Education Sciences. "Fast Facts: Distance Learning" National Center for Education Statistics. 2017. https://nces.ed.gov/fastfacts /display.asp?id=80.

International Federation of Library Associations and Institutions (IFLA). "Statement of Principles Adopted by the International Conference on Cataloging Principles Paris 1961." Accessed November 1, 2017. https://www.ifla.org/files/assets/cataloguing/IMEICC/IMEICC1 /statement_principles_paris_1961.pdf.

Intner, Sheila S. "Evaluating Technical Services." *Technicalities* 36, no. 5 (October 9, 2016): 6.

Jackson, Andrew P., Julius Jefferson, Jr., and Akilah S. Nosakhere, eds. *The 21st-Century Black Librarian in America: Issues and Challenges*. Lanham, MD: Scarecrow Press, 2012.

Jakubs, Deborah. "Technical Services on the Move." Fall 2007 ASERL Membership Meeting Presentation Slides. New Orleans, LA, November 27, 2007.

James, Norene, Lisa Shamchuk, and Kathrine Koch. "Changing Roles of Librarians and Library Technicians." *Canadian Journal of Library and Information Practice and Research* 10, no. 2 (2015). https://doi .org/10.21083/partnership.v10i2.3333.

Josey, E. J., ed. *The Black Librarian in America*. Metuchen, NJ: Scarecrow Press, 1970.

Josey, E. J., ed. *The Black Librarian in America: Revisited*. Metuchen, NJ: Scarecrow Press, 1994.

Josey, E. J., ed. *What Black Librarians Are Saying*. Metuchen, NJ: Scarecrow Press, 1972.

Josey, E. J., and Ismail Abdullahi. "Why Diversity in American Libraries." *Library Management* 23, no. 1/2 (2002): 10–16. https://doi.org/10.1108/01435120210413544.

Kelley, Tom, and David Kelley. *Creative Confidence: Unleashing the Creative Potential Within Us All*. London: William Collins, 2015.

Kniffel, L. "Tech Services Consolidation Looms Over Massachusetts' Five Colleges." *American Libraries* 40, no. 12 (2009): 26–27.

Kotter, John. *Leading Change*. Boston: Harvard Business Review Press, 2012.

Kowalski, Meghan. "Breaking Down Silo Walls: Successful Collaboration Across Library Departments." *Library Leadership and Management* 31, no. 2 (February 2017): 1–16.

Krajewski, Markus. *Paper Machines: About Cards and Catalogs, 1548–1929*. Cambridge: The MIT Press, 2011.

Krug, Steve. *Rocket Surgery Made Easy: The Do-It-Yourself Guide to Finding and Fixing Usability Problems*. Berkeley, CA: New Riders, 2010.

Library of Congress. "BIBFRAME Frequently Asked Questions." Accessed April 5, 2020, https://www.loc.gov/bibframe/faqs/.

Library of Congress. "Resource Description and Access (RDA): Information and Resources in Preparation for RDA." Accessed October 24, 2017. https://www.loc.gov/aba/rda/.

Library of Congress. "Subject Heading and Term Source Codes." Network Development & MARC Standards Office. 2017. http://www.loc.gov/standards/sourcelist/subject.html.

Littletree, Sandra, and Cheryl A. Metoyer. "Knowledge Organization From an Indigenous Perspective: The Mashantucket Pequot Thesaurus of American Indian Terminology Project." *Cataloging & Classification Quarterly* 53, no. 5–6 (2015): 640–57. https://doi.org/10.1080/01639374.2015.1010113.

Loesch, Martha Fallahay. "Inventory Redux: A Twenty-First Century Adaptation." *Technical Services Quarterly* 28, no. 3 (2011): 301–11. https://doi.org/10.1080/07317131.2011.571636.

Long, Kara, Santi Thompson, Sarah Potvin, and Monica Rivero. "The 'Wicked Problem' of Neutral Description: Toward a Documentation Approach to Metadata Standards." *Cataloging & Classification Quarterly* 55, no. 3 (2017): 107–28. https://doi.org/10.1080/01639374.2016.1278419.

Lorenzo, Lisa. "Agile and Scrum in the Michigan State University Libraries Digital Repository." Presentation at the ALA Annual Conference, Chicago, IL, June 22–27, 2017.

Lovins, Daniel. "'Agile' as a Key to Collaboration on NYU Digital Collections Discovery Initiative." Presentation at the ALA Annual Conference, Orlando, FL, June 23–28, 2016.

Lowry, Charles B. "ARL Library Budgets After the Great Recession, 2011–13." *Research Library Issues: A Report From ARL, CNI, and SPARC* no. 282 (2013): 2–12. https://doi.org/10.29242/rli.282.2.

Lynch, Frances H., and Mary Charles Lasater. "Government Documents and the Online Catalog." *Bulletin of the Medical Library Association* 78, no. 1 (January 1990): 23–28.

Maddox Abbott, Jennifer A., and Mary S. Laskowski. "So Many Projects, So Few Resources: Using Effective Project Management in Technical Services." *Collection Management* 39, no. 2/3 (July 2014): 161–76. https://doi.org/10.1080/01462679.2014.891492.

Manahan, Meg, and Nathan B. Putnam. "Moving From Print-Centric to E-Centric Workflows: A Reorganization of the Technical Services Group at Mason Libraries." Presentation at the Annual Meeting of the Potomac Technical Processing Librarians, Annapolis, MD, October 17, 2014. Accessed December 4, 2017. https://www.potomac techlibrarians.org/Resources/Documents/Annual%20Meeting%20 Presentations/manahan_putnam.pdf.

MarcEdit Development. "Features." Accessed August 8, 2017. http:// marcedit.reeset.net/features.

MarcEdit Development. Home page. Accessed August 2, 2017. http:// marcedit.reeset.net/.

MARCIVE. "MARCIVE Company History." Accessed July 21, 2017. http:// home.marcive.com/history.

McCann, Laura. "Conservation Documentation in Research Libraries." *Library Resources & Technical Services* 57, no. 1 (2013): 30–50. https://doi.org/10.5860/lrts.57n1.30.

McGurr, Melanie J. "Remote Locations for Technical Services: An Exploratory Survey." *Technical Services Quarterly* 28, no. 3 (2011): 283–300. https://doi.org/10.1080/07317131.2011.571596.

Meszaros, Rosemary L. "Western Kentucky University and the CRDP." *FDLP Connection* 6, no. 4 (2016). Last updated August 25, 2016. https:// www.fdlp.gov/all-newsletters/community-insights/2670-western -kentucky-university-and-the-crdp-under-community-insights.

Miller, Steven J. *Metadata for Digital Collections: A How-to-Do-It Manual.* How-to-Do-It Manuals, no. 179. New York: Neal-Schuman Publishers, 2011.

MIT. "MIT Facts 2020: Enrollments 2019–2020." http://web.mit.edu /facts/enrollment.html.

MIT Libraries. "MIT Libraries Vision, Mission, and Values." Adopted September 2017. https://libraries.mit.edu/about/vision/vision -mission-values/.

Morales, Myrna, Em Claire Knowles, and Chris Bourg. "Diversity, Social Justice, and the Future of Libraries." *Portal: Libraries and the Academy* 14, no. 3 (2014): 439–51. https://doi.org/10.1353/pla.2014.0017.

National Center on Universal Design for Learning. "About Universal Design for Learning." Accessed April 5, 2020. http://www.udlcenter .org/aboutudl/whatisudl.

New Mexico State University. "Be Bold. Shape the Future." About NMSU. Accessed March 2, 2020. https://www.nmsu.edu/about.html.

New Mexico State University. "Factbook 2017." Accessed February 19, 2020. https://oia.nmsu.edu/data-reports/factbooks/.

New Mexico State University. *New Mexico State University Quick Facts 2019–2020,* 1. Accessed February 19, 2020. https://oia.nmsu.edu /files/2019/11/Quick-Facts-2019-20.pdf.

New Mexico State University. "NMSU Leads 2025." About NMSU. Accessed March 2, 2020. https://nmsu.edu/about_nmsu/index .html.

New Mexico State University. "Our Heritage." About NMSU. Accessed March 2, 2020. https://home-p.nmsu.edu/about_nmsu/Our%20 Heritage%20.html.

New Mexico State University. "Points of Pride." About NMSU. Accessed March 2, 2020. https://www.nmsu.edu/about_nmsu/universal -page.html.

Nielsen, Jakob. "The Use and Misuse of Focus Group." Nielsen Norman Group. January 1, 1997. https://www.nngroup.com/articles /focus-groups/.

Nielson, Jakob. "Why You Only Need to Test With 5 Users." Nielsen Norman Group. March 19, 2000. https://www.nngroup.com/articles /why-you-only-need-to-test-with-5-users.

Noh, Younghee. "A Study on Metadata Elements for Web-Based Reference Resources System Developed Through Usability Testing."

Library Hi Tech 29, no. 2 (2011): 242–65. https://doi.org/10.1108 /07378831111138161.

Novak, John, and Annette Day. "The Libraries They Are A-Changin': How Libraries Reorganize." *College & Undergraduate Libraries* 22, no. 3–4 (2015): 358–73. https://doi.org/10.1080/10691316.2015.1067663.

OCLC home page. Accessed August 2, 2017. https://www.oclc.org/en /home.html.

Oder, Norman. "Permanent Shift?: Library Budgets 2010." *Library Journal* 135, no. 1 (2010): 44–46.

Olin, Jessica, and Michelle Millet. "Gendered Expectations for Leadership in Libraries." *In the Library With the Lead Pipe*. November 4, 2015. http://www.inthelibrarywiththeleadpipe.org/2015/libleadgender/.

Olson, Hope A. *Power to Name: Locating the Limits of Subject Representation in Libraries*. Dordrecht: Kluwer Academic, 2002.

Ostergaard, Kirsten, and Doralyn Rossmann. "There's Work to Be Done: Exploring Library–Vendor Relations." *Technical Services Quarterly* 34, no. 1 (2017): 13–33. https://doi.org/10.1080/07317131.2017 .1238196.

Ostergaard, Kirsten, and Doralyn Rossmann. "Vendor Relations Strategies for Libraries." *Against the Grain* 27, no. 6 (2015): 14. https:// doi.org/10.7771/2380-176X.7222.

Pinfield, Stephen. "The Changing Role of Subject Librarians in Academic Libraries." *Journal of Librarianship and Information Science* 33, no. 1 (2001): 32–38. https://doi.org/10.1177/096100060103300104.

Playfair, William. *The Statistical Breviary: Shewing the Resources of Every State and Kingdom in Europe*. London: J. Wallis, 1801. https://books.google.com/books?id=Y4wBAAAAQAAJ.

Pollitt, Christopher. "Institutional Amnesia: A Paradox of the 'Information Age'?" *Prometheus* 18, no. 1 (2000): 5–16. https://doi.org/10 .1080/08109020050000627.

Preston, Gregor A. "How Will Automation Affect Cataloging Staff?" *Technical Services Quarterly* 1, no. 1–2 (Fall/ Winter 1983): 129–36. https://doi.org/10.1300/J124v01n01_21.

Program for Cooperative Cataloging. *URI FAQs: PCC URI Task Group on URIs in MARC*. September 26, 2018. http://www.loc.gov/aba/pcc /bibframe/TaskGroups/URI%20FAQs.pdf.

Rawan, Atifa, Cheryl Knott Malone, and Laura J. Bender. "Assessing the Virtual Depository Program: The Arizona Experience."

Journal of Government Information 30 (2004): 710–26. https:// doi.org/10.1016/j.jgi.2004.11.004.

Regazzi, John J. "U.S. Academic Library Spending, Staffing and Utilization During the Great Recession 2008–2010." *Journal of Academic Librarianship* 39, no. 3 (2013): 217–22. https://doi.org /10.1016/j .acalib.2012.12.002.

Remy, Charlie. "Libraries Are From Mars and Vendors Are From Venus? Understanding One Another Better to Achieve Common Goals." *Journal of Electronic Resources Librarianship* 25, no. 3 (2013): 233–40. https://doi.org/10.1080/1941126X.2013.813318.

Richardson, Lee M., and Barbara Rochen Renner. *Better Together: Technical Services & Public Services*, 2018. https://doi.org/10.17615 /h8tm-2s87.

Riva, Pat, Patrick Le Bœuf, and Maja Žumer. *IFLA Library Reference Model: A Conceptual Model for Bibliographic Information*. The Hague, Netherlands: IFLA, 2017. Accessed January 2020. https:// www.ifla.org/files/assets/cataloguing/frbr-lrm/ifla-lrm-august -2017.pdf.

Rosa, Kathy, and Tom Storey. "American Libraries in 2016: Creating Their Future by Connecting, Collaborating and Building Community." *IFLA Journal* 42, no. 2 (2016): 85–101. https://doi.org/10 .1177/0340035216646061.

Ryan, Susan. *Public Services Annual Report FY 2010–2011, 2011–2012, 2012–2013, 2013–2014, 2014–2015, 2015–2016*. https://www2 .stetson.edu/library/about-us/library-publications/annual-reports/.

Ryan, Susan. *Public Services Annual Report FY 2016–2017*. https://www2 .stetson.edu/library/about-us/library-publications/annual-reports/.

Sandstrom, John, and Liz Miller. *Fundamentals of Technical Services*. ALA Fundamentals Series. Chicago: Neal-Schuman, an imprint of the American Library Association, 2015.

Sanville, Thomas J. "A Method out of the Madness: OhioLINK's Collaborative Response to the Serials Crisis." *Serials* 14, no. 2 (July 2001): 163–77. https://doi.org/10.1629/14163.

Schmidt, Ben. "A Brief Visual History of MARC Cataloging at the Library of Congress." *Sapping Attention* (blog). May 16, 2017. Accessed May 20, 2017. http://sappingattention.blogspot.com/2017/05/a -brief-visual-history-of-marc.html.

Schonfeld, Roger C., and Ross Houseright. *What to Withdraw? Print Collection Management in the Wake of Digitization.* New York: Ithaka S+R, 2009. https://doi.org/10.18665/sr.22357.

Scrum Alliance. "Learn About Scrum." Accessed November 2, 2017. https://www.scrumalliance.org/why-scrum.

Senge, Peter. *The Fifth Discipline: The Art and Practice of the Learning Organization.* New York: Doubleday Currency, 1990.

Shoaf, Eric C. "Transparency Means Greater Payoff in a Planning Process." *North Carolina Libraries* 71, no. 1 (Spring–Summer 2013): 11–14. http://tigerprints.clemson.edu/cgi/viewcontent.cgi?article=1028&context=lib_pubs.

Sicignano, Charles. "Emerging Roles and Opportunities for the Technical Services Manager." In *Rethinking Technical Services: New Frameworks, New Skill Sets, New Tools, New Roles*, edited by Bradford Lee Eden. Lanham, MD: Rowman & Littlefield, 2016.

SimplyAnalytics, Inc. "SimplyAnalytics: Analytics for Everyone." http://simplyanalytics.com/.

Sommers, Hannah. "Two Weeks at a Time: Applying Agile Frameworks to Library Practice." Presentation at the ALA Midwinter Meeting, Atlanta, GA, January 20–24, 2017.

Stamison, Christine, Bob Persing, Chris Beckett, and Chris Brady. "What They Never Told You About Vendors in Library School." *Serials Librarian* 56, no. 1–4 (2009): 139–45. https://doi.org/10.1080/03615260802665555.

State University of New York. "History of SUNY." Accessed March 18, 2018. https://www.suny.edu/about/history/.

State University of New York College at Cortland. "Memorial Library." Accessed March 18, 2018. http://www2.cortland.edu/library/about/.

Sung, Jan S., John A. Whisler, and Nackil Sung. "A Cost-Benefit Analysis of a Collections Inventory Project: A Statistical Analysis of Inventory Data From a Medium-Sized Academic Library." *Journal of Academic Librarianship* 35, no. 4 (2009): 314–23. https://doi.org/10.1016/j.acalib.2009.04.002.

Tbaishat, Dina. "Using Business Process Modelling to Examine Academic Library Activities for Periodicals." *Library Management* 37, no. 7 (2010): 480–93. https://doi.org/10.1108/01435121011071184.

Texas A&M University-Central Texas. "Library Receives Special Project Grant Funding." News release, October 21, 2016. https://news .tamuct.edu/library-receives-special-project-grant-funding/.

Thomale, Jason. "Interpreting MARC: Where's the Bibliographic Data?" *Code4Lib Journal*, no. 11 (2010). http://journal.code4lib.org/articles /3832.

Thomison, Dennis. *A History of the American Library Association: 1876–1972*. Chicago: American Library Association, 1978.

Tizon, Christian. "Current Term Enrollment Estimates—Spring 2016." *National Student Clearinghouse Research Center* (blog). May 23, 2016. https://nscresearchcenter.org/currenttermenrollmentestimate -spring2016/.

"To Be Black and a Librarian: Talking With E. J. Josey," *American Libraries* 31, no. 1 (2000): 80–82.

Turner, Carol, and Ann Latta. *Current Approaches to Improving Access to Government Documents: An OMS Occasional Paper Produced as Part of the Collaborative Research-Writing Program*. Washington, DC: Association of Research Libraries, Office of Management Studies, 1987.

Turner, Laura, and Alejandra Nann. "Venturing From the 'Back Room': Do Technical Services Librarians Have a Role in Information Literacy?" *Charleston Conference Proceedings*, 2013. https://doi.org/10 .5703/1288284315293.

Turner, Nancy B. "Librarians Do It Differently: Comparative Usability Testing With Students and Library Staff." *Journal of Web Librarianship* 5, no. 4 (2011): 286–98. https://doi.org/10.1080/19322909 .2011.624428.

United States Census Bureau. "QuickFacts: United States" (2017). https:// www.census.gov/quickfacts/fact/table/US/PST045217.

United States Department of Labor. "Household Data Annual Averages" (2019). Bureau of Labor Statistics. Accessed February 28, 2020. https://www.bls.gov/cps/cpsaat11.pdf.

United States Department of Labor. "Labor Force Statistics From the Current Population Survey" (2017). Bureau of Labor Statistics. Accessed February 28, 2020. https://www.bls.gov/cps/cps_aa2017.htm.

United States General Accounting Office. *Information Management: Electronic Dissemination of Government Publications*. Report to Congressional Committees (Report no. GAO-01-428). Washington,

DC: United States General Accounting Office, 2001. https://www.gao
.gov/assets/240/231303.pdf.

United States Government Publishing Office. "Mission, Vision, and Goals:
Keeping America Informed." Accessed February 27, 2020. https://
www.gpo.gov/who-we-are/our-agency/mission-vision-and-goals.

U.S. Army Fort Hood. "History." Last modified March 8, 2019. https://
home.army.mil/hood/index.php/about/history.

University of Dayton Libraries. *Strategic Plan 2017–2020*, 2017. https://
www.udayton.edu/libraries/_resources/docs/strategic-plan-2017
-20.pdf.

University of Denver University Libraries. *University Libraries Five Year
Strategic Plan: 2017–2022*, 2017. https://library.du.edu/media
/documents/university_libraries_strategic_plan_2017.pdf.

University of Illinois at Urbana-Champaign Library. *Framework for Strategic Action, 2015–2021*. Adopted December 7, 2015. https://www
.library.illinois.edu/staff/wp-content/uploads/sites/24/2017/10
/ADOPTEDFramework_for_Strategic_Action.pdf.

University of Massachusetts Amherst Libraries. "IRM Evolving Workflows." Information Resources Management Staff Wiki. August 25,
2017. Accessed January 16, 2018. https://www.library.umass.edu
/wikis/acp/doku.php?id=evolving_workflows_-_2016.

University of North Carolina at Greensboro. "Course Adopted Texts by
Department: Course Adopted Texts by Subject." University Libraries.
http://uncg.libguides.com/c.php?g=532866&p=5423390.

University of North Carolina at Greensboro. "Faculty Representatives and
Library Liaisons." University Libraries. http://library.uncg.edu/info
/faculty_liaisons.aspx.

University of North Carolina at Greensboro. "Information Technology
Services." https://its.uncg.edu/.

University of North Carolina at Greensboro. "Office of Accessibility
Resources & Services." https://ods.uncg.edu/.

University of North Carolina at Greensboro. "Research Guides by Subject." University Libraries. http://library.uncg.edu/research/guides/.

University of North Carolina at Greensboro. "Research, Outreach, and
Instruction." University Libraries. https://library.uncg.edu/info
/depts/reference/.

University of North Carolina at Greensboro. "UNCG Online." https://
online.uncg.edu/.

University of North Carolina at Greensboro. "University Libraries." https:/library.uncg.edu/.

University of North Carolina at Greensboro. "University Teaching and Learning Commons." https://utlc.uncg.edu/.

University of South Alabama. "About USA." Accessed January 25, 2018. http://www.southalabama.edu/aboutusa/.

University of South Alabama. *History of the University Libraries, University of South Alabama.* Last updated June 5, 2015. http://www.south alabama.edu/departments/library/resources/libraries-history.pdf.

VanDuinkerken, Wyoma, and Pixey Anne Mosley. *The Challenge of Library Management: Leading With Emotional Engagement.* Chicago: American Library Association, 2011.

Waber, Ben, Jennifer Magnolfi, and Greg Lindsay. "Workspaces That Move People." *Harvard Business Review* 92, no. 10 (2014): 69–77. https://hbr.org/2014/10/workspaces-that-move-people.

Walters, William H. "Evaluating Online Resources for College and University Libraries: Assessing Value and Cost Based on Academic Needs." *Serials Review* 42, no. 1 (2016): 10–17. https://doi.org/10 .1080/00987913.2015.1131519.

Ward, Suzanne M. *Rightsizing the Academic Library Collection.* Chicago: ALA Editions, 2015.

Weiss, Amy K., John P. Abbott, and Joseph C. Harmon. "Print Journals: Off Site? Out of Site? Out of Mind?" *Serials Librarian* 44, no. 3/4 (2003): 271–78. https://doi.org/10.1300/J123v44n03_19.

Weng, Cathy, and Erin Ackerman. "Towards Sustainable Partnership: Examining Cross Perceptions of Public and Technical Services Academic Librarians." *Library Resources & Technical Services* 61, no. 4 (2017): 198–211.

Wesolek, Andrew, Jan Comfort, and Lisa Bodenheimer. "Collaborate to Innovate: Expanding Access to Faculty Patents Through the Institutional Repository and the Library Catalog." *Collection Management* 40, no. 4 (2015). https://doi.org/10.1080/01462679.2015.1093986.

White, Hollie C. "Documentation in Technical Services." *Serials Librarian* 49, no. 3 (2006): 47–55.

Williams, Priscilla R., Tatiana Barr, Daniel Cromwell, Jimmie Lundgren, and Betsy Simpson. "Relocation or Dislocation: Optimizing Change in Technical Services." *Technical Services Quarterly* 20, no. 1 (2002): 13–27. https://doi.org/10.1300/J124v20n01_02.

Womack, Jim. "Inventory or Stockcheck?" *Christian Librarian* 53, no. 3 (2010): 111–13. https://digitalcommons.georgefox.edu/tcl/vol53/iss3/4.

Xu, Hong. "The Impact of Automation on Job Requirements and Qualifications for Catalogers and Reference Librarians in Academic Libraries." *Library Resources & Technical Services* 40, no. 1 (2011): 9–31. https://doi.org/10.5860/lrts.40n1.9.

Yeo, ShinJoung, and James R. Jacobs. "Diversity Matters? Rethinking Diversity in Libraries." *Counterpoise* 9, no. 2 (2006): 5–8.

Zhu, Lihong. "The Physical Office Environment in Technical Services ARL Libraries." *Library Collections, Acquisitions, & Technical Services* 37, no. 1–2 (2013): 42–55. https://doi.org/10.1016/j.lcats.2013.09.001.

Zhu, Lihong. "Use of Teams in Technical Services in Academic Libraries." *Library Collections, Acquisitions, & Technical Services* 35, no. 2–3 (June 2011): 69–82. https://doi.org/10.1016/j.lcats.2011.03.013.

Contributors

Mary C. Aagard, Head of Access Services, Boise State University, Boise, Idaho

Martina S. Anderson, Acquisitions and Appraisal Librarian, Massachusetts Institute of Technology, Cambridge, Massachusetts

Gail Perkins Barton, Interlibrary Loan Librarian, Auburn University, Auburn, Alabama

Edith K. Beckett, Head of Technical Services, New Jersey State Library, Trenton, New Jersey

Meghan Banach Bergin, Head of the Metadata Unit, University of Massachusetts at Amherst, Amherst, Massachusetts

Mary Bevis, Serials & Acquisitions Librarian, Jacksonville State University, Jacksonville, Alabama

Paromita Biswas, formerly Metadata Librarian at Western Carolina University, now Continuing Resources Metadata Librarian at the University of California, Los Angeles, Los Angeles, California

Ellen Bosman, Head of Technical Services, New Mexico State University, Las Cruces, New Mexico

Sommer Browning, Associate Director of Technical Services, Auraria Library, Denver, Colorado

Rebecca Ciota, Discovery & Integrated Systems Librarian, Grinnell College, Grinnell, Iowa

Kevin Clair, Digital Collections Librarian, University of Denver, Denver, Colorado

Laurel Sammonds Crawford, Head of Collection Development, University of North Texas, Denton, Texas

Emy Nelson Decker, Associate Dean for Research & User Services, University of Alabama, Tuscaloosa, Alabama

Christine Korytnyk Dulaney, Chief, Germanic and Slavic Division, Acquisitions and Bibliographic Access Directorate, Library of Congress, Washington, DC

Scott M. Dutkiewicz, Cataloger, Clemson University, Clemson, South Carolina

Kimberley A. Edwards, Head, Database Integrity & Analysis, George Mason University, Fairfax, Virginia

Erin Elzi, Design and Discovery Librarian, University of Denver, Denver, Colorado

Bridget Euliano, Assistant University Librarian, Access & Resource Management, George Mason University, Fairfax, Virginia

Cheri A. Folkner, Head of Cataloging, Boise State University, Boise, Idaho

Karen Glover, Associate Dean for Content, Access, and User Services, Georgia Institute of Technology, Atlanta, Georgia

Monika Glowacka-Musial, Metadata Librarian, New Mexico State University, Las Cruces, New Mexico

Peggy Griesinger, Metadata Technologies Librarian, University of Notre Dame, South Bend, Indiana

Samantha Harlow, Online Learning Librarian, University of North Carolina at Greensboro, Greensboro, North Carolina

Jia He, Cataloging Electronic Resources Librarian, University of South Alabama, Mobile, Alabama

Emily A. Hicks, Director of Information Acquisition and Organization, University of Dayton, Dayton, Ohio. Emily passed away on October 7, 2019, at the age of 50. She will be greatly missed by her friends and colleagues

Katherine Hill, Electronic Resources Librarian, University of North Carolina at Greensboro, Greensboro, North Carolina

Marlena Hooyboer, Manager of Receiving and Collections, Boise State University, Boise, Idaho

Lisa Kallman Hopkins, Head of Technical Services, Assistant Director of the University Library, Texas A&M University-Central Texas, Killeen, Texas

Fred W. Jenkins, Associate Dean of Collections and Operations, University of Dayton, Dayton, Ohio

Rhonda Y. Kauffman, Metadata Management Librarian at the University of Connecticut, Storrs, Connecticut

Laura Kirkland, Cataloging Librarian, Stetson University, DeLand, Florida

R. Cecilia Knight, Discovery & Acquisitions Librarian, Grinnell College, Grinnell, Iowa

Sally Krash, Associate Dean for Content and Discovery, University of Massachusetts at Amherst, Amherst, Massachusetts

Jennifer Kronenbitter, Director of Libraries, SUNY Cortland, Cortland, New York

Mary S. Laskowski, Head, Collection Management Services, University of Illinois at Urbana-Champaign, Urbana, Illinois

Bethany Latham, Electronic Resources/Documents Librarian, Jacksonville State University, Jacksonville, Alabama

Kara D. Long, Coordinator of Metadata Technologies, Virginia Tech, Blacksburg, Virginia

Tricia Mackenzie, Head, Metadata Services, George Mason University, Fairfax, Virginia

Jennifer A. Maddox Abbott, Collection Management Librarian, University of Illinois at Urbana-Champaign, Urbana, Illinois

Stacey Marien, Acquisitions Librarian, American University, Washington, DC

Susanne Markgren, Assistant Director of the Library for Technical Services, Manhattan College, Bronx, New York

Courtney McAllister, Library Services Engineer, EBSCO Information Services, New Haven, Connecticut

Muriel D. Nero, Head of Cataloging, University of South Alabama, Mobile, Alabama

Maaike Oldemans, Interim Associate Director of Libraries, SUNY Cortland, Cortland, New York

Jodi Poe, Head of Technical Services, Jacksonville State University, Jacksonville, Alabama

Allyson Rodriguez, Assistant Director of Library Services, Tarrant County College, South Campus Library, Fort Worth, Texas

Nancy Rosenheim, Head of Acquisitions and Collections, Boise State University, Boise, Idaho

John Sandstrom, Acquisitions Librarian, New Mexico State University, Las Cruces, New Mexico

Rachel Elizabeth Scott, Integrated Library Systems Librarian, University of Memphis, Memphis, Tennessee

Jessica L. Serrao, Metadata Librarian for Digital Collections, Clemson University, Clemson, South Carolina

McKinley Sielaff, Academic Engagement and Research Librarian, Colorado College, Colorado Springs, Colorado

Kimberly W. Stevens, Senior Catalog Librarian, Jacksonville State University, Jacksonville, Alabama

Elizabeth Winter, Knowledge Manager, North Highland Consulting, Atlanta, Georgia

Index

Page numbers in italics refer to tables and figures.